The Nomads of Mykonos

New Directions in Anthropology

General Editor: Jacqueline Waldren, *Institute of Social Anthropology, University of Oxford*

Volume 1 *Coping with Tourists: European Reactions to Mass Tourism*
Edited by Jeremy Boissevain

Volume 2 *A Sentimental Economy: Commodity and Community in Rural Ireland*
Carles Salazar

Volume 3 *Insiders and Outsiders: Paradise and Reality in Mallorca*
Jacqueline Waldren

Volume 4 *The Hegemonic Male: Masculinity in a Portuguese Town*
Miguel Vale de Almeida

Volume 5 *Communities of Faith: Sectarianism, Identity, and Social Change on a Danish Island*
Andrew S. Buckser

Volume 6 *After Socialism: Land Reform and Rural Social Change in Eastern Europe*
Edited by Ray Abrahams

Volume 7 *Immigrants and Bureaucrats: Ethiopians in an Israeli Absorption Center*
Esther Hertzog

Volume 8 *A Venetian Island: Environment, History and Change in Burano*
Lidia Sciama

Volume 9 *Recalling the Belgian Congo: Conversations and Introspection*
Marie-Bénédicte Dembour

Volume 10 *Mastering Soldiers: Conflict, Emotions, and the Enemy in an Israeli Military Unit*
Eyal Ben-Ari

Volume 11 *The Great Immigration: Russian Jews in Israel*
Dina Siegel

Volume 12 *Morals of Legitimacy: Between Agency and System*
Edited by Italo Pardo

Volume 13 *Academic Anthropology and the Museum: Back to the Future*
Edited by Mary Bouquet

Volume 14 *Simulated Dreams: Israeli Youth and Virtual Zionism*
Haim Hazan

Volume 15 *Defiance and Compliance: Negotiating Gender in Low-Income Cairo*
Heba Aziz Morsi El-Kholy

Volume 16 *Troubles with Turtles: Cultural Understandings of the Environment on a Greek Island*
Dimitrios Theodossopoulos

Volume 17 *Rebordering the Mediterranean: Boundaries and Citizenship in Southern Europe*
Liliana Suarez-Navaz

Volume 18 *The Bounded Field: Localism and Local Identity in an Italian Alpine Valley*
Jaro Stacul

Volume 19 *Foundations of National Identity: From Catalonia to Europe*
Josep Llobera

Volume 20 *Bodies of Evidence: Burial, Memory and the Recovery of Missing Persons in Cyprus*
Paul Sant Cassia

Volume 21 *Who Owns the Past? The Politics of Time in a 'Model' Bulgarian Village*
Deema Kaneff

Volume 22 *An Earth-Colored Sea: "Race," Culture and the Politics of Identity in the Postcolonial Portuguese-Speaking World*
Miguel Vale De Almeida

Volume 23 *Science, Magic and Religion: The Ritual Process of Museum Magic*
Edited by Mary Bouquet and Nuno Porto

Volume 24 *Crossing European Boundaries: Beyond Conventional Geographical Categories*
Edited by Jaro Stacul, Christina Moutsou and Helen Kopnina

Volume 25 *Documenting Transnational Migration: Jordanian Men Working and Studying in Europe, Asia and North America*
Richard Antoum

Volume 26 *Le Malaise Créole: Ethnic Identity in Mauritius*
Rosabelle Boswell

Volume 27 *Nursing Stories: Life and Death in a German Hospice*
Nicholas Eschenbruch

Volume 28 *Inclusionary Rhetoric/Exclusionary Practices: Left-wing Politics and Migrants in Italy*
Davide Però

Volume 29 *The Nomads of Mykonos: Performing Liminalities in a 'Queer' Space*
Pola Bousiou

THE NOMADS OF MYKONOS

Performing Liminalities in a 'Queer' Space

Pola Bousiou

Berghahn Books
New York • Oxford

First published in 2008 by

Berghahn Books
www.berghahnbooks.com

© 2008 Pola Bousiou

All rights reserved. Except for the quotation of short passages for the purposes of criticism and review, no part of this book may be reproduced in any form or by any means, electronic or mechanical, including photocopying, recording, or any information storage and retrieval system now known or to be invented, without written permission of the publisher.

Library of Congress Cataloging-in-Publication Data
Bousiou, Pola, 1967-
  The nomads of Mykonos : performing liminalities in a 'queer' space / Pola Bousiou.
    p. cm. -- (New directions in anthropology ; vol. 69)
  Includes bibliographical references and index.
  ISBN 978-1-84545-426-5 (hardback : alk. paper) -- ISBN 978-1-84545-466-1 (pbk. : alk. paper)
  1. Ethnology--Greece--Mykonos. 2. Gays--Travel--Greece--Mykonos. 3. Gays--Greece--Mykonos--Social life and customs. 4. Group identity--Greece--Mykonos. 5. Geographical perception--Greece--Mykonos. 6. Culture and tourism--Greece--Mykonos. 7. Mykonos (Greece)--Social life and customs. I. Title.

DF901.M9B68 2008
306.76'60949585--dc22

2008014246

British Library Cataloguing in Publication Data

A catalogue record for this book is available from the British Library

Printed in the United States on acid-free paper

ISBN 978-1-84545-426-5 (hardback)

Contents

Acknowledgements	vii
Note on transliteration	x
Introduction	xi
1. Mykonos: the building of a liminal space-myth	1
2. Narratives of belonging: the myth of an 'indigenous' otherness	35
3. Narratives of the self: an eccentric myth of otherness	65
4. Narratives of place: a spatial myth of otherness	139
5. Narratives of difference: an aesthetic myth of otherness	175
Conclusion	215
Epilogue. A beach farewell	231
Appendix I. The problem of agency in the Greek ethnographic subject	249
Appendix II. The emergence of the sensual post-tourist: consuming 'cultures', multisubjective selves and (trans)local spaces	263
Glossary	271
Bibliography	277
Index	293

In memory of the uncompromising
John Edward Read
1947–1999

Acknowledgements

This book would never have seen the light of day were it not for the cajoling of my old friend and research companion from my London School of Economics (LSE) years, Dimitris Theodossopulos. As soon as I had taken my viva voce in 1999, I did what I had promised myself I was going to do: forget all about anthropology and my thesis and turn to film-making. I turned to a new vocation. But Dimitris continually reminded me that I had 'unfinished business', until one day he insisted on my writing to Jackie Waldren, who had produced a comparable ethnography, as well as having lived in a comparable mythologised tourist space on a Mediterranean island, where she became an integral part of her own ethnographic setting. Jackie was kind enough to read my monograph and the rest is history or not quite so ... the Ariadne like thread of the transcript's progress was apparently lost for a year or so, somewhere between Jackie Waldren and the publisher Marion Berghahn, until one day Marion informed me that she had found the 'thread' and a contract was on its way.

Now, flashback to my viva voce: A University College London (UCL) conference room with dark wood panelling and heavy furniture; me waiting for Charles Stewart and Nigel Rapport, the 'external', in company with my Leica and a copy of the thesis. All went well, and I was urged to publish my work, but I replied I was going to pursue another venture. I was somewhat alienated by my research years at the LSE, where I had to keep mute about my self-reflexive auto-ethnographic endeavours, which were out of favour at the time in the anthropology department. I took a picture of both Charles and Nigel, as a remembrance of my 'anthropological' years. In the context of the viva, my Leica acted symbolically as a key signifying my transition to yet another 'liminal' state, that of my apprenticeship in film-making. I will always remember that day. Their exciting suggestions fitted with my own ideas for an alternative conclusion to my ethnographic scenario. This discussion eventually became the epilogue: 'a beach farewell', and a full ethnographic realisation of my theoretical argument – and I thank them for that.

Acknowledgements

During my revisiting the text, I took on-board the publishers' suggestions to expand on the current literature on embodiment, mobility, tourism and travel, as well as widen my theoretical discussion on performativity and gender to include a more thorough exploration of the literature on performance. I also took on-board Nigel's and Charles's suggestions, which encouraged me to take on a more adventurous, self-reflexive mode of representation that allows for the reader to decipher my self-transformation under my long Mykonian apprenticeship. My fieldwork locus, given its aesthetic pluralism, eventually created an alternative identity scenario for myself; my ethnography became autobiographical. I was in a sense, through my auto-ethnographic writing, 'fictionalising' ethnography. I invented a 'collectivity' my 'unconventional self' could safely identify with. This realisation eventually led me to update and rephrase the whole theoretical argument by shifting it from notions of style, extreme individuality and consumption, to a conscious performative self-play *à la* Schechner and thus the auto-ethnographic crescendo of the epilogue. I turned to anthropological writings on [the self as] fetish, the politics of performance in gender theory and contemporary transient/tourist contexts, and on identity displacement where movement becomes 'home'.

The monograph finally obtained a more mixed ethnographic and theoretical style of writing, exemplified in the interchanging voices within the same text. The varying voices do not monosemantically stand to delineate different forms of writing; conversely, sometimes the different forms of writing intentionally overlap. What this mixing of voices is meant to accomplish is my own inner predicament as partly the ethnographer/the outsider, and partly the self-reflexive insider – ultimately the fictionalist of my own story and ethnographic construction. The theoretical and self-reflexive updating of the text thus led to this invented textual heteroglossia.

After a long gap in my cognitive development as a 'mature anthropologist' and my consequent return to this text, there were a number of people who helped enormously to shape this work. First and foremost, Henrietta Moore, my only supervisor at the LSE, without whose courage and encouragement I would have never been able to realise this project. Secondly, my colleagues – the Greek gang I should call them – Leo Economou, Marios Sarris and Venetia Kantsa, and our Greek ethnography patrons: Peter Loizos and Akis Papataxiarchis. Also, Despina Nazou, from the University of the Aegean, Mytilene, who was 'fieldworking' at the same time on Mykonos, and with whom I exchanged notes. My 'dyslexic' thinking process often makes it impossible for me to progress with any ideas without interlocutors. I had been accompanied on this long editing journey with some generous supporters gifted with the required stamina to tolerate my perpetual and initially largely unstructured theoretical and textual inventions as well as personal insecurities. I need to mention here Dimitris again and Elisabeth Kirtsoglou and my proofreader, Valerie Nunn. But this long editing process would not have been possible without the invaluable support, hard work and empathy, as well as creative antagonism with my long-time friend and research assistant in both the early and late stages of this book, Roger Smedley. For he acted as a thinking 'punching bag' for my sometimes wacky ideas. It would also be fair to say that a lot of the ideas in this monograph were born out of many long, indulgent nights with a group of 'diasporic' Greeks friends, who were also students at the time of my fieldwork and later: Amina and Hercules Moskoff, Marianna Michalaki, Marina Fokidis and Sophia Kosmaoglou. Together we fantasised and projected our own liminalities.

Finally, I owe a debt of gratitude to the *Mykoniots d'élection*, the protagonists of this ethnographic performance, and especially to those who were already or eventually became a 'family', on our respective quests for performative self-assimilation: George Karaoglou, Arrianna Samouri, Michael Chairetis, Eleni Karida, Babis Pasaoglou, Marili Tsopanelli, Thelgia Sistovari and Kostas Koniordos. I will never forget the encouragement I received early on in embarking on this ethnographic journey from Spiros Vrachoritis.

Lastly, a great thank you to my brother for his invaluable input vis-à-vis information technologies and personal/cyber insecurities, and to both my parents – Despo and Lefteris – for their unflagging support; but most of all to Jason, my constant friend, lover and companion.

Note on Transliteration

αι	ai
β	v
γ	g before the vowels a, o and consonants y before vowels i, e and 'ipsilon'
γγ	ng
γκ	g initially ng medially
δ	d
ντ	d initially nd medially (except in names, e.g., Antonis)
μπ	b initially mb medially (except in 'synpotiasmos')
ει	ei
οι	oi
η	i (except in Delos, delos, adelos, Deliana, Deliani)
ου	ou
υ	y (but after γ: i)
ευ	ev/ef
φ	f
χ	h (except in Pascha, erchetai)
θ	th
ξ	x

INTRODUCTION

The construction of the Mykonian pleasure ground: nomads in a 'queer' space?

This book is an anthropological study of consumption and self-construction on the Greek island of Mykonos, the place I have been enchanted with since my late teens. It is a study of the *Mykoniots d'élection*, who, as their invented group-designation reveals, are a group of people who have been visiting the island of Mykonos for the last thirty-five years or so and have formed an alternative community. Their constant return to the island and their insistence on living, acting, working and creating in a tourist space offers them an alternative identity, which in turn is aesthetically marked by the transient cultural properties of Mykonos, the space they have fetishised in their lives as 'nomads'.

The ethnographic material was collected from a series of performers in the Mykonos rurban tourist scene of an, initially, heterogeneous cultural background and with a highly individualistic discourse, who, paradoxically, form a 'group'. The identity of this new Mykonian group of exogenous 'locals', the *Mykoniots d'élection*, was self-created and draws on several 'local' myths. Therefore, the ethnography concentrated on the discursive making of these myths.

The characteristic all these myths shared was that they revolved around a common theme: symbolic 'otherness'. This discursive otherness, was initially reflected in the emerging myth of the cosmopolitan place in which it was performed, the liminal place-myth of Mykonos. But symmetrically, in this ethnographic case, the liminal myth of the place, counter-reflects the myth of its subjects. Through their performing liminalities, a series of invented 'heroes' gradually prospered in the mythical space of 'otherness': first the reckless, unorthodox locals; then the eccentric 'first visitors' followed by the alternative groups of the seventies, the subcultural groups of the eighties and the 'tribestyles' of the nineties.

The myth of this spatial 'otherness', apart from the peculiar groupings which it simultaneously attracted and created in the tourist space, was also a propagator of self-myths. The ethnography explores the construction of sensual selves and affective communities through their consumption patterns, aestheticisation, invented rituals and a distinctive set of social practices, but primarily through their discursive otherness and performative liminality. The myth of the idiosyncratic space is echoed in the myth of their unclassified and fetishised selves. During my fieldwork years (1991 to 1997) and my subsequent returns to the island, I collected a long list of fetishised references for the Cycladic space of Mykonos. In this assembling, I realised that the 'anarchic' property of the Mykonian space is its only consistent pattern and, in turn, a source of communal identity. The discourse of locality that arises out of these 'mythologies' celebrates a highly subjective pattern of an aesthetic and sensual 'otherness'. The bonding of all these myths lies precisely in their taste for 'difference'. The fetishisation of the self reflects upon the fetishisation of space; just as the fetishisation of space reflects upon the fetishisation of the self.

The performance of liminality in the Mykonian space

Mykonos' space-myth developed as a sign of liminality. Places like Mykonos which carry the image of their 'marginality' exploit, so to speak, this marginality in order to build their cultural status. Semantically, Mykonos signifies otherness in the global cultural agenda. This 'marginal' image is due to an antithesis: Mykonos attracted both the status quo and 'fringe' cultures alike. More importantly, what the Mykonos space reflects is a constructed 'otherness' especially tailored for the Athenian bourgeoisie; Mykonos is close enough to Athens to become both its anomie and its extension (cf. Shields 1991: ch. 2). Among other things, the island was chosen to perform the role of the 'anti-structure' against the organised life of the centre.

Mykonos, in the modern Greek context, was the catholic signifier of an aesthetic 'otherness', since it stood for an unrestricted, disorganised, hedonist, marginal and glamorous lifestyle. Different groups appropriated Mykonos' myth of 'otherness' in different periods. These gradual appropriations, however, always revolved around the themes of marginality and desire manifested in conspicuous extravagance: i.e., excessive drinking, drug-taking, sex and partying. Reputedly, marginal identities, as well as cosmopolitan ones, were and still are highly fetishised in the discourses of 'modern' Greeks. Mykonos, in the aforementioned context, represents an 'amoral' space. Its sign invokes – in readers who are familiar with it strong feelings, either positive or negative. Indicative of the above was the typical reaction – which I came to terms with over the years – to the mere mention of this ethnography's research space: Mykonos was synonymous with hedonism and marginality. In fact, the association of the Mykonian space with pleasure was so entrenched, that supposedly no 'proper' piece of research could possibly be produced out of it.

Mykonos' sign acquired a 'classless' connotation, mainly as an internally employed logic of distinction rather than as a reputation. Systems of classification based on social position were replaced by alternative criteria such as beauty (physical and body capital) and the level of deviation from a 'proper' bourgeois prototype. All this happened mainly during the seventies and eighties, before Mykonos' 'liminal' sign became a simulacrum of alternativity. There was also a romantic element involved in the projection of 'marginality' onto the Mykonian space; its visitors traditionally simulated marginality. They performed a self, supposedly liberated from the social constraints of modern urban life, by converting themselves into 'locals', 'hippies' and so forth.

The ruling discourse of an initially spatial and eventually symbolic liminality produces both a positive and a negative place image, a marginal and a glamorous one, a 'decadent' yet 'alive' space. In no case, though, did the pattern deviate from the principle of otherness. This liminal space-myth has created a chain of semantic associations and contradictions; by-products of this spatial liminality include positive discourses concerning one's symbolic seduction by the idiosyncratic space, as well as negative discourses of aesthetic resentment (class based, puritan, anti-elitist or otherwise) that focus on an ideological 'uneasiness' originating in Mykonos' prevailing element of invented (i.e., superficial) 'difference'.

The *Mykoniots d'élection* live in their heroic past and decadent present. Mykonos for them is the symbolic spatialisation of their ideological nomadic subjectivities. The first to arrive embraced the myth that Mykonos is a 'queer place'; via their sensuous bodies, an 'organised' act of subversion beyond any social, cultural or gender roles gradually emerges. Mykonos' liminal space-image is ultimately reflected on the 'mythical' subjects who occupy this liminal space. As one can see in the conclusion of this monograph, the definition of *a* space – i.e., the Mykonian space – as 'queer' operates in the text less literally (where the term 'queer' equates the strange, atypical, liminal semantics of the space-myth of Mykonos) and more metaphorically connoting to 'queer theory' (where performativity is a 'political' identity displacement). In other words, 'queer space' here connotes to an eternal desire for fluidity; a space of (structural) liminality where performing subjects can project – as it were – their liminal subjectivities. Furthermore, it connotes to the *Mykoniots d'élection*'s strategic shifting between different subject positions and 'political' self-transformations, a lived-out identity-repertoire which emerges out of their need to transcend every category. Mykonos, from the nineties, is openly advertised as a 'gay' island. The term 'queer place' in this sense goes far beyond the recently developed discourse and image of Mykonos as a massive homosexual pleasure dome, to how a tourist space can acquire its own semiotic power which subsequently manipulates and transforms the profile of its performers.

Following the reader's queries as to what happened to the group since the completion of my fieldwork, the epilogue – written in a more personal style – in an implicit way also introduces us to the present-day Mykonian reality and the fading myth of the *Mykoniots d'élection*. The ethnography here undertakes a definitive self-reflexive overtone; the self (as a theoretical construct) finally becomes an integral part of the ethnographic narrative; the self finally becomes part of the 'group'. My informants' idiosyncratic aesthetics/ethics are here ethnographically recreated through a narrative of loss. The mythologisation and commemoration of one of the *Mykoniots*, arguably the 'mentor' of the group, is epitomised in a beach farewell ritual. The epilogue, in a lyrical fashion, following my mythologisation of a mentor's death, also describes the end of an era for the 'Nomads of Mykonos' and the opening of a new 'global' cosmopolitan reality for tourist Mykonos, where the 'idiosyncratic' being appropriated – becomes obsolete.

My distance from and revisiting the text made me revise my theoretical stance on what is the key issue vis-à-vis identity in the case of the *Mykoniots d'élection*. In such extreme contexts – 'non-places' like Mykonos – identity, especially for actors who belong to a 'transgressive' category vis-à-vis their locality, becomes a conscious construction. The theoretical ideas that emerged were: conscious self-performance, self-transformation and liminality as 'structure'. Thus, this theoretical revisiting accounts for this monograph's subtitle: *Performing liminalities in a 'queer' space*.

Finally, I decided not to include any images of the characters in this ethnography because, I believe, it would reduce its 'liminal' protagonists to literal representations – otherwise, to misrepresentations. To protect the identity of my informants, names as well as personal details have been altered.

1
MYKONOS: THE BUILDING OF A LIMINAL SPACE-MYTH

The *Mykoniots d'élection*: a performance

'By their performances shall ye know them.' Is it a play? Or rather is it a performance one plays by oneself? I wrote this ethnography without having any idea what the theoretical notion of performativity was. 'My informants' led me to this existential topos. Prior to this encounter I saw Greece, my auto-ethnographic topos, as comprised of imitative social actors who were prescribed to perform a stereotypical role. There was a repertoire of roles, of course, but it was a limited one. Why was I seeing my auto-ethnographic 'other' like this? Was it because they were passively acting out this imitative 'role'? Or was it because the 'marginality' of my new *Mykoniots d'élection* informants made them appear to me, for the first time, more ludic, more 'performative'? Why wasn't I seeing my own mother, for example, as an equally competent 'performer' of a similarly playful role?

I know now what I did not know then. I should blame it on my fixated ethnographic translation of any 'stereotypical' category: Greek-woman-middle-class equals uniformity in performance. Anthropology, but most importantly my middle-class cultural upbringing, made me think of myself as part of a fixed category, be it either of a family, a culture, or of a much-troubled gender group. I do not want to declare either a relativist or a syncretist manifesto. But within a 'restlessness' always to seek the 'other', the different, one can find the way for a more personal political performativity. This does not mean that the *Mykoniots d'élection* are fully self-conscious, as well as perfectly integrated human carriers of a universal-humanist-individualist consciousness. Yet, by just being with them, I learned that one can be many things, acquire many roles, in this ludic process of 'playing' with the self.

'By their performances shall ye know them'; Schechner and Appel open their edited volume on performance, ritual and theatre with this characteristic quote from Turner (1990: 1). Schechner – following Turner's principles of the 'universals of performance' – perambulates from fragments of ritual, to fragments of theatre to the conscious performativity of everyday life. Turner clearly believes that within ritual and theatre performances there is a transformative element that brings self-awareness to the cultural or personal level. Irrespective of which emerged first, theatre or ritual performativity, performance is always described as a conscious act and a constitutive part of life. Schechner describes the transformative experience of the performer as a paradox: one side of the performer is totally immersed, and the other remains the observer. There is an element of control and awareness in the process; the transformation is not permanent. Myerhoff (1990) in the same volume, drawing on Turner's state of *communitas*, accepts that in performance, heightened subjective states can account for the performers' 'transformation of consciousness'. This can also acquire a 'collective dimension' involving groups and communities. Myerhoff, following Turner, also observes a 'dark side' to *communitas*; this transformative experience may provoke intensive feelings of self-loss and rapture (ibid. 248).

The *Mykoniots d'élection*'s playfulness with their self-images can border on the edge of eccentricity, self-indulgence and liberation. The *Mykoniots d'élection* provided me with an opening towards a performative self and this, in turn, provided me with the aesthetic impetus to utilise performative auto-ethnography [and by other means such as film-making]. This provided me with the challenge to de-codify how consciously we could perform the role of playing ourselves, using one role, then another, and then another. This ethnography is thus a narrative assemblage of multi-performativity in self-representation. In other words, it was the *Mykoniots d'élection* themselves who were performative and not the theory of performativity applied to them: they were practising performativity. Schechner (1995) establishes his notion of performance as embodied playing. This embodied form of performing-being-playing takes place in daily life beyond art and ritual (ibid. 42), Schechner's subject is constituted in the 'playing': 'the process of making performances does not so much imitate playing as epitomise it' (ibid. 41).

Thus, I will propose that ethnographers as well as the auto-ethnographers involved in writing about performativity, should try to reveal the (more) personal 'root' of this sort of reflexivity. My 'roots' were the *Mykoniots d'élection*. I therefore dedicate this book to them. Because they taught me to 'play' without guilt. So I moved onto somewhere else, but now I return to my 'roots' and publish this ethnography.

This is a *longue durée* ethnography; it took me seven years to complete the writing, but it continues. In return I gained a 'home', a 'displaced' sense of an oxymoronic collectivity of extreme individuals.

The 'group' in its space

This is a study of the *Mykoniots d'élection*, who, as their invented[1] group-designation reveals, are a group of people who have been visiting the island of Mykonos for the last thirty-five years or so and have formed an alternative community. Their constant return to the island and their insistence on living, acting, working and creating in a tourist space offers them an alternative identity, which, in turn, is aesthetically marked by the transient cultural properties of Mykonos, the space they have fetishised in their lives as 'nomads'. During my fieldwork years (1991 to 1997) and my subsequent returns to the island, I collected a long list of fetishised references for the Cycladic space of Mykonos.

Emma, a Londoner 'by descent' who has been living on the island since the late sixties, compares Mykonos' image to that of the (female) womb. Mykonos for Emma and her friends signifies a place of 'protection' and desired 'exclusion'. Following Dubisch's analogous description of the nearby island of Tinos, the spatial image of an 'island' immediately becomes something more than a mere 'physical setting'. Dubisch argues that 'the very fact that it [Tinos] is an island helps to give it a unique identity' (Dubisch 1995: 120). For example, in Mykonos' case, the island becomes engendered, personified and unique.

Emma goes on to portray the 'travellers' who became enchanted with and anchored on Mykonos, as mysterious individuals who have the distinctive ability to 'incorporate' with great ease – as if they were merely 'passing it by'- a new collective self. This newly acquired Mykonian identity is apparently aimed at a boundless communion that ideally draws no distinction between the 'self' and the 'other', between 'them' and the 'indigenous'. In other words, they all arrived alone as individuals, but became affiliated to the 'magic' properties of this small protected island and 'transformed' themselves into 'mystic' participants in an ideal socialisation. Mykonos is thus represented as a perfect 'mother', a perfect 'home'. Common to all members is the fact that this element of fetishisation of the Mykonian space has contributed to the development of an alternative collective self, but one which paradoxically does not contradict their uncompromising individuality. The *Mykoniots d'élection* might have established a collective self, but one based on a counter-collective discourse of accentuated individuality. This notion of a collective self cuts across established social categories of exclusion and belonging. The result is a struggle for 'exclusivity' projected onto the symbol of Mykonos. Mykonos, as an all inclusive sign of freedom and protection, has created in the *Mykoniots d'élection* the traveller's addiction for a space that somehow reflects her 'transitory' identity, a place that she can fearlessly identify with, a place that feels, at last, familiar. This study is about how the *Mykoniots d'élection* construct their illusive, and exclusive, sense of a collective self.

Locating the 'group'

The word Mykonos, stands for both the island as a whole and the locale called Mykonos town which is the concentrated centre of the island; this urbanised centre is also traditionally called the *Hora* of Mykonos.[2] Since the sixties, tourism has been built upon a space/aesthetic myth of exclusivity and liberality, and the fetishisation of the island by the Greek media. The diversity of visitors created 'routes' of action for distinct (aesthetic) groups, who appropriated the island and created their own identity niches by slowly parcelling out the Mykonian *Hora*. The reader should bear in mind that 91 per cent of the overall 'indigenous' labour force (out of approximately 6,000 registered inhabitants) are employed in tourism (cf. Backos 1992: 32). One should add to the above population an unrecorded number of several thousand 'permanent' summer residents and occasional workers who, in their turn, mingle with the hundreds of thousands of tourists in the six-month tourist season.

During the last decade, Mykonos' population has dramatically increased since many of its seasonal residents, both Greek and foreigners, chose to settle on the island. The once migrant Mykonians, now receive a stream of immigrants from Albania, Bulgaria and Poland. Paradoxically, the prosperous economy of the formerly impoverished Mykonos makes it an attractive place for those trying to 'improve' their lives (Nazou 1996:16). According to the local press, by the late nineties the official number of the much contested category of 'the Albanians' had already reached 3,200 (cf. Katsoudas 1998).

It is thus evident that the demographic composition cannot be confined to the recorded group of the 'indigenous'. The fact that it attracts many 'permanent' and 'transient' exogenous inhabitants, thanks to its successful mystic place-image and local economy, gives Mykonos town a very complex system of socialisation. The cultural complexity created by this tourist space is evident in the appropriation of various Mykonian haunts by diverse stylistic groups, which represent distinct tribal-like gatherings. The *Mykoniots d'élection* act and work in such a space; their daily reality reflects this network of aesthetic tribes. The *Mykoniots d'élection* are a counter-local group who act as the representatives of the myth of 'otherness' for all those tourists who come to Mykonos aspiring to find 'something different'.

This study is not about a 'simple' rural society that has been invaded by tourism nor a homogenised image of a 'local' culture that has changed beyond recognition. My research focuses on the *Mykoniots d'élection* aesthetic group as one among several in this complex setting. The members of this group have lived for more than thirty years in the shadow of the place-myth of Mykonos, and have survived only by fetishising it.

The transgressive ethnographic category of the *Mykoniots d'élection* is akin to Waldren's 'outsiders', the artistic colonisers of Deia, Mallorca. These foreign Deianecs represent an alternative spatial designation of belonging in the tourist space – quite distinct from the homogenised category of the 'local' (Waldren 1996: xi). It is interesting to make this inversion in the tourist space: to ethnographically read it from the point of view of the exogenous 'locals'.[3] Mykonos, an ex-romantic cosmopolitan and now mass tourist destination for hundreds of thousands of tourists, is a place that may evoke the idea of locality, the idea of translocality and the idea of an artificial locality to the tourists, the indigenous population and exogenous locals alike. In such a space, a traditional anthropological approach (cf. Stott 1982) would probably examine ethnographically how the 'local' population has been affected by the invasion of 'outsiders'. A sociological one would concentrate on the identity of the 'tourist' as a generic category of post-modernity (Urry 1990). However, throughout this book, I maintain that in this hybrid space, there is an alternative category of (trans)locals who fall in-between: they are neither outsiders, nor insiders and most importantly they have no real home to return to. Nonetheless, one can become caught up in a dualistic ethnographic exercise. Waldren's 'Insiders and Outsiders', for example, reconstructs 'alienated' encounters in the contemporary tourist space. This dualism is justified at least at the discursive level: discourses that favour development against preservation are equally employed by both the 'strata of the indigenous' – Mykonians and Deianecs alike – and set them against the 'exogenous', who prefer their discovered paradise untouched (Waldren 1996: xvii). Yet, the huge cultural and class-based gap between the cosmopolitan bourgeoisie of the artistic newcomers and the peasant background of the indigenous Deianecs, although indisputable, can overshadow alternative cultural dynamics that emerge in the (trans)local tourist *topos*. In today's Mykonos, cultural politics is far removed from this form of explicit dualism. What sociologically informs contemporary Mykonos is a series of rurbanised overlapping networks of individuals with diverse cultural and class backgrounds. This multiplicity undermines the dichotomy of the insider/outsider. In a sense, the anthropological [re]construction of the *Mykoniots d'élection* could be seen as an ethnographic continuation, but also as a deconstruction of Waldren's 'outsiders' in the age of 'touristification', when the once elitist model of the traveller with an 'extremely individualist lifestyle' is appropriated by the masses.

Tracing the 'group'

To identify the members of the group, I started by approaching a few members I was familiar with through my earlier visits when I had spent some time working and holidaying on the island. These people led me eventually to the whole network. I established my presence gradually among members of the group. The fact that I was working – that is sharing a temporary identity in the tourist space – linked me to a wider group of people who already felt connected. Hence, rather than treating me as just the 'ethnographer', they eventually regarded me as 'one of them'.

The principle of random socialisation that a 'snowball' technique prescribes for the ethnographer reflects a 'natural' way of socialising practised by several elitist and marginal groups in the Greek context. Based upon a general consensus, this principle rules the social lives of the *Mykoniots d'élection* and thus this type of gradual initiation into the 'Mykonian' network was actually the only way for me to socialise. In order to decodify this idiosyncratic socialising system and become 'part of the same *sinafi* (i.e., part of the same aesthetic and sensual category[4]) I had to be recognised as consistently exposing myself to the *Mykoniots*'[5] peculiar understanding of sharing.

The Mykonian network as a whole – of which the *Mykoniots d'élection* were only one group – operated through several distinct subgroups and its participants were occasionally connected with one or more *parees* (singular, *parea*, circle of friends). Individual alliances obeyed a similar rule of transience. The 'local core' belonged to a larger context of socialisation comprising various '*Mykoniot* nomads' who were affiliated with each other and played a part in analogous cosmopolitan networks which connected spaces like Mykonos, Athens, London, New York, Bali, India, Ibiza and so forth.

It would be impossible to explore the cultural signs of all the different Mykonian groups and *parees* in detail, since each of them engaged in different sets of practices and appeared to belong to different aesthetic 'tribes'. Initially, it felt like an overwhelming ethnographic task to put such a diversity under the usual anthropological scrutiny. I eventually decided to concentrate on the *Mykoniots d'élection* because I had had some acquaintance with them during my earlier visits as a summer worker. I can suggest that in broad terms, my informants were aesthetically and socially affiliated with a larger group of 300 to 500 'exogenous locals' who composed the diachronic core of the exogenous 'cosmopolitans'. In turn, the members of this larger aesthetic group seemed only occasionally to establish various alliances within the boundaries of a peculiar and much fetishised set of practices relevant to membership of the group of the *Mykoniots d'élection*. Moreover, the transient quality of the tourist space was clearly reflected, both in the foundation and in the easy abolition of group roles and their aesthetic configurations.

This category of workers, whom Urry terms a 'service group', are defined by a special labour property which stems from the particularity of their style of work. Urry evaluates the special conditions and services of the tourist and catering industry in general, as offering a specific type of 'emotional work' (Urry 1990: 70). Further, Shields (1991: 112) draws on Bakhtin in order to 'morally' exculpate the image of the liminal/pleasure zone as something counterproductive. For Shields, what distinguishes the beach (pleasure zone) semantically from the factory floor (work zone) is not the production-consumption dichotomy. It is rather a 'spatial division' that depends on the principles of another semantic, antithetical pairing: libidinal versus rational. In the latter dichotomy, the libidinal energies are historically restored as 'real and productive' (Deleuze and Guattari quoted in ibid.).

This kind of emotionally charged labour in Mykonos' pleasure zone, which creates a special bond among the island's summer workers, offered me a shared identity with my informants. The identity of the group is dictated by a logic of 'setting the local scene' for the transient groups of tourists. Thus the *Mykoniots d'élection* 'transgress', and become 'local'; in Mykonos' cultural heterotopia they perform as the 'host community'.[6] Interestingly, this 'service-identity' is shared both by those *Mykoniots d'élection* who work in tourism on a professional basis, as well as by those whose work or existence bears no apparent relation to tourism.

Boissevain (1996) was amongst the first to ethnographically focus on the 'performances' of the host community in an era of mass cultural tourism; here the 'host community' is represented as a homogenous cultural category through its [structural] resistance pattern: the 'hosts' are struggling to sustain their privacy. Their Goffmanesque i.e., performative yet quotidian 'back-regions' – the private places where they take off their masks – remain intact (Goffman 1959). Therefore they manage to recolonise the invaded tourist space, only by displaying to the tourist a staged version of their daily routine and liminality. The agonistic/performative play in question works somewhat like this: an outsider (the tourist) voyeuristically desires to 'look in' and momentarily be part of the 'inside'; an insider protects the inside, by organising a fake authenticity that pretends to introduce the visitor 'backstage'. Yet, as Damer's (2004) ethnographic account on the tourist island of Symi suggests, tourist performances can also be improvisational. Not everything is staged 'staged authenticity'; 'front' or 'backstages' in the tourist performative space acquire a Schechnerian mode of interactive play.

Ironically, performance here is not solely a technical sociological term, nor a prop for the anthropological analysis: it is a fully realisable, as well as conscious artistic project on behalf of the individual, be they a tourist or a host. Performance regains its 'sensuality'. The tourist is involved in a penetrating act: to deconstruct the constructed performance. She becomes an avant-garde reader of the performance, 'where the experience itself is more important than the hermeneutics' (Bruner 2001: 902).

A new wave of reflexive anthropology, like Frank's (2000) autobiographical fictional ethnography makes the performative notion of a 'staged' backstage implicitly redundant. Here the ethnographic 'setting', which by poetic licence could work metonymically as the 'tourist space', is a fictional strip club somewhere in America. Frank herself is both an ethnographer and a sex worker, i.e., the host, the connoisseur of the 'backstage', who unravels for us – the readers of her *roman-à-clef* – both her own and her client's staged 'backstage' performance. Curiously, they both know that in their regular clandestine weekly meetings in the club they only 'act out' a fake intimacy. In other words, both the 'insider's' and the 'outsider's' performances remain a re-enactment of a 'front-stage' while being conscious, at the same time of each other's 'backstages'.

Mapping the signs of Mykonos 'city'

Mykonos 'city'[7] can be described ethnographically as a hybrid spatial construct. This could best be represented by browsing through the different cultural connotations which the signs and stylistic patterns of its different haunts and neighbourhoods reflect. The *Hora* (central part) of Mykonos functions semantically as a cross-cultural sign for aesthetic consumption, and as an 'exhibition' space for diverse lifestyles and types of entertainment. This aesthetic configuration takes shape through different spatial trajectories which during the high tourist season are occupied by different style groups. The differences may be semiotically established in 'ethnic' spaces, for example, the 'Italian' neighbourhood, the 'Scandinavian' or the 'Irish' bar; or, alternatively, in simulated 'cult' zones like Pierro's bar, the greatest tourist attraction for 'gay culture' and its occasional associates. An additional element of stylistic *attraction* is the 'aesthetics of locality'. It consists of revised or imposed 'examples' of traditionality, such as the institutionalised conservation of the local vernacular architecture, that also act as 'cult' zones. An alternative spatial code of distinction is the music played in the various haunts. Zones of sound ambience create further classificatory divisions in the polysemic tourist space: simulated seventies Greek bouzouki spaces where enthusiastic participants perform traditional Greek machismo; zones of 'rock music', that are remnants of the glamorous seventies and eighties Mykonos scene when rock 'n' roll was the dominant ideology. Finally, there are the drinking and dancing establishments that have formed the local status quo in Mykonian nightlife for the last two to three decades. Their names have created a tradition beyond classification; then there are the nineties replicas of the above styles, as well as the current buying-up of the original establishments by characterless arrivistes that has led to an imposed impersonality on these – once notorious – haunts.

The extremely sophisticated classificatory rules of the tourist space follow the aesthetic and consumption principles of different groups which are, in turn, reflected spatially. There is an elaborate coding as to where one should reside, eat, swim or dance. These spatial and aesthetic categories are imposed onto contemporary 'visitors', who in contrast to their seventies predecessors, do not appear to mingle, following instead predetermined aesthetic paths.

The reader should try to visualise the densely packed Mykonian settlement as an all-encompassing aesthetic forum which displays these different zones of identity in-between the traditional households, Orthodox churches, souvenir shops, fashion retailers and fast food outlets. Mykonos tourist guides usually give an extensive list of clubs and restaurants and an accompanying text which leads the 'consumer' to the legendary Mykonian nightlife, an essential part of cultural sightseeing. As shrines to a local system of spatial fetishisation, Mykonian haunts (bars and clubs) act as semiotic references for the unsuspecting visitor who maps the Mykonian *Hora* and its culture accordingly. The reader can imagine the 'protected' settlement of the *Hora* of Mykonos as a series of open doors that create a feeling of 'intimacy'. In Mykonos everything seems to be public. The typical late afternoon scene on a 'Greek' island where the local women are sitting outside their homes crocheting and exchanging gossip – turning the whitewashed lanes into a 'private space' *pace* Hirschon (1982, 1985) – is designated by Damer (2004: 218) as the 'domestication of the street'. In Mykonos, this 'domestication' becomes more of a dialectical 'staged performance' where the visitor, the 'other', can immerse themselves in the scene and cohabitate. Mykonos streets come to signify the democratisation of this 'domestication of the street' in the performative polysemic tourist space.

The constant 'entering' and 'exiting' creates an endless motion of the masses in the labyrinth-like inner *Hora*; the local tourist tradition dictates 'strolling' or rather 'parading' in the Mykonian streets, dressed in one's loudest garments, combined with a generous consumption of alcohol. Penelope, the librarian and one of the local cult figures, draws parallels between this practice and a traditional local custom of the old days – which she refers to as a 'bacchanalian remnant' – when during the period of carnival the locals used to dress up in costume and attend public dances, the so-called *kasina* or *balosia*. These dances took place on the ground-floor halls of the two-storey houses located in the main street of the *Hora*. A series of houses were transformed into public spaces where meeting, dancing and flirting took place. The old custom of *balosia* reminded Penelope of the 'wild situation' of the seventies when Pierro's crowd used to parade in 'themed' costumes. Penelope promoted a discourse which indicated that the ambience of anarchy and enjoyment was actually familiar to Mykonians, and not just a newly established order.

The way the semiotic mapping of the Mykonian 'city' is constructed invites the visitor to consume its 'myth'. In recent years there has been a dramatic increase in internal tourism. Greeks have invaded Mykonos in order to be part of the island's cosmopolitan myth. The reality of contemporary Mykonos is crowded streets. The 'Mykonos experience' does not feel real anymore. The objective of the Mykonos visitor is less to enjoy himself and more to accumulate signs. Like the visitor to the Expo exhibition in Seville in 1992 described by Harvey, the visitor to Mykonos fetishises the accumulation of signs (Harvey 1996). As Urry suggests, 'tourism itself involves the collection of signs' (1990: 3). In New York's post-

Second-World-War Greenwich Village, the early tourist expected to collect signs of bohemia (Wilson 1998); in nineties Calcutta, the backpacker expects to collect signs of poverty (Hutnyk 1996); in nineties San Francisco, the gay-pilgrim expects to find a queer homeland (Howe 2001); in post-*Captain Corelli's* Cephallonia, the tourist expects to visit an ahistorical romanticised Mediterranean island space (Tzanelli 2003). In today's Mykonos, one can hear conservative members of the aspiring Greek bourgeoisie boasting about the fact that they have been to Pierro's, the 'gay place', as if it were just another section of a rock 'n' roll museum.

In line with Harvey's suggestion, I can see an identical pattern in relation to the consumption of Mykonos: 'the accumulation of ... signs was more important than the content of the exhibit itself' (1996: 156). The same applies to the European or American traveller who visits the Cyclades or the Greek islands in general. People usually tend to visit two or three islands, and sometimes it is difficult for them to remember their names; the touring is what matters.[8] Once again, in this instance, the object of the 'tourist gaze', the Greek islands, the Mykonian haunts, the Expo pavilions are 'consumed' in the style that Baudrillard talked of: 'not in their materiality but in their difference, in the evocation or simulation of relationships and experiences where reality is less important than signification' (Harvey 1996: 157).

In this sense, the parading and viewing of Mykonos' nightlife for many visitors does not include the actual experience itself, as recorded by their predecessors; the excitement, the symbolic 'seduction' are absent. Just as Expo is for Harvey 'the key institution in constituting the world as representation', Mykonos is a key representation of an easily accessible symbol of cosmopolitanism ready-made for local consumption. The tourist space, in this sense, breaks the chains of locality, of a Greek culture that lies on the 'margins of Europe'. Thus, Mykonos' sign, constitutes multiculturalism and cosmopolitanism as its spatial representation. The visiting tourist is turned into a museum visitor in one of the most cosmopolitan and notorious haunts of the seventies. The 'museum' includes a hippie section of which the *Mykoniots d'élection*, the main protagonists of this book, form a part. The *Mykoniots d'élection* perform and instruct their 'descendants' on how to continue or rather how to experience, at least for a few days a year, the lifestyle of the 'Greek beatnik'. For the visitor, Mykonos' *Hora* semiotically represents itself in sections, as a multi-tribal setting of different aesthetic choices.

The trouble designating these 'extreme' individuals

The people I portray in this study are certainly not typical 'anthropological subjects'. The *Mykoniots d'élection* are not an isomorphic group in the sense that they belong exclusively to an established social category based on class, gender or ethnicity. However, in order to avoid any further theoretical complications, I generally excluded data I had collected from some non-Greek members of the group. My intention was to explore diversity through cultural homogeneity.

One could argue that the study of 'trans-national', 'trans-local', 'trans-class' processes[9] is likely to be resistant to conventional anthropological classification. 'Alternative' classifications – for example, group and individual identities based on aesthetics, on 'marginality' and/or on extreme individuality – destabilise the traditionally homogenised 'cultural' self. The theoretical emergence of the 'conscious' and 'unconscious' subject in the anthropological text and the subject's fragile relationship with established and superficially isomorphic categories of a monolithic 'cultural identity' are, I think, one of the greatest theoretical challenges facing the discipline at present.

Those acquainted with eighties and nineties Greek ethnography will probably find the aforementioned theoretical predicament a commanding one. Any rhetoric on individuality was susceptible to stereotypical interpretations. It almost automatically connoted discourses of Greek machismo and hidden nationalism (Herzfeld 1985, 1995). I will return to this constructed notion of a culturally fetishised 'Greek' individuality. For the moment, I intend to focus on the constructed myth of Mykonos, which will prove a useful analytical tool. What several Mykonian groups share vis-à-vis their communal identity is precisely the fetishisation of the image of Mykonos. Each aesthetic group conceptualises Mykonos as its spatial reflection. Its members, in turn, conceptualise Mykonos as the reflection of their extreme individuality. My informants, for instance, mostly employed highly individualistic discourses and disliked being associated monosemantically with a single identity category such as Greek, local, hippie, gay and so forth. In parallel with the fetishisation of the space of Mykonos as unique and boundless, there is an extreme element of self-fetishisation. The discourses of my informants suggest that their life is lived through style. Their absolute commitment to style[10] makes them, with reference to Bourdieu's model of social emulation, very sensitive receivers of cultural change (Bourdieu 1984: 56, 57).

This study could be described first and foremost as an attempt to account ethnographically for an extreme eclectic group located in a highly hybridic space. Critics could argue that it is only an invented fetishisation of exclusivity, consistent with a (Greek) cultural context that is recorded to have strategically employed similar rhetorics of exclusivity and deviation for purposes of cultural survival in an otherwise unequal confrontation with the dominant westernised discourses of power. The aforementioned interpretative model could further suggest that the cultural self of a Greek ethnographer is reflected upon a seemingly 'atypical' ethnographic example of Greekness, yet recreating the same version of Greekness, a Greekness inclusive of familiar elements as an already ethnographically justified performative fragmentation. In Appendix I, I will attempt to theoretically challenge this view.

Instead, Mykonos can stand for the performative space – ultimately a space-fetish – and the *Mykoniots d'élection* as a performative oxymoronic collectivity with uncommitted peripheral members that make their acquired Mykonian identity, *pace* Taussig (1998), an 'interiority' fetish that betrays a similarity, a sense of belonging to a collectivity. In this interlaced scenario, the fetish ceases to be a thing – it is instead related to some abstract notion: interiority (ibid. 236). In other words, *fetish* is not monosemantically inscribed onto a thing or a category, rather, it is, its property – i.e., the fetish's inscription – that 'moves'; there are 'fissured, performative spaces where the fetish moves (as it were !) … ' (Spyer 1998: 2). The fetishisation of (the tourist) space and the fetishisation of a performatively-acquired 'local' identity with its constructed narrativity and semiotic paraphenalia constitute the *Mykoniots d'élection* performance. Their 'wardrobe of selves' (an identity-repertoire), then, accompanies them as their transient fetishes – their performing props, their conscious and unconscious intentions that rename their subjectivities. Are they 'naked' without them? Are these personae merely their masks? Taussig argues that 'demasking is a peculiar form of defacement' (Taussig 1998: 232). There is no transparency: her 'naked' face/body becomes her 'mask'. There is an interesting analogy between Taussig's identity fetish – mask as defacement – and the *Mykoniots*' playfulness with their 'naked' face/body and their image construction. For their seasonal performances, the *Mykoniots*' naked sensuous bodies become their masks. In the summer months, their self-image becomes synonymous with their beach attire, their *pareos*. Their interiority fetish, then, is a product of their self-transformations.

There is an interesting link between Taussig's notion of the fetish as interiority and symbolic defacement (a symbolic constituent of their 'collective' fluid subjectivities) with an idiosyncratic notion of a ritualistic quotidian performance in the tourist space and the *Mykoniots*' performativity in general. Demasking attempts to restore faciality, Taussig declares. For the *Mykoniots*, every spring signifies the 'removal' of the masks: the 'naked body' has been deformed by the claustrophobia of the winter. Still, they have to confront one another, exhibiting the withered body/face at the beach; alienated every new season from last years' friendships, they return to the island's *maya-leela* (literally 'illusion-play') performative playground only in order to regain 'faciality' (cf. Schechner 1995: 27–36). They put their masks back on. This year in, year out, soul-searching enterprise, to lose and find a collectivity, to lose and find self, endows them with their self-transformative properties. After some time, the neglected body – isolated from the winter's inertia – will return to the Mykonian stage. This hyper-masking defines the *Mykoniots d'élection*. Unmasking makes no difference, because there is no transparency behind the mask. Imagine the fetish power of the 'naked body' of a *Mykoniot* as her mask. The 'naked' face/body becomes her fetish. And fetish is this double property: the 'naked' face/body as window, and at the same time, as mask of the soul. This disproportionate property of the face/body is for Taussig (1998: 227) what links it with the notion of the fetish.

The *Mykoniots d'élection*'s self-narratives, their 'wardrobe of selves', both in their rhetoric and in my discourse, are ethnographically revisited in order to talk about the power of self-transformation. Do their self-transformations, then, ultimately constitute the *Mykoniots*' fetish? Is their tranformation/performance 'political' (*pace* Parkin, Caplan and Fisher 1996)?

Marcus (1998) makes a link between the construction of fetish and eccentricity. The *Mykoniots d'élection*'s *habitus* is clearly dependent upon notions of eccentricity and fetish construction. Their habitual fetish construction is equally applied to their garments and distinctive household paraphernalia, their symbolic and performative attributions to the Mykonian space, as well as to themselves, who are mythologised and thus fetishised due to their extreme individuality/eccentricity. Their eccentricity though – given the plurality of their social backgrounds – is not orchestrated without self-awareness. In other words, their eccentricity is not determined by a *habitus*. Their fetishistic acts are performative and volatile. Things and ideologies, selves and spaces can be turned into obsessions and fetishes; yet, all this lies at the level of a conscious self-performance. This performative element of their eccentricity, as we shall see in their self-narratives, essentially removes them from the essentialist category of the 'eccentric' as part of a collective *habitus*. Unlike Marcus' socially 'elect' eccentrics, the *Mykoniots*' eccentricity is a self-conscious act of resistance and reinvention. Their self-mythologising is due to their trivial obsessions. And these became their fetishes: 'Mama India', a Mykonian beach, a sarong. Obsessions and fetishes are not solely 'the collective emblem of distinctive identity' (Marcus 1998: 169), neither are they solely a 'mimetic faculty' *à la* Benjamin (1986) and Taussig (1993), but rather the metonymy of their creative resistance.

Fetishised spaces, fetishised selves

Mykonos: the building of a liminal place-myth

'What time is this place?' By employing this rhetorical question, Lynch argues that the establishment of the tourist/romantic gaze has in its turn created images of places connected with particular times and histories (Lynch 1973, quoted in Urry 1990: 126). In this sense, Mykonos' tour de force was its primitive characteristically vernacular and cubist-like architecture that initially inspired the modern artists. From the early stages of its tourist development, the reproduction of a local vernacular style (the so-called post-modern vernacular), combined with a sense of modernist cultural non-placeness was initiated. Both those elements promoted an 'amoral' representation that in its turn attracted different and diverse tribestyles. Consequently, the sense of time in tourist Mykonos is not singular, since what is enacted is both a 'traditional' backdrop and a cosmopolitan and eccentric ambience. This aesthetic and cultural mixing gave the visitor a spatial and temporal sense of déjà vu, a sense of familiarity, that was later exploited in favour of a local myth of otherness.

Mykonos: an image of the 'authentic' vernacular

> There are clearly many holiday destinations which are consumed not because they are intrinsically superior but because they convey taste or superior status. (Urry 1990: 44)

The above quotation accurately describes the emerging sign of tourist Mykonos which, unlike many other Greek tourist islands, has obtained a worldwide reputation. To be more precise, Mykonos has built a stylistic myth of exclusivity and acquired aesthetic 'superiority' over other Greek tourist destinations. The second chapter of the book describes the legendary 'coming' to the island of various individuals and groups who promoted a myth of exclusivity that gradually established Mykonos' aesthetic identity. Mykonos acquired its status partly because it happened to be near the archaeological sites of the ancient shrine of Apollo on the nearby island of Delos. Even so, the locals did not rely solely on this proximity and created a counter place-myth, a modern one, based on the originality of the islanders and their craftsmanship.

Left impoverished after the war, Mykonos, an infertile island,[11] had little to offer the visitor but the islanders' hospitality and tolerance. The first modern visitors admired the simplicity and the repetition of the all-embracing whitewashed stonework. Thus the locals decided to 'respect' their visitors' tastes and preserve everything 'as it was back then'. Moreover, new houses were built according to the old style.[12] This slowly created a form of 'staged' vernacular. This spatial performativity was reflected in the actions of the locals and, as we shall see later, in the *habitus* of the whole exogenous community, thus creating what Urry calls a 'post-modern vernacular' where the representation of time in space is faked to create a picture of authenticity.[13] Mykonos' later notoriety was acquired through an aesthetic capital which reputedly derived from its 'inherent taste'. In this sense, the place-myth remained faithful to the romantic gaze by constantly recreating a local vernacular architecture. Timelessness defines the island's performative space, not unlike Tzanelli's (2003) place-myth of Cephallonia where – instead of its architecture – it is its unalterable landscape that is romanticised.

Lawerence Durrell is largely responsible for the semiotic acquisition of Mykonos space as timeless with no definite style – haphazard and harmonious at the same time. Mykonos, the 'miracle' of modernist architecture 'has so little history to intimidate one' (Durrell 1978: 231). Yet, unlike Cephallonia, Mykonos – due to its overdevelopment – suffered a semantic mutation: from a romanticised ahistorical rural landscape, into a cosmopolitan 'metropolis' that semiotically works as a rurban space, constantly expanding through sophisticated contemporary architecture, contiguous with the picturesque signs of the vernacular. The prevailing discourse is one of a historical catastrophe due to the vandalisation of the romanticised Mykonian landscape by the invading visitors and the greedy locals.

Mykonos' myth of its 'unique style' grew to arbitrarily represent a generalised category of Greek island-style architecture, a style copied by other resorts. Indicative of Mykonos' stylistic success is Zarkia's ethnographic account of a Skyrian 'staged' authenticity (Skyros is another Greek island relatively close to the island of Mykonos). She reports that Skyrians have happily imported a so-called 'Mykonian' style architecture, dramatically different from their own traditional one in order to stage a resort-like setting and advance tourism (Zarkia 1996: 160).

What type of spectacle, then, does Mykonos offer the tourist gaze? Mykonos is a polysemic place that bombards the tourist with conflicting signs. It is a full and exciting aesthetic kaleidoscope. Mykonos as a polythetic sign can also afford to invoke different desires, as well as perform different spectacles for different groups. For Greek tourists, for instance, Mykonos' image may signify cosmopolitanism, a 'cultural quality' they themselves feel deprived of. In this sense, Mykonos performs for them the ideal, the miniature mapping of a cosmopolitan city with its subcultures, hedonism, transculturalism, multi-neotribalism; in short, the object of desire for their hungry 'gaze' is the boundless element of the post-modern space. On the other hand, the attracted tribestyles of the nineties, groups like the gays or the ravers or some aesthetic simulators of the hippie-style, satisfy their desire through identification with diverse bodies of spectacle that 'democratically' coexist in the polysemic space: Mykonos' clubbing, alternative communions with 'old' friends, or the group of fetishisers of the special (metaphysical) properties of the island's natural setting. In any case, the discourses on what the Mykonian spectacle consists of may also, in many cases, overlap. Yet, each tribestyle strategically occupies different parts of this small tourist island. Their performative distinction game is conspicuously displayed through a set of 'distinct' aesthetic preferences which are, in turn, spatially re-presented, thus, overtly demarcating the territorial map of Mykonos.

The tourist, confused in the narrow cobbled streets of the maze-like Mykonos 'city', engages in the most 'significant' act: voyeurism. By satisfying every anticipation, the polythetic Mykonian sign locates the tourist in the place-myth. She is strolling around the central arteries of the town only to watch where the 'others' go. Without realising it, she is part of the parade, part of the spectacle.

Once upon a time, in Mykonos, the streets were clean and the explorer/tourist walked barefoot, enchanted, seeking to catch up with 'local' time and forget his own, taking pictures of old ladies weaving at their looms. Nowadays, the picturesque old ladies are a scarce spectacle for the tourist gaze. The ones that still exist simulate the image of the 'Mykonian woman' and her act of weaving by displaying the old loom without actually using it. Some women still knit caps near their windows and sell them during the summer months, especially around sunset when the tourists return from the beaches. For a moment the eye can be enchanted: what time is this place? Greece in the fifties, or further back? Next to the window with the old lady knitting, there is a small chapel with its door modestly open. With just one glimpse, time can change here and now. The next snapshot is of Pierro's. Soon after sunset its fame will transform the Mykonian neighbourhood: laughter and extravagant clothes, leather, boots, beers. What time is this place? The eighties, I should say. Youth, subcultures, and all that. Tourists do not bother to explore the many short cuts of the town. There is nothing 'left' there to discover. They have already decoded their own haunts. Some will end up at Pierro's, some at the Irish bar, some at the Scandinavian, some will exhaust themselves in 'celebrity' spotting. Some old-fashioned romantics visit Mykonos off-season, admire the architecture, talk to the locals. They will perhaps find cheap accommodation in the freaks' camping site on Paradise beach. What time is this place? Definitely the seventies.

The subject who consumes the aforementioned polysemic image becomes automatically part of it. The inspecting subject is, at the same time, converted to an object of appropriation and consumption in the tourist setting of Mykonos. The inspecting subject can feel a sense of 'belonging' and 'non-placeness' simultaneously. As Urry states, what people 'gaze upon' are ideal representations of the 'view in question', and I would like to add that the pleasure gained from it is not the actual appreciation of the spectacular scenery or street happenings (Urry 1990: 86); rather, it is the ideal identity (a mutable, performative one) they acquire through the act of participating/consuming this organised and versatile space.

Theories of spatialisation: a theoretical solution?

Shields (1991) uses discourses of space as a useful guide to actors' conceptualisations of themselves and to their representations of reality. He proposes a Barthesian analysis of the tourist space. He actually expands his spatially determined analysis to wider contexts, such as various consumption sites like the shopping mall (Shields 1992a). The shopping malls as social spaces, operate semantically in a similar way to tourist places. In Shields' theory of spatialisation, a place becomes a sign, or even better, a cluster of different and sometimes conflicting signs. The same place can simultaneously symbolise a variety of things and/or stand for different social and cultural groups. By incorporating this 'polysemy', space creates a symbolic ambiguity, which in turn is attached to its identity. Space as a flexible 'structure' 'can acquire contrasting connotations' (Shields 1991: 23).

In cases like Mykonos, where the place-myth rests upon a liminal image based on pleasure, this conflicting polysemy creates a spatial idolisation that turns a place into a fetish. The reason is simple: the different semantic dimensions are governed by the principle of pleasure. In this sense, images of space are processed libidinally.

Shields uses the notion of spatialisation in order to solve the problem of creativity and change in more static notions such as Bourdieu's *habitus* (1977). He ambitiously attempts to question the theoretical predominance of the 'structuring structures' in order to accommodate apparent contradictions and discontinuities. For Shields, the notion of spatialisation does not assume the coherence of an ordered structure. It is a formation rather than a structure, a function rather than a principle. Spatialisation, as an organising concept, entails an intrinsic flexibility. Space-myths form mythologies based on oppositions. As flexible formations, space-myths have the capacity to carry reshaped meanings. Thus, they are capable of accounting for change and continuity. Shields argues that 'spatialisation as a cultural artefact is inherently unstable because it is always challenged by reality' (Shields 1991: 65).

Eventually, Shields attempts to deal with the problem of subjectivity by proposing the abolition of the 'unfruitful' dichotomy between the agent and the structure, since: 'if anywhere, the "real" structure or "system" is within the position of an "agent" or a "subject"' (1991: 272). In his theory, the predominance of the spatial functions as a basis for classification upon which social divisions and separations may be articulated.

His focus on marginality is important to this study, since it could offer a theoretical solution to the dilemma raised by the urge to ethnographically classify a 'marginal' space, Mykonos, and a collection of *ex-centric* subjects (i.e., the *Mykoniots d'élection*), as representatives of either modern or post-modern discourses. 'Marginality', in his words, 'is the central topos in both the modern pluralist utopias and postmodern, radical heterotopias, following the logic of exclusionary incorporation in the former and a tactic of singularity in the latter' (Shields 1991: 277). And he concludes: 'it is from a place on the margins that one sees most clearly the relativistic, so-called post-modern features of the modern. In this sense, margins have long been "postmodern", before the growth of the popularity of this term among the intellectuals of the centre' (ibid. 278).

The Mykoniots d'élection: a group of worshippers of an aesthetic cosmopolitanism?

'There is a search for and delight in contrasts between societies rather than a longing for uniformity or superiority' (Urry 1995: 167). This is part of Urry's definition of an emerging aesthetic cosmopolitanism which belongs to a post-modern project that sets the subject in constant motion. This 'motion' is either literal through travelling, virtual through communication and information systems, or, finally, reflexive through the performance of different subjectivities. Whether one can fully accept Urry's definition as suitable to describe the

Mykoniots' cosmopolitanism is debatable. The concept of the post-tourist (whose emergence I discuss at length in Appendix II) is connected with the wider theoretical notion of the 'post-shopper', the protagonist of all consumption sites, be they tourist spaces (cf. Urry 1990), shopping centres (cf. Shields 1991), or world exhibitions (cf. Harvey 1996). The point that all of the above theorists are trying to stress is that the process of globalisation is becoming a dominant phenomenon. This phenomenon, it is argued, will not result in cultural homogeneity, but instead, in the proliferation of multiple popular and (trans)local cultures. These new groups, as Lash and Urry claim, are not determined by their subjects' relation to production, and thus they only partly correspond to 'dominant ideologies' (Lash and Urry 1994: 306, 319).

My problem with the above approach is that it does not clearly account for groups, or individuals for that matter, who were already 'alternative', so to speak, before the emergence of this overriding rule of cultural globalisation. Has the position of these groups changed in the new order? Do they still continue to exist? Are they transformed? For instance, this study deals with a 'transient' group that practises an ideological/romantic aesthetic cosmopolitanism, rejects dominant classifications, invents communal rituals and lives in a constant liminality. However, this group happens to have been practising all of the above for some decades now; the discourse of its members clearly includes elitist, extremely individualistic, in short modernist, patterns. On the other hand, the appropriation of diverse semantic subject positions by the members of the group could possibly be reduced to an overriding rule which categorises them as post-modern cosmopolitans, rather than the romantic travellers they would probably prefer to see themselves as. *Mykoniots* are consumers of culture itself, just as the post-modern subject seems to be. Even so, they fetishise and constantly recreate a discourse of marginality which, in turn, ascribes to them the social profile of an *ex-centric* group.

In this book, I attempt to reconstruct an ethnography about a group, self-created out of the diversity of a 'tourist space'. Mykonos is, for the *Mykoniots d'élection*, an 'affective' community, capable of keeping them together as a group while tolerating their idiosyncratic selves. This might sound consistent with the alternative aesthetic classification of the post-modern project. What is not consistent, however, with the aforementioned project, is the fact that these people, discursively, do not belong to any collective category whatsoever. Their discourses are intentionally marked by inconsistency; irrespective of their given position, they can contradict themselves and criticise this position at any time.[14]

My application of an eclectic/invented identity to the group reflects my belief that individuals, in principle (and beyond post-modernity), are capable of consciously creating alternative groups. This process, i.e., of 'affectively' forming a group, is considered by my informants as a 'natural' process. According to an established collective discourse, the 'like-minded' automatically share a communion. Yet, sharing, a commitment to a group is incidental, and not a lifelong commitment, since the central 'cultural' project is to reflexively transform the self. The group is itself constantly in the 'making', since its members eclectically adopt or reject, imitate or abort certain stylistic elements through the group's consumption practices ('consumption practices' here refer to choices, action, discourse, ideology, self-narrative). I therefore agree with theorists like Rapport who argue that individuals actively shape and reshape groups (1997: 6), as well as having the capacity to guard their lives 'against an impersonal, socio-cultural or institutional power' and construct an autonomous creative existence dedicated to their own life projects, their works of art (Rapport 2003: 5). I also maintain that individuals may also draw their self-identity from multiple sources and feel part of many different hybrid and fluid collectivities, beyond their fixed social, cultural and gender subject positions.

The establishment of the *Mykoniots'* communal identity stretches back some thirty-five years, when the first of them arrived at the place-myth of Mykonos. They returned every year and eventually connected their lives and their self-discourses to the 'marginal' space-myth. The emergence of a group *habitus*, i.e., a set of practices, is claimed to have developed almost 'accidentally'. They 'accidentally' came to Mykonos, they 'accidentally' kept returning there for thirty-five years or so, just as they 'accidentally' committed themselves to the group's practices. They shared some fashionable, and yet at the same time political, discourses on unconventionality and anarchy which semiotically matched the 'liminoid' property of Mykonos' place-myth.

The *Mykoniots d'élection* are totally unaware of their invented group name. According to Wagner, the anthropologist always invents the culture he is studying. 'In the act of inventing another culture', he invents his own (1981: 4). His 'invention' has to be entered as a world of his own; it feels 'like a schizophrenic's endeavour' (ibid. 9). Ultimately, 'what the fieldworker invents … is his own understanding' (ibid. 12). Wagner argues for an invention within a recognised collectivity. But what if you invent a collectivity par excellence such as the *Mykoniots d'élection*? Is this then fiction or is this ethnography? Wagner goes so far as to claim that 'invention … *is* culture' (ibid. 35). So, is fiction culture as well? This invention, that the ethnographer builds for her understanding is, in turn, the context that will eventually turn into text. This 'invented system' is the beginning of a dialogical relationship with the other (*pace* Dumont 1978). More radically, Clifford is for an 'invention' of culture through the mechanism of collage and [the practice of] ethnographic surrealism that brings to the fore all the incongruous and bizarre elements that 'betray' any consistency with a pseudo-realistic ethnographic text. Clifford argues that the two phenomenologically diverse attitudes, of anthropological humanism and the practice of ethnographic surrealism, actually presuppose one another and they are both inclusive in the cultural process (Clifford 1988: 145).

The appropriation of the term *Mykoniots d'élection* is my romantic device aimed at conforming to the strict yet arbitrary rules of traditional anthropological thinking, as to what constitutes a group, what defines a culture, what demarcates a category. Although their collective name (*Mykoniots d'élection*) is invented, my informants are definitely a group since they feel bonded, protected in their constructed community, and have invented their own counter-local cosmology. In addition, they have been practising/inventing communal actions/rituals, as well as discourses, for many years now. Yet, many of them consistently avoided defining themselves according to any collective category. In short, these people consciously refuse to identify with anything; they refuse to belong.

Finally, this 'nameless group' is by no means a cult, or a residue of some 'new religious movement', as we shall see in the following section of this chapter. They cannot be reduced to a party of 'Greek' leftovers who have meditated in India and used Mykonos as a hippie resort. Rather, their most important 'cultural' characteristic is that they are just another group who have actively promoted individual agency.

Since they see themselves as social beings with agency, I think that they should be theoretically treated as individuals with agency. Their celebrated creativity is manifested in their idiosyncratic relations. It is evident in the way they manipulate time and aesthetics, and in the fact that they employ a central communal rhetoric of desire (as an infrastructure). Their predominant group discourse consists mainly of a mythology of 'transcendence': first and foremost it promotes the escape from established social and cultural boundaries, and celebrates the creative and unrestricted bricolage of identity categories. This celebration of individuality (rather than of individualism) cannot be subjugated to some universalistic or metaphysical order. It is not a form of group ethic. Their celebration of *ex-centricity* – in other words their conscious choice to remain on the periphery – does not just derive from a Foucauldian type of aesthetics. It involves residual elements of libertarian and humanist discourses. Rapport's 'transcendental individual', defined as a creative 'Nietzschean ego' who acts in a liberal humanist context, may prove theoretically relevant to the subjectivities this study accounts for (Rapport 1997: 4–5). The 'nameless group' *Mykoniots d'élection*, which translates as 'Mykonians by choice' (an arbitrarily ascribed self-identity, that in anthropological terms initially corresponds to a 'virtual' locality against some 'real' 'Mykonian' identity), did not emerge as a counter-group and for this reason the group did not need to acquire an identity (label) in opposition to something else. In contrast (although these people do not define themselves as a counter-culture), they can be defined spatially through their (dis)placements, as well as reflexively through their radical personal transformations.

I will propose a double cultural configuration drawn from my extensive fieldwork on the lifestyle of the *Mykoniots d'élection*. There is a twofold element of fetishisation: the fetishisation of space and the fetishisation of self. In turn, these two discursive fetishes are interdependent: the one reflects upon the other, the one empowers the other. What is the result of this combination vis-à-vis the subjectivities in question?

The *Mykoniots*, following the *transient* quality of the tourist space, keeping up with the pace of the constant movement, contextually transform their cultural and social markers according to the season. Time is, as we shall see, a great fetish for the *Mykoniots d'élection*. It follows that changes occur in the habits and styles of the *Mykoniots*: for instance, they can move from a seventies hippie style to an eighties subcultural style and then onto a nineties yuppie 'neotribal' one.

The *polythetic* subjects I describe can perform with great ease the demanding and multiple roles that the discourse of nostalgia, a dominant one in the tourist space, requires. They can equally well perform the role of 'progressive' marginality that the cosmopolitan place-myth evokes. What's more, the *Mykoniots d'élection* have made this performativity a way of life. The *Mykoniots'* tribestyle (a personal neologism) is, in a Maffesolian sense, a cultural neo-tribe with an unfixed and renewable syllabus of praxis (Maffesoli 1996a). Yet *Mykoniots* also belong to the 'old' tribe of the hippies. In this sense, they belong equally to modernity and to post-modernity.

While the *Mykoniots'* discourse is predominantly elitist and cosmopolitan in a Romantic/modernist sense, they act out the post-structuralist project of the reflexive and versatile self. This aesthetic project is reflected in the image of the place-myth they chose as their place of residence. The *Mykoniots'* subjectivities lie at the interface between the post-structuralist and the post-modern subject: the subject in our case has a performative identity, which is not habitual, but conscious and convertible, in other words, a polythetic one.

An aesthetically reflexive self set against a strategically polythetic subject

This performative ethnography, by personifying the ethnographic subject, and by refusing for the most part to pre-classify her under established cultural categories, addresses the problem of self-conscious and self-reflexive identity, largely a taboo topic in anthropology. The problem of accounting for self-reflexivity in anthropological representations is, in turn, connected to a theoretical uneasiness with reference to notions such as human agency, individuality and creativity (Moore 1994: 54; Rapport 1997: 41).

It is of particular interest to this research to explore the problem of subjectivity in hybrid contexts, or otherwise, in (trans)local cultural realities. In my opinion, the problem is not solely a sociological one, i.e., how to solve the agency/structure dualism. By emerging as a prevailing theoretical position, the reflexive project of the modern subject (cf. Giddens 1991, 1992; Taylor 1989; Lash and Urry 1994) poses the question of individual consciousness, which, in its turn, re-emerges as an overriding theoretical predicament for the ethnographer. Is it all a mere simulation of reality? Are we, in line with Baudrillard, passive observers? Is it all chaotically 'democratic', in the fashion of a Derridean deconstructionist democracy? Is it all a series of stylistic/autistic tribes *à la* Maffesoli? What is the anthropological/ethnographic answer to reflexive subjectivity?

According to many theorists, what happens in post-late-modernity is that aesthetic reflexivity is an all-pervasive mechanism that governs social processes, everyday life, as well as subjects (Featherstone 1991; Giddens 1991; Lash and Urry 1994; Maffesoli 1996b). Post-modernity, it is argued, has radical consequences for subjectivity (Lash and Urry 1994: 3). Lash and Urry (ibid.) view post-modernity as an exaggeration of modernity, where the only structures that organise the reflexive individual are 'economies of signs and space'. In this sense, Lash and Urry do not take the fatalist end of the spectrum in post-modern theory like theorists such as Baudrillard and Derrida. Instead, they offer a more optimistic model of post-modernity which does not choose to reflect the 'emptying out' and 'flattening' of the subject, but the 'development' of reflexivity (ibid. 31). Equally, romantic post-modernists, such as Maffesoli (cf. Maffesoli 1993, 1996a, 1996b), allow some room for the blossoming of new possibilities in 'post-modern' social relations.

Lash and Urry criticise Giddens's view of late modernity, by arguing that his theoretical schema of reflexive subjectivity entails a cognitivist bias against the body, in opposition to other similar theoretical schemes, such as Bourdieu's notion of *habitus* that do not reside in a subject–object dualism (Lash and Urry 1994: 46). Bourdieu's *habitus* is psychoanalytically 'informed', thus allowing the subject some inner flexibility (Bourdieu 1977: 78–79). Nevertheless, Bourdieu's reflexive subject is aesthetically predisposed by a class-based internalised and almost unconscious classificatory system that allows no space for individual reflexivity or autonomous improvisation. Thus, his notion of *habitus* becomes hermeneutic and aesthetic, while producing an inadequately creative and ultimately compliant subject. Bourdieu's system of aesthetic reflexivity entails the inherent problem of every structuring principle, namely, a certain bias vis-à-vis change and individual idiosyncrasy. In other words, the role of the unconscious in Bourdieu's schema is over-exploited by a social parameter, thus leaving the conscious side of the making of this integral body atrophied. On the other hand, Giddens's strategically organised ego entails the cognitivist bias according to which, the self masters the body.

The notion of aesthetic reflexivity has turned out to be an important one in recent theorising on subjectivity, since modern systems of classification entailed the element of aesthetic judgement that diverted theory from a set of moral or cognitive (in other words, universalistic) principles. As Lash and Urry (1994) point out, the problem with this type of less mediated theory of the subject, is that it upsets the balance between the ethical and the aesthetic parts of the individual's judgement. Instead, they propose a (post-modern) return to a new type of 'tribalism' which entails a principle according to which classifications are not purely, but only partly aesthetic. Furthermore, they stress a common principle in traditional tribal societies, which is that the aesthetic, the moral and the ethical are not differentiated from one another. This 'traditional' principle is transplanted into the 'post-modern tribalism' and manifested in the cultural elements of bricolage (Lash and Urry 1994: 48).

Employing Taylor's (1989) search for the origins of modernity, Lash and Urry detect the emergence of the reflexive subject. They distinguish Giddens's mechanical reflexivity as relying too much on the 'leftovers' of a rational discourse, where there is no place for aesthetics, and strongly object to this omission. They also criticise Bourdieu's more inclusive, less mechanical notion of the body for including a socially determined aesthetic reflexivity. Taylor's modern subject, instead, is defined as being critical of rationalism, thus signifying the shift to the aesthetically reflexive subject. Taylor is a neo-communitarian philosopher whose theory is that, at the political level, the hermeneutic tradition made the modern Romantic movements realise themselves through their protest against a rationalist reality. Nevertheless, Lash and Urry (1994: 49) hasten to stress that the 'rejection of modernity' is in essence a modernist characteristic.

Lash and Urry further emphasise a point that will be of interest to the following section of this chapter, which is theoretically concerned with the position of the new social and political movements in post-modernity. Their point is that in modernity there is a very conscious creation of 'universals' through the processes of daily repetition of various symbolic systems (Lash and Urry 1994: 50). These new forms of action, which involve a larger form of agency, make their participants conscious 'makers' of these systems and not mere followers of 'cults'. The difference between new and 'traditional' forms of communities 'is not that the symbol-systems are reflexively created in the former, but that people are not born into them' (ibid.). The process of creating various new symbolic systems is not an unconscious, imitative one, but rather a discursively conscious and reflexive one. These same theorists are quick to argue that consciously choosing to join these new symbolic systems or not involves an 'identity risk' because these systems 'involve new forms of identification'. I will show eventually that my data disagrees with such assumptions. In my case, the element of (post-modern) risk is complicated by an (aesthetic) element of marginality already ascribed to the symbolic representation of these new systems since 'modernity'; but there is no real indication of a new identity, since in the 'consumption mode' of appropriating signs, choices are not fixed or final. The very concept of self-identity cannot be described following one track. The reflexive subject by acquiring one subject position or another is not necessarily in conflict with established social parameters.

The *Mykoniots d'élection* will be presented as a group of individuals primarily related to each other with an anarchic principle of 'not belonging' to any category, an existential thesis which has romantically survived out of older social movements (especially the hippies). Their 'anarchic' principle is further reflected discursively in space; Mykonos as the chosen space, semantically operates so as to justify a paradox: the bonding of a sense of non-placeness with a place. Mykonos is the symbol of this aesthetic positional plurality.

The *Mykoniots* themselves, on the other hand, as polythetic subjects are not solely romantic locals, fetishised old hippies, devotees of some peculiar variation of a Hindu or Buddhist cult. Yet, they may have obtained in the past analogous provisional identity titles. But all these (titles) are temporary. They are part of a bricolage process of identification and multi-positionality. Defining the self polythetically is, thus, part of the self's social definition; is part of the 'self in the group'. The invented identity of the '*Mykoniot d'élection*' is yet another 'acquired' identity among continually negotiable others. The principle of provisionality is the very essence that marks the *Mykoniots*' mode of socialisation and fertilises their versatile subjectivities. In line with Butler's gender performativity, the *Mykoniots*' identity performativity entails the political overturning of monothetic categories, as well as the overturning of the essence of the notion of social 'performance' (Butler 1993: 14). Space is central to the notion of the polythetic subject. Space semantically works in accordance with the polythetic subject as a meta-structural organising principle. The localisation, the context of these multiply constituted subjects, is defined by a space that is treated as equally polysemic. Mykonos, as the context of the *Mykoniots*' polythetic subjectivity, or rather as its reflection, operates as the consumption site where the *Mykoniots* reflect their instantaneous desires. In our case, the polythetic subject is conveniently 'located' in and reflected upon a 'marginal' space myth.

The Mykoniots' sense of 'distinction'

The *Mykoniots d'élection*, a cluster of 'creative' individuals, share an aesthetic identity which derives from the consumption of their own self-image and in essence the conscious consumption of culture itself.

I wish to acknowledge that the inspiration of this ethnographic project was Bourdieu's (1984) theoretical manipulation of aesthetic reflexivity through the act of consumption and distinction. In retrospect, I found Bourdieu's notion of distinction and style fundamentally inappropriate to theoretically discuss the subjects of this ethnography. Bourdieu establishes an ideal model of endlessly reproducing fixed aesthetic and social categories. But as the reader will see, the *Mykoniots d'élection* celebrate the individuality of style rather than a 'common' style. Their practice of 'difference through style' is thus not imitative, yet is still distinctive. Their main act then is the consumption of their own life history. But this is, in essence, an act of production; it is more than a reflexive project, it is a creative praxis.

Nevertheless, the logic of Bourdieu's social distinction has 'habitually' put its mark on this text and my anthropological urge for 'social classification'. Thus, the strategies of difference between the various Mykonian groups are discursively organised, in Bourdieu's fashion, through the notion of style. Still, Bourdieu's work overtly relies on people adhering to categories. There is no real individuality involved in his schema, just socially organised aesthetic dispositions. In our case, the *Mykoniots* are extreme 'individuals'; yet, they form a group through their common practice of renewing aesthetic values and inventing their 'social' category. Their consumption project, then, is their performative celebration of 'difference'. Different styles, diverse aesthetic choices that traditionally 'belong' to different social groups are performatively exploited only to establish their individual 'difference'.

Gender performativity plays an important role here. For example, the second chapter of the book ethnographically explores a seemingly 'macho' and antagonistic distinction game between the male patrons of the group vis-à-vis legendary stories of exemplary recklessness and endurance. Yet, this 'normative' role-modelling of 'agonistic' masculinity – very suitable for the Mediterranean ethnographic context (*pace* Herzfeld: 1985) – is not due to a fixed-engendered male-cultural-self that the *Mykoniots* subconsciously reproduce; rather, it is a conscious and strategic exhibition of a simulated 'male' persona only to be interchangeable with a series of further gender simulations. For the *Mykoniots*, gender performativity is an alternative means of acting out their idiosyncratic distinction game.

Improvised syncretism

As in 'improvising' gender, an improvised cultural syncretism (i.e., not confined to the religious) further indicates to the *Mykoniots*' desire to shift from a classificatory distinction game to a performative one. In Mykonos, syncretic metaphysical discourses are a shared practice amongst the different groups that occupy the tourist space. Following a local historical practice, the *Mykoniots d'élection* restore paganism – while at the same time consuming 'official' Greek Orthodox Church dogma and their insights from eastern esotericism – reproducing as a result discourses on the island's spatial supernatural properties. The fourth chapter of this book initiates the reader into this performative syncretic group practice.

In order for the reader to have an idea of the syncretic profile of the tourist space, I will briefly describe the different expressions of 'Mykonian' syncretism. Greek Orthodox rituals discursively coexist with 'Dionysiac' celebrations (*paniyiria*); rationalist discourses from the locals merge with pagan ones. On the other hand, there are conscious 'pagan constructivists' who are 'trained' to educate the tourists on the 'special' properties of the place. There are younger locals who have embraced New Age type self-religions. The local Mykonian, easily renounces *laikes doxasies* (local beliefs relating to the supernatural), as signs of 'backwardness' but equally adopts a metaphysical theory about the special 'energy field' in which (the space of) Mykonos belongs.

In the above complex metaphysical model, there are reflections of the image of a cosmopolitan visitor in search of remnants from the 'Classic supernatural' and expressions of a 'naïve locality'. The Mykonian (trans)locals are very well aware of the high demand for the image. They may even, up to a point, consume it themselves. They occasionally employ compatible or conflicting discourses. They might choose to speak 'rationally' among themselves, both 'irrationally' and 'rationally' to the anthropologist and sometimes entirely 'irrationally', employing a plethora of supernatural semantics to seduce the visitor. Moreover, the indigenous Mykonians appear to direct their 'irrational' discourses mostly to their tourist audience rather than subscribing them to themselves.[15]

The *Mykoniots d'élection*: a subculture or a tribestyle?

Is the sociological theorising on new religious movements at all relevant?

The *Mykoniots d'élection* are individuals with primarily diverse social and 'cultural' backgrounds, who are connected by an acquired identity, which is, in turn, defined by their desire to be 'on the move'. The *Mykoniots*' mobility is literal, since it entails 'moving' in between different spaces and cultures, as well as metaphorical, involving the dissolving of cultural boundaries and the strategic blurring of their location between different aesthetic and cultural categories in order to keep themselves unclassifiable. Their notion of home is equally 'unstable': *Mykoniot* nomads choose to reside only 'temporarily' in certain places, such as Mykonos, a cultural context that (not accidentally) is also defined by a predominant element of 'transience'. In effect, Mykonos for the *Mykoniots d'élection* is their permanent 'stopover'; in this sense, their regular 'coming back' discursively projects onto Mykonos' space an allegorical (discordant) notion of 'home'.

The *Mykoniots* are a group of independent nomads who literally move between the 'East' (they actually make a point of visiting 'exotic' places) and the 'West' (Mykonos, in this sense, plays the part of the post-modern cosmopolitan space). The connotations of 'transience' combined with discourses of a(n amoral and aesthetic) principle of perpetual self-transformation, could indicate the group's affiliation with, and its sociological definition as a self-cult.

Before I proceed with the notion of self-cult, I would like to incorporate the 'subcultural' connotations that the practices of the group may acquire; firstly, through the fetishised consumption preferences of its members, namely, the use of illegal substances; and, secondly, through an overriding aesthetic principle of hedonism, sensuality and freedom. The combination of drug consumption with discourses of freedom and obedience to the 'anarchic' realm of the senses relate to modernist and subversive discourses introduced by the new social movements of the late sixties. So far, one could say that the group has aesthetically preserved a 'subcultural' outlook – i.e., subculture as style, autonomy and resistance (cf. Hebdige, 1979). In other words, these fetishised practices and discourses are no longer part of personal/ideological statements. Rather, they are largely re-enacted in the nineties simply as only one set of aesthetic choices. In addition, as we shall see in the ethnography, the ideological echo of a 'subcultural' praxis does not always require the subject to exclude from his social 'performance' other more traditional, more conventional, roles.

Self-religions

Exploring the theoretical body of new religious movements as new cults of the self, one is confronted, as Heelas suggests (in line with theorists like Lasch 1991; Giddens 1991; Taylor 1989 and Lash and Urry 1994), with an obsession with the self, rather than metaphysics, ethics, religion or tradition.[16] The modern subject is obsessed with perfection (Heelas 1982: 69). Self-religions have become in the West a part of a new monistic tradition that promotes exhaustive self-exploration. The capacity to (*pace* Giddens) 'monitor the self' on many levels, such as ethical and/or spiritual, turns the conscious individual into a 'control freak' of her own monitoring. However, it is not only through spiritual enquiries that this characteristic emerges in late-modernity/post-modernity. Obsessive monitoring of oneself is symptomatic of an epoch of aesthetic reflexivity. Rather than being peculiar to weak-willed or eccentric individuals, it covers diverse subject positions, such as professionals, healers, theorists, conceptual artists. In contrast to Heelas' views, I maintain that the model of self-perfection does not necessarily lead to a new religion. Even so, it has become a very popular 'vocation' in post-modernity.

Heelas' analysis of Californian self-religions concentrates on the subjective (Heelas 1982). He wishes to relocate the subjective and abolish the 'splitting' which places the subjective outside the social. In short, he is 'socialising' the subjective (ibid. 70). Self-religions, it is maintained, fuse the social with the psychological. The subjective in Heelas' theory (projected in the ethnographic examples of Californian self-religions), struggles, so to speak, to become part of the 'structure'.[17]

Heelas, in order to study self-religions, employed as a case study a Californian group called the Kerista, that was active mainly during the weekends when its members gathered together. During these weekend sessions, each member of the group, sought to individually explore his/her own creativity. The maxim of the Kerista was to monitor their individual experiences, 'savouring them to the fullest'. The author reports that the Kerista participants did not keep their subjective experiences private. Instead, they were 'ethically' obliged to 'project' them onto the group following a gestalt process (Heelas 1982: 76).

In the *Mykoniots'* context, the art of open 'gossip' and direct cathartic confrontations or otherwise intense interrogations performed in a communal manner have a similar function: turning the subjective into social. In both groups the subjective experience is communicated, or in the case of the *Mykoniots* is extracted, in order to become part of the collective. The private–public boundaries are vague. Intimate details and harsh criticisms are openly communicated among the members, but easily consigned to oblivion. The *Mykoniots* do not tend to be secretive. This is part of a greater self-liberating project to abolish boundaries and taboos. The *Mykoniots* do not use psychobabble or a defining gestalt method in order to share their subjective experiences. Their type of 'sharing', although the main principle in forming the group, is rather random. Random commensality is an unwritten rule, as is their belief in non-commitment and the liberation of the libido. Furthermore, the *Mykoniots'* group identity is constructed through difference (distinction is accomplished through the 'otherness' of the self) as opposed to mono-semantic traditional/modern/subcultural social frameworks. In the same way as Heelas describes, in respect of the group of Kerista, the *Mykoniots* play their identity game by inventing new rituals, or otherwise by 'intersubjectively constituting objects of attention' (ibid. 78).

Nevertheless, self-religions, at least as described in this early part of Heelas' work, do not share the same principles of organisation as the *Mykoniots*, who basically sustain their identity bonding as a group in aesthetic terms rather than as a commitment to an organised syllabus of self-exploration. In the cases described by Heelas (1982), the religious element eventually controls subjective experiences within an internal system of evaluation. In the *Mykoniots'* case, the subjective becomes public, and part of the social, but there is no other rule. The self is reflected in collective discourses, but there is no definite cultural processing of the subjective. The praxis of the *Mykoniots* fuses the subjective with the aesthetic in order to further secure the principle of difference.

Their ethnographic case paradoxically demonstrates that the more fetishised the personal autonomy (as in the case of Hercules in chapter three), the more intricate the personal structure. For instance, getting out of the house, in other words out of his own symbolic structure, is, for Hercules, a daily ritual that can last for hours. In this way his subjective structure is symbolically ritualised and thus safeguarded.

Heelas, in his more recent work, deals with the New Age, another self-religion, yet a non-organised movement (Heelas 1993: 105, 1996). He employs Taylor's (1989) definition of modernity as a complicated construction of differing moral orientations. One of these moral orientations, according to Heelas, is the deification of 'nature' and a very optimistic version of humanism as found in Romanticism; New Age belongs to this tradition (Heelas 1993: 106, 1996: 42).

Although New Age entails pre-modern elements, it is largely de-traditionalised. Heelas further argues that it makes sense to see the New Age as post-modern (Heelas 1993: 110).

Elsewhere, Heelas (1996) has defined New Age as a superficially heterogeneous phenomenon which is organised around a common theme: self-transformation. As I noted earlier, Heelas resists the definition of New Age as either another example of a new religious movement or merely a syncretic combination consisting of various similar movements. Heelas maintains that the phenomenon of New Age is largely undertheorised, since academics cannot do justice to the essence of the New Age which is 'the wisdom of the experiential'[18] (Heelas 1996: 9).

The *Mykoniots d'élection* in their discourse promote similar 'structuring principles' to that of the New Age, as described by Heelas, and especially to the New Agers' core logic that we all 'malfunction' because we have been 'brainwashed' by mainstream society. 'We' are competitive, performative, tied to obligatory institutions, such as the family, education and so forth. 'We' are all part of an 'unnatural' lifestyle (Heelas 1996: 18). The *Mykoniots* seem seduced by this type of discourse. 'The self', according to Heelas' description of New Agers' values, 'must be liberated'; the ego, a mere performer, must lose its authority; (ibid. 20). There is a striking resemblance with the *Mykoniots*' main discourses of de-identification. Heelas' catholic model, however, cannot account for the type of inconsistent de-identification promoted by the *Mykoniots*. The group appropriates conflicting discourses and practices on processes of de-traditionalisation. When it is convenient they employ a very unsettling, rebellious discourse about the 'social order'. At other times, traditional notions are selected. Subject positions change to suit the audience. They can also change according to personal and unstructured aesthetic principles. On the one hand, the *Mykoniots*, as we shall see, employ mainstream localist discourses connecting their practices with certain aspects of ancient Greek culture. Based on their [aesthetic] principle of a gender-less similarity, they display an otherwise 'politically incorrect' affiliation with indigenous macho heroes. They also aesthetically promote 'traditional' elements, such as the prototype of a local vernacular architecture. On the other hand, they reject any official status quo by being consciously uninvolved in local and national politics. They avoid voting, they avoid 'steady' employment, they avoid paying taxes. They avoid planning anything permanent; they avoid 'family'. They challenge traditional gender roles; yet they can marry and perform mainstream religious ceremonies, as well as consume indigenous esotericism.

The *Mykoniots* share an alternative spiritual ethic with the New Age dogma. To achieve liberation from social constraints one has to work constantly at resisting compliance. The ideal state of being, the liberated self, will eventually emerge as a result of the work invested in the self. Here, the prototype of subjectivity reminds us of the project of the Foucauldian subject who has reflexively acquired agency over her constraints and the personal ethical targets of the self; this is the only recipe for success.

If New Age is symptomatic of post-modernity, how can it be that a similar discourse fashioned by the *Mykoniots* has its ideological and aesthetic roots in the new social movements of the late sixties? The fact that the founders of the group are now in their fifties (in other words, are part of the 'hippie generation'), hints at the answer: for them, all that was just an ideology. But, if one accepts the above, a series of questions arise: what remains of the original ideology? how much of that is lifestyle? how much of this remaining ideological discourse is transformed into a mere (post-modern) aesthetic choice? For Possamaï (2002), New Agers inhabit a post-modern mode of existence, where they can appropriate, consume (and discard) any religio-cultural tropes, artifacts as well as ideological fragments that appeal to them. Their tastes for belief are only 'perennist'.

Heelas points to people like Jung, Reich and Gurdjieff as the spiritual forerunners of the movement. These thinkers are also frequently mentioned, as we shall see, in the *Mykoniots'* discourses. The history of the New Age movement, as reconstructed by Heelas, is traced back through references more or less common to those favoured by the *Mykoniots*: cult works of literature like those of Aldous Huxley, cult movements like the initially small-scale beat movement of the fifties which was later transubstantiated into the hippies, the most popular move towards 'inner spirituality' in modernity (Heelas 1996: 50–51). The sixties and the hippies signified the creation of a communal non-organised counter-culture which basically promoted the spiritual quest 'within'.

Through the self-narratives of my informants the connection with these movements will be evident. The problem starts when one projects 'subcultural' discourses, created in the hippie era, in time, and especially when one attempts to connect all the rhetoric concerning self-spirituality with post-modern notions of aesthetically reflexive subjects in the process of existential self-monitoring. Everything that used to be alternative, an ideology, now is, at best, just a choice, a style. Everything that Heelas calls New Age or self-religion may be merely aesthetic and in any case a provisional consumption choice (cf. with Bauman's [1998] redefinition of the so-called 'post-modern religions' as 'consumer religions'). As Heelas characteristically points out: 'True, Goa still attracts "hippies"; but many are on holiday, resting from their careers – for example, exporting batik from Bali to Amsterdam' (Heelas 1996: 128).[19]

The reason I am including part of the theorising on self-religions, is that I need to find alternative theoretical classifications beyond the established dichotomies between mainstream cultures and marginal subcultures, as well as between local and global, traditional and modern, modern and post-modern. There seems to be a major structural difference when negotiating categories in the post-modern order: the pattern of following internal classifications within a category, as well as the fact that categories are diffused, becomes (structurally) predominant. When projecting this new, post-structural order on the notion of subjectivity/ies, it seems that there are many alternative fields, 'compartments of identity' to reflect upon and experiment with. Likewise, a review of recent theories of space indicates a radical transformation of the way space is symbolically classified in this new order.

This is reflected in St.John's (2001) ethnographic scenario of 'cultural heterotopia' at the Australian 'ConFest': a huge alternative life-style event which includes a range of alternative spiritualities, music, drugs, eco-workshops, 'transgressive happenings' that coexist. Spaces such as the ConFest act as contemporary pilgrimage sites where an alternative notion of liminal spatiality and corporeality is invented. In order to describe the innovative liminal spatiality of the ConFest, St.John replaces Turner's notion of 'communitas' with that of 'alternative cultural heterotopia' (ibid. 48). These new spatial communities of resistance are defined as islands of segregated different tribestyles where hedonistic consumption practices are sanctioned. Similar to Foucault's 'counter-sites', these alternative cultural heterotopias are 'destinations for expatriates of, and exiles from, the parent culture' (ibid. 51). Equally, Mykonos' space performatively operates as a symbol of an aesthetic and sensual 'otherness'.

The 'upgrading' of sociological categories like new religious or new social movements from cults into mainstream discourses, signifies the theoretical emergence of an alternative classificatory order beyond the dominant/peripheral, culture/subculture dichotomy. In this sense, I think that the discipline of anthropology needs to redefine itself. The once progressive classificatory anthropological model based on cultural heterogeneity has turned into a sterile and outdated form of relativism that offers no theoretical challenge to this post-structuralist/post-modern fusion of boundaries. Cultures do not fit comfortably into *either* symmetrical *or* asymmetrical models: traditional fuses into modern, modern into post-modern, post-modern into traditional and so on. This theoretical context of a series of (de)classifications is, furthermore, informed by a (post-modern) philosophical humanism. The subject, within the realm of unlimited (cultural) moulds of this post-structuralist order, has regained creativity. I think that anthropology should ethnographically (re)turn to these sub-categories, since this is how it would regain a theoretical perspective of what Lévi-Strauss originally proclaimed as its destiny: namely, safeguarding heterogeneity (1978). It is indeed alluring to be confronted with creative informants who consciously improvise in-between cultural categories, struggling through their 'preordained' classification.

The descendants of the old 'subversive' social movements, the new 'communes' of the post-modern era are governed by a pervasive aesthetic element: they are consumption movements consisting of creative individuals whose aim is to existentially/socially 'overcome' their fate by playing in-between the categories of belonging and not belonging. This positional 'instability' creates their theoretical appeal and formulates their post-modern 'ideology'.

Notes

1. An anthropologist's invention and actually an appropriation from Lawrence Durrell's (1978) characterisation of a Greek group of thirties Mykonos visitors who had formed their 'little club' there (for more details, see the introduction to chapter 2).
2. The topography of Mykonos and especially the *Hora*, the town of the island, is unusual. The island is divided into two communes: Mykonos town (the so-called *Hora*) and Ano-Mera. It seems that since medieval times, the *Hora* has been the only settlement on Mykonos. The rest of the island was studded with private Mykonian *horia*, self-sustained household units. A Mykonian *horio* was a confined and established space where the Mykonian rural family used to live and work. Apart from its own land, a Mykonian *horio* consisted of a stall, a hayloft, a storeroom, a dovecote, a traditional oven and water source, and even its own chapel. 'The *horio* is the representative residential unit of rural Mykonos, a detached habitation cell ... ' (Yangakis 1985: 18). The *Hora* lies on the western coast of the island; its spatial organisation and more precisely the fact that it is built upon a level area makes it characteristically different from the rest of the Aegean and especially from its neighbouring Cycladic settlements (Romanos 1983: 14). The planning of the Mykonian *Hora* is a characteristic piece of vernacular architecture. Despite the fact that the settlement is the result of additions and gradual development of different areas over a period of at least five centuries, 'as a whole, it has a characteristic cohesion while at the same time, the individual elements remain idiosyncratic' (Romanos 1983: 16). The aforementioned author describes the *Hora* as a labyrinthine 'interior' space which creates the strong feeling of being somewhere 'inside' rather than 'outside'; the impression of its interior provokes a feeling of 'great intimacy and protection' (ibid. 14). The *Hora* is divided into twenty neighbourhoods. Very characteristic are the large two- and even three-storey houses, known as the 'captain's houses', that date back to the nineteenth century (Stott 1982: 12). Up until the seventh century, the *Hora* was probably confined to the area around the *kastro* (fort) that exists to this day. The dense buildings within the *kastro* made it look, according to Kyriazopoulos, like the interior of a pomegranate (1972: 348–49).
3. Damer's performative tourist space of Symi is another rare ethnographic account, in the Greek island context, that entails only a passing reference to a group of 'outsiders' similar to that of the *Mykoniots d'élection*; a group of Greeks who are neither 'locals' nor 'tourists' (2004: 216).
4. I will largely employ the term *sinafi* throughout the book, a fetishised and emotional term which connotes to a sense of belonging to an idiosyncratic collectivity, like a group of friends or a clique of the 'like-minded'.
5. *Mykoniots* will be an abridgement for the term *Mykoniots d'élection*, set against the 'real' Mykonians (i.e., the 'indigenous').
6. St.John's (2001: 55) ethnography describes an analogous group of volunteers who cooperate to organise and service the alternative Australian lifestyle event, the 'ConFest'. As the 'tourist' who transgresses and becomes 'local', they acquire the status of the 'ideal pilgrim'. The festival's crew become the 'local' in this 'alternative cultural heterotopia', they become the 'host community'.
7. I think that the Mykonian space works semiotically like a cosmopolitan city, in other words, as a complicated and polysemic space, rather than merely a 'Greek town' or 'Greek village'. For this reason I have rhetorically renamed the central Mykonian settlement of the *Hora* and its suburbs 'Mykonos city'.
8. The Greek islands – as tourist spaces – semantically compose a common body whereby different places have become arbitrarily identified with distinct properties. These (superimposed) properties have nothing whatsoever to do with the 'nature' of the local culture. Instead, they reflect the characteristics of their 'transient' visitors. Extending their notion of aesthetic cosmopolitanism, which 'presupposes extensive patterns of mobility', thus establishing the ability to judge and aesthetically reflect upon different places, Lash and Urry argue that disorganised capitalism involves, among other things, the 'end of tourism' (1994: 259). Given

the abundance and fluidity of signs and images, people are permanent 'tourists', since they perpetually travel either literally or virtually. 'Images of space are endlessly manufactured' and this results in radical changes to the initial spatial significations (ibid. 260).

9. See, for example, Augé (1995); Clifford (1997); Amit and Rapport (2002).
10. Cf. with Bourdieu's appropriation of the Weberian 'stylisation of life' (1984: 55)
11. It has been widely argued, or so the local discourse goes, that the reason for Mykonos' playing a marginal role in history – a fact that also created a significant difference between Mykonos and some of the nearby (prosperous) islands – was its lack of fertile soil and water. According to Kyriazopoulos: 'While Mykonos' location on busy shipping routes attracted traders and invaders, its poverty [due to the infertility of the land and the small seasonal rainfall] discouraged them from settling there permanently. This is the reason that neither the Turks, nor the Venetians left any vestiges of their presence, work, or buildings as they did on other islands of the Cyclades' (Kyriazopoulos 1972: 334).
12. As early as the late sixties, the preservation of Mykonian architecture was protected by law.
13. In a similar way, what is called 'traditional performance' in Bali is an invention. Bali, sponsored by its Dutch colonisers, was 'staged' as a tourist paradise by a means of a reconstruction of 'Balinese' traditions and performances (cf. Hobsbawm 1992). The spatial performativity thus re-enacted was that of a lost cultural and artistic paradise: 'Paradise was not simply discovered; it was created' (Yamashita 2003: 25).
14. The term *Mykoniots d'élection* is an invention. My informants avoid all kinds of permanent self-classifications, since they consider them self-restrictive. Indeed, they are eclectically involved in a project of perpetually reinventing themselves through 'aesthetic' reflexivity. In other words, their judgement is not moral or cognitively based on a set of universal rules, but rather is a more idiosyncratic and creative one. It is initially a Kantian aesthetic judgement (cf. Bourdieu 1984: 5, 41; Lash and Urry 1994).
15. A similar case is demonstrated in Okely's ethnographic account, where the traveller-gypsy fortune-tellers are presented – against the stereotype – as employing rationalist discourses opposed to their 'gorgio' (i.e., non-gypsy) English clients (Okely 1996: 94–114).
16. The model of these 'New Age' movements departs from a theocratic dualism where God is superior to the individual. Instead, it embraces a monistic prototype. The new religious movements, according to Barker's analysis, offer the potential follower a liberating form of self-expression in relation to the highly bureaucratised and ritualised 'traditional religions', as well as 'a more immediate promise of salvation' (Barker 1984: 250).
17. Heelas distinguishes self-religions from counter-cultures, since they appeal to a wider audience, such as his middle-aged Californian informants, who can, under no circumstances, be considered 'subcultural'. According to Heelas, consumer expectations at the material level, have been saturated. In short, the American dream has ceased to satisfy the consumer on the purely material level. The pervasive act of consumption has now expanded to spiritual discourses. Heelas shows that all this obsession with the self, the post-modern version of the Foucauldian 'taking care of the self', is a consumption project.
18. *Mykoniots* employed a similar rhetoric about my ethnographic research: I could not possibly understand them by applying any kind of theory. In fact, there was nothing to understand or learn, I had to 'experience'.
19. In conclusion, Heelas argues that the New Age is, 'in measure being popularised', since it is no longer in the hands of 'elites' (Heelas 1996: 128). The 'New Age traveller', it is argued, has become a 'familiar figure' in the West. 'It is no longer so much a matter of "cults" as it is of "culture"' (ibid.).

2
NARRATIVES OF BELONGING: THE MYTH OF AN 'INDIGENOUS' OTHERNESS

Apprenticeship in the Mykonian sinafia: myths of Mykonos and 'maleness'

The primary purpose of this chapter is to familiarise the reader with the aesthetic plurality of the Mykonian context and to discuss one means through which the myth of Mykonos is constructed. This type of a hybrid cultural context shapes and is shaped by conscious subjects with multiple subjectivities who sustain alternating group affiliations. Classificatory attempts are arbitrary since they portray a complex social reality where group classifications experiment on different aesthetic/social levels. Hence any category is recreated through a freeze-frame of these alternating discourses of group affiliations. In this sense, ethnography could not work as a 'total' representation of the *Mykoniots*', otherwise fragmented, reality. Similarly, it is worth noting that when the actors of this chapter incorporate a [traditional] 'masculine' model into their multiply-constituted subjectivities, they [consciously] *perform* this model as simply part of another discourse. The performative category 'male', 'maleness', here, is part of an aesthetic rhetoric based on the eclectic consumption of diverse cultural practices and discourses and thus could stand for a virtually transgender quality. The identification of the actors with a[n aesthetic] category, in this case masculinity, as well as with the predominantly masculine ethos of Greek culture, is only a provisional one.

The two worlds of 'maleness'

Aristos had become westernised; Markos had made money out of selling jeans in Kansas; and Patrick had bummed around the East. Migration was a religion with them. Faithful followers of the travel trail, they had picked up a certain cosmopolitanism. In the basements of the King's Road in London they learnt about world music. In New York they bought 501s, the real thing in jeans, and all the second-hand clothes that made them different. Then came the age of the East, virgin territory for wanton Western pleasures, mysticism and 'pure' substances. But, for them, coming home always meant returning to Mykonos, to their own 'personal' shrine. There they got to know some mystical teachers, gurus of a 'sacred culture'; the culture of the *andras potis* (a male who consumes legal and/or illegal substances 'skillfully'). The so called *rembetes* [members of the underground] were another generation who had been over the hill for some time; but they had their own local subculture to imitate. At the very shrine to sex and drugs and rock 'n' roll – the rock 'n' roll sprang from a handful of uncompromising natives. A gang of Mykonians that had been [literally decimated] worn down over the years, but had remained a legend among the *sinafia*[1] ('gangs') of wandering *Mykoniots*, and automatically became a myth for the *kosmikoi Athinaioi* (Athens' socialites) who deigned to join the party. Among those leftover from this (Mykonian) gang were Spathas, the refuse collector who grows roses, Baroutis, an Olympic-class alcoholic, Nenes, who has never been seen sober and Jimmy, who goes in for orgiastic *hoirosfayia* (pig-slaughtering). The boys from Athens came to them and to the other Mykonian 'pirates' who 'departed before their time' (i.e., died early) to learn that highly desirable lesson, *to andriliki* or 'how to be a man'. Drunk on the pleasures of 'brotherhood' and absorbed in their all-male society, occasionally they gave their manhood a boost, with fascinated women holiday-makers proving easy prey. This is a place where the *andras kamaki*[2] (ladykiller), the legendary male, the *andras potis*, is king; someone who doesn't give an inch where his passions are concerned, who is faithful to the bottle and faithful to the alliances of the *pioma*[3] (illegal drug taking), a communal activity in which the greatest joy is the secret conspiracy.

Thousands of young Athenians flood into the island nowadays, equipped with their freshly laundered, trade-marked sweatshirts; Mykonos dilettantes and johnny-come-lately fans of the place. What these ecstatic devotees of the *sfinakia* (shots of alcohol) 'culture' in Antonis' bar want is to take part themselves in this sort of – in their case 'low fidelity' – game of *methexi* (sacred commensality). Antonis himself, and every other Antonis, is a conduit for this sacred culture. He in his turn enchants these unsuspecting *leledes* (mother's boys) from the northern suburbs of Athens and 'ordains' the stalwarts of contemporary *mangia*[4] (street cred), offering them work and 'promoting' them on the island. Antonis, himself once a silent disciple of the local gang, and the other enchanters of the cosmopolitan element, is nowadays a conduit for that diachronic *mangia*. This aspirational quality of *mangia* is not spread simply by acquiring the style, but has to be taught in secret, like a form of hermetic knowledge. It is deciphered via a strictly 'male' quality of directness coming from men who have survived the trials they themselves devised as artificial goals. And, thus, within this secret conspiracy the myth of 'maleness' is created, a cultural feature, which at least in the multi-semantic context of Mykonos, extends beyond the biological definition of sex. Antonis had already constructed his own myth by the time he was in his forties. A lot of people know him, but he recognises only a few. What makes them admire him?

Mykonos is an endless client 'network' which recycles itself through apprenticeships or discipleships (call it what you like), under the aegis of certain mythologized guardians of the local 'subculture', certain decadent gurus from a variety of social backgrounds, members of the various 'Mykonian *sinafia*'. The initiate into Mykonos' closed society undertakes a long 'apprenticeship', through continual *sympotiasmos* (drinking commensality) where the stakes are each individual's personal limits. The teachers in the 'Mykonos school' are a few charismatic cripples, pseudo-philosophers of the 'art of living', descendants of a line of 'genuine characters', already 'done for', descendants of the heroes of the *pioma*, heroes who have seen the notorious mandragora root.[5]

Mykonos was built on a myth. The *sinafi* of *kosmikoi* (Athens socialites) would like the island to be seen as their creation. Through the same myth, the *sinafi* of local 'pirates' lay claim to being the genuine article, using their power of *endopiotita* (locality). Then again the hippies threw off their clothes, and were entrusted with the Dionysiac revelry proper to Apollo; by giving themselves up to pleasure they transformed the island. The present-day neo-Romantics, having finished with drugs and rock 'n' roll, are rediscovering their own island possession, by reviving theories which glorify the special energy of this particular geographical location. The 'conspiracy of the *pioma*' brought together the disparate *sinafia* and constructed a tightly knit circle with strict codes of behaviour, survivals of 'maleness', which are reminiscent of the original '*rembetika* *sinafia*[6] (Damianakos 1976). Mykonos, a tourist resort dedicated to pleasure, was built on a myth. The myth-symbol is not the creation of any one 'class', any one *sinafi*. The myth was created through the coexistence and the 'kneading together' of heterogeneity. Those amongst the international set who dared, mixed with the 'honourable men' among the Mykonian 'plebs'. In their turn the latter had codes akin to those of the *frikia* (freaks) who had come back from their 'discipleships' in the East. While they taught the locals about the 'new' drugs, the locals taught them how to take them *andrikia* ('like a man').

I could never precisely understand the extent of the intimacy within that orgiastic mysticism based on hashish and random drunkenness in the *andropareá* (all-male society), which had created a vast number of audacious and enticing practices. The myths about local heroic characters reconfirm the manliness of the storytellers, men who have a share in the mystical essence of manhood[7]. This is how the current descendants of the Mykonian *mangia* became obsessed with their own *mangia*. The common denominator is the perpetual chase after the ceremonial commensality (*sympotiasmos*), pursued with sang froid and emotional aloofness, a long-term commitment which simply gives access to the more advanced stages of the Mykonian apprenticeship/discipleship.

In the accounts given both by the 'old school' and the new converts in their twenties, the privilege of the lowly apprenticeship/discipleship under some great man is presented as something natural. The rules of the game require a long period of indenture under the island's most colourful characters. Thus Hercules had his disciples, whom he taught how to utilise 'a Mykonian mode of exchange'. Orpheus had his army of workers whom he looked after each season, providing them with temporary work in his second-hand shop. Armies of young men looking for the 'real thing', living the communal life in their Mykonian *kellakia* (cells), vouchsafed to them by their bosses-cum-mentors. Antonis accordingly organised and sustained his 'kids', the Delos Bar team, a group which usually stayed together for some years. Eleonora had her 'girls', whom she lodged in her isolated 'castle', and with whom she indulged in yoga and long giggling sessions about men and karma. Then there was Artemis and her 'powerful' girlfriends, the so-called 'sorceresses'.

There is a mythical discourse of seniority (*o mythos tis palaiotitas*) in the client relationships of the present-day 'big' patrons on the island. Those who have established themselves as 'outstanding' personas have endured the 'cruelty' of the island, and above all they have rubbed shoulders with the 'old-timers'. They know the local Zorbas, the 'brains' behind the Mykonian lifestyle, even those who – due to circumstances beyond their control – are currently to be found in other worldly paradises, together with all the well-known and little-known legends which the island has occasionally attracted. The myth spreads 'mystically', and in the struggle for seniority the mythologised local *personae* seek out supporters, promoting derring-do, hermeticism, pleasure and primitivism and the personal pain of the social misfit survivor. Some of them remain disciples, some failed gurus from another age, long gone. Others go on attracting supporters, by 'selling' their image, in order to 'get by' (*yia na ti vgazoune*).

On Mykonos, wherever you go you are haunted by the issue of 'stylistic authenticity'. Throughout the silent apprenticeship, in withdrawal from petit-bourgeois cultural models, the apprentice remains silent and plays the part of the enthusiastic 'courtier'. Once she has come through this process and established her presence and her bona fide on the island, she has a right to spread her own version of the 'Mykonian lifestyle'. Mykonos is a small conspiracy, with the unsuspecting tourists, the *ohla*[8] *tou ohlou* (the din of the mob), acting as a backdrop to the scene so that the 'teachers' can come and go unnoticed, while they are choosing whom they will 'bewitch'.

In the distorting mirror of the myth, the *kosmikoi* (Athens socialites) learned how to be *manges* from the local 'gangs' in the early seventies while the *manges* themselves got to know the VIP visitors of the modern era. The VIPs were coming to learn simplicity and primitivism from the sun and stone of the Cyclades. Alongside them the rootless followers of the 'international culture' had made the eccentric style of the elite tourist resort their own, and were continuing their progress along the route of non-assimilation to the social and cultural identity that was their lot in life. It was a journey of fleeting alliances and completely individual choices. The society of 'exogenous Mykonians'[9] is a host of solitaries, united by the common myth of the place, which they themselves created as a construct for reasons of survival.

Introduction to the Mykonian sinafia

The common denominator in the broad category that I set out to study, that of the 'exogenous Mykonians', resides primarily in each individual's making a personal choice to move to Mykonos. This move is accounted for in narrative fashion by a chance first acquaintance with the island. A gradual mythologising of the specialness of the place and its inhabitants follows. The island dweller is fully aware of the way in which the place, and its actors are transformed from summer to winter, from season to season, from day to day, from one cruise ship to the next. She is conscious of daily dealings with demanding and ignorant tourists, dealings regarded as 'soul destroying' by the summer workers. On the other hand, such dealings often avoid the bureaucracy and routine of 'occupational stability'. The army of 'summer workers' is attracted by the temporary nature of the work, the high *merokamata* (daily wage), and the opportunity to systematically exploit an 'up-for-grabs' economy. Given, on top of all this, the island's cosmopolitan status, would-be immigrants experience a greater sense of freedom and the chance to broaden their identity.

The potential future immigrant is gradually initiated into the process of mythologising this barren place. There are countless notorious 'ethnographic' explanations worth collecting. What they have in common is a rhetoric repeated by both locals and the exogenous group alike. The common rhetoric, a crucial building block in the process, is characterised by the need to mythologise the place and its associated heroes. In order to account for the island's reputation, the unique aesthetic of the landscape is deployed, with its fabulous beaches, primitive architecture and its genuine simplicity. 'Energy theories', which were at their height in the sixties, are revived, attributing metaphysical properties to the place, such as the amazing sunlight, the proximity to ancient Delos and the Dionysiac types which it attracts. Even negative myth-making about money-mad Mykonians, penniless arch-hedonists and every kind of lunatic that the place attracts, provides elements that contribute to the making of the spatial/cultural myth of otherness. So for my informants, Mykonos, as the scene of action, is marked out as a currently rich, cosmopolitan and extremely mythologised place both for the active 'players' as well as for its visitors.

Mykonos has a reputation, or at least had a reputation until recently, for attracting a particular 'brand' of tourist. Expressions such as 'everyone who goes to Mykonos is a bit ... ' are very widespread among regular visitors. At least until the end of the last decade at Athens airport you could guess which gate led to the little planes for Mykonos by its passengers' conspicuously eccentric sense of style compared with those at neighbouring gates.

Looking for the first visitors to the island I went back to the early thirties, when Helen Vlachos (a well-known editor and publisher of a Greek newspaper) describes the 'first Mykonos', raking up her memories using her private collection of snapshots (Vlachos 1987). She describes a group of bourgeois intellectuals who arrived on the island at the invitation of some Mykonians[10] from, as Vlachos emphasises, the same 'exigent and exclusive social circle' (ibid. 21). Almost instantaneously the island became the bourgeois group's fetish,[11] an unspoilt earthly paradise which belonged to them because they had discovered it. But what gave Mykonos the edge, that 'bit extra', according to Vlachos, was 'the Mykonians themselves' who had no 'provincial inferiority complex'. The genuineness of the Mykonian, the way in which she appropriated and made her mark on the infertile land with stone and whitewash and lopsided curves, the cleanliness, the spontaneous hospitality and liberality,[12] are all virtues of the Mykonian 'clan'. Virtues which were almost automatically acknowledged, together with an innate and chronic amorality, a species of cunning and courage, a seductive quality which accounts for the islanders' need to roam the world and become smugglers and pirates.[13] I, too, heard about these qualities of the locals; qualities that, according to the same rhetoric, remain virtually unchanged today from the way that Vlachos described them. Nevertheless, the historical perspective helped me to understand that the modern semiology of the 'exclusive' place might also be the product of the eclecticism of the social group which discovered it.

Laurence Durrell, describing the Greek islands, makes an explicit reference to the special nature of the visitors to Mykonos. The island is presented as an exclusive club which the 'elect' keep for themselves. Their enthusiasm for the place, evidently prompted him at this early stage (he must be talking about 1939 onwards and especially the sixties) to create the category of Mykoniots 'd'élection', members of an exclusive caste of Athenians, which he describes as follows: 'a remarkable body of spirits – some of fortune, some poor ... they could live like nabobs or like tramps, without ever losing their taste for life, without ever yielding before adversity. These young men were an education in themselves' (Durrell 1978: 235–36). The author continues with a detailed description of one member of the above-mentioned group who initiated him and his wife into the pleasures of the island and particularly into the officially illegal overnight sojourns on the sacred island of Delos.[14] We can already discern a deviation from the norm of the, by definition, strictly bourgeois group of visitors of the first tourist period, which Vlachos had described. In Durrell's narrative, his link with the island was Stephan Syriotis, who spent his summers in solitude on a small boat. The examples of these 'heroes', the *'Mykoniots d'élection'* led Durrell to rave about their 'attitude to life and ... intrinsic Greekness'. It should be pointed out that the members of the Athenian group he describes are all men, while in Vlachos' case one or two women are at least mentioned.

Thus the sense of exclusivity attached to the island was established early on; it was taken over by charismatic and privileged groups who in their turn initiated, in the first instance, the 'elite' of their day and age. The cosmopolitan Greeks, ship owners, artists, intellectuals and their keepers arrived and thus begins the whole snowballing scenario of acquaintanceship. For quite a few decades, by virtue of the fact that it tended to attract people from the same *sinafi*, the island remained a paradise for the few. At the same time some footloose travellers were also stopping off there, but the difficulty of access to this windy island, with its inhospitable harbour built on its north side, delayed the advent of mass tourism. In those first exclusive decades, the *sinafi* of the 'elect' put its stamp on its 'personal' paradise. This was when the first homes for outsiders were built. At an early stage, the Mykonians developed a tolerance for bourgeois tastes; they were indifferent to Melina Mercouri's short shorts, just as later they would be indifferent to the first nudists and *frikia* (hippie freaks) on the beaches of the south coast. The beaches were to be classified around the beginning of the seventies. Beaches for the gay community, beaches for *frikia*, beaches for the Athenian 'nobs' and so on. The locals blended in with the new scene, with the same ease and a total lack of any element of puritanism. They kept their customs, at least the style if not the content, and very quickly recognised the benefits of the folkloric element. The place's reputation spread, the exclusivity was relaxed and more and more people came to share in the miracle of 'cubist' Mykonos. This is when the real tourist exploitation began, a harbour was built for the ferries from Piraeus and by 1969 there was a heliport. In the sixties and seventies, the island acquired both tourism and new permanent residents.[15]

Coming to the island is turned into a form of cult by the various groups, so that the Mykonian *sinafia* are always gradually being reformed. The proximity to Delos, which besides being the island of Apollo is also the island of the arch-hedonist Dionysus, creates a new category of mythologised context for the place. In conjunction with the absence of moral limits laid down by the locals, Mykonos becomes an effective tourist paradise for the unconventional elements of the period. The island became a magnet for homosexual men in the 1970s, something which remains true to this day; the island's reputation makes it 'part of the scene'. Mykonos is recognised as one of the 'meeting places' for hippie travellers. The island's reputation made it part of the scene for the international jet set once the airport was built in 1971. The *sinafia* of regulars continued to be formed and tourism creates opportunities for many temporary and seasonal activities. The wealthy clientele provide the potential for innovation and experimentation.

During the seventies, among the groups who took over the 'new order of things' there were some cosmopolitan figures, Greeks or otherwise who, when they were not travelling around the world, set up businesses on the island. Mykonos led the way worldwide in the leisure industry, and in fashionable drugs. The haunts which mark the island's history were opening up. Pierro Amversa, a legend in the intrigues of the nightlife, is finally kicked out after he has established an alternative artistic and gay culture with his famous happenings revolving around his eponymous bar (Pierro's).

During the same period, more or less, the 'terrible tribe' of a newly constituted local 'subculture' led the way in establishing haunts of a predominantly 'male' culture. Patrick, a semi-Greek traveller, creates the urbane 'Casablanca'; Baroutis, a politicised local and member of the 'pirates' gang sets up the 'Mourayio' ('The Jetty'). Along with the intellectuals and the bourgeoisie of the earlier period the fashion world is now arriving, the world of the aesthetically privileged, as well as the hippies who occupy the caves at Paranga. The period of the seventies on Mykonos has assumed mythical proportions. The island was the 'most *in* place in the world'.[16] Drugs and every kind of illicit substance were glorified, despite being totally illegal. The island was a sort of free zone until the end of the decade, simply because, as my informants would proudly tell me, 'it had only three police officers'. The secret 'communicants' of an alternative 'drug culture' were created and the local bohemians exchanged and interchanged information with the cosmopolitan crowd, but they never imitated one another, or as Aristos put it: 'They just borrowed from one another, silently ... *mangika* [streetwise fashion].'[17]

Mykonos became the island of freedom and of illegal substances and, as a place which mainly attracted the haute bourgeoisie, it remained for a while free of special attention from the 'forces of law and order'. By the eighties, everything is changed by mass tourism. Yet an echo of hedonism remains. Remnants of the old gang and new admirers of that lifestyle still try their luck on Mykonos. The *palioi* (old-timers), in accordance with the unwritten laws of the island, have a certain 'authority'. Over and above the ideologies they had embraced, each of the *palioi* had acquired a special link with the place and with the community of 'outsiders'. The 'Mykonian' identity which is acquired as a result of long-term residence on the island has of itself only symbolic value. The immigrants' real place of origin and their family ties, when they are not forgotten, take on secondary importance. Even for those who are going to spend the winter in the large urban centres, marginalising their glamorous 'Mykonian' identity, the only collective noun that satisfies and sustains them is that of *oi Mykoniates* (Mykonians). The same goes for those who travel regularly during their absences from the island. On their cosmopolitan 'identity card', the only recognisably Greek part is the assumed Mykonian element.

The established groups who have moved to the island in recent decades have acquired some prestige in the area but above all they have created, through storytelling and fictionalised accounts of the island's 'crazy bygone days', the bridge which incorporates them in the common myth. The takeover of the place and its history, through storytelling, sets up a new underground authority, which is consolidated by exploiting the ancestral symbols of the 'Mykonian lifestyle'. Their shared mentality, unconventional lifestyle, consumption of illegal substances and above all the philosophy of an exclusive caste led me to designate the various groups with the euphemistic term 'Mykonian *sinafiá*'.

At first sight relatively arbitrary, the categories I created are basically classified according to the particular consumer preferences of the members of the *sinafi*. In most cases, using the sphere of consumption as a guideline for classification works well, given that their employment status is unclear and the occupational identity of the members fluid. Moreover, there is often no maintenance of ties with the traditional family or operation of the basic laws of kinship. One of the main problems I had to face in fieldwork was obscurity concerning the means of livelihood of a large numbers of my informants. Consequently their role as consumer became paramount.

The type of work associated with a tourist resort is the provision of services to people who are in a special situation (in a liminal state), not engaged in their everyday routine. On the other hand, this inversion of the 'normal' state of affairs, which the holidaymaker considers a special time, is for my informants part of their everyday routine. In terms of this reversal of the 'norm' then, work has been discursively converted into symbolic and artistic creativity. Thus, Karl from Germany, who knows a little about horticulture and has spent quite a few years travelling around, will 'get by' on the island as a 'garden designer' or 'sculptor of the plant kingdom'. Themis' 'genuine' wooden seagulls sell for twice the price of roughly hewn imitations. Finally, Hercules can charge much higher daily rates than skilled Mykonian builders, because he is a(n untrained) craftsman with a personal style. The *Mykoniots d'élection*, who chose to colonise the tourist resort, share many similar ideological characteristics, such as their attitude to work. The question 'What do you do?' is often answered by some general reference to various 'occupational identities'. This in turn leads to a more general obscurity regarding identity, which makes up a common structural characteristic of the small community of *Mykoniots d'élection*. Understandably, this way of thinking generally infiltrates the reasoning of the local residents. Gradually they seem to have abandoned their farming and fishing, and in their turn adapt to the (tourist) logic of selling 'Mykonian wine' (a demanding product they rarely take the trouble to produce any more) at unrealistically inflated prices. *Kyr*-Thodoris,[18] at eighty odd, either as a labour of love, as he himself claims, or to avoid his wife's nagging, goes to his fields every day and continues his agricultural labours, at the same time as keeping a small flock of animals which he personally takes to and fro Delos. In point of fact, he has income from property which is sufficient for the family expenditure right down to his great-grandchildren, and he retired from the business of production long before growing old. I show this other side of the coin to illustrate very briefly here how work, even in the mindset of the local traditional type, can be transformed into something other than 'productivity'.

The principal rationale behind the anthropological representation that follows is to (arbitrarily) classify the cosmopolitan 'immigrants' into categories which correspond to individual aesthetic/social contexts. But it must be understood from the beginning that over and above this conventional classification we are looking for a sort of similarity, an integrated code which defines a 'new identity' that not only validates its obscure boundaries, but above all establishes a new internal logic of power; a transcendent identity in relation to each individual's biography, whose function is to create some sort of (arbitrary) hierarchical order out of the island's aesthetic melange by mythologising the shared 'ideals' of common expressive codes.

The ethnographic construction of several aesthetic groups (i.e., the Mykonian *sinafia*) in this chapter intentionally involves some elements of romanticisation and naïveté. Nevertheless, these alternative forms of group classification will familiarise the reader with the Mykonian context where, through a series of performative identifications, social relations are intertwined on several levels of meaning. I have borrowed the notion of the *sinafi* in order to account for the 'models' of an aestheticised 'masculinity' operating on the island. I shall not be referring in any sense to the totality of the island's inhabitants, immigrants or regular summer visitors. I shall be concerned with a particular segment, which in the case of Mykonos is by no means easily overlooked, of exogenous and endogenous Mykonians who provide the basis for a shared, fetishised local 'subculture'. The limits of this ethnographic study extend, in fact, only to the exogenous Mykonians. The endogenous group, especially with regard to the theme of aesthetic masculinity, summon up the myth of a local clique with all the hallmarks of a fringe group. The element which dictates this local 'subculture' is a 'masculine' 'agonistic' transgender property similar to the expression of the 'agonistic model' of traditional male-gender as described by Herzfeld (1985) and Papataxiarchis (1992b). In our case, the existential goal of the 'agonistic' property of the actor is to remain unclassified, to stay 'underground'. In other words, a metaphorical aestheticised masculinity is in the *Mykoniots'* case the yeast of their mythologised collective identity. The deviation from a traditional model of the gender role is clear. Masculinity is not culturally dictated but alternatively becomes an aesthetic choice, a provisional identity, one amongst many others. The 'traditional' representation of masculinity is a consumption-based status quo in the tourist space, like the numerous (constructed) myths narrated to the 'tourists' about the legendary cult-locals and their 'high' technologies.

While working on the anthropological material I noticed the frequency with which different groups wove a unifying Mykonian myth with common heroes, the 'great old local gangs'. The way in which various stories reproduced the past helped me to distinguish between the *parees* (cliques) which had established the myth of the 'subcultural' Mykonian *andropareas* (male club) and by extension their own personal myth. The majority of men, who are members of this 'club', are intensely attached to it. Being accepted into the bosom of the Mykonian *parees* is the 'open sesame' into the idealised 'shared world' of the Mykonian *sinafia*. This is how the collective operation of the Mykonian *sinafia* began, which for the purposes of our story started around the mid sixties and continues to this day. Many of those who have been through this process are still on the island today and, although no one would have thought the Mykonian 'subculture' would have no age limits, the reality shows that restless seekers after truth have found a spiritual home here.

The use, or to be exact the abuse of substances, gives the clique its charm. The absence of limits leads to the excess which is the defining factor in the autonomous shared identity, over and above the various personal contexts. Within the context of a dramatic reconstruction of Mykonian society, the logic of the *sinafi*, that is of the codified exclusive group, can go beyond the conspiracy of the '*pioma*' (for a definition see n.3). Groups that share other types of 'unconventional' practices also exist. There are the homosexuals, the penniless artists, those who subscribe to the philosophy of 'just getting by', scions of the haute bourgeoisie who have come to live the simple life, ghettoised groups of English speakers who turn their backs on their social origins and engage in menial work, as well as commercial artists – the bearers of 'symbolic creativity' in this tourist space. Being diasporic in a tourist space like Mykonos, being part or not of the tourist industry, curiously makes one more like a monad rather than a nomad in this surreal cosmopolitan classless Mykonian milieu. So what defines your identity in a place like Mykonos is not anymore where you come from but it is your newly acquired Mykonian cosmopolitanism. So you turn into: Emma, the Mykonian Englishwoman (cf. Clifford 1994).

There are a number of Mykonian *sinafia* that fetishise aspects of masculinity through a reconstruction of a mythical past peopled by local heroes. Here are some examples. The first *sinafi* is the gang of local heroes, 'the pirates', a term borrowed from a short story by Chadjifotiou, an Athenian socialite, journalist and Mykonos' regular (1992) who refers to a similar group of reckless locals. They were originally discovered by Athenian bourgeois visitors and mythologised as archetypal models of 'male' behaviour. They were fishermen and builders, 'who had grown up in the sea', distinguished by their 'superhuman' endurance, their specialist knowledge of the natural world and their charisma. They quickly adapted to the new circumstances, took charge of the 'new situation' and became the entrepreneurs behind the island's leisure industry. Though they did not stay 'fishermen', and thus subservient to the modern invaders, they nevertheless carried on fishing. They had control of the nightlife, opening up the first nightclubs on the island, but they still went on being the heart and soul of the Mykonian *paniyiria* (traditional feasts) where they occasionally played along with the local bands. They had families, though they never saw them, because their ruling passions left them no time. They discovered whisky, but to this day they are still extremely keen to ritualistically prepare the *souma* (their traditional firewater) at the *hoirosfayia* (ceremonial pig-slaughtering), and continue to get drunk on it. The *sinafi* of the 'pirates' are said to have been the bane of the island. A state within a state, they would stay up all night playing music and getting drunk. Anyone who wanted to establish themselves on the island had to serve an 'apprenticeship' under the *sinafi* of the 'pirates'. Despite the fact that some of them had families, in their admirers' eyes their role continues to be seen strictly in the context of the *androparea* (male club). They portion out their time almost religiously, in a life of endless *sympotiasmos* (drinking commensality), and it becomes a vicious circle: the more they drink, the more they have to drink. Sometimes they are to be found at their 'businesses', sometimes at the local *paniyiria*, where they always play a leading role, sometimes at the endless *glendi* (carousing) with their mates and in their improvised dope dens; wherever they are, their ritualised commensality goes on and on.

The second *sinafi* is made up of those who introduced the modern drug culture to Greece. Most of its members are Greeks who had adopted the ideology of 'the road'. The first 'Greek beatniks' embraced the international culture of the sixties in the backstreets of the planet and made it into a way of life, not just a philosophy. Mykonos became a shrine for them. The *sinafi* sang the praises of distancing oneself from the embrace of the family and of the 'petit bourgeois model'. It introduced the drug culture, rock 'n' roll became a religion and a life without constraints or pre-planning an object of worship, an eternal bumming around. I shall call this *sinafi* by the somewhat arbitrary name of the *hippie sinafi*, because the arrival of its members on the island coincides with the first mention of hippies. The subjects of this monograph, the contemporary *Mykoniots d'élection* aesthetically originate from the *hippie sinafi*.

The third *sinafi* consists of members of the first group of modern visitors to the island (as early as the 1930s), a clique of Athenian and later international socialites and their descendants. For some of them, though their relationship with the island has remained close over the years and has been decisive in terms of their identity, they have not entirely shed the restraints of a bourgeois lifestyle. They either support families, or have professional obligations in Athens or elsewhere in the world. This leads in some ways to a 'dual' identity, since despite the fact that they keep homes on the island and spend long spells there, their socialisation is not restricted to the Mykonian *sinafia*. This category is in some ways an imitation of a Mykonian *sinafi*. Enjoying a certain intimacy with the 'archetypal' elements of the 'real' island culture, the *sinafi* of the 'pirates', the group can lay claim indirectly to a 'fringe' identity.

A fourth *sinafi*, I have called the 'neo-pirates', comprises the would-be successors to the 'pirates' and their *mangia* (streetwise ways). The members of this group are quickly assimilated and attempt to imitate aesthetically the archetypal 'males' of the pirates' *sinafi*. The 'neo-pirates' sing the praises of the *rouhla*,[19] learn the various codes of 'drinking commensality' at the islands' *kafeneia* (traditional coffee shops), learning at the feet of the senior gurus of the older generation. The distinguishing feature of this (exogenous) *sinafi* is that they spend the winter on the island, adopt local customs, and change their work roles from winter to summer. At the same time, they rhetorically distinguish themselves from a different aesthetic category of settlers on the island who do not need to redefine their identities and who keep well away from the natives.

There is a clear correspondence between the Mykonian subcultural lifestyle promoted by the pirates' *sinafi* and the traditional Greek rembetika *sinafia*,[20] a subculture based on music and hashish consumption which flourished from the turn of the twentieth century onwards (Damianakos 1976; Holst 1975; Petropoulos 1972, 1987; Tsiki 1981). In both cases, the discourses the members promote is of shared 'ideals' and, above all, identification with and allegiance to the group. They are united by special dress codes, shared *stekia*[21] (haunts) which serve as their meeting places to which they display blind allegiance, their ability to improvise on musical instruments and perform a spontaneous dance while 'under the influence'. Within this closed circle a whole world develops, 'turned in on the values of the *sinafi*' with strictly hierarchical relationships, accompanied by 'a shared psychological ambience' and a shared rhetoric (Damianakos 1976: 119, 134). Among the ideological elements common to both the old *rembetika sinafia* and the Mykonian pirates' *sinafi* are the image of a socially 'aloof' personality, the glorification of hashish, an ardent hedonism, and a dislike of any kind of 'representative of the law'. Anger is never politicised and generally speaking there is distancing from the politicised self.

In concluding this brief introduction to the world of the Mykonian *sinafia*, it must be stressed that the way in which this material has been reproduced reflects the point of view of the *Mykoniots d'élection* on whom the fieldwork concentrated. I have attempted this reconstruction of the image of several Mykonian groups as affective *sinafia* because I believe that their hero-protagonists, through their storytelling, have created a mythologised image of the old cliques, which in its turn reinforces the 'mysterious essence of maleness', a symbolic and aesthetic identity which can be acquired and then passed on. In this sense, Mykonos emotionally and aesthetically functions, at one discursive level, as a boundless great big *kafeneio* which propagates transcendental ties that resemble the model of the 'friends from the heart' described by Papataxiarchis in his analysis of male friendship (Papataxiarchis 1988, 1991). The difference is that in Papataxiarchis' *kafeneio* what is re-enacted – through the male-collectivity of the drinking of the *parea* – is the most egalitarian type of social grouping (Papataxiarchis 1992b: 223). Nevertheless, this egalitarian state is always displaced by the male actors' social roles. It is no accident that *Mykoniots d'élection* rarely employ such self-definitions of [egalitarian] group formations, codes of familiarity with reference to closed systems like the notion of *parea*, since they prefer to refer vaguely to a broader category of 'Mykoniot' friends. Semantically, Mykonos performs for them the context of an 'affective' familiarity.

In the Mykonian *sinafia* you find the genuine article and the ersatz, types that do not exist in everyday reality but which have moral and aesthetic resonances within the group. The subject of my enquiry is to decodify the need to reproduce on a grand scale an aesthetic 'male' persona which very quickly becomes mythologised and borrowed by an autonomous group consciousness.

The two worlds of 'maleness': the ethnography

I tehni tou stisimatos: the art of 'setting up' a space, or Mykonos as the space of fetishised masculinity

On a trip to Volos I met a friend who had attended the 'Mykonos school' a decade before my own fieldwork. Lefteris had 'served an apprenticeship' with the *hippie sinafi* and especially under the Mykonian master Hercules (see the relevant self-narrative in chapter 3) in the early eighties. Now thirty-three and having already set up three businesses of his own in his hometown, he could take a detached view. On one of the rare occasions when he told a story in detail, he gave me his view of how the Mykonian *sinafia* worked.

One spring, he left school and went to Mykonos. Being bright and exceptionally hard-working he found various jobs and short-term contracts. First he took a job at 'Pepes', a fashionable Mykonian café, where as they used to say at the time '*varagan fixakia* (they would get a fix) in the toilets'. The early eighties was the golden era of *preza*[22] (heroin) on the island. You used to see the gangs of style-conscious *frikia* sallying forth from their haunts 'beyond the statue of Mando'[23] to rove the cobbled streets in their cowboy boots, their leathers and dark glasses. For them it was one continuous 'scene': *preza* in their urban setting and *preza* on Mykonos.

The next summer, Lefteris got a 'transfer' to another breakfast bar, the 'Suzy Q'. Hercules, the first guru of the 'breakfast culture' on the island, had agreed to set it up. His breakfasts in the urbane rock bar attracted all the avant-garde of the island. Lefteris lived and worked with Hercules or, to be precise, Hercules lived in the house while Lefteris was lodged in the small courtyard at its entrance. Hercules had transformed the courtyard of the Mykonian stone-house into an outdoor sitting room with a view of the stars and the sculptured rocks of the south coast of the island. They worked 'together', that is to say Lefteris did twice as much or more, and Hercules, who was 'setting up' (*estine*) the operation, and besides was 'known for *stisimata ton magazion*' (setting up businesses), piled more and more onto his shoulders. Nevertheless, the 'Susy Q scene' was the ultimate in island terms and all the 'elect' used to drop in. The organisation of the service offered was something entirely new. When you went in, the bar where you had danced the night before, had everything attractively set out. You felt you could have anything you wanted, the atmosphere and presentation were very simple, just as if you were a guest in someone's home. You could stretch out a hand and nibble. Hercules, all affability, maintained order with a sprig of basil tucked behind his ear. He designed exclusive interiors for 'ambience', played his avant-garde music and did the PR. He set Lefteris to work and charged his guests whatever he fancied (according to their wallets). The consumption of alcohol began at an early hour. The place was full of undercover policemen on duty. The nineteen-year-old Lefteris, who had a taste for 'forbidden' substances and above all for bumming around, worked hard under the protective 'roof' of Hercules' courtyard and was initiated into the idiosyncratic 'underworld' of the island.

Hercules was a builder and a furniture maker; all in all he was the ideal handyman, specialising in his own personal style. Already thirty-something and having spent a decade on the island, he was one of the *vasikous* (founder members) of the *hippie sinafi*. By his very presence he enticed the other members of the *sinafi* into his enterprises, so that they made his current year's project-*kafeneio*,[24] their haunt for the season. And so passed the days of Lefteris' apprenticeship, under his eccentric master Hercules. Members of various *sinafia* used to gather at the Susy Q and thus Lefteris gradually learnt to recognise the various styles. He was initiated into the *sarong* culture[25] and the early morning drug-sniffing. He got drunk, stayed up all night and went to work in the morning, serving glassy-eyed customers with wonderful local produce. Living close to Hercules he was often disappointed at being on the wrong end of 'bad deals'.[26] Lefteris wondered why, despite the fact that Hercules upset his customers with his capricious tariff and annoyed him by the unequal division of labour, neither he nor the customers left. During the three years of his apprenticeship on the island, as he said outright, he learnt from Hercules how to *stinei* (set up) businesses. He learnt how to *stinei* (design) spaces in his own way, having been 'trained' in the personal style of his 'master'. Lefteris admitted verbatim: 'I learnt the cosmopolitan *stisimo* (set-up), which is all that you can hold on to afterwards to get something out of it.'

As he described to me the experience of his apprenticeship under the supervision of the local 'boss' Hercules, it seemed to me that Lefteris had really benefited. Unlike most people, he learned to set up (*na stinei*) the 'businesses' by himself, not following the expensive craze for going to a 'specialist', and he did it in perfect taste. Despite the beneficial influence of his apprenticeship and the good reputation he acquired there, I realised that Lefteris now finds it hard to stay on the island more than a few days at a time. In response to my enquiry about this he began to tell me about '*to Mykoniatiko mentality*' (the Mykonian *mentality*).[27] He spoke with some disappointment about the 'psychology' and the 'make-up' of the people who settle on the island. In a nutshell, 'Few of them pass muster, when you come right down to it.' And he went on: 'To give you an idea, when Schizas died,[28] there was deep mourning throughout the island. Well, all of them [from the *hippie sinafi*] flaunted themselves in the front row at the funeral, next to the relatives.' And 'Not,' he judged, 'for sentimental reasons.' He continued, 'I also knew the man, but I was embarrassed to go to the funeral; I didn't feel that close.' Lefteris saw how the ostentatious presence of the rock 'n' roll heroes of the *hippie sinafi* at the funeral of the local *mangas* (streetwise guy) was just a front for their impudence and an attempt to justify their own futility, by appropriating the myth of the deceased's *mangia* (street cred). This is an example of the affected solidarity which I have come across many times in the rhetoric of the 'junkies', a cockeyed version of *pallikaria* (derring-do), shared by the *potes* (users of [illegal] substances).

This was as far as Lefteris' commentary went. Though somewhat obscure, it was nevertheless important because it was spontaneous and he was talking about feelings, a rarity in the endless tales of *pallikaria*, of the heroes of the Mykonian 'subculture'. And it was this retrospective comment about the *sinafi* of the 'wannabe Mykonians' which excited my interest. From the written sources relating to the island's recent history and mainly in the oral accounts, which now that they were getting to know me were becoming more and more frequent, I discovered a mythologised 'male' world of values, (a world) which was always situated in the past, 'when Schizas was still alive' and when everything on Mykonos was '*pure*' and '*original*'. From the accounts of my own male informants I began to discern an indirect glorification of their own *mangia* in the narration of the achievements of their 'local' or their 'cosmopolitan' friends.

The moving atmosphere of Schizas' funeral, which I will describe later with the help of other testimonies, could not help but bring to mind Eleni's death. (Incidentally, there is no need to be surprised at her sex, as Eleni was a worthy member of the *hippie sinafi* and ideally there is no gender discrimination here.) She was buried on Mount Olympus, after struggling for many years against cancer, a struggle which never prevented her from coming to the island and participating fully in the life of the *sinafi*. I remember her constantly allaying the fears and anxieties of others, offering them hospitality and/or nursing them, and then getting bored again and becoming indifferent while going off in search of her own pleasures. Eleni was a typical member of her *sinafi*. Towards the end her condition deteriorated and she went to visit the *ashram* of her late spiritual teacher 'Bhagwan' in India. She was buried on Good Friday, which was in early April that spring. Just when the members of the *sinafi* were slowly coming together on the island to usher in their worldly season, their 'new year'. Eleni, who had spent her life surrounded by people, who had been hospitable, offering nourishment for body and soul, was buried in the presence of just a few friends.

The reverberations of mourning on the island were subterranean. The subject was not mentioned, it was taboo. They pretended not to notice that one of them was missing. I wondered if this was a matter of transcendence or of pure futility. Several days went by before someone from the *sinafi* mentioned the event. It was one afternoon at Hercules' house and he was 'purifying' the place by burning sage leaves, when he told me that he felt the presence of Eleni around. His usual composure showed slight signs of emotional upheaval for a few seconds. Then he became reconciled to it and putting all the force of his unconventional existence once again into his metaphysical rationalism, he smiled and carried on burning incense.

On the other hand, the sudden death and the subsequent memorial services in memory of the local hero, Schizas, prompted emotion and admiration for years afterwards in the *sinafi*. If we look at the two cases side by side we find a different attitude to bereavement and the commemoration of a companion.[29] There may perhaps be a simple explanation for this difference, if we bear in mind the 'distance factor' in the case of Eleni's funeral.[30] Nevertheless, we still have to explain the commemorative aspect.

On the death of the archetypal hero, Schizas the active part played by the members of the *hippie sinafi* may indicate a conscious attempt at embodiment, whereby they reinforced and validated their own 'Mykonian' identity. Maybe identifying themselves with an aesthetic super (male) role model is less painful. Then, again, perhaps the problem simply lay in the fact that Eleni, as well as being a member of the *sinafi*, was also a woman (although I am doubtful about this interpretation).

Men's tales: men's apprenticeships

The following are two individuals' accounts of their socialisation into the legendary Mykonian *sinafia* of the 'hippies' and the 'pirates'.

Markos' tales

Markos had deservedly earned a name as a raconteur in the *hippie sinafi*. His stories enchanted the elderly members of the gang [*sinafi*], the wannabe rock 'n 'rollers and whatever enchanted 'chicks' happened to be in the company at the time, and ended up as marathon storytelling sessions. Usually in the early evening, when the strong sun had left the beach, or at the *sinafi*'s get-togethers on autumn evenings, Markos took on the role of the wizard and unearthed old stories about the gang with a unique talent. Here, narration and authenticity play a role. Following Graburn (1978), Bendix (2002) reconnects with the ritualistic and liminal aspect of the tourist's travelling experience. She accounts for narrativity as the underlying structure for the emergence of tourism in modern society; she further argues that: 'the process of narrating the experience recovers the moment' (ibid. 473). Likewise, the worst travelling experience can come across as a success thanks to Markos' skills as a raconteur. For example, our disastrous road trip in Rajasthan has been utterly romanticised in his later narrative reconstructions as recounted to our shared *Mykoniot* friends. The reconstruction of narrative through experience banishes any feelings of incompetence and powerlessness that were evoked in the 'tourist-field' (ibid. 474). Travelling like the pilgrimage site holds 'tremendous narrative potential' (ibid.), and therefore proliferates self myth-making; an opportunity to uniquely express one's experience, i.e., one's individuality. Travel stories, be they good or bad, are therefore spontaneous displays of cultural capital. The worst experiences often make the best stories.

Before Markos re-established himself as a permanent resident on the island for the second time in the early nineties, he usually arrived on Mykonos towards mid September. Each year, Markos' return coincided with the end of the tourist season and the beginning of the closed sessions of the *sinafi*. A bon viveur from Istanbul, Markos, who had been a dealer in unisex clothes somewhere in Kansas for many years, gave the *parea* (his [*Mykoniots d'élection*] circle of friends) a certain cohesion by his very presence. The annual *Mykoniots*' trips to Delos, the shared meals and the cooking sessions that took place in members' homes, seemed to organise themselves automatically.

The members of the *parea* would sit on the built-in sofas of Hercules' house with whoever happened to be around and cast the '*animal cards*',[31] smoke dope and Markos, usually reclining, would begin to tell his tale. He would tell tales of 'Constantinople'[32], and of his childhood, of Mykonos in 1968 ... 'unrecognisable now', of London in the seventies and the Picasso Bar on the King's Road and the basement bar, Mykonos, in Fulham. He would interweave his tales with incidents from travels in the Orient, journeys with wealthy girlfriends, and starring the gang members themselves as penniless lady-killers. Markos acquired special status in the *sinafi* by virtue of his close relationship and experience of travelling with Patrick. Patrick, though still alive, was already a mythologised character in Markos' *sinafi*. He had 'set up' (*estise*) the whole new culture of the Mykonian bar and attracted a new type of person to the island. He set up businesses, which, even after they changed hands, were still leading the way in the island's leisure market well into their second decade. He was, however, obliged to leave Greece, having violated the drugs laws, and was supposedly never able to return. Since then he has been leading a similar life on another of this world's island paradises. Patrick became a legend because he was an 'adventurer' from birth. When the rest of them had yet to leave their 'provincial' homes, he was already travelling the world, gathering experiences. He appeared in American second-hand clothes when the others were still discovering jeans. Whatever Patrick was wearing became the fashion for the avant-garde. Patrick had style, and he was also notoriously handsome. He inspired love in strong and wealthy women, or at least this is how the myth goes. From time to time he sold goods from both East and West, which became the fashion on the island. He had a huge collection of clothes and antiques. Patrick had discovered the 'other paradises' early on and had already appropriated some of the 'other cultures', using his talent for becoming accepted and surviving anywhere. He played with the various styles and he was accepted by different Mykonian *sinafia* on account of his cosmopolitan upbringing. The details of this hero's curriculum vitae are vague. Of bourgeois descent and from a Greek family with some obscure European ancestor from whom he got his foreign name, there had been many women but no serious attachment. Patrick not only plays the part of a hero in Markos' tales but to a greater extent functions as a 'legendary' symbol for that glorious bygone age 'when Mykonos had only three policemen'.[33]

Mykonos, where the drug culture of the rebels of the 'new consciousness' flourished, was undeveloped in the seventies. Patrick and the other refined fashion freaks had found their paradise. As Markos relates, with tourism and the increasing worldliness of the island, 'came the first *dioikitis* (police chief)'.

One of the *sinafi*'s favourite stories is about the 'cops and robbers' period which ended, ingloriously for many in the eighties. 'But in the old days,' continues Markos 'everybody used to drink (*na pinei*) ... All together, us and the locals. And Schizas used to dash out into the fields with the *kommates* (large chunks of hashish) and shout "I'm no thief," as a form of protest,' thus ritualising a form of resistance. At that time, as Artemis also says, 'there was a revolution going on through drugs.' In the *pirates' sinafi*, Schizas' gang, and in Patrick's cosmopolitan *hippie sinafi*, there was a shared rhetoric of resistance to the 'forces of law and order'. There were exchanges of 'substances', exchanges between the old and the new attitude to the *pioma*. The two *sinafia* may not have had shared codes of 'male' behaviour, but there was certainly a requirement for stamina and a facade of sangfroid in the face of the existential requirements of the 'fix'.

Aristos' tale about the death of Schizas: the bourgeois model of mythologising a local hero

Aristos, who owns the Casablanca, the bar that Patrick set up, is wandering around the 'office' blind drunk. The 'office' is what Aristos and his friends called one of the *kafeneia* (traditional coffee-shops) in the harbour. That was where the locals gathered and where Aristos, as a consequence, could hide away from the sophistication of the area 'beyond the statue of Mando' (preferred by avant-garde tourists). For Aristos, the 'office' is in effect his point of contact and place-where-he-gets-drunk with his local Mykonian friends. Theoretically, it remains an exclusively male assembly, and it involves obligatory *kraipali* (excessive drunkenness/crapulence). It was the news about Baroutis' accident that made Aristos miss his midday swim. Baroutis, one of the last remaining members of Schizas' *sinafi* (the *pirates*), on his way to his celebrated dip, being dead drunk, came over dizzy and hit his head as he fell over. He was transferred straightaway to Athens. Aristos fell prey to his existential demons. He is also a heavy drinker and so he seized the opportunity to show solidarity and get legless. Later on, while conveying to me the glum atmosphere of the *kafeneio*, he babbled: 'Rumour has it that they've saved him, but he didn't want to be saved, he wanted to go. A subconscious suicide in other words. Well, there you are ... people like that aren't cut out for a sick bed.' Baroutis had had severe liver problems for years and his facial features had been transformed by drink. Nevertheless, his friends and admirers confronted the melancholy notion of the legendary Baroutis' potentially suicidal inclinations with endless whiskies in the 'office'. Aristos, in his authentic 'Mykonian' afternoon *kraipali*, was as one inspired. He recalled the local gang (the 'pirates') and Schizas' unexpected end. Later on, when he had sobered up, I sat him down to tell me about it. According to Aristos, his end was an inglorious one: 'It was shitting that killed him!'

The stories I heard about Schizas' sudden death show no consistency. There are a number of versions. Some say that he ate too many blackberries, others that he saw a mandragora root, and others that he was found with a fix in his arm. The multiple versions are fitting for a local legend, but Aristos' version seemed to me to be plausible. Nevertheless, even in this scenario, the myth of perpetual *kraipali* is fulfilled. 'Heroes die with their boots on' (lit. standing up). 'Well, ... they had drunk a lot the night before,' continued Aristos, 'and Schizas, as was his wont, went to work without having slept.' According to the Mykonian *theriaklides* (abusers of any substance), this was because 'Sleep sobers you up, spoils your drunkenness and then you have to start all over again.' 'So that day, as he was going to the toilet in a rather woozy condition, he strained a bit too much, suffered a stroke and that was it.' Schizas, we should remember, undertook the difficult work of digging wells, something which requires first-rate physical condition and skill. When they heard of his death, his mates were inconsolable. And it came just when the group was in its heyday, when they all believed they were immortal, As a result of his sudden death, the reputation of the extraordinary diminutive *mangas* automatically increased. Whenever he mentions Constantis Schizas, Aristos becomes reverent. His name has the same effect on all the *sinafia* from the bourgeois Athenians to the cosmopolitan *prezakia* (heroin sniffers).

As he continues his tale, Aristos describes with evident emotion how the *pallikaria* (the fearless men), inconsolable at the pointless loss of their friend, went along with their instruments and some wine to his grave, filled their glasses and clinked them against one poured out for him, saying, 'Good evening, Constanti!'[34] Then they began playing their instruments to keep him company and pass the night. The 'village' was scandalised. Once again the deceased's family did not approve of the 'friends' behaviour. The dead man had not had a chance to rest, *den eihe sarantisei* ('he hadn't even got to the forty-day mark yet' as in Orthodox tradition the deep mourning lasts for forty days until the soul of the deceased finally abandons this world). As he was telling me all this, Aristos was almost in tears. The nostalgia for those times, times when he was part of the 'essence of maleness', together with the power of the tale about the 'derring-do of the other', the friend, the drinking companion, gave the vulnerable and melancholy Aristos an excuse for his own consuming passions and a feeling that he and Constantis were made of the same stuff.

Aristos liked to get drunk and flirt with whoever he was talking to, using this sort of melodramatic storytelling.[35]

Aristos, then, had arrived on the island as a reserved eighteen-year-old. He studied under the great masters of the *pioma* in Schizas' local *sinafi*. We do not know exactly how close the relationship was. Now forty-five, Aristos wears the knitted Mykonian cap that Baroutis' mother makes, plays the *toumberleki* (a traditional Turkish drum) skilfully, '*mangika*' (in an exhibitionist manner, like a *mangas*), and despite having the most sophisticated bar on the island, has no hesitation in putting *rembetika* on the record player when he is making merry with his friends. Having a somewhat politicised past, Aristos laid the foundations of his culture when living in Berlin in the early seventies. When he returned to Mykonos, he bought the bar that Patrick had set up and gradually transformed it into a shrine for the 'old style' Athenian *haute bourgeoisie* who had been going to the island for years and who trusted the old haunts.

As a twenty-year-old conscript, he used to read the *kosmika* (gossip columns and social diaries) in the *Vradyni*[36] newspaper: hair-raising stuff for his father, who had fought with the leftist resistance group, ELAS, during the war. He also had a *daïs* (powerful macho) granddad, as he put it, who played the mandolin and painted. Aristos, however, took after his uncle Menelaos 'who lived in Syntagma', in the centre of Athens, and was always well-turned out. In Athens, where he spends the winter, and where he also runs a restaurant-cum-bar, he takes off his Mykonian caps and wears cashmere waistcoats. For some time now he has been planning to open up a 'café *aman*'[37] so that his friends can play live music on instruments, without amplifiers. He looks back over his 'apprenticeship' in the *sinafi* of Costantis' local gang, where he grew to his 'other' manhood, and continues to dream of *mia oraia lantza* (a 'beautiful' motor boat), like the one Nicholas Baroutis had.

Aristos is an example of a collaborative apprenticeship among the Mykonian *sinafia*. His was a more petit bourgeois lifestyle, with bourgeois and family examples which he stuck to, at least ostensibly. As far as he is concerned, he was influenced by Patrick, who is still earning a living in the style of a rock guru, and by Schizas' brand of 'manhood', but also by the citified, well-tailored uncle. A sophisticated bohemian, married to an Australian woman, he is bringing up two daughters and hopes to stop bringing them to the island before they reach adolescence.[38]

Improvising masculinities

The bourgeois, enchanted by the power of the super-daring 'masculinity' they find in this 'traditional' space, attempt to appropriate it. In this way they gain aesthetic access to the elements of power they find so attractive. Admiration for and mythologisation of the place itself and the inhabitants of Mykonos is perhaps the most important common element to come out of the stories I have collected. This perpetual process of mythologisation underpins the *Mykoniots' d'élection* decision to move to the island and constitutes the fundamental building block on which they will construct their new 'Mykonian' identity.

By taming the forces of nature, the 'alcoholic philosophers',[39] the Mykonian *pirates*, have become models for the construction of a mythologised identity, a construction which suited the outsiders. In the tales told by the wannabe Mykonians, the locals were always more *manges* (had more street credibility) because while the sobered-up city kids were looking for cigarette papers to roll their joints, 'Costantis improvised *nargiledes* (hookahs) out of airbricks on building sites.' The wannabe 'locals' needed a new identity. They needed the support of their personal image in the midst of the mythologised models which they found in the confines of this tiny, timeless island, at times in the mythologised anti-heroes who worshipped at its shrine and at others in the unruly, cosmopolitan survivors.

It is clear that, by extolling shared models of 'masculinity', the narrators are attempting to transcend their personal and social contexts. The shared ideology is a product of the glorification of certain super role-models of 'masculinity', which are in this case the phantoms of a modern tourist resort, and creates the contradictory prototype of a strictly socialised 'man' who, nevertheless, constantly needs to demonstrate 'his' marginality. Playing the *pallikari* is a profoundly conscious and effective social practice. The thinking behind Mykonian 'networking' proved to me that to be 'different', to transgress by virtue of your eccentricity, your style, and your marginality, is a consciously organised social act in the Mykonian *attraction*, a way of reaffirming a new 'self' in the endless process of adapting to cosmopolitanism.

There is, perhaps, an existential affinity between the *Mykoniots d'élection* as 'marginal' performers and Bauman's theoretical allocation and predicament of the contemporary subject; in other words, between Bauman's post-modern 'vagabond' and the 'piratical' *Mykoniots*. Bauman (interviewed in Franklin 2003: 206) has characterised our central role as consumers in 'liquid modernity', not unlike tourists. Tourism stands as a metaphor for the contemporary condition, being in a place only temporarily, not belonging to that place: 'Being *in* but not *of* the place' (ibid. 208). The name of the game is lack of commitment vis-à-vis spatial and emotional belonging. Bauman juxtaposes the 'tourist syndrome' of liquid modernity with its transient predecessor the 'pilgrim syndrome' where the pilgrim lives for the next stop. The tourist syndrome is about restlessness, neurotic arrival and not about the process; it is not about becoming. Bauman's transient 'tourist' aspires to an oxymoronic contemplative state: 'living from one moment to another, living for the moment' (ibid. 209). The dark side of Bauman's transient subject, the alter ego of the tourist is the 'vagabond'. What's interesting in his concept of the vagabond in 'liquid modernity' is that one need not travel to turn into one. For Bauman, the tourist and the vagabond are 'two poles of a continuum' (ibid.). The old-fashioned 'traveller' seeking for cultural exchanges is now being replaced by the soulless tourist who seeks no otherness; because 'otherness' is only superficially desired and immediately consumed and discarded. People long for communities they miss, instead they indulge in substitutes: conferences, festivals, or visiting pleasure domes such as Mykonos. Bauman's 'cloakroom communities' here act like tourist destinations: short-lived and over-idealised (ibid. 214). '... substitutes are instant cures' (ibid.). Vagabondage attempts to fulfil the desire for community. *Mykoniots d'élection* act as the representative public performers of this existential impetus; travelling metonymically stands for this desire for a mystic community.

Bauman's 'cloakroom communities' resemble Augé's non-places (1995): defined as spaces of supermodernity that dictate newly emerged temporary affiliations. Mykonos, a paradigmatic non-place, operates as a spatial signifier haphazardly orchestrating aleatory encounters. This exposure to aleatory encounters through frequenting non-places, i.e., 'acquainting others' through the frequent visits of the 'solitaires' in the impersonal places of supermodernity is a phenomenon, according to Augé, which is historically unprecedented (ibid. 117–18). Likewise, the non-place acquires its allure. Non-places become fetishes of narrative, as well as fetishes of sensuality; non-places, very much like tourist spaces or contemporary pilgrim sites, are amalgamated in an extremely individualistic restlessness principle; a restless wandering to and from different fetishised non-places becomes a[n existential] driving force, as well as the foundation for an emerging self-narrative *à la Mykoniot*.

For Augé, conclusively, non-places are a metaphor for new types of oxymoronic non-relational collectivities. 'The community of human destinies is experienced in the anonymity of non-place, and in solitude' (ibid. 120). In other words, 'the traveller's space [inclusive of the traveller's ritualised stopovers] may thus be the archetypal non-place' (ibid. 86). It is very useful to imagine Mykonos, as well as similar modernist temples of extreme individuality, as the ritualised stopovers, the non-places of Augé's solitaires. Travelling and solitude are characteristic companions of Augé's de Certeauian space: the non-places (cf. Certeau: 1984).

Finally, Bauman's identity metaphor of the tourist and his alter ego, the vagabond, reminds me of groups like the *Mykoniots d'élection*. Their once-upon-a-time glamorous marginalisation per se is now becoming obsolete in a tourist space where every otherness is semiotically consumed irrespective of its content. The *Mykoniots d'élection* are only one display in the rock 'n' roll museum of

Mykonian unconventionality. The museum hosts other unconventional categories: the uncompromising locals, the gays, the cosmopolitan eccentrics, the global adventurers who migrated there, aspiring to no special status. In the winding Mykonian streets there is no real mixing anymore; there is no immersion in the other, *à la* Bauman.

Composing the myth, composing identities

The theoretical approach to the above anthropological material does not confront masculinity in general, but examines it in a particular context, that of gaining a place in the myth of the Mykonian *sinafia*. I am interested here in how the modes of a codified 'male' behaviour become part of the discourse of a multi-influenced 'Mykonian' society, and I consider that this constitutes the fundamental mechanism that supports an inner circle of client relationships. Within the bounds of this artificially constructed, hierarchical society of *mangia*, skilfulness, extreme individuality and aesthetic discrimination, there are masters of style and apprentice followers of the spatial/cultural myth of otherness.

The myth-making (storytelling) and more specifically the appropriation of the legendary heroes through the storytelling functions as 'symbolic/aesthetic capital' in the Mykonos paradise of subjectivity. This capital in turn offers a place in the strictly hierarchical context of the over-idealised Mykonian 'commune'. The myth-making and the establishment of a shared narrative of accepted models of behaviour in effect promotes the smooth incorporation of the members into the shared myth; in other words, it assists their entry into the group (cf. Waldren 1996: 201). By creating a myth about their master/teacher they incorporate themselves into it. In this way, they boost the already existing client relationship based on 'seniority' and strengthen the position of their teachers, and in addition become part of the chain of those carrying on the myth.

On one level, therefore, the idealised narrative promotes the bonding of the group, laying the foundations for a special community made up of idiosyncratic personalities, assembled 'by chance' on the island and who share in the common past of the place and its inhabitants, with all its oddity. The idealised narrative reinforces the 'equality', putting all the narrator participants on an equal footing. The bond of sharing a 'common destiny' is bolstered by the ideal of the collective *pioma*. Incorporation into the *parea* (circle) of Mykonian 'bachelors' through learning about the local history of *mangia*, does result in some benefits accruing to the initiate. By borrowing from the other fellow's myth, the 'newcomer' acquires 'women', work and kudos on the island; the kudos act as symbolic/aesthetic capital which translates as incorporation of the member into the group with access to the codified logic of power within the boundaries of the tourist resort.[40]

However, this same pattern of positive myth-making, which creates models and establishes a codified [aesthetic/experiential] logic of power[41] can at the same time function hierarchically and antagonistically. The role models are unbeatable, because they are forever in the island's glorious past, an idealised time which the newcomer has missed out on. All they can do is follow the hierarchical structure and hand on the torch of the old days to worthy followers who can overcome their personal limitations through their blind identification with the group. As to the rest, the bourgeois can never become an old salt, nor the cosmopolitan adventurer a traditional Mykonian 'buccaneer'.

The established 'institution' of apprenticeship in the Mykonian *sinafia* is the mechanism through which the 'outsiders' authenticate their authority on the island. They are assimilated in two ways: through the silent apprenticeship, in which they acquire an understanding of the 'male' behaviour of the group-culture of the *pioma*, and the active training, which is rewarded with entry into the shared myth and the symbolic constituents of 'collective knowledge'. Within these constituents lies the myth of the essence of 'maleness', the myth of a ['male'] otherness, which the apprentice must develop.[42]

The elitist space-myth of Mykonos is suitable for this sort of idealisation. Within the tourist space the myth has 'survival' value over and above its symbolic worth, because it can be sold. It is sold to the tourist, the visitor, the traveller, the sign collector who needs to exceed[43] her limits, to 'unwind'. In the fiefdom of the 'temporaries' in this mythologised tourist space the myth can be sold, the aesthetic signs can be easily appropriated because the communicant purchasers do not go there for the 'truth' but for 'its legend'.

Notes

1. *Sinafi* has its etymological root in the Turkish word *esnaf* and literally means a (craft) guild. Metaphorically it connotes a cohesive group of people that functions as a clique. *Sinafia* is the plural of *sinafi*.
2. Zinovieff proposes a definition of *kamaki* as 'the act of a Greek man pursuing a foreign woman with the intention of having sex' (Zinovieff 1991: 203).
3. The *pioma*, the act of consuming a 'fetishised' substance, literally means 'drinking'. *Pioma*, is a slang expression used as a codified way of referring to the consumption of illegal substances, e.g., I 'drink' a cigarette or 'drink' drugs, whereas you are in fact drinking wine while smoking a joint or snorting cocaine.
4. *Mangia*, an old-fashioned word that is best rendered as 'street cred'/'street-wise ways'. The origin of the word is the term *manga*, common to both Spanish and Turkish, which stood for a group of disorderly soldiers.
5. The mandragora root, an intensely hallucinogenic plant, which is reputedly easily available on Mykonos and Delos, is considered a very dangerous substance by local people. Apart from the powerful consciousness-altering properties of the plant itself, its root, which goes very deep and is difficult to uproot, is traditionally thought to be anthropomorphic in shape and, according to local superstition, anyone who comes face to face with it will die.
6. Members of the 'underground' affiliated to a group.

7. The traditional (male) prototype of a transcendental expression of masculinity is frequently portrayed in Greek ethnography through the practice of (*sympotiasmos*) drinking commensality (cf. Gefou-Madianou 1992: 125; Papataxiarchis 1991, 1992b).
8. *Ohla* is a slang expression referring to an unpleasantly noisy situation in any large-scale assembly.
9. The term 'exogenous Mykonians' refers to those who have chosen to move to the island, without any bonds of kinship.
10. According to Loukissas (1977), most probably Mykonos was 'predestined' to turn into a tourist community by a few (bourgeois) Mykonians who were living in Athens at the time (during the early thirties). They realised that the early attraction for several groups of artists, intellectuals and other elites interested in the remains of Delos could transform the nearby Mykonos into a successful tourist stopover.
11. To sketch the spatial representation of Mykonos as a fetish, I will briefly refer to an account offered by an offspring of this bourgeois group of early Athenian visitors and an ex-Mykonos regular himself. Interestingly enough for Kostis, Mykonos is a place that does not deserve his visits anymore. Nevertheless, his discourse on Mykonos remains an enchanted one. Kostis is hooked on Mykonos' glorious past: 'Mykonos was freedom. It was freedom because it was mixed. Nowadays, each season is dedicated to a different group. June for the gays, July for the Greek petit-bourgeois holiday-makers and October for the old "regulars". This beach is for the gays, the other for the hippies and so forth. Once upon a time freedom [in Mykonos] was embodied in the "mixing". Everybody was mingling ... In reality, back then, everybody was a member of the same [social] class; only some were [performing the role of] the "hippies", some the "straight", some the "artists". Think about it! At the time only a few knew about Mykonos, and could travel anyway'.

    The space-myth of Mykonos seems to have passed from a class-based elitism (disguised in an aestheticised discourse), through an elitist 'deviant' discourse, to being a sign available to the aesthetically 'aware'. In other words, Mykonos used to belong to the 'elect', then to the 'liberated', and nowadays to the sign-creators/appreciators.
12. The discourse on locals' liberality/tolerance is also promoted by the *littérateur* Karantonis (n.d.) as an 'inherent' cultural quality of the Mykonians. In order to promote an amoral space-myth, convenient for the aesthetic groups that initially gathered on Mykonos, Karantonis maintains that the actors'/tourists' tendency towards exhibitionism is exceptionally well taken and respected by the locals.
13. Romanos (1983) reports that, up until the seventeenth century, the Greeks were involved in piracy. Most particularly, the Aegean islands are reported to have suffered from piratical raids since Minoan times, as well as during the classical period (Keffaliniadis 1984: 113). In the sixteenth and seventeenth centuries, when pirates, both Christian and Muslim, were rife across the Aegean, piracy in Mykonos became a form of 'community business' (Romanos 1983: 11); in other words, the boundaries between legitimate mercantilism and piracy, 'legal' and 'illegal' practices, were unclear. Keffaliniadis characteristically calls Mykonos the 'nest of the pirates' (1984: 113), as Mykonos and nearby Delos were reported to be an appropriate shelter for them until the nineteenth century (Tsakos 1996). Today's locals, seem discursively to fetishise and promote their 'piratic' and 'anarchic' identities.
14. Durrell's discourse on Greece and the Greeks in general reminds us of the obvious connection between the first tourist flow in modern Greece and the long-established Philhellenic movement. According to Pettifer (1993), the 'ancestors' of the modern European tourists in modern Greece were the nineteenth-century travellers/philhellenes. At the time classicism, very popular amongst the Western intelligentsia, was the motive for the Romantic travellers of the era to visit Greece, the 'birthplace' of 'their' civilisation, as well as of the Italian Renaissance. In 1916, Greece was connected to the rest of Europe by rail. In the 1920s, the Hellenic Travellers' club would characteristically include in its travelling itinerary historically and

mythologically charged places like Ithaca, Athens, Kos, Rhodes, Mycenae, Olympia and Delos, among others. However, as Pettifer suggests, up to this point (apart from Byron's romanticisation of the 'Sweet Souths'), modern Greeks (i.e., the locals) were not within the scope of interest of the European traveller. Thus, it is no accident that 'today's holidaymaker on upmarket Swan Hellenic Cruises is in direct line of descent from these Victorian upper middle-class journeyers' (Pettifer 1993: 73).

15. One can roughly divide the recent history of Mykonian tourism into several different phases: the first can be said to have started in the thirties when the first cruise visits are reported; a second period commenced after the Second World War and lasted up until the end of the sixties, during that time the island was still relatively 'underdeveloped'. There was no airport, not even a proper dock: the visitors had to fight to overcome the unfriendly local winds to arrive on the island's coast, which they could only reach in small boats after leaving their ship some distance from the harbour. As a result, Mykonos attracted only those who were 'determined' to go there; this 'inconvenience' was later, paradoxically, converted into nostalgia, only to support the space-myth of Mykonos. Helicopters could arrive on the island by the end of the sixties and, in 1971, the first aeroplane landed on Mykonos. This signifies the third period of tourist development and the island's welcome to mass tourism. However, Mykonos retained for some time its exclusive image; at the beginning of the eighties the island was finally equipped with a dock, and largely affordable passenger ships brought more and more tourists. The resort for the international jet set became an accessible sign available for mass consumption. In 1983, the annual arrivals rose to 398,865 (Yangakis 1985: 20); according to the statistical data of the Greek Tourist Board, during 1993, 543,000 tourists stayed overnight on Mykonos. The island still attracts the young and affluent tourists, while it has also established a name as a gay resort. However, the profile of the tourists who go to Mykonos for their summer holidays has clearly changed and is largely a heterogeneous one. The first tourists usually arrive at the beginning of March, while charter flights start in April, and tourist activity does not end until November.

16. Or at least this is the place-image promoted by the Greek lifestyle magazines of the nineties for an already mythologised seventies' Mykonos.

17. A similar cultural pattern of a silent exchange of knowledge (i.e., silent copying) is offered in Herzfeld's account of carpenter apprenticeship which is dictated, according to the author, by the logic that 'a good craftsperson does not speak in order to teach an apprentice' (1995: 137); in order to learn, the apprentice needs, in a sense, to 'steal' the artisan's skills.

18. *Kyr*, is an informal (rural) mode of address, actually a contraction of *kyrios*, which means 'Mister'.

19. A term indicating a state of excessive and long-term drunkenness: a 'bender'.

20. The *rembetika sinafia* consist of *rembetes*. *Rembetis* in turn has its root in the term *rembetas*, a good-for-nothing person. Eventually, *rembetis* came to signify in general a member of the 'underground'.

21. The etymological root of the Greek word '*steki*', according to Papataxiarchis, is the verb *istamai/steko*, that literally means to stand (1992b: 214). *Steki* (haunt), as the context of the traditional *kafeneio* described by Papataxiarchis, is defined as a fluid and open-ended identity-space vis-à-vis the more stable domestic realm. In contradistinction, for my informants, *steki* functions as an extension of their identity, thus reminding us of the 'absolute' affective properties of belonging to the old type 'subcultures' of the *rembetika sinafia*.

22. *Preza* literally meaning a snort and used as a synonym for heroin.

23. An area in the centre of the Mykonian *Hora* that initially attracted the avant-garde.

24. Hercules uses the word 'project' in English to describe his 'business' enterprises.

25. Sarong: a piece of cloth, known in Greece as *pareo*, which was being introduced at that time mainly from India and Bali. The swathes of material that Orientals wrapped around their bodies became a distinctive feature of the dress of the *Mykoniots d'élection*, mainly in the

eighties. At that time it was a rare commodity, a perk reserved for those who travelled in the 'Orient'. Later it entered into common use, and thereafter became a symbol of the Mykonian lifestyle and an essential accessory-cum-fetish.

26. The boundaries of the multiple modes of *Mykoniots*' exchange are vague.
27. Here the word 'Mykonian' is used in Greek whereas the word 'mentality' is used in English. That is the reason I keep 'mentality' in italics. The reader should be aware of the double use of italics, as both signifying a word foreign to the English language (i.e., Greek), as well as a word foreign to the Greek language (i.e., English) that the informants themselves use. The second case will be rendered in the text by the use of inverted commas together with the English word italicised. The *diglossia* or rather *triglossia* of the text is intended to reproduce with a greater degree of verisimilitude the Mykonian *sinafia*'s way of speaking, especially that of the cosmopolitan *sinafi*, the 'hippy' one, with which a large part of this research is concerned. The frequency with which they use English expressions is worthy of note, mainly when they are used to express abstract connotations or the worldviews of the *sinafi*'s members. Then again, slang is used mostly as a secret code in respect of illegal activities and moreover as a special code for the *sinafi* and the wider community of outsiders. Greek is the lingua franca, used for descriptive purposes. I should add that there is a marked tendency to idealise the Mykonian dialect, which is used by certain *sinafia* in an ostentatious manner. In this case, adapting to the local linguistic idiom is not (considered) aesthetically degrading. On the contrary, the *Mykoniots d'élection* deliberately emphasise their acquired, sing-song Mykonian intonation, thereby emphasising their equally acquired 'Mykonian' identity.
28. Schizas, one of the pirates' *sinafi*, became a legend in the story-telling of the *hippie sinafi*, on account of his uncommon degree of authenticity and his outspokenness.
29. For an ethnographic exploration of death and bereavement in the Greek rural and urban contexts, see the relevant ethnographies: Danforth 1982; Panourgia 1995; Seremetakis 1991.
30. She was buried at her home on Mount Olympus, far away from Mykonos.
31. An Indian divination method, according to which the different species of the animal kingdom are used like totemic symbols – extensions of human characteristics and behaviour.
32. The Byzantine version of Istanbul, much preferred by the modern Greeks to its contemporary appellation.
33. In Waldren's ethnography of the Mallorcan outsiders, stories about the pre-eminent patrons of the group like Graves and the Archduke, as well as other heroic figures of the past, propagates the self-myth of the exogenous locals and the continuation of their community-colony of the 'elect' (1996: 201). This appropriation technique via the storytelling about the adventurous past colonisers is also a common practice amongst the *Mykoniots d'élection*.
34. The drinking commensality described here shares common elements with Papataxiarchis' principles of *raki* drinking, *rakoposia* (1992b: 240). As in his ethnographic case study, the drinking commensality at Constanti's grave is dictated by expressive elements (i.e., pure giving, emotionality, generosity) rather than by reciprocity.
35. Theorising emotions according to the ethnographic prototype of Abu-Lughod (1990) and Lutz (1988) could prove to be helpful in our case. Aristos is describing a performative organised expression of grief. By contrast, Eleni's death is marked by an uneasiness on the part of her *sinafi* to express any reaction to her loss. Following Dubisch's proposition that 'emotions must be studied as part of the constructions of culture itself', the aforementioned inconsistency re-validates the element of (aesthetic) bricolage present in *Mykoniots*' practice, this time vis-à-vis sentiments (1995: 213).
36. *Vradyní*: a conservative, right-wing newspaper.
37. Traditional type of *kafeneio* with music that was transferred from Asia Minor – but does not exist any more in its prototypical form.
38. One of Aristos' customers, a worldly-wise Athenian himself – in the myth which he acts out on Mykonos – enthusiastically described a similar gang of local 'pirates', which is where I borrowed

the name from for the *sinafi*. Chadjifotiou (1992) uses admiring expressions about the tough nuts (who) 'do as they like all over the island ... the island belongs to them.' Thus the writer introduces his prospective girlfriend to the charms of the island. The prestige of his local 'friends' and the entrée which he has into their society reinforces his own charm. He extols their attitude to life and their superhuman tolerance of alcohol. He describes one of them to the girl by telling her how, when he was very drunk, he swam home (covering a distance of two kilometres or so) because he had drunk too much to walk that far.

39. As Chadjifotiou (1992) puts it.
40. Thus the *Mykoniots d'élection* – in line with Bourdieu's (1984) culturally dominant groups – reinvent an internal game of distinction by controlling the reproduction of the 'valuable' Mykonian myth. This is how the 'Mykonos experience' is recreated. In order to establish this idiosyncratic 'distinction' game, they have created the aforementioned aesthetic 'masculine' ethos – an ethos the newcomer is cultivated by – that operates, in an 'exclusive' and 'self-assuring' manner, similar to Bourdieu's notion of taste (cf. 1984: 174).
41. This is the power that belongs to anyone who has 'experience' of the subculture, the keys of knowledge that open the way to incorporation into the over-idealised 'male' world.
42. It must have become obvious by now that the property/category 'male', in our case, is but an aesthetic/experiential and acquired quality perpetually verified through the synthetic performance of the actor/actress but more importantly through (eclectic) *mimesis*.
43. Likewise, the space-myth is aesthetically qualified through acquired elements of extremity. 'Extremely' windy, 'extremely' bright, a sign of 'extreme' hedonism and 'excessive' drinking. Extremity and constant liminality are precisely the properties the Mykonos' space-myth offers to the tourist who, in turn, experiences her own personal liminality. The 'unconventional', the 'marginal', the 'carnivalesque'; in other words, the 'other' are the most popular elements of the Mykonian *attraction*, thus fully justifying the 'subcultural' myth invested in the Mykonian *sinafia*.

3
NARRATIVES OF THE SELF: AN ECCENTRIC MYTH OF OTHERNESS

Narratives of the self

The self-image as fetish

This chapter explores how the self, through acquiring alternating subject-positions formulates an eccentric self-myth of *otherness*. In this ethnographic context, individual and group identities can be seen as manifestations of the same thing. The *Mykoniots d'élection* consciously do not employ a collective discourse. Their 'group identity' and sense of belonging is instead exemplified in a common praxis, which revolves around the theme of the constant revalidation of each one's extreme individuality based upon a silent consensus. Thus, their narratives of the self are always implicit references to some common 'other' who equals the self, but who, nevertheless, remains unacknowledged at the rhetorical level. Paradoxically, discourses of a celebrated extreme individuality, instead of abolishing group identity, actually become its (only) binding force.

Introduction

Autobiographical confessions? Narratives of the self? Or self portraits? I was puzzled. Which term should I use? What would be the appropriate title to epitomise my endeavour to reconstruct and portray my informants' personal stories?

After some consideration of theoretical terms, I decided to employ the phrase 'narratives of the self',[1] since what I had were not linear narrations, straightforwardly constructed life-histories. My informants, in any case, would not provide me with life-histories as such. As will be demonstrated, such monolithic self-representations would be in contradiction with their conscious identity experimentation, their multiple/aesthetic subjectivities.

The next task was to determine who narrated the stories and precisely whose 'self' the narratives reflected. How much of the text was strictly 'narration', how much interpretation and how much reconstruction? How much of the text was imaginary? Most importantly, who was the real author, in other words the agent of the interpretation underlying the narration: the informant or I, or both? Following Behar's (2003) insistence for an ethnography realised in a variety of forms, as theatrical vignettes, as poetic auto-ethnography or video-diary, ethnography is given its performative dimension. 'Every ethnographer,' Behar argues, 'to some extent, has to reinvent the genre of ethnography to make it fit the uniqueness of his or her fieldwork experience' (ibid. 35). In other words, it is the ethnographer who 'constructs' the field; ethnography becomes 'personal' and the ethnographic context a construct of the ethnographer's imagination; the fieldworker becomes the set designer of her own ethnographic context. In this process, ethnographic texts need not necessarily be distinguished from fictional texts.

In the introduction to this chapter I attempt two things: first, to offer some methodological clues as to what decided the style of the text; and second, to establish that the style of the text is also linked to the theoretical implications of ethnographic self-narrative.

While I was transcribing my field notes, I had to reconstruct my informants' self-portraits out of the reflexive information they had given me about themselves. Self-narratives were a 'valuable commodity' in the *Mykoniots'* aesthetic/cultural quid pro quo. My informants had built a 'myth' surrounding their past by being extremely reluctant to speak directly of it or relate it to their social and family background. On the other hand, the *Mykoniots* loved to recount the stories of their *sinafi* and narrate the derring-do of the 'other'. By reflexively dealing with their frequent storytelling, their occasional intimate self-narratives and their rare confessions, I could slowly put together the pieces of their 'private' puzzle.

Without any prescribed 'ordering' – that is, hierarchically contextualising my informants' self-reflexive accounts – I assembled the pieces of self-narrative they had consciously offered me and created elliptical self-portraits. My theoretical aim was to explore the different discourses of the self in order to reveal potential common 'structuring' patterns. *Mykoniots*, however, disliked classifying themselves as members of any larger group as much as they disliked talking explicitly about their own past. Their interpretative tools were drawn from monistic philosophical doctrines rather than collective (political or ideological) discourses.

I soon realised that these people were conveying information about themselves to me in a very indirect way through unarticulated self-narratives, or alternatively, through 'gossip'. By creating a reputation, a 'glorious' past, for this or that member of the group, my informants were reciprocally constructing each other's myths.[2] Part of the process of building this eccentric reputation was to abolish any fixed identity category and this probably explains why the *Mykoniots* avoided relating to their family past.

The collection of *Mykoniots'* self-portraits, beyond its superficial diversity (class, personal, ethnic), could produce significant representations of their narrated extreme identity. More importantly, it could finally place them in a group that produced a peculiar homogeneity based on analogous examples of extreme individuality.

I present four self-portraits: two of men and two of women. In order to sustain some underlying 'cultural symmetry' I have chosen only Greeks. I intentionally decided to portray two of the key people who guided me while in the field: Hercules and Eleonora who were both pre-eminent 'patrons' of my Mykonian experience. The self-narratives in this instance were indirect, stemming from naturally occurring everyday encounters and mostly from my experience of living with them. They were the product of a continuous dialogue rather than a product of an interview or a direct linear self-narration. Thus, the element of indirectness in this case was not indicative of my level of intimacy with them. On the contrary, the self-narratives of Artemis and Angelos were collected over a fixed period of time, in the form of a series of interviews; the recording of their self-narrations became an established process. Nevertheless, my relationship with both of them was not nearly as close as that with Hercules and Eleonora.

In a sense, the whole game of reciprocity between the 'anthropologist' and the 'informant' was acted out in a metaphorical (patron/client) relationship. I was seeking anthropological 'subjects' and they were seeking an 'audience' and a 'disciple' willing to learn their way of living. Part of my 'apprenticeship' was to be 'seduced' by the culture and then initiated, and, eventually as the *Mykoniots* saw it, to learn how to 'liberate' myself and surpass all my 'guilt syndromes' without further help from my 'patrons'. One should be careful here not to read my metaphorical presentation of the internal power games as evidence of manipulation by some sort of 'cult', or as the chronicle of the seduction of the 'ignorant anthropologist' by some 'superannuated hippies' of the nineties. In fact, to an extent, I have consciously chosen to present my personal experience in the field in an exaggerated fashion[3] for purely methodological reasons.

I was twenty-three when I started my fieldwork. My informants were a very 'alien' category to my cultural self. As opposed to people who are members of another 'culture', the *Mykoniots* had, to my mind at least, no apparent reason for being culturally 'different'. They were claiming to be 'survivors', 'bricoleurs', 'artists', people without fixed identities. This manifestation of fluidity vis-à-vis self-identity was a provoking element since I was trained to treat my identity as something fixed and stable; I was the anthropologist and they were my anthropological 'subjects'. Alas, they immediately attacked my 'anthropological' identity. My status as an anthropologist was at risk. I had no interpretative power, no real role. I was just a 'disciple'. I chose to 'become assimilated'. In order to offer me the data I wanted, my informants stripped me of the role of interpreter. To establish a relationship, both sides forgot all about my 'enquiry'. Instead, I was given alternative roles in the community. In other words, the game of reciprocity I had to play with them demanded that I should question my own identity and its parameters. Paradoxically enough, as soon as I gave up defending my anthropological expertise people started accepting it. My discipleship was over. Unfortunately, this happened towards the end of my fieldwork.

A comment on methodology

> instead of conceptualising the self as a replicate in miniature of society, we could begin by paying attention *to the ways in which people reflect on themselves* and then see in what ways these reflections are indicative of social and cultural context, or require such contextualisation to be intelligible to us. (Cohen 1994: 29, my emphasis)

My fieldwork could be considered as highly reflexive. I was a 'Greek' studying a group in 'Greece' whose members were largely 'Greeks' in origin, and some of them my friends, too. In this respect it was auto-anthropology. One could initially refer here to Strathern's notion (1987) of auto-anthropology, understood as the study of one's own 'culture' without employing discourses which favour 'authentic' interpretations and thus reproduce [theoretically] undesirable fixed dichotomies of the 'insider'/'outsider' kind. The kind of reflexivity suggested by Strathern is according to Bakalaki, not only 'personal' but mainly 'conceptual' (1997: 512). Bakalaki builds upon Herzfeld's claim that Greek identity, due to its marginality in the European cultural/political agenda, encases (like anthropology) both the notions of 'selfhood' and 'otherness'. Thus, she establishes that 'anthropological work in Greece could probably be cast in Strathern's category of auto-anthropology' (Bakalaki 1997: 513).

The notions of auto-anthropology and auto-ethnography (cf. Reed-Danahay 1997) further relate to a diverse body of ethnographic expertise that the 'anthropologist' has invented in order to consciously deal with the ethnographic task of reflexively producing cultural representations either by clearly including oneself in the group of the 'others' as in the case of the anthropologies produced 'at home' (Jackson 1987), or by monitoring the self and its potential alienation during the ethnographic process (due to the ethnographer's gender, for example) in an otherwise familiar context, as in the case of Hastrup's 'anthropology among friends' (1987). Reflexivity also engages ethnography in the form of anthropological autobiography, in other words, in a text that blends in autobiography and ethnography (Crapanzano 1980; Kenna 1992; Loizos 1981; Okely 1975, 1996; Okely and Callaway 1992; Rapport 1992). The politicised writing about one's own culture in negotiation with other more 'dominant' ones also reveals an alternative, reflexive twist in the production of ethnography (cf. Pratt 1992).

The above theoretical approaches establish the production of the reflexive experimental ethnographic text by theorising the 'personal', turning the focus to the 'totalising' effect of fieldwork experience (Okely 1992: 3) rather than seeing culture and anthropology as a 'written' Derridean 'deconstruction'. In fact, Okely (1975) has argued that the affective 'personal' experience of fieldwork is absolutely valid and relevant here, and thus it cannot be separated from the production of 'anthropological knowledge'. Nevertheless, going into the field with the self-consciousness of preparing an autobiographical account is not a common practice among anthropologists. Although, in the Greek ethnographic context the reality of the ethnographic production is that 'Greeks' tend to study 'Greeks' and this phenomenon is 'culturally' as well as politically justified by anthropologists (cf. Bakalaki 1997), fieldwork as an autobiographical project is clearly demonstrated on rare occasions like the type of ethnography produced by Panourgia (1995) who has reflexively employed herself and her family as her 'informants' in her urban study of death rituals. Apart from the above piece of 'experimental' ethnography, the self of the author, her anxieties, presuppositions, splits and displacements, rarely intertwine with the ethnographic description in a straightforward manner, except in cases like Dubisch's ethnography of Greek women on pilgrimage, where the ethnographer's as well as her subjects' emotions are reflexively described and theorised in the author's text (1995).

It has to be underlined that it is no accident that this type of reflexive/experimental ethnography is very frequently related to issues of gender and is actually politically favoured by many women anthropologists and feminist thinkers alike (Okely 1992: 4; Moore 1994). Self-experience, according to de Lauretis (de Lauretis 1984 in Callaway 1992: 37) is an intersubjective reality that, in turn, is tested and re-enacted through different subject positions. In this sense, experience plays an important role in de Lauretis' analysis of subjectivity. Subjectivity is not considered a fixed given position but rather a constantly reformulated one. Previously treated as 'experimental' texts (i.e., drawing on reflexive information), the above type of ethnographic writing has been recently 'granted' a special place in anthropological thinking, establishing a 'new' way of [reflexively] writing about culture and the highly 'personal' experience of fieldwork. Feminist theorising replanted into the ethnographic text urges the ethnography-producer to account for her own engendered experience (Caplan 1988). In this sense, not only the 'personal' is relevant in this auto-ethnographic experience, but the 'subjective' as well.

Yet, if one were willing to see the same (auto-ethnographic) setting from a different perspective one could alternatively define it as a hybridic culture emerging out of a tourist and cosmopolitan resort which has undergone such rapid change as to preclude a 'homogenous' culture. In addition, my preoccupation with my self-identity, or rather my preoccupation with the ambitious bourgeois self which I aspired to get rid of, made me choose the most 'unorthodox' ethnographic group in this hybridic setting; neither the locals, nor the tourists, but the unclassified 'others' of Mykonos.

These 'others' were the 'nomads' of Mykonos; they were not officially part of the Mykonian community, neither were they just visitors. They were always coming and going. Moreover, while they were clearly a group and the founders of an alternative culture that had influenced the island since the seventies, it was very difficult to define the group's underlying principles of cohesion. Where could one 'locate' them? Were they part of the traditional setting or part of the local folklore? Were they (remnant) radical modernists, or the epitome of the aesthetically pluralist 'subject'? Were they replicas of some 'original' hippie culture? Or were they just repudiators of a rigid ethnic identity? Were they, as they themselves maintained, the trendsetters, or simply the 'deviant' subjects of some [conventional] subcultural classification? Were they telling me something new about the context of Greek ethnography, or, in the end, were they just culturally unclassifiable since they acted in a post-modern setting?

My initial difficulty as regards starting with a bounded group or a coherent category within the corpus of *a* culture paradoxically proved to be helpful in the long run. My hesitance in consolidating the identity of my ethnographic 'subjects' and that of their group led me to start linking my ethnographic enquiries to issues of self-identity. I followed what Cohen proposes (see above), and explored 'how people reflect on themselves', thus employing the self as a conceptual tool.

This chapter is designed to represent the cultural specifics in my informants' discourse on the self. It comes at the beginning of the ethnographic corpus because it played an organising role in the reconstruction of my data, and in my understanding of my ethnographic 'subjects'. The reader should treat the four texts that follow as particular forms of self-narrative which sometimes employ direct speech, but also utilise forms of consumption and specific ritual and spatial practices to construct a sense of self.

The aim of the chapter is to initiate the reader, as I was initiated myself, into the state of 'discipleship' that produced this data. The *Mykoniots*' intentional 'mysticism' about their 'selves' seduced me into their personal myth. My informants' self-definitions rarely related them directly to a collective identity and at a discursive level their arguments never stemmed from a collective ideology. All their views were presented as being strictly personal. They systematically avoided classification and professed a purely idiosyncratic rhetoric. Only later did I realise that this was how the group's distinction-game (cf. Bourdieu 1984) was established.

The overriding methodological problem in constructing these self-portraits was the issue of my own authorial status in interpreting the discourse of the *Mykoniots* and constructing that interpretation as text. Reflecting on others' self-narratives made me realise that my memory, my reconstruction, constituted an additional narrative. In the corpus of the growing production of 'experimental' anthropological writing the issue of reflexivity emerges with the ethnographic appropriation of life hi/stories (for a discussion on the difference between the concepts of life history, life story in the Giddensian sense [cf. Giddens 1992] and life narrative see Svensson 1997: 94). This type of 'meta-anthropological literature' (Tedlock 1991, quoted in Brettell, 1997: 224) influenced by feminism and later post-modernism, celebrates the autobiographical experience of the ethnographer. Life stories of anthropologists, as well as their informants, increasingly become the centre of attention in ethnographic politics (Herzfeld 1997b, 1997c; Okely 1996; Rapport 1992). The importance of self-narrative lies in the fact that through the narrative of the 'other' the [anthropological] self emerges. A pioneering example of an ethnographic account that concentrates on a single informant is Crapanzano's self-portrait of Tuhami (1980). As Moore (1994: 118–19) points out, Crapanzano's ethnographic textualisation of another's life history actually conveys more information about the author than the informant, thus reflexively producing knowledge about the anthropologist himself. Ethnographic biography, in this sense, is directly related to ethnographic representation. Another pioneer of the reflexive anthropological project, Dumont (1978: 11–12) believes in a dialectical relationship between an 'I' and a 'they' in fieldwork that transform one another. This reflexive transformative process, the so-called 'anthropologising subject' is not exhausted in the field but is more crucially reintroduced in the ethnographic text. In Dumont's inter-subjective enterprise, the rule is to let it all happen. The observer becomes part of the experiment: in his monograph, Dumont becomes the adopted brother of the 'Headman' he studies, and finds himself in a state of transference vis-à-vis his 'brother'.

As Okely (1992) and Loizos (1994) have argued, reflexivity forces the ethnographer to reconsider the moral and political dimension of her stance. In turn, Brettell (1997) aims to divert our attention to the 'complex blending of voices' (ibid. 225) in ethnographic accounts offered by authors who employ life-histories of women's lives in order to put their own ones into perspective. The focus of attention vis-à-vis life history in this case, shifts from the question of 'representativeness' and 'objectivity' to the debate of 'shaping the text', in other words, the authorship and authority of the ethnographer with reference to her textual product. Abu-Lughod (1993) admits that she has reshaped the stories of her Bedouin informants in order to appeal to Western audiences. Like many of us, I had also been imbued with Clifford's 'historical predicament of ethnography' which apparently involved 'inventing' rather than 'representing' cultures, by creating only 'partial' ethnographic 'truths' (Clifford 1986: 2, 7). The classic work *Writing Culture*, strongly influenced by hermeneutic philosophy, promoted the idea of textual polyvocality; an 'expanded' ethnographic text, an ongoing cultural *poesis* that constructed the 'self' as much as it constructed the 'other' (Clifford and Marcus 1986: 16, 24). Together with its companion volume, *Anthropology as*

Cultural Critique (Marcus and Fischer 1986), it produced a long debate in anthropology challenging the discipline's 'collective' and 'epistemological' representations, the authority of the fieldworker, and the 'authenticity' of the ethnographic experience reworked as an 'authentic' piece of ethnography. This debate 'alarmed' anthropologists; some felt obliged to condemn it as a misleading 'post-modern' approach that essentially reproduced the 'authority it was seeking to destabilise' either by taking the agency away from the actor, or by mystifying gender issues[4] (Sangren 1988; McDonald 1988; Bell 1993; James, Hockey and Dawson 1997: 1–14).

The issue of ethnographic authority is treated diachronically, drawing on Clifford's historical retrospection of the discipline which schematically identifies the different periods in which the anthropological authority is validated. Anthropological authority is initially validated through 'experience' (fieldwork, i.e., by 'being there'), later on through 'interpretation', by assembling culture into text, moving to a 'discursive' model of ethnographic practice that emphasises the importance of an intersubjective model of writing, and finally to a 'polyphonic' model where the writing of culture is treated as a multisubjective activity (Clifford 1988: 21–54). In his analysis of this complex transformation, Clifford assures the reader that, nevertheless, 'ethnography is, from beginning to end, enmeshed in writing' (ibid. 25).

More radically, Clifford Geertz – one of the pre-eminent figures of 'interpretative' anthropology – had already promoted a semiotic and literary approach to culture. He proclaimed that he was committed to an approach which viewed any ethnographic assertion as 'essentially contestable' (Geertz 1973: 29). Geertz's ethnographic model of 'thick description' promotes an ethnography that interprets the 'flow of social discourse' and also requires the 'author' of this cultural interpretation to 'converse with them' (i.e., the subjects) (ibid. 13, 20). Influenced by Ricoeur, Geertz maintains that anthropological writings are acts of inscription, they are fictions; they are 'something made' out of social discourse.

In a later essay, Geertz distinguishes his position on ethnographic authority from the experimental writing of Clifford and his 'cohorts' by reassessing the particular but non-homogenous experience that the anthropologist as the I-witnessing subject of the text has acquired by 'being there' (Geertz 1988). He argues for a counter-reflection beyond 'the comprehension of the self by detour of the other' (Rabinow 1977: 5, quoted in Geertz 1988: 92), by unfolding the different positions of the 'I'. He implicitly criticises the author-saturated text where the self the text creates and the self that creates the text are treated as identical (ibid. 97).

Moore (1994), drawing on Geertz and de Lauretis, takes a similar line: the interest is shifted from ethnographic allegories and the process of textualisation per se to a process of identification. To put it more accurately, the underlining process in Moore's analysis is the process of constructing a self through the process of textualisation, a process similar to the function of narrative (ibid. 119). She

Narratives of the self

goes on to argue that the relationship between the author in the text and the author of the text is fictive, since the one is the imaginary product of the other. The product of this relationship, more precisely, is a self-in-process.

The process of identification, Moore argues, is particularly important in ethnographic writing. Apart from the identifications of the *author of* the text who wishes to identify with the *author in* the text there is also the reader, who is encouraged by the *author of* the text to identify with the *author of* the text through the medium of the *author in* the text (Moore 1994: 121–22).

For Derrida's subversive theory of textualisation (1974), the production and 'reading' of a text is not an autonomous process. It is an imaginary continuum with all the pre-existing texts and 'readings'. This 'intertextual weaving has a life of its own' (Harvey 1989: 49). Ultimately though, the written text is seen by Derrida as 'a construction in its own right' (Okely 1992: 1). Derrida's 'deconstructionism' is based on the inherent heterogeneity of the text itself. Minimising the authority of the producer of the text, according to Derrida, leads to better opportunities for popular 'participation'; thus ironically celebrating again the power of subjectivity, this time from the other side – that of the reader.

The reinterpretation of my ethnographic text

The text I have prepared on the *Mykoniots*' self-narratives is a particular and mostly indirect form of narration, since my informants would often only speak indirectly about themselves and refused to provide conventional life-histories. I was puzzled as to how I could present an understanding of their sense of self/ves. Eventually, I realised that their specific practices of consumption – objects, space and time – had to be understood, alongside explicit discourse, as forms of self-narration and self-reflection.

I experienced my fieldwork mainly as a long series of fragmented self-narratives. The entire process comprised of different space-zones, and several long and distinct apprenticeships under the supervision of one *Mykoniot* or another. The texts that emerge must therefore be understood as a set of intersubjective narratives.

In some of the stories, the 'I' is the organising author of the narrative. In other instances, the self-narration is strictly reflexive and the biographical information chronologically inconsistent. In this sense the text might not be conventionally ordered, and follows the informant's random reflexive discourse which glorifies fragmentation and the self's versatility in adapting and constantly transforming. All the cases of self-narrative that I present in the following pages share a common discourse on the infinite sources of alternating identity-repertoires. The result is a celebration of the fragmented self (which is) revealed through discourse. The shared discourse of the fragmented self is the organising principle of the group's underlying structure. This fragmentary and transformative experience of the self through narrative symbolically abolishes continuity in the *Mykoniots'* lives; ultimately, it abolishes time itself. The reader must be aware of the protagonists' protean nature; moving in and out of their past experiences and past lifestyles. Nevertheless, one should be very careful not to define this characteristic as an ideological platform on which the *Mykoniots* stand and act, but rather to appreciate this transformative experience as part of the narrative process.

Mykoniots as 'Foucauldian' subjects

> Modern man, for Baudelaire, is not the man who goes off to discover himself, his secrets and his hidden truth; he is the man who tries to invent himself. (Foucault 1984a: 42)

While I was transcribing the data on which this chapter is based, I realised that the discourse of my informants was somehow akin to Foucault's work on sexuality. One could assume that the reason for this connection is that Foucault's references to classical Greek ethics seem to match the cosmopolitan and historical constructivist attitude of the *Mykoniots*. My informants could be described as extreme syncretists, mentors of a patchwork summer culture, who imitate the pagan ways of classical Greece. In fact, the *Mykoniots'* discourse on the group's way of life suggests a similarity to the culture of classical antiquity. However, what led me to Foucault here, was not my informants' discourse, but rather the ideological platform emerging out of his own later work. Foucault's notion of difference as a conceptual tool was essential for the theoretical organisation of this chapter.

Foucault maintained that classical Greeks had a different understanding of morality from that which predominated in the Christian age, based on the so-called 'aesthetics of existence' (Foucault 1984b: 343). By analysing classical texts as discourses (McNay 1992: 76), Foucault created his theoretical argument of a distinct mode of subjectivation. He suggested that one of the problems of modernity was that nobody seemed to be pleased with the fact that ethics were founded on religion or a legal system, in other words, they were externally imposed codes of behaviour. Instead of moralities which emphasised codes, Foucault counter-posed moralities (exemplified in classical Greek thought) oriented towards *ethics of the self.*

Likewise, *Mykoniots*, both at a discursive level and at the level of practice strongly endorse a rhetoric that questions the origins of modern ethics and aims to repudiate them. They promote an alternative rhetoric that places all the (ethical) agency on the self. Ethical norms, in the *Mykoniots'* actions are replaced by aesthetics. The *Mykoniots d'élection* claim to be conscious 'historical constructivists' with 'attitude'; they love to perform acts of 'paganism'; however, they have adopted a widely syncretic (rather than a purely nationalistic) discourse which they relate to the 'Greekness' of the space rather than to their own 'Greek' identity. But is that all? Or is there a more complex identity quest lying behind their syncretic discourse?

A grandiose rhetoric on pleasure occupies the *Mykoniots*' self-narratives. Pleasure in the *Mykoniot* discourse is connected to the senses rather than to the emotions. If I follow Foucault's line of thinking, my informants' discourse clearly influenced by the ethics of oriental *ars erotica*, is opposed to the preoccupation with desire that has its roots in both Greek and Christian ethics, as well as to the Western idea of *scientia sexualis* (Foucault 1978: 57–58). On the other hand, the aesthetic principles of the '*art of living*'[5] constitute a discourse shared by classical Greeks and *Mykoniots* alike. The *Mykoniots*' existential question is 'how to live' and they have constructed a collective and extensive discourse on the subject. Their life-project is to 'cultivate' the self (Foucault 1984b: 348). 'Discipleship' is part of this project.

According to Foucault's model, the mode of subjectivation attributed to the classical Greeks is to build one's existence as a 'beautiful' existence. The aesthetics of existence, as an ethical formula free from any normalising pressures, could also apply to the *Mykoniots*' subjectivity. Their mode of subjectivation is an aesthetic mode in that the self requires 'training'. The perfect government of the self is precisely the expertise the *Mykoniots* seek through styling their lives. *Mykoniots*, through their self-training, reflexively transmit a perfect demonstration of self-government to their 'disciples': meditation, abstinence, writing. Similar methods of 'strategic' self-management are described by Foucault in his examination of how the Greeks trained the self (Foucault 1985: 11).

Foucault's analysis of the technologies of the cultivation of the self as a social practice is a useful analytical tool. His theory of the subject, however, offers no real agency to the unconscious; yet, the subject – through the process of active self-fashioning – is constantly negotiating her subject-position.

As McNay suggests, Foucault's shift of interest from the body to the self signifies a 'modification' of his previous intellectual concerns. His later work on sexuality sets out to explain how the individual understands itself as a subject (McNay 1992: 49). Foucault has been criticised as regards his earlier writings for analysing and placing power as a monolithic and paralysing dominant force. But his thesis in the later work, that the individual actively fashions her own existence and does not solely reflect structures, ideologies and systems of belief, suggests a dynamic relationship between individuals and social structures. Foucault further argued that it is, paradoxically, through 'techniques of self-government' that individuals can resist the 'government of individualisation' (ibid. 68).

The decline of 'grand narratives', according to Foucault, opened the way for a modern aesthetics of existence where there is a considerable degree of agency, of having the choice to determine one's own 'becoming'. Nevertheless, his theory of the actively self-transforming subject obscures the theoretical position of the subject as a social and cultural entity. In other words, as McNay suggests,

Foucault fails to distinguish between practices that are imposed and practices that are 'suggested'; how much is reproduction and how much autonomous, creative and authentic (McNay 1992: 74).

Finally, to focus once again on my ethnographic 'subjects', my attempt to incorporate style and self-fashioning as a conceptual tool to account for the *Mykoniots*' discourse on the self could alternatively be seen as addressing Taylor's theory of authenticity as a historically emerging modern idea of self-ethics. Taylor (1991) places authenticity in an 'expressivist' tradition, linked with the modern notion of the individual; he argues that from the late eighteenth century onwards, together with Herder's romanticism, an 'expressivist' understanding of human life emerges. Artistic creation becomes the prototype by which people can define themselves. An alternative definition of authenticity which involves originality derives from the reformed essence of the aesthetic judgement of art. Art comes to be understood as a creation and not as it used to be as *mimesis*, as imitation. Authenticity, in this sense, is equated with creativity. This idea is transplanted to the self. Each one of us has a unique way of being human. The revelation of this 'uniqueness' comes through 'expression'. 'Self-discovery requires *poiesis*, making' (Taylor 1991: 62). Two big shifts towards a 'modern' subject are gradually accomplished out of this notion of 'expressivism': authenticity is linked with the aesthetic, and beauty and art cease to be defined in terms of the reality depicted and are expressed in terms of the unique feelings they arouse in the individual. In this sense, the *Mykoniots* remind us of Maffesoli's manifesto about the 'new' communitarian ideal of the post-modern *tribus*. In Maffesoli's 'neo-tribes' the 'aesthetic style' is the organising principle of this emerging (post-modern) cultural ideal which, in turn, paradoxically invents an (affective) social solidarity. This 'aesthetic style' is 'at the conjunction of the material and the immaterial and tends to favour a being-togetherness not seeking an objective to attain ... ' (1996b: 33). Belonging is not context-specific; it disengages from both time and space. Instead, the Maffesolian subject engages in the Foucauldian 'care of the self'. The 'self' meets the 'other' consciously omitting commitment from the agenda, in order only to 'share a few common emotions and sentiments' (ibid.). Aesthetic 'wholeness' becomes an independent goal; a struggle between authenticity and morality begins. Authenticity, in its new sense, involves originality and further demands a revolt against convention (Taylor 1991: 65).

In the following ethnographic text, I intend to show how through the 'narratives of the self' the *Mykoniots* achieve their (collective) self-tranformation. Discursive self-transformation, in turn, safeguards the Foucauldian existential/aesthetic principle of 'taking care of the self', as well as paying homage to the 'expressivist' mode of existence, highlighted by Taylor, thus creating an 'authentic' self.

Narratives of the self: the self-image of Eleonora

People that find it hard to grow older

*The epitome of the Mykoniots' existential agony,
or a tribute to timeless Mykonos*

Eleonora is a woman who has no age: the female Dorian Gray of Mykonos. For many years her age has been an ever-popular topic for discussion among the *Mykoniots d'élection*. Nevertheless, nobody dares to ask this exotic ginger-haired woman with the lithe provocative body and sharp gaze what age she is hiding behind her large sun-induced wrinkles. Admittedly, the face suggests maturity, but her aura is light and teen-like. This mystery around her identity develops more intensively once one gets to know her more intimately. I never found any serious clues as to her social background, her source of income or an accurate definition of the origins of her personal 'culture'. The reason being that Eleonora disliked defining herself in those terms. On the other hand, she would disclose to me intimate details of her current circumstances. Eleonora, very much like the rest of the *Mykoniots*, preferred to live in the 'here and now'.

I knew only what I could see: a completely 'independent' woman, both financially and emotionally; well off, without ever working, or resorting to the 'status' of the 'married woman' and without even, or so it seemed, having inherited money from a rich family relative. All these made her an unclassifiable social case of a 'Greek', 'mature', 'female'.[6] The fragmentary and enigmatic manner of her self-narration revealed a general uneasiness with 'the past'. I could never break through this uneasy feeling. She would only speak about herself when she felt like it, employing a rather distant narration. Her 'patronising' attitude reflected her personality: she employed a passionate and a distant discourse. I used to think of her as a really 'lonely' person and that made me sympathetic to her sometimes explosive behaviour.

She was living on a large piece of uncultivated and rocky Mykonian land. The dangerous road up the hill leading to her house was restricted to 'specially equipped' cars and 'local connoisseurs' only. At the top of this abrupt road Eleonora's temple-like house was suddenly revealed facing the southern part of the island. The visitor was first introduced to a spacious split-level terrace, covered with an orange awning; the cushions scattered on its floor and the breathtaking view induced an immediate feeling of relaxation. The yard-terrace was surrounded by big clumps of marguerites that were cultivated a few years ago by a yogi friend who came from Santa Fe. The untypical light-green painted door, near the area with the cushions, led the visitor into a big central space. This door was always kept open during the summer period. One had to leave one's shoes outside before entering.

The house was not a typical Mykonian construction (mostly in terms of size), but it did follow the simple forms which the local architecture dictates. The interior felt large due to the open central space, its big windows and the exceptional views. The tremendously tranquil feeling made one automatically whisper, thus copying Eleonora, in order to avoid the slight echo. The house's remoteness, its high ceilings, and the immediate coolness and silence one could feel combined with the pure empty form of the white walls gave it a sacred feeling. For the last few years Eleonora had been living there alone. As she characteristically said, she did not care to 'look after' anybody in particular. She had had enough, she said, of all those men in her life that she had had to 'mother'. Therefore, she cautiously picked up her occasional guests, but insisted on being alone in the long term. Eleonora could be generous and hospitable, but, at the same time, being a highly temperamental person, it was hardly ever possible to predict her moods. Her life was divided between Mykonos and India. Winter was India, summer was Mykonos. She had no other permanent residence apart from this house. Her name on the island was linked with extravagant rumours about her past lifestyle, since Eleonora was among the first to establish the mythical seventies Mykonos scene. A trendy Greek magazine of the nineties published an issue dedicated to seventies Mykonos. Eleonora was pictured taking part in an improvised performance called 'the children of the universe'. The caption of the picture raised the kudos of the seventies Mykonos group by mentioning a Greek member, namely Eleonora, qualifying her as 'the international jet-setter Eleonora'. Two decades later Eleonora was taking part in the first Mykonos raves of the nineties. *Pace* the London raves described in Hutson (2000), which took their lead from the Balearic islands' entertainment scene – a return back in time through a simulated disco extravaganza re-enacted in the tourist night clubs – Mykonos equally operates as a sign of entertainment extravaganza which later acquired its own rave scene. One can draw parallels between today's Mykonos rave scene with the seventies cross-dressing and wild disco-partying, hallucinating on LSD, as well as creating impromptu hippie performances, like the ones referred to here, with the 'children of the universe'.

The rumours among her *sinafi* would either exalt her seductive beauty, or alternatively speak of an immensely rich past lover who was a grandee, and how she abandoned the glamorous lifestyle he offered her and left for India. Before I ever visited her house, I was already informed about the idiosyncratic nature of the house's private chapel which caused an additional wave of gossip.[7] Eleonora has been a resident of Mykonos for more than thirty years. She is known to the locals as '*kyria* Eleonora' ('lady' Eleonora). No one among the local group of Mykonians has ever managed to have any closer contact with her beyond this formal greeting. Over the years she has developed a patronising attitude based on the fact that she was one of the first long-term cosmopolitan 'settlers' to buy a sizeable plot on the island. Eleonora has never managed to see the locals as anything other than the indifferent and homogenised category of the 'indigenous'. She would likewise advise me, 'always keep a distance from them, they do not need to know what you are doing.'

When she first arrived on Mykonos during the sixties land was cheap. Initially, she bought a beautiful old Mykonian town house on the edges of the Mykonian *Hora* with a jungle-like mature garden and a small private chapel. There it was that Eleonora spent the 'hippie' years, the 'ecstatic summers' of the seventies. This is how she described this period: 'The *flower-power kids*[8] appeared in Mykonos; by the early *seventies* they had gathered and lived in the caves of Paranga beach. Mykonos was fun. The constant happenings and the *acid* both aroused a feeling of spiritual alertness. The first group of people left for India then. The turning point came soon after: some got trapped into the "*sex* and *drugs* and *rock 'n' roll*" myth, others became *creative directors* and some remained hippie freaks.'

Eleonora herself was among the first to choose the 'spiritual' pathway of Eastern syncretism. She was a modest devotee of Maharaj Ji, comparatively little known in the West, whose *ashram* was in Vrindavan, a sacred city for the Hindus situated in the northern part of India. Maharaj Ji, otherwise called Nim Karoli Baba, was Eleonora's spiritual teacher, but he died many years ago. She was one of his favourite followers, but this is something Eleonora would hardly ever share with others. In general, Eleonora avoided talking about her spiritual quests with people she did not respect. Her devotion was great, but never explicit. She continues to return to his *ashram* in Vrindavan every year and has established long-lasting relationships there. She remains very sceptical about the retreat centres in India that eventually became 'fashionable' in the West, like the '*Sannyasin* culture' in Poona which became a favourite destination for *Mykoniots* in the eighties. The term '*Sannyasin*' (a renunciator) stands for a 'spiritual' password grandiloquently used by some of my informants to address the *Mykoniot* followers of Bhagwan Shree Rajneesh.[9] Eleonora thought that the whole concept of Bhagwan was too flashy and commercial to be spiritual at all: 'It was all an *overacting*; Bhagwan himself was only selling Dionysiac "*partouza*" [a slang Greek expression for group sex]. He was only giving a *show*, he was playing Hollywood when he appeared to his stunned American devotees [descending] from a helicopter. His "divine descent" was ridiculously accompanied by some *chicks* sprinkling him with flowers! You know here the people who come to Mykonos [implying the *Mykoniots*' group] were very easily hooked on this *trip* since they were looking for anything hedonistic, only this time the issue was not an "artificial" [connoting drugs] but a "real" paradise.'

During the period of the seventies, when Eleonora was first acquainted with the island, Mykonos' devotees were an exclusive cosmopolitan crowd drawn from an international network. Firstly, there were the members of the artistic and aesthetic elite, a culture that glorified youth and beauty which attracted the 'rich and famous'. Soon, the recently developed groups of gays and hippies would follow. They were all in search of the pan-hedonistic symbol which derived from a modern reconstruction of an 'ancient Greek culture', and more particularly from the 'Dionysiasm' and cosmopolitanism of the classical era in nearby Delos. The 'amoral' image of the Dionysiastic Delos commanded the new ethics of Mykonos and was already 'selling' to the tourists. Mykonos was constructed as the 'island of the elect' whether of a mainstream or more marginal nature. Mykonos attracted those who either in financial or ideological terms could afford to belong nowhere. The creators of the Mykonos scene were talented and charismatic people who did not have to be productive in the conventional sense. Mykonos for them was the perfect excuse. Tourism offered them a flexible, thus creative, lifestyle.

Eleonora herself could become anything she desired: a top model, a dancer, an actress; she is an excellent and glamorous performer, but she managed to 'do nothing'. Although she is always fashionable and can intuitively de-codify every new style, she hates being just trendy. Her Mykonian aesthetic repertoire (following the local tradition of thematic appearances on the Mykonian streets – a must in seventies and eighties clubbing) is always exclusive and constantly evolving.

Eleonora has never 'worked' in her life. Within the boundaries of her *Mykoniot* milieu she has a modest rather than a conspicuous lifestyle. She is a strict vegetarian and has strong opinions about 'habits' (meaning anything that can become habitual) in general. Nevertheless, she very occasionally takes 'drugs' herself. Eleonora has periods of strict seclusion and abstinence and although she practises meditation and yoga, she says she could never become solely a 'judgemental' health freak, or indeed be a freak of any description. Being opposed to any sort of habit, she commented on the widely accepted drug consumption amongst the *Mykoniots*: '*Drugs* are [an indication of] the individuals' laziness to work with themselves.' Eleonora thought that Mykonos was full of lazy 'hermits' of this sort.

Eleonora's 'sacred' time is clearly differentiated from the pattern of her *Mykoniot* friends. *Mykoniots* mainly mark their ritualistic time through the communal act of 'getting high' on all sorts of substances or by spontaneously celebrating their 'communal identity'. In this sense, Eleonora proves to be quite an exceptional case vis-à-vis the milieu's lifestyle since her seclusion and renunciation is an imperative for her. She occasionally manages to distance herself from the group retreating to her own sacred 'space'. Nearly half of her year would be termed 'retreat' by Eleonora. It would either be the Vrindavan *retreat*, or various New Age *retreats* in the West (mainly the States combined with frequent trips to New York), as well as her personal *retreats* on Mykonos when she disappears for a while from the social life of the island. She practises meditation early in the morning everyday by visiting her private chapel. Additionally, she initiates periods of 'alienation' with others, using among other methods, straightforward aggression that she calls '*purifying confrontations*'. She extends her daily meditation with a long swim and a yoga group that usually practises in her

Narratives of the self

large living room, a session followed by tea. The group's composition varies since people come and go and some just disappear after a few sessions. To be consistent and committed to a daily schedule is reputedly not an easy task in Mykonos. During the high tourist season Eleonora is normally more sociable. She will also organise her annual open house to honour the July '*full moon*', a party given for the *Mykoniots* but dedicated to her late spiritual teacher.

Eleonora was brought up in the centre of Athens. Straight after school, she disappeared. She travelled a lot, ending up living in Madrid for some time. The only member of her family she mentioned frequently was her late mother, whom Eleonora had cared for obsessively during her lifetime. Eleonora's mother had lived in the old town house Eleonora owned in the Mykonian *Hora*. Her mother had long been divorced from Eleonora's father. After her death, to honour her mother's memory, Eleonora organised annual meals for an orphanage in Athens, replacing the usual family commemorative ritual[10] and thus avoiding any meeting with her relatives. Apart from vague references, I never heard Eleonora talk about her kin. She acted as if she had nobody in the world apart from her spiritual and *Mykoniot* friends. Furthermore, although her father was still alive, contact between them appeared to be non-existent.

Eleonora's discourse about aesthetics and social inequality shares very little with a mainstream 'feminist' one. Nevertheless, with or without a partner in her life, Eleonora cannot afford to be less independent than she is since this is her ideal type of existence. Given that, it was no accident that she was euphemistically called one of the rare 'true' feminists by Eurydice, another *Mykoniot* female friend.

As well as crossing the boundaries of Greek stereotypes of gender aiming for a predominantly 'male' ideal of being independent, *anexartitos*,[11] Eleonora further attempts to defy other mainstream cultural classifications. A characteristic linguistic example is how she addresses others. The boundary between boyfriend, partner, or friend is not clear-cut with Eleonora who employs a genderless, emotionally non-indulgent and unified definition of 'friend' for her relationships in general. In Eleonora's discourse, every type of relationship is discreetly classified under the 'affective' category of a 'friend'. This 'friend' might be a man she had spent ten years living with or equally somebody she had met in Vrindavan a year ago. Eleonora applies her private 'politically correct' norms of existence and classification to the way she perceives others' identities as well. For example, she abolishes another important identity classification for herself and for others, that of age. Crossing the boundaries and defying mainstream cultural classifications does not mean that Eleonora will not share with her girlfriends a popular discourse accusing men of exploitation and domination.

During the first year of my fieldwork, I spent a lot of time socialising with Eleonora. It was very helpful for me to follow her everyday discipline, through which I discovered the codified elements and the social organization that underlie the *Mykoniots*' superficial anomie. Since she had vast experience of the island's rhythms, a fact that was also reflected in her everyday choices, I started, through

Eleonora's moodiness, unravelling the *Mykoniots'* concept of time and space. All the obscurity of how and why the *Mykoniots* never firmly arranged an appointment but still managed to be in the right place at the right time, or the fact that there was no apparent logic governing what to avoid or what to choose, was made clearer to me by observing Eleonora's practice of correctly dividing 'Mykonian time'.

Her cyclic notion of time consists of distinct phases that transform Eleonora's lifestyle and consumption habits. Eleonora is socially transformed according to the season. In this respect I will try to unravel Eleonora's different selves, or even better, I will attempt to display Eleonora's 'wardrobe of selves'. I will attempt to describe the cyclic cultural order of the *Mykoniots'* lifestyles, as reflected in Eleonora's practices throughout the year that I followed her daily routine. I will assume that the beginning should be, according to the inherent rhetoric, the spring period where everything starts 'growing', when *Mykoniots*, too, are finally 'awake' after their long winter sleep; this is when they get a bit more creative, a bit more organised in their thoughts and actions and are likely to become over-optimistic about the summer to come.

Mykonos in the spring: Eleonora's disciplined self

It was early March and Eleonora had just returned from her long winter retreat, first to India and then to the States. She was very enthusiastic about the new meditation techniques she had collected from the Buddhist retreat she had visited in California, as well as being keen to demonstrate and practise something she called '*progressive movement*'. Her season on the island started as usual with a period of deliberate solitude and meditation, long walks in the Mykonian countryside and some dynamic yoga before sunset. Her daily programme also included some modest and healthy suppers.

The beginning of the season signified the 'painting period', so Eleonora began her search for a group of workers who would 'sterilise' her house with whitewash, as well as refresh the paintwork of the doors. During this 'opening' period, Eleonora's communication with the rest of the *Mykoniots* was distant and suspicious. 'They are always the same; they never change,' she would frequently complain.

My eagerness to learn about Eleonora's attractive lifestyle and our proximity in terms of residence that March produced a new 'bonding' in the constantly negotiable alliances between the *Mykoniots* themselves as well as between them and their 'disciples'. My role among them was clearly to follow this discipleship. We could alternatively trace, in this instance, a gender-specific ethnographic occasion for 'female bonding'. Eleonora and I came close through, among other things, 'performing pain'. By exploring our 'old', 'bad' relationships with men, we shared our 'traumas' from our [respective] self-destructive encounters with the 'other' sex. Papataxiarchis' review of the Greek anthropology of 'women', drawing on Caraveli's (1986) and Seremetakis' (1987) ethnographies on death and lament, highlights the common ethnographic assumption that women use the 'aesthetics of pain as a means of constructing a metaphysical [mutually shared] communion' (Papataxiarchis 1992a: 59–60). According to Caraveli, 'pain' is a 'distinct' performative domain which represents an, otherwise, 'mute female world'. Likewise, 'lamenting' the 'old' or 'bad' relationships and counselling one another, as ever-present elements of female bonding, could be viewed as comprising a context-specific, almost metaphysical means of communication between Eleonora and myself. However, it should be noted that female bonding among the *Mykoniots* discursively promotes an [aesthetically] syncretic set of techniques beyond the strictly 'female' performance of pain. For example, *Mykoniot* 'women' like to individually 'drink', 'smoke' and 'fuck around'; in other words, to 'overcome' pain experientially and autonomously, in a 'streetwise' manner.

The Easter Supper

Although the Greek Easter was early that year, the Mykonian countryside was already at its best. The usually infertile Cycladic landscape was temporarily blooming with vivid wild flowers that the *Mykoniots* collected and dried out with care for their summer decorations. I joined them in collecting big bunches of lilac, occasionally helping Eleonora or Hercules with their summer decorations. Mykonos' countryside was patiently awaiting the invasion of the Athenian bourgeoisie that would soon ruin Eleonora's 'devotional' feeling for the 'Greek' spring and holy Easter.

Eleonora warned me in advance that we should protect ourselves from the '*vibes*' of the 'barbarian Athenians' and hide. In that spirit she decided to take command of the situation and organise a private feast in her house to honour the Orthodox celebrations of *Megalo Sabbato* (the Easter Saturday when the moment of the resurrection is re-enacted).

Knowing how to avoid the 'couleur locale' atmosphere of the crowded Mykonian *Hora*, Eleonora arranged for us to attend church services at the monastery of Ano-Mera, an admittedly less touristy location. Despite the fact that we never managed to actually make it to Ano-Mera's monastery, we did achieve our aim of 'abstaining' from the practices of the Athenian visitors who paraded to the many churches of the Mykonian *Hora*. We also arranged to shop outside the centre. Eleonora provided herself with dairy products and seasonal vegetables from the nearby Mykonian *horio* (household) of *Kyra*-Lena,[12] and with sweet wine from an elderly Mykonian who still cultivated grapes and prepared the Mykonian wine himself.[13] With *Kyra*-Lena's 'Mykonian' cheese and the old man's 'Mykonian' wine we were able to play at being 'authentic' settlers, distinguishing ourselves from the 'tasteless' bourgeois invaders from Athens. For Easter dinner, we managed to recreate the 'old days' when the *Mykoniots* were emerging as the 'pure' back-to-naturists of Mykonos. Nevertheless, in order to back up this authentic identity, we had to pay handsomely for these fetishised 'Mykonian' products. On the morning of *Megalo Sabbato* (Easter Saturday), we started the preparations:[14] we cleaned the house and placed a huge Tibetan carpet in the middle of the otherwise empty space of the central room. We dressed the sofas with pieces of embroidery that Eleonora had brought from Kashmir and filled the vases with seasonal wild flowers. The centre-piece of the 'sacred' white room, was a big piece of light-green silk with a gold-brocaded border. We managed to fix it with pins to the top part of the wall, letting the long fabric fall to the floor. At the foot of the fabric, Eleonora placed a carved wooden figure of Ganesh.[15] We 'offered' this cross-legged deity big trays of fruits and garden flowers and olive oil, and lit the impressive brass oil lamp Eleonora had recently brought from India. Fruit 'offerings' were also placed in other parts of the large room. To complete the sacred atmosphere a number of candleholders, as well as a tray full of candles were arranged. Eleonora prepared and placed, strictly on her own, the special 'offerings' for her private chapel. Later she called me to inspect the setting. It was the first time I had had the chance to see Eleonora's 'mysterious' chapel that she carefully kept out of sight. Later on, she explained that she respected the local culture and was trying not to be provocative. She had placed in the otherwise traditional Mykonian chapel a mixture of Indian and Christian deities. One had to take off one's shoes to enter. A carpet and a *zafou*[16] had been placed on the floor for the purposes of prayer. The festive atmosphere in the chapel was heightened by the 'offerings', the smell of Indian incense, and the hanging oil lamps, typical of an Orthodox church.

After completing the decoration, we started cooking a vegetarian meal, highly atypical for the occasion. Eleonora has been a strict vegetarian for many years. For our 'Resurrection supper' we prepared a local speciality, a 'Mykonian' spinach pie following the recipe of *Kyra*-Lena. The traditional 'resurrection supper', consisting mainly of the Easter soup (*mageiritsa*) made out of the entrails of the lamb cooked on the spit the following day, was transformed into a vegetarian substitute. Improvising on the ingredients, our *faux mageiritsa* was accomplished after some hard work, using mushrooms instead of the lamb entrails. By the time the 'vegetarian' Easter menu was almost ready, the Orthodox evening service for Christ's Resurrection had begun. We avoided watching it on the television since it would 'ruin' the atmosphere; to follow the touching Orthodox service, we chose the radio instead. Eleonora went inside her private rooms and dressed herself in a strong red. She offered me a dark-red cashmere dress with a hand-embroidered border of flowers. I finally matched the decor and the festive atmosphere. We gave the final Easter touch to the table setting: some red Easter eggs and a pair of red candles. The spiritual background to the Easter table was the kitchen noticeboard with two illustrations: one was the monkey-like Indian deity Hanuman and the other a Byzantine icon of Jesus Christ.[17] The kitchen

Narratives of the self

table was lit by a seventies mushroom-shaped lamp. The 'Mykonian' wine was the most exclusive commodity on the table. Our eagerness in searching for it had given our dinner a distinctive taste. We were pretty well ready and all we needed was for our guests to appear. Eleonora's final move was to burn her 'natural' incense[18] all over the house, in order to elevate the 'exchange value' of the party. In Mykonos, one of the rare commodities most appreciated, second only to good quality hashish, is good quality incense.[19]

Although I have described the whole preparation of the resurrection supper as if it happened in an organised and consistent way, preparations in reality were more complicated. We actually needed to drive back and forth to the supermarket five times in order to complete Eleonora's erratic plans and shopping list.

Soon after the 'Resurrection', that took place as usual according to the Orthodox ritual at midnight, our guests arrived hungry and we sat down to the Easter Supper. Later on in the night we moved onto Eleonora's magic carpet with the red dragons, after carefully removing our shoes, we shared some dope and relaxed deeply, in some cases to the point of sleep. The guests were Hercules (my landlord and Eleonora's neighbour), another younger *Mykoniot* and his occasional girlfriend, and a couple of friends from Athens who were in the fashion business.[20]

The philosophy of Easter Sunday

After Eleonora's Easter supper on Saturday, the festive atmosphere continued. The next day was Easter Sunday, the *Agio Pascha*, when all Greeks have a wild party. Our group did not consume the traditional 'lamb on the spit' and the vast quantities of alcohol. Instead we enjoyed the 'seductive' Mykonian landscape, consuming food and alcohol in moderation. The 'party' this time was in another house also belonging to the *Mykoniots*' network, that of Hercules. The spring and my anthropological 'interrogation' inspired Eleonora to philosophise that day. Her elaborated theory concerned an idea about an 'ecstatic Cycladic triangle' which produced a special 'energy' and Delos was its generator.[21]

Later she switched the topic of our 'metaphysical' discussion to an exercise in comparative philosophy. She began her favourite game of Eastern and Western philosophical analogies, which compared the ancient Greeks' temperament to the characteristics of the *gyani* yogis (according to Eleonora, the ascetic, or otherwise the yogi who works via the intellect). She chatted pleasantly about the different types of love: 'their [the Greeks] attitude makes them swing between *agapi* (love), and *erotas* (falling in love). But still, this is the charm of the Mediterranean type. During the spring, Delos is covered with poppies, she turns red as if she's bleeding. Falling in love stops you from reaching God, which is the pure love.' And she went on and on improvising and playing with ideas without ever intending to seriously persuade anybody or construct an argument. She continued by elaborating the difference between the Mediterranean people and the Hindus:

> All life is a tragedy, but the Hindus discovered its comic side, since they became aware of *plani* (seduction); Greeks conceived the notion of *plani* but only intellectually. In Greek tragedy, *erotas* (Eros) is equivalent to *ponos* (grief). There is no such thing as an uplifting *erotas*, in the form of pure love. This big difference is characteristically revealed in the conflicting reactions of Shiva who first cut off his son's head but later on regretted it and replaced it with an elephant's head; but look at the dramatic story of Medea, she ate her own children due to her grief. *Hronos* [Time] is another mythological persona in Greek mythology who also ate his children. *Hronos* is the equivalent to the Indian karma, the good and bad debts. The big difference between the two philosophies lies in the apotheosis of *tyhi* [luck] and *pepromeno* [fate] which is predestined, as opposed to karma, which is a flexible fate.

After our philosophical Easter 'symposium', Eleonora decided that we should finally hit the clubbing side of Mykonos' eclectic culture. We got into our fashionable clothes and went dancing.

Guru Purnima: Eleonora's big annual feast

In the *Mykoniots'* social organisation, the monthly occasion of the full moon signified liminality for the group. The full moon of July traditionally belonged to Eleonora. She had established her annual gathering, an 'offering' to the *Mykoniots'* commune. The selection of guests for each year's party would depend on Eleonora's moods. By contrast, the cooking and general party preparations were identical every year. It would be vegetable *biriyani*, a Mykonian onion pie (a gift from *Kyra*-Lena), and the delicious apple pie that Eleonora made with brown sugar. The full moon of July, as she explained, was the day of celebration for all spiritual teachers. During that day, Eleonora was obliged to transform herself into a limitless giver. Therefore, she established her annual party as an offering to her teacher, the late Maharaj Ji, an occasion where she would open her house and tolerate all the eccentricities of her guests. She usually prepared the house and the food for the party alone while simultaneously practising her *'devotional singing'*. She also decorated her chapel and offered 'food' to her metaphysical honoured guests to further generate *'positive vibrations'*. The year 1992 was the first time I attended her feast. It was quite a successful gathering with the hostess dressed in an orange silk sari, her forehead painted with gold dust. Eleonora was happy that day.[22]

During the 1992 celebration of *Guru Purnima*, a group of senior members of the *Mykoniots' sinafi* recalled some scenes from Eleonora's celebrations in earlier years. One of them, Orpheus, amused the circle of old friends by mentioning the 'junkie' years of the 'eighties' when the consumption of 'hard' drugs was an imperative at all parties. The story was that the group of friends had gone, with a legendary provider of heroin, into Eleonora's chapel to consume 'hard drugs'. When Eleonora realised what was going on, she ended up quarrelling with them (not seriously) about their desecration of the holiness of the place and the holiness of the day. Orpheus narrated all this scene nostalgically, like a memory that brings satisfaction to somebody who had been the 'naughty child' of the family. Now, all this madness was past, Orpheus said. This year's full moon party was dead calm. No hard drugs, only dope. The younger set were into chemical drugs like 'ecstasy'.

The 1992 party ended up with another typical scene. A jam session at sunrise with Eleonora improvising her Indian songs. People were dead stoned mainly from '*grass*'. Some were sleeping in different corners of the house, some were jamming wildly and some were still just arriving from town. Orpheus forgot all about his 'nostalgic mood' and became active as soon as he realised that the party was turning into a jam session. He went to Eleonora's kitchen, took whatever he could find that would produce a loud noise, and provided the rhythm for the jamming.

The aesthetic emphasis of the 1992 celebration was, according to Eleonora: 'on a different style of party. Nearly everybody was *tripping* naturally, they were like on an *acid* trip.' This natural 'tripping', Eleonora explained, was a form of 'welcome' to the sober '*Aquarian*' reality of the '*nineties*'.

The 'dissolution' of the summer: the hedonistic August

The phrase 'don't let them lay a trip on you' was the most frequent 'counselling' received during my discipleship with Eleonora. I spent four months in a group practising dynamic yoga and some *vipasanas* (breathing techniques) with Eleonora as the '*teacher*'. People would easily join in and equally easily drop out of the yoga group, since there is no concept of regularity in the *Mykoniots*' regime of the temporary (the idea of regularity is exhausted in frequenting the local haunts). The inconsistency of her yoga 'disciples' drove Eleonora mad. She had a habit of impatiently searching for them and making their status in the 'yoga group' a probationary one.

The yoga lessons took place till the end of July. The chain of events, the so-called 'debauchery', started emerging slowly after the *Guru Purnima*. Eleonora was continually complaining: 'If you have alcohol inside you for two days in a row, there can be no yoga *nidra* [deeper level of consciousness].' The constant arrival of 'friends' who were seeking accommodation in the houses of the *Mykoniot* mentors changed the daily programme of the *sinafi*. The 'yoga group' decided to cease commitment to the weekly gatherings for the next month or so. The new regime under Eleonora's patronage was the following: 'after the August craze follows a pilgrimage to Tinos. After that, follows *detoxification* and *purification* with a grape diet only. In-between everything is allowed, all substances, any Dionysiac behaviour.' Eleonora initiated the practices of the summer period with a philosophical statement: 'We need dissolution in order to perform discipline.' The 'girls'[23] spent their summer at the rave parties of the nineties and the local *paniyiria*, dancing under Eleonora's influence both the fashionable '*Goa acid*' rhythms and the long-established *ballos* (a local traditional dance).

September: the pilgrimage period

September was the most beautiful time of the year. Everything was still warm but not that windy. Eleonora began her usual period of warmly socialising with her *Mykoniot sinafi*.

The stages of transition in the organisation and sociability, mentioned vis-à-vis Eleonora's seasonal schedule, are a characteristic of the *Mykoniots*. Old friends come in September. Dinners are organised and everybody is slowly turning inwards to the practices of the group. October is more intimate, but more or less the same. It is when Eleonora makes her winter arrangements. Who she will travel with, where will she go? At the last minute she usually decides to travel alone, always to India. Before departure, Eleonora has to pass through Athens for several days and this is where one realises how 'peculiar' she can be among other Greeks. She cannot synchronise herself with anybody else's schedule, she cannot stand the pollution. She constantly complains. She feels and simultaneously looks 'exotic' in this context. November to February is the 'India period' for Eleonora. Later on is the return to Mykonos where her life cycle is initiated again.

Eleonora's engendered Mykonos: a seductive female

During my discipleship under Eleonora, she would frequently reply to my shower of questions concerning the local lifestyle by ascribing metaphysical properties to the geographical space of Mykonos. I realised later that the constant reference to the properties of Mykonos was an indirect way of talking about herself.

Mykonos in Eleonora's discourse is like a human character and stands for the personification of *plani*, a Greek word connoting 'a strongly seductive illusionary force'. Eleonora's rhetoric of a personified Mykonos is not unique and is common to other *Mykoniots* as well. Eleonora would often say: 'Mykonos is like a beautiful woman who only cares to seduce. She gets her victims into an uncontrollable state; they get drunk from pleasure. Mykonos acts as the contemporary Circe who takes her victims, like Ulysses, out of their way but not beyond their karma, since it is within the law of their karma that they must be misled.'

'The countryside in spring makes one so spontaneously lazy,' Eleonora stressed. 'Everything changes as soon as the sun reaches one's body.' This theory about laziness somehow resembled the one about the Mykonian *plani* that Eleonora loved to talk about; it also resembled the psychological *plani* that my junkie friends were well acquainted with. What was important for me as the 'interpreter' was that all this *plani* was part of a rhetorically 'timeless' space; that of Mykonos.

The modus operandi for the majority of the *Mykoniots* is epitomised by a constant rhetoric about the insignificance of the emotions which they view as deceptive. Challenging the deceptive quality of the emotions produces an alternative rhetoric: the superiority of the 'authentic' senses that know of no manipulation and should thus govern one's existence.

Eleonora would never take '*Greeks' dramatisations*', as she called them, seriously. Her reaction to her Greek friends' over-emotional and passionate attitude would be distant, as if the sufferers of 'Greekness' belonged to an alien culture. However, she would be completely passionate about her own affairs and then her otherwise considerable analytical potential would just disappear.

Although Eleonora was highly sceptical about the notion of *plani*, she was a great seducer herself. She would also maintain that *plani* is a constant game, similar to the game of life. 'Life is *leela*,[24] to live is a constant game, since everything changes continuously. *Plani* is the *visible* and the *invisible*. The whole creation is God's *leela*; just an illusion.' I remember years later when I joined Eleonora on a Buddhist retreat in Devon she was talking about the same thing: 'If you grasp this game of constant change in life, you have got it all.' Eleonora's discourse here vis-à-vis performance is akin to Schechner's decoding of performance as embodied 'playing' (1995: 24–44).

For quite a long time Eleonora attempted to teach me about Mykonos' special reality, where one has more chance to confront oneself. While I was desperately trying to get my anthropological data, she would disapprovingly mutter: 'Mykonos is going to be a big school for you. Mykonos is a *meeting place* of ourselves. We come to meet a part of ourselves that nobody really expects to meet.'[25]

Eleonora, like the majority of the *Mykoniots*, could be extremely bored by and full of complaints about my 'anthropological' inquiries. 'Too much analysis. Analysis is old-fashioned! This is *eighties* stuff. It is tiring for the soul. We are entering the Aquarian era, back again to the hippie terminology: *waves, vibes,* energies, alternative families, universal love. So, move on!'

Eleonora herself, after her long wandering in Eastern philosophies, rejected all sociology, psychoanalysis and rational thinking long ago. Whereas, I was still interpreting Eleonora and the world in those terms. And I could not explain how the same woman who could stay patiently in her meditative pose could get angry, jealous and intense in reaction to the scary shapes that her own mind had created. Then, an endless stream of criticism would flow out of Eleonora. Everyone around was to blame for her inner turmoil. Yet, it took her only a moment to get out of her *plani* (literally 'illusion' or 'fallacy'). After all, the game of life for

Eleonora is not to be taken too seriously. After a long winter meditating in India, Mykonos is the place that gives to Eleonora's 'passionate self some *feedback*'. With Eleonora one could be a 'friend' and possibly an 'enemy' on the same day.

Beyond her occasionally oppressive attitude, Eleonora had a positive influence on my dietary shopping list and my potential for concentration. I turned into a health freak. I was part of the group of the so-called *koritsia*, the girls,[26] who gathered and organised the daily schedule of their existence under Eleonora's sphere of influence. This group of girls would normally gather in Eleonora's house or at the beach, or in the haunts in town and talk about astrology, art and male predators. Some eclectic clubbing was always an imperative for Eleonora's occasional groups of 'girls'. Through the medium of yoga and dancing, Eleonora had the ability to transform herself into a carefree teenager, seducing her 'disciples' into her timeless reality.

Narratives of the self: the self-image of Hercules

Hercules, the transformer of his multi-faceted identity
His maxim: 'I am everything, I am the Universe, I am love'

Hercules has been the most difficult informant to describe, owing to his dramatic influence on me. Apart from being an excellent example of a much fetishised authentic 'Mykonian' lifestyle, Hercules taught me a deeper 'existential' lesson: how to internally justify my presence and work on the island.

My apprenticeship under Hercules made me realise that according to the *Mykoniots*' ethical code there is not a single thing we feel, think or practise for which we need to get hooked into a '*guilt trip*'.[27] By observing him being so consciously 'amoral', 'asexual', 'apolitical' and, at the same time, charming and self-conscious, I experienced both threat and relief. How could his persona have such a catalytic effect on other people? Was it the way in which he played with his own identity, or any kind of identity? Or was it the complete absence of judgement or criticism of any other human being, group or attitude? His unique, idealist, neutral predisposition somehow created a 'demonic' but yet enticing self. Moreover, his emphasis on commensality and sharing in any aspect of everyday life, revealed a highly romantic naïvety.

Until the end of our house-sharing, I kept feeling suspicious of him being manipulative, fantasising secret sufferings inspired by his contradictory personality. Hercules was giving but yet distant; he was a strange mixture of craftiness and sobriety; an old-time 'gigolo' and a 'guru'. Moreover, Hercules belonged to a gender-less performative category that had no fixed sexual persuasion.

While I was organising my fieldwork methodology, I decided to live with and share the everyday life and reality of my informants. I did not know at the time that the local 'mafia' would make it impossible to realise this project in any other

Narratives of the self

way, since long-term rentals were effectively unaffordable for the unsuspecting visitor. This was the reason why Hercules agreed to 'pick me out' (at the time I thought *I* picked him out) and introduce me to the *Mykoniots*' lifestyle. I automatically became another 'apprentice' under the patronage of the *Mykoniot* 'patron' Hercules. At the time, I was completely ignorant about my new position and how the group operated.

Hercules usually spent eight months on the island every year. I could describe him as an almost archetypal *Mykoniot d'élection*. He rented a traditional old Mykonian house, his own Mykonian *horio*, at a bargain price. This house was on the still rural periphery of the otherwise overdeveloped tourist island. Many other *Mykoniot* friends lived nearby. They all preferred to mix with the locals, sharing a part of their Mykonian *horia*; alternatively, some of them had already built their own houses somewhere in the area.

I had visited Hercules' home in the past, and retained a very idealised memory of its magical setting. The Mykonian *horio* of *Kyr*-Thodoris (the name of the Mykonian owner of the large tract of land that included the house and the cultivated fields) had stayed untouched by time. *Kyr*-Thodoris entrusted the house where he himself had been born to Hercules, since Hercules would invest skill and artistry in it every new season. The house represented the kind of typical folkloric image that any ethnologically-minded photographer longs to immortalise. I remember that once one of them actually passed by and asked permission to take a picture. Hercules stared at him impassively and proposed: 'Let's toss a coin. Heads or tails?' The photographer unfortunately lost and left the house quite reluctantly. Hercules stared at him departing with a sardonic smile.

There was nothing glamorous about Hercules' *horio*, but its sublime simplicity, combined with some personal *meraki* (artistry), managed to create a unique composition in harmony with the local architecture and landscape, a house that was fully functional without being pretentiously 'folksy'. The house consisted of a very well-organised tiny kitchen, along with a bed-sitting-room, an outside bathroom and a distinctive blue and whitewashed guest room.

Having entered Hercules' courtyard, one entered a different space-time. Its seductive rhythms were slow, almost motionless. You soon realised that you had entered into Hercules' time zone. Fifty people would make no more difference than one to this motionless feeling. Hercules' aura was so dominant over his own space that his guests quickly adopted his rhythm. The gusts of the summer *meltemi* (strong local winds) would stay out of its well-protected southern terrace, letting the vines climb and the Mykonian *vasilikous* (basil plants)[28] release their persistent odour. All of a sudden, the endless whistling of the wind seemed far away. And at the front of the house the huge rocky Cycladic landscape appeared as motionless as ever.

Piraeus' harbour: the beginning of fieldwork and my apprenticeship with Hercules

Nearly all of Hercules' belongings were carried in two large, black cloth bags every spring. The 'passage' from Piraeus to Mykonos has been a constant one for something like thirty years, dating back to the times when not a single ferry-boat reached the unfriendly northern harbour of the island. Back then, the regular means of transport were local boats that sailed once or twice a week and which did not even dock alongside the pier but anchored further out and transported passengers back and forth in small launches. It was mid April and *Megali Pempti* (the Thursday before Easter). The ferry was full of aspiring nouveaux Greeks.[29] Hercules had delayed his arrival this year because some work had 'turned up'. For me it was the official opening of my fieldwork, and my initiation into a second role among the *Mykoniots*: Hercules' housemate.[30]

The house

We 'opened up' the house and left it like that in order to get rid of the winter dampness. I tried to follow Hercules' ritualistic 'return' to the Cycladic land. The *strosimo* (the setting up of the house for the new season) and the cleaning of the basic furniture and household goods lasted for two whole days. The preparation reminded me of a meticulous petit bourgeois housewife who arranges everything in a perfect and unchangeable order, except that Hercules really took his time; he managed to relax and enjoy the preparations. After the basic arrangements of the 'opening' had been completed and the house had been aired and the cobwebs removed, Hercules opened the black cloth bags and carefully arranged his portable 'treasures', each in its proper position. The heavy bronze Indian cigarette box had to go on the left side of the old wooden table, the collection of handmade leather cases brought from North American Indians which accommodated his flutes went to the place awaiting them on the upper part of the bedroom wall. Then he carefully chose the order in which to hang the *sarongs* across the opposite wall, a big collection assembled over many years. After that, he took out his wooden hand-engraved box which was filled with his special coins and placed it next to the candleholder on the old wooden table. The arrangement of Hercules' 'treasures' on the old wooden table was completed by placing the *I-Ching* Book of Changes on the right-hand side. Finally, after arranging some clothes and his collection of tiny stones, and ornaments, he took out his 'travelling' library and placed it on the old wooden trunk in display fashion. Hercules' choice of reading reminded one of a naïve anthropologist's book collection. When the 'treasures' were safely in their proper places, Hercules went to the well of *Kyr*-Thodoris to fill his pitcher with 'Mykonian' water or, as he called it 'this earth's water'. On his way back, he picked some wild flowers to dry them out for the vases. He also collected some ears of corn from the nearby fields and replaced last year's decorations. Later, around sunset, he lit all the candles in the house, made his *pujas* (incensing and purification rituals) with his sage incense and slowly settled himself again after this long procedure, in his normal 'sitting posture' near the old wooden table.

For Hercules, his 'removal' from one place to the next was a lengthy affair. He did not appear downtown in his friends' haunts until he felt 'settled'. He was not into trips and travelling like the rest of his circle, since, as he at least claimed, he personally did not 'need' them. He characteristically stated: 'I retain strong impressions of other places from my previous lives.'

During the general state of the house's *strosimo* (setting up), I felt completely incompetent. Even my attempt to arrange the temporary place of the sofa cushions while they were still drying in the courtyard was wrong. Even in this instance, Hercules would urge me to rearrange them in their 'proper' order or, preferably, rearrange them himself. It took me a little time to understand that even some unusually shaped stones outside the house had their proper 'Herculean order', just as every activity in the house had its sacred sequence. The good thing was that sooner or later one realised that it was unnecessary to follow it, since in any case it was Hercules' personal, eccentric order. '[T]hrough their [i.e., Greek women's] religious praxis, they transform the house into a spiritual shelter and a microcosm of orderliness' (Dubisch 1983; in Papataxiarchis 1992a: 57). Surprisingly, this ethnographic description of Greek women precisely matches Hercules' 'domesticated' image.

While in Hercules' house, I copied his radical and ecologically aware attitude towards nature; the watchword was to consume only fresh products and throw the remains straight onto the fields for immediate recycling. Furthermore, Hercules had intentionally closed the drains, so his guests had immediately to recycle used water onto the rose bushes, carrying it in large plastic buckets. (It took a while until I really accepted this habit and stopped cheating by throwing the water directly into the cesspool.) The radical 'recycling' habits of Hercules' home became normal activity after a while. My cultural norms of cleanliness altered somehow, yet without any ecological hysteria. The scraps of food were given to the cats and birds, consumption of toilet paper or any paper was limited and the use of detergents was confined to real emergencies only. The regular *liasimo* (exposure to the sun), the frequent whitewashing, and the *meltemi* (strong wind) were the strongest 'disinfectants'. This alternative natural 'cleanliness', the moderate consumption of goods, and a Spartan order in Hercules' life, brought the house to a certain state of 'beauty' which also came from the esoteric discipline of its tenant. This beauty also came at night from the tranquil light of the candles, the smells of Hercules' personal use of incense with Greek herbs, and the monotonous meditative music he preferred to listen to. But most of it was brought about through Hercules' deliberate stillness; after finishing with the morning housework, he would light his personal incense pot and swing it around him. Then he would sit cross-legged in meditation posture, with his second Turkish coffee at his side, in a tiny cup, and eventually roll his first miniature-size '*joint*' of the day. He would then consult the Book of Changes, the *I-Ching*, or alternatively use his more recent divination method, playing the animal cards, as if invoking totems, a situation where humans take on features and qualities from the animal realm. He would never miss being still for a 'long while', even if he had to leave the house for his occasional job-projects.

The summer preparation of Hercules' *horio* took two months. He first waited patiently to get rid of the damp, and then started painting everything inside and out. The painting session came every year with a new idea for a building project of either a decorative or functional nature; an open fireplace *à la Mykoniata*, or a Spanish pergola, a built table or whitewashed chimney extensions which were asymmetrical works of art. This year, he decided to build a second courtyard and organise a new lighting system for his outdoor parties.

The 'reconstruction' of Hercules' personal semantics on Mykonos (i.e., his house) simultaneously signified his inward 'opening'. Hercules got rid of his clothes and worked naked at his building works. He stayed naked as long as possible. He was naked in the house, he was naked at the beach and when walking on the island's rocks nearby. He slowly regained his 'strength', his tan, and he eventually managed to 'rejuvenate his cells'.[31] By the end of that spring, Hercules looked impressively young again and renewed. The change was obvious. The whitewashing and the Mykonian sun brought about 'regeneration'. For Hercules, as for the rest of his group, all it takes is the 'return' to this small Cycladic island.

The work on the house, Hercules' 'care of the self', and his simultaneous energetic 'opening' was developed methodically by his paying equal attention to important and unimportant details alike, such as the collecting in season of the purple amaranthus, the varnishing of the old doors with oil, and his annual washing of the household blankets, white linen, Indian textiles and wonderful mosquito nets (under which a large number of bodies would rest).

His next step was to go to the local women to beg for some Mykonian basil for his courtyard. He also provided himself with good quality incense brought by his friends who had just returned from India, since he himself never travelled that far. Then Hercules had to make his final steps towards his Mykonian 'opening': he had to persuade his cat to come back to the house after her long winter absence. The external whitewashing of the house signified the end of the 'reconstruction' period. The symbolic seasonal 'opening' of Hercules' home for the *Mykoniots* was celebrated with a delicious *briam* (a traditional vegetarian recipe with mixed vegetables in fresh tomato) which he cooked over a very slow fire, in the old fireplace of his 'Mykonian' kitchen. Hercules specified to me that the fuel for the fire of the old 'Mykonian' fireplace was not wood but *frigana* (brushwood), which one could find in plenty in the dry Mykonian landscape.

As soon as the long circle of transition and incorporation into the Mykonian setting was completed, Hercules gradually grew more extrovert, either seeking a new '*project*',[32] or, if he had worked enough during the winter, just socialising.[33] Even if his financial situation was very bad, he would still spend his two-month 'incorporation period' in the same way. At the end of this 'reconstruction', he would ask for an old *kilim* or a bamboo chair from his friends' shops on credit or in exchange for some building job or a decorating 'commission'.

Occasionally, Hercules' living expenses were credited to a local businessman and friend who decided to hire him to 'create' something for his new business or for his home. Eventually Hercules would have free access to food and drinks there. As a general rule, Hercules and the *Mykoniots* paid symbolically rather than directly to the local bars and taverns. In this sense, there was no need for Hercules to be restrained in how he spent his money. Any of the cosmopolitan habits he enjoyed were easily affordable, since he was part of the milieu of the *Mykoniots* who supported one another.

Before Hercules' socialisation period, we used to spend the nights indoors, in the main building of the house which consisted of two connecting rooms. One was a kitchen and a 'wardrobe' combined. Everything in there was on 'display', handmade shelves with hand-decorated ceramic plates and a work-table made from a large piece of rock; bunches of dried oregano, mint and other aromatic herbs were hung on the whitewashed wall; the fruits and vegetables were in woven baskets on the floor; the water in an old pitcher inside an alcove. A stylish Mexican textile divided the two rooms. In the main room, there were also an antique pot, taken from the remains of Delos, an old linen chest and small cross-cultural curios; a painting from Carolina, the local naïve painter. The head of a caryatid was placed near his bed as the base for his bedside table. Hercules' personal fetishes were placed on the top: an old snake bracelet, and the clay pot for his personal 'incensing'. The room had two extra wooden tables with their edges roughly finished. Big, totem-like kites, remnants of the pre-rave parties held under the full moons of the eighties were hung from the ceiling.

Every single corner of this tiny space was softly lit, a fact that helped bring out its various angles; a blue light hidden behind the vase which held the wheat, a pale white coming from behind natural sea shells placed high on its walls; yellow, on the main outer doorway to repel the mosquitoes; various small colourful psychedelic night lights close to the guests' beds; finally, a spotlight was turned towards the wickerwork of the ceiling, also illuminating the upper borders of the colourful sarongs all hung in a line. In earlier days, the possession of a sarong also symbolised membership of the *Mykoniots d'élection:* Hercules would offer them to his most 'beautiful' visitors, the ones he wanted to incorporate into the community.

On the terms 'brotherhood' and 'joint ownership'

Right from the very beginning of my fieldwork and house-sharing, Hercules initiated a rhetoric of a grandiose commensality. Right up to the end of our house-sharing, I had constant suspicions about Hercules' manipulations. I even felt that he was sometimes 'exploiting'[34] me. I remember once he persuaded me to buy a second-hand motorcycle at a bargain price. The deal was that we would share the expenses, but the unwritten deal was that he was the master of the motorcycle. The fact was that this motorcycle was hardly ever used by me when Hercules was around. Hercules also charged me with the whole amount of the yearly rental on the house, while I thought I was only contributing to the rent. When I discovered the truth, I decided not to confront him because, given the island's normally high cost of living, the rent for Hercules' house was admittedly low due to a special deal between him and *Kyr*-Thodoris, the owner. Hercules had his own idiosyncratic ethical rules in mind that were difficult to follow, and sometimes they caused me a great deal of frustration and a feeling of mistrust. On the other hand, dealing with him at the material level gave me a more holistic picture of how *Mykoniots'* commensality relationships really worked. Apart from my occasional frustration, needless to say I benefited a great deal from my experience of living with Hercules. Firstly, I conceived the core of the *Mykoniots'* mentality, personified in Hercules' attitude. Secondly, I realised that there were alternative measures and parameters of give and take I had never thought of before. But more importantly, Hercules performed a spiritual role, quite unpretentiously valuable to me. I would say that the practical circumstances combined with Hercules' free handedness and commensality in the community, gave me the perfect opportunity to describe my ethical dilemma with the group. His inconsistent and almost amoral attitude would put me off only when I overlooked his mainly giving and guiding side.

Hercules loved to talk about the 'hard times' of modern life, preaching in favour of understanding and commitment to an ideology of sharing, proposing an extended family as the only plausible and beneficial solution. The idea was to have an overlapping network of groups or individual friends who would appreciate mutual reciprocity on the basis of giving whatever one might want or could afford. His romantic perception of commensality also included an ideal revival of a barter-like system. He 'offered' with his lifestyle a taste of hippie folklore to the island's visitors and 'refugees'.[35] For example, he carefully organised his cosmopolitan gastronomic celebrations, along with his manual and inspired labour. He offered an ideology of simplicity and sexual freedom that included no guilt. His idea of reciprocity, however, also included asking an enormous amount for renting his Mykonian house as a short let to a rich German friend. Yet, he was equally eager to offer hospitality to some 'hysterical' and 'traumatised' human beings, giving them comfort and kindness and expecting no reciprocity. All that might sound inconsistent but Hercules spoke about the inner balance that made him choose either the one or the other attitude.

Hercules' discourse presents us with sophisticated ideas of exchange. His model is more like a bricolage of diverse aesthetic and political discourses of exchange, than a culturally specific one. One could initially consider the re-emergence of patron–client relationships in the *Mykoniots'* context. The tourist space creates a peculiar sense of a constant 'liminality', as well as egalitarian discourses vis-à-vis inner group relationships through only occasional alliances. Nevertheless, the element of ephemeral 'patronage' on the part of the *Mykoniots* exists towards the newly 'initiated'. This type of patronage, unlike Campbell's suggestion, does not aim at established and asymmetrical personal relationships through some kind of 'moral obligation' (1964: 259). In the fluid tourist setting, any sense of obligation directed to some 'benefactor' is ephemeral and beyond an established context like kinship, or any fixed set of class-based social obligations like the political type of patronage frequently described in Greek ethnography (Herzfeld 1985: 106; Campbell ibid.; Mouzelis 1978). In the Mykonian context, alliances are short-term transactions and patrons short-lived. The absence of any element of establishing or reproducing 'permanent personal relationships' leaves out, in our case, the element of 'moral obligation'. The *Mykoniots'* patronage provides them with a temporary and ideally reversible power. After the actual initiation of the 'new' member into the Mykonian scene comes incorporation which aims to transcend the initial and arbitrary power of the patron-initiator.

Hercules' house was something of a refuge to which, after leaving it, I would eventually return for long visits, most of which gave me a ritualistic sense of being on a personal retreat. Every time I entered Hercules' home, I felt at home.

Hercules' life history

Hercules' roots were back in Crete. He was brought up there until he was eleven. Although he has strong photographic memories of this place in the Aegean sea, he has never been back since he left. He confessed he was even reluctant to claim his share of the ancestral land. His only enthusiastic relationship with his homeland was his admiration for the Minoan period in Crete, which he took as the highest expression of culture; mainly because, as he maintained, the Minoan civilisation was an exception among the great civilisations having the sophistication to place women at the top of the social hierarchy.

Hercules adored women and treated them in a way which distinguished him from his 'macho' peers. His 'ambivalent', gender-free behaviour would sometimes lead him to extreme declarations. For Hercules, there was no clearly defined male or female attitude. Every attitude belonged to every human being beyond one's sex. Hercules ideology for the most part abolished fixed categories. His personal attitude could be equally qualified as purely hermaphrodite according to the cultural semantics of a mainstream Greek male. He has been and still is a very attractive man, always surrounded by women, mostly younger in age (although he has spent a long period of his life with an older woman). Another great characteristic of Hercules' anti-macho attitude was that in his house he liked to gather a lot of 'female energy', as he called it. He was one of the rare exceptions among the male Greek *Mykoniots* because he accepted female discourse absolutely without underestimating it. On the other hand, although he himself did not adopt a macho attitude in his own discourse, he was part of the 'boy's gang' that consisted of the male patrons of the *Mykoniots d'élection*.

During my 'apprenticeship' under Hercules' guidance, I constantly swung between feelings of enormous anger at his apathy and manipulativeness and feelings of deep relaxation and satisfaction within his realm of aesthetic perfection. When the moon was full, and whenever any occasion arose that Hercules wished to celebrate, anyone around could experience a sacred feeling arising out of the ultimate Herculean commensality. Hercules' commensality did not rely upon equality, the point was not equal 'offerings' but an offering based on a sliding scale related to circumstances and idiosyncrasies of each individual. Hercules expended all his money and energy on his parties without ever complaining about anything.

Hercules was another mentor for the home and outdoor celebrations of the group, which he designed and executed perfectly by himself, no matter how many guests there were. He enjoyed equally his solitude, and the company of friends.

Hercules could sometimes be extremely didactic about his cosmology, as well as his theories of reincarnation. He was not a follower of any 'dominant' religious ideology, since he avoided empathising and taking a fixed persona and a fixed life history. He preferred rather to craft his own eclectic theory of practice. Hercules hated strictly personal conversations; he felt as if he had nothing to say. He also hated gossiping and judging other people's lives. He would instead take his flute out of its case and play what was sometimes a unique and inspired improvisation.

Hercules' rhetoric, in line with Eleonora's, would passionately advocate: 'You should not be driven by your *emotions*, but you should simply follow the *senses*. *Emotions are a folly*. Energy should be converted from negativity and aggressiveness, from an *ego trip* and *possessiveness* to *brotherhood*, a *universal love*.'

Hercules, the 'breakfast' mentor: an 'authentic' role play in 'eighties' Mykonos

Hercules is said to be the founder of the still fashionable 'breakfast ritual' on the island, a practice perhaps copied from Ibiza. As he himself described it, the whole concept started soon after his arrival from London in the late seventies where he had lived and worked for some years. He brought with him his personal music collection[36] and established the new trend in Mykonos: the breakfast 'happening'.

Narratives of the self

The innovation in this whole concept of breakfast was that it was held in the busy night spots of the island. Mykonos' more eclectic visitors had the chance to create an additional meeting time in a familiar meeting place. The whole concept supported the lingering notion of the hippies' collectivity. In the dark rooms of the Mykonian bars and clubs which he chose as the occasional setting for his 'breakfast happening', Hercules as mentor performed a great transformation.

His success was that he managed to amass the few local dairy products of exceptional quality by visiting their producers every morning. He brought all these along together with beautiful fresh Mykonian flowers to decorate his breakfast setting. Locals adored Hercules because he spoke 'the same language' as them and they did not feel intimidated by him, as they did by other 'outsiders'. That was the reason why they took care of him and his breakfast happening by supplying him with their best products. On the other hand, the 'visitors' also liked Hercules because he was charismatic. During the 'high' season, Hercules managed to keep his enormous energy for his 'morning happenings' and personally undertook to lift the morning spirits of his guests.

In the breakfast history of Mykonos, Hercules was reputedly the most successful and the most 'expensive' manager. As the joke went among his fellow *Mykoniots*, Hercules charged his breakfast guests according to his whim. Yet, Hercules was the orchestrator of the morning game of 'distinction', and he cautiously calculated the dynamics and potential of his guests so as to make everybody happy.

Hercules' breakfast-setting started with coffee and freshly squeezed juices, but could easily switch to a morning beer (in order to treat the hangover), chilled vodkas and champagne for the eccentric. The local *sinafia* of the aesthetically 'privileged' displayed their youth, their beauty and their decadence by slowly arriving one by one every morning in an aloof and individual manner, just to crowd into the scene that was set for the Mykonian distinction game: they entered the bar in their 501s and cowboy boots. Their colourful *sarongs* were draped over their bodies, a sign that they were ready for a swim. They were always protected behind their avant-garde sunglasses. The 'Mykonian fashion' of the eighties had a common dress code for both 'girls' and 'boys'. In a sense beauty made them faceless; *pace* Waldren 'a new and attractive person was accepted at 'face value' (1996: 166). The 'sarong' was sometimes carried from the night before as if the interlude of the night had never happened. After a while, Hercules' rock and jazz music would make them groove into the rhythm again. For 'eighties' Mykonos the principal rule was minimal sleep.

I cannot really put in writing what it was about Hercules' *stisimo* (setting up) that made it unique, but yet I know that it was unique. Hercules' 'breakfast rituals' managed to transform the act of taking breakfast into a spontaneous morning 'happening'. It was not uncommon for the 'breakfast ritual' to turn into a party.

An additional fact that made Hercules' breakfast a distinctive setting was that there was nothing touristy or really expensive about it. His own seductive presence behind the bar made his breakfast happening unpretentious, yet exclusive due to his 'special care'. What maybe made it fashionable was the absolute importance of style. Hercules himself would say: 'I set the scene, because I really liked it myself. In those days an elite crowd was arriving on the island. It was exclusive. Nice boys and girls. That was enough. You would *get high* just at the sight of them.'

Hercules was one of the core patrons of the local underground culture of the cosmopolitan island of Mykonos. What made him special were his manual skills and his charismatic persona, but most of all his survivalist attitude that made him a local leader. In today's Mykonos, where the aspiring nouveaux riches and the petit bourgeois Greeks have invaded the island and its haunts in order to appropriate the cosmopolitan symbol, our group of the 'elect' *Mykoniots* have become marginalised. Those associated with the seventies scene, like Hercules and his peers, are left feeling like 'outsiders' in a culture that they themselves had once created. The change to mass tourism leaves the *Mykoniots* with no cultural space on Mykonos. But any sense of ambition they might have in the new situation is overwhelmed by their principle of spontaneous pleasure.

Hercules and his fellow *Mykoniots* still live exclusively, since they enjoy 'simple' pleasures, work as little as possible and try to stand out as much as possible. Hercules indirectly asserts his role play of the 'authentic' *Mykoniot* by searching for new disciples. The tragic irony is that the island which was 'chosen by the gods' according to the Greek tourist campaigns of the fifties, has fallen prey to a myth in Barthesian fashion, and been consumed by the masses. Hercules was one of the creators of the 'original' Mykonian lifestyle, when Mykonos was another 'meeting place' for an emerging cosmopolitan culture. Yet, he is no decadent. In his late forties, he keeps moving on to new 'projects' as a form of survival.

Hercules never served in the obligatory institution of the Greek army, he has never paid any taxes and never had a driving licence. The only official document he possesses, apart from his early identity card, is a recent bank account book. He does not look after anyone in particular, nor does anyone look after him either. Hercules is not into self-destructive rituals, he lives constantly in a harmonious apathy, playing the photographer in the seventies, the breakfast mentor in the eighties and lately for the last seven years or so, the interior designer and the naïve architect.[37] Mykonos offers Hercules his yearly transformation from winter hibernation to the *stisimo* (the setting up) of the body, the *stisimo* of the Mykonian *horio*, but first and foremost, the *stisimo* of his self-image. His already strained financial resources will soon be exhausted but he will keep staying on, still enchanted by the transformation. And he will continue to 'expend himself', as the others do: letting the sun consume their bodies, giving themselves over to dancing and to love. They will fall in love only platonically, no strong emotions are recorded in their diaries, since they care mostly for themselves. Their 'kick' is the art of adding style to their living. They know how to act out their lives, so they have glamour. Empathy, for them, is only imitative. Perhaps this is the result of drug-taking in the seventies, perhaps the result of the oblivion-inducing sea and sun of the Aegean and the rhetorical Dionysiac effects of Apollo. Hercules' rhetoric would describe this whole idea of personal transformation as a long process that starts with a first obligatory step, namely *'erasing one's personal history'*.

The 'Mykonian' communal ideology has persisted through personal style and symbolic creativity in reaction to the alienation of the mass urban lifestyle. The motif is: 'making style out of a breakfast, or out of a good dinner; having a satisfying fuck'. By spreading the dream to a few available bourgeois and making them admire it, the *Mykoniots d'élection* keep the keys of free membership to a fleeting worldly paradise: today Mykonos or Bali, tomorrow somewhere else.

About relationships and commitment

Hercules is the only informant for whom I perhaps do not need to designate a pseudonym.[38] Hercules had no nagging ideas about his personal identity as if it was something respectable, vulnerable or, more precisely, something fixed. He wouldn't mind how he was addressed. He left his family a long time ago. Likewise, Hercules strongly maintained the philosophy that 'a person's assimilation to a fixed identity is the most *misleading path*'. And he would likewise extend his eclectic existential theory by proposing that 'all of us have both a male and female side'. Moreover, according to the 'Herculean' theory, one should be a lover and a friend, attached and independent at the same time.

Hercules considered that his random relationships with other people happened in order to 'advance' them as much as to advance himself. He strongly maintained that human relationships involved no authentic roles. Therefore, no rules were needed. In 'Herculean' theory gender roles were abolished when that was convenient. Moreover, a 'fixation' with a concrete life history, a rigorous self-identity, a stable profession, a single social class, an exclusive spouse, were all destructive factors that only made one's self shrink. Popular ethical dogmas, in respect of a 'proper' behaviour concerning the exclusivity of intimate relationships, could equally detract from one's potential in life. The 'Herculean' theory on relationships replaced the salient position of *the* 'significant other' with numerous combinations of relationships and occasional 'significant others'.

His *Mykoniot sinafi* exemplified the ultimate pattern for relationships. Hercules called his *Mykoniot* friends *'brothers*' and 'co-warriors of life'. Mysteriously enough this uncommitted 'group' of *Mykoniots* which emerged back in the late sixties has managed to survive and can still be traced in Mykonos, that is after nearly forty years.

In seventies Mykonos, well aware of his charm, the young Hercules quickly learned to expose his beauty and charisma, and in a way to 'prostitute' his persona. This was manifest in a great easiness with his naked body. He would always dress smartly and behave flirtatiously. If one had to stereotype him, he must have been a typical cosmopolitan womaniser. During his time in the breakfast business, flirting was 'part of the job'. But as he said: 'That was the *seventies*. Everybody was open'.

Nowadays, he 'saves his energy' for rare occasions. 'Solitude is the only way to creativity,' he loves to state. He no longer plays the mature gigolo. He prefers to speak about rituals of 'purification' that he performs with friends during long retreats in private houses outside Athens, that include fasting, hot baths, and *chilum* smoking (an Indian pipe filled with dope). Or his participation in the 'earth celebrations' – ecologically-minded feasts celebrating 'planet earth' – by playing his flute. Or he would rather talk about Franz Boas, and Joseph Campbell and his favourite Gurdjieff.[39] But mostly, he would practise his self ritual, the so-called 'sacralisation of daily life'. For Hercules, everyday action belongs to the sacred realm. His 'sacred' daily routine, what he calls '*the art of living*', builds his unique 'Herculean' style: 'We came here for a while and we don't have to take ourselves for granted, we came here to *enjoy* living. This is the most difficult thing: *the art of living.*'

Hercules' personal lifestyle and general aesthetic predisposition has been long appreciated by the *Mykoniot* circle, as has his idiosyncratic nature. Likewise, friends would generously pay him to spend the winter in New York and transform their lofts *à la Mykoniata*. In the end, he may take twice the expected time and charge them twice the agreed money, simply by repeating his ritualistic slow everyday practices. Hercules would never do this, however, i.e., 'share' and 'offer' his inspiration, to an unknown rich guy or a 'straight'. He always works for 'friends'.

Psychological insecurities and 'social security'

The absence of any type of commitment, and Hercules' consistent ambivalence towards his 'professional' identity never ceased to surprise me. Yet, I could not feel that this was due to personal insecurities, since I have to admit that Hercules was a very relaxed and carefree human character. My own existential anxiety for social reward, personal security, a stable income, a permanent social circle, a stable relationship, a bank account, would revolt against his lack of any long-term desire or ambition to establish a secure 'social' self.

Hercules had no 'property in his own name' since he disliked being taxed. Nor did he have a reliable salary, nor any insurance, nor even a social security number after thirty years of work. Back in the seventies, he married, in England, to obtain a residence permit; there he worked as a sales manager and engaged in other

Narratives of the self

mysterious occupations. Only recently has he acquired a bank account, though he habitually deals only in cash, something that he carries with him at all times.[40]

During one of my frequent 'ritualistic' returns to Hercules' *horio* which always felt like 'coming home', I stayed as usual longer then I intended. Carried away in Hercules' time zone, I spent the night and the next day there. But this time I had a sudden panic attack over Hercules' future. We were sitting indoors, since spring had only just begun. The refrigerator was not in its usual state of abundance, containing only some tomatoes, and a piece of feta cheese. There was also half a bottle of red wine and some dried barley bread. Hercules was in a complaining mood, mainly concerning 'friends' who owed him money from his latest 'project', the *stisimo* (setting up) of a bar. Only later did I realise that his uneasiness was because he had hardly any money left. Yet, this fact would not stop him dreaming of building new extensions in the backyard. In Hercules' mind, obviously some solution would appear sooner or later, as far as his financial difficulties were concerned. I, on the other hand, was admiring his sangfroid about the future. My fieldwork was over and I was anxious to turn to the future phases of this work, but Hercules was there the same as ever; he was equally caring no matter what his actual financial circumstances were, and he cooked for us.

He was still sitting in his normal meditative position on the built-in sofa near the wooden table and he was still rolling small joints. He was wearing a semi-winter outfit, and was looking weak and a bit older, I thought, from winter and seclusion. An immediate tenderness combined with anxiety overtook me. And I thought that this person was the most complete example of solitude. He had no business or family or cash, he just had his personal skills and good health. (In Greek culture, the stereotype of the complete and successful person presupposes someone who looks after his or her 'future'; so only when one grows older and is financially and emotionally secure can one be characterised as a wise person.) Thus, in absolute cultural terms, according to the stereotype of a Greek complete person, Hercules was a complete failure: no children, no companionship, no ownership, no money, no future pension.[41] On top of his economic 'insecurity', he would rarely visit any relatives not even his mother. Hercules never felt like talking about or belonging to his real kin group. He lived on the cheap, as in the rooming house he occupied in the centre of Athens. This was in a very picturesque building with an internal courtyard which was shared with other housemates. The building had been saved by some miracle from the seventies developers and it was managed by another *Mykoniot* friend. His quite 'unsettled' life circumstances would not 'show' at all on him or in his private space. Hercules would work eclectically and as little as possible for some periods of the year, and he would pass the rest of his time calmly in his house which remained in a nearly manic order.

For some reason,[42] that night I could not see this order in his life, nor his calmness, perhaps because the setting was not yet summery and carefree. In addition, in the back of my mind I had this persistent thought that the big project in Athens was over, and that he would be awaiting the big job that would never come. There was still some more money owing to him but his pockets were nearly empty and rent not yet paid. I could not stop myself from returning to this persistent idea, coupled with the anxiety of him being old. I over-dramatised the situation in my mind: who is going to take care of him once he is old and ugly and incapable? When he grows older, which is not a very distant reality in his case, he will no longer hang around friends' bars. He will not have anything to offer then. He will be useless. He might even feel too intimidated to cross his friends' thresholds and look for shelter, commensality and food. On the spur of the moment, I suggested he should get a private pension scheme immediately. There was hardly any time left, I said, since he was about fifty. Hercules refused to share my anxiety[43] and explained, indifferently, that there was no reason for him to do a thing like that. And stated in his seemingly wise way: 'If I were to have anxieties of this sort, and live the way I do, I would have already killed myself with stress.'

For Hercules, as he had explained many times to me during my long apprenticeship in his Mykonian *horio*, existential anxiety is a natural thing that one can only negotiate during every minute of one's existence, and observe the next minute that comes, only to renegotiate. He has built his metaphysical and existential understanding from a bricolage of cross-cultural thinking. The anxiety which led me to make this proposal about a private pension initiated a bilingual dialogue. (Hercules loved to recite his existential theories partly in Greek and partly in English.[44]) Parts of this dialogue we had had many times before:

Hercules: In order to live as I do, one has to be aware of the *universality* of one's being. *We are all travellers in this universe, eternal beings.* Insecurity comes when someone does not know who he is. They told us that we were born there and that is our personal history. But this is just a small piece of the cake of *existence*. The rest of the cake is untouched. Shouldn't we eat it? And as for your concern with work, sometimes it comes by itself and sometimes you have to go out there and find it. You do everything.
(I kept insisting on my bourgeois dilemma.)

Me: Yes, but what about when you get older, and what if you become ill?
(Hercules replied laughing.)

Hercules: I perceive things quite differently; look, as I grow older I feel more creative. Inspiration is bigger. Completely the opposite, you see, more *energy*. And don't forget all these worries, *they come from the mind…*

Me: And your mother, doesn't she feel *marazi* [heartache] for you?

Hercules: No, do I look like somebody that provokes heartache? I do not really care about being 'secure'. Maybe tomorrow *a big project* comes along. And logically it will happen. But let's take the opposite scenario, me with no home, no 'fortune'. Me and my saddlebag wandering around. There will be a house that will need care. My friends would love me to take care of their houses. I cannot see any problem, *the world out there is for you*, whatever you like you can do, I could even go to Mount Athos. Let's say you get bored and old, then you go to the holy mountain to 'give birth'. Problems are always there but they are of a different sort. They are only for people who have desires and vanities.

Me: This human emotion called insecurity has it ever applied to you?

Hercules: In the past, yes. Lately, I have not felt it.

Me: Feelings like jealousy, anger, or 'getting the blues'?

Hercules: Those things happen, but they are so unstable and they do 'pass'. As everything else does. As we, ourselves, pass on.

Me: And when, for example, you seek divination from the *I-Ching* book, what is it that you would like to know?

Hercules: What is the appropriate step for the time being, what is the right position I should hold in order *to be in accordance with the flow*. Or, if you like, one has to decide her or his own attitude to things and then check: *is it in accordance?*

I was taken by his theories (despite the fact that it was the first time after a year of sharing a home that I was meticulously keeping notes in front of him), and soon afterwards I abandoned my existential and cultural projections and switched the topic of conversation to the consumption of illegal substances, after he had finally reassured me that his lifestyle was the kind of life that he had always wanted.

Our late night discussion would close with an identity game that amused both of us. The question was what were the 'professions' he had experienced in his life so far: the latest was an architect and occasional interior designer and builder. He has also been a photographer, which is the profession written on his official identity card. Later, he was the creator of the breakfast trend in Mykonos. Before that, he was a manager in a retailing business on Carnaby Street (during this period, he was also a musician). He had also been a waiter, house-cleaner, gardener, drug-dealer, a pimp who was paid, for a short time, by some beautiful girls, and a supermarket 'boy'. He also used to run his father's taverna, in some small Athenian neighbourhood. His most stable occupational identity through the years was that of a musician performing with various groups. He had also spent some time in the past experimenting with producing handmade jewellery. He had also learnt carpentry, a skill that turned out to be very useful in later years. He once played in a movie, not an important role – a bit part. But all the above are unimportant details of his identity, since the important thing is that he had been an 'amateur' virtuoso all of his life, and maintained that he had liked every single thing that he ever did equally.

Hercules: I did most of them just for the sake of the *experience*. Some because I could not do otherwise at the time. During the *breakfast* period, I would say, I was a photographer. But creativity is the important thing. Every single human being has chosen to come into this life with a certain lifestyle that fits him. Some are hard workers and some lazybones. Just learn from that!

So our conversation that night ended with much laughter. I contemplated the idea of Hercules the magician of identities, who every five years or so would have to reconstruct a new, appealing identity, just by labelling himself according to whatever job had come along.

Narratives of the self: the self-image of Artemis

Artemis' 'rough' glamour

During one of my boat trips to Athens, I engaged in a long conversation with Antonio, a long established member of the *Mykoniots*, concerning the elitist discourse on aesthetics that predominated in all conversations about Mykonos and its visitors. The *Mykoniots*' great preoccupation with beauty and glamour further established their game of distinction and also indirectly acted as a prerequisite of membership. I was actually seeking for an explanation and some further insights from Antonio, who must have been among the creative founders of the group's image. He himself looks something like Mick Jagger. Due to his extraordinary appearance, it might be difficult for some people to culturally and aesthetically locate Antonio's bodily 'habitus', and recognise his purely 'Greek' origin. Antonio is gentle and effeminate, and a real womaniser still in his sixties. There is something intangibly glamorous and decadent about him that revealed his frenzied lifestyle. Antonio verified my constant observation that the *Mykoniots*' milieu had consisted of individuals of characteristic beauty and charm. People's narratives, in general, included stories about legendary figures, like the guy whose Mykonian nickname was synonymous with his charisma: he was called the 'Saint'. Another one was 'Patrick', a seminal figure for the local 'subcultural' milieu of the *hippie sinafi*. These legendary figures were distinguished in the arena of cosmopolitan Mykonos not purely by their actions and style, but also by a charisma that was linked to their exceptional physical appearance. Antonio further validated my comments by poetically paying tribute to the countless unidentified 'visions of beauty' that used to overwhelm the Mykonian streets. They were just 'beautiful tourists', he said, 'who were passing by like comets during the *seventies*'.

It was through this long conversation I had with Antonio that I recognised the importance of self-image for the *Mykoniots*. It began with his captivating description of Artemis, which was due to his enchantment with her. Antonio epitomised Artemis' image in two words: 'rough beauty'. Artemis is one of the legendary figures of beauty within the *Mykoniot* circle who is still on the island. Nevertheless, what I could not understand at the time was why this association with beauty was so salient in people's narratives. I was aware of Artemis' bizarre radiance, a characteristic actually shared among the *Mykoniots*, but I could not clearly identify its 'function' in the group. I should perhaps also mention an analogous popular rhetoric among the *Mykoniots* that concerned the grandiose aesthetic of the 'rough' Cycladic landscape, and its combination with the 'unique' energy created out of the so-called 'Delian light' that allegedly had the potential to attract 'beautiful' people and also bring out the 'best' of one's performative 'repertoire'.

This concern with beauty might almost be termed an aesthetic 'racism' and was exemplified in eighties Mykonos where there was a snobbish tendency among the *Mykoniots* to exclude the 'ugly', the 'square' and the 'petit bourgeois'. Back then the prerequisite for membership was charisma, beauty, individuality, existential wandering. In line with Taylor's definition of beauty (1991), there is a clear correlation between the notion of 'beauty' and 'authenticity' in the *Mykoniots*' discourse. Following the modern 'aesthetic' project of the self, 'beauty', once de-moralised, becomes an end in itself. This elitist 'predisposition' must have had its roots in various historical and circumstantial elements.[45]

It seems that there is nothing more 'discriminating' than the undeniable effect of 'good looks'. The reputation-code of Mykonos as a tourist *locus* used the most direct classification based on physical capital, one that was 'even' beyond the power of style itself, in order to keep attracting its visitors. The *Mykoniots d'élection* might or might not have had cultural or economic capital, but they surely had this physical one, an asset that helped them survive the exclusive setting. Thus they built an alternative myth of exclusivity in order to sufficiently 'compete' and 'survive' the elitist parameters of the space-image of Mykonos by discursively investing in the group's exemplary 'visions of beauty'. In line with Bourdieu's notion of physical capital, the body peculiarly works (independently of its social parameters in our case) as cultural capital in the form of an aesthetic/ethical embodiment (Shilling 1993: 149n). The *Mykoniots*' myth about an occasionally 'natural' or otherwise 'developed' physical charisma (discourses vary dramatically at this point) is a myth that is created for others to 'consume', and for the self to revalidate his/her 'individuality' through the 'monadic' style of relating to the group. Since there is no other collective principle or ethics, apart from the aesthetics of the 'monadic', *Mykoniots* stress their narcissistic treatment of the body (cf. Lasch 1991). Like an end in itself, like a 'mirroring body', the self reflexively keeps producing her/his own 'superficial desires through consumption' (Shilling] 1993: 96).

In the case of the *Mykoniots d'élection*, physical capital is consciously cultivated through discourse (as I have already shown in the self-narratives of Eleonora and Hercules). The reason for that must be that physical capital, in the cultural context of Mykonos, entails a great deal of symbolic and exchange value both within the open-ended boundaries of the group and the wider social setting of the tourist space. If somebody were eager to push Bourdieu's argument on physical capital beyond the subconscious reproduction of class-based social identities, physical capital could be viewed as a powerful vehicle for developing strategic self-mystifications at multiple levels. In fact, both the 'built-in' and the 'cultivated' cultural capital, once creatively embodied, can easily produce 'counter-naturalised' discourses on aesthetic 'difference', in the same way as the *Mykoniots* have strategically organised discourses about their members' 'physical charisma'. For them, the legendary element that derives from one or the other member's personal beauty or charisma is transformed into a 'shared' aesthetic capital and validates them as an 'elect' group. In crude terms, it justifies their alternative 'distinction' game. If we follow Bourdieu's analysis of the physical capital (1978, 1986, 1993), it is hard to theoretically validate beauty as something other than an arbitrarily accepted 'shaping of the body', similar to sport practices where the self is 'performing' for others to 'gaze at' (Bourdieu 1993: 351). Following, once more, Bourdieu's analysis of the bodily *habitus* of the dominant classes, the body in the *Mykoniots*' discourse seems to be treated similarly as a 'sign of one's own ease' (ibid. 355), except that, in our case, the members of the group of *Mykoniots d'élection* do not necessarily share the same social and cultural backgrounds. This performative 'ease' with the body is especially evident in the *Mykoniots*' discourse. I can characteristically recall the commanding manner that both Eleonora and Artemis used to employ, in order to persuade me to dance in front of an audience so as to successfully 'direct' a carefree self-image for me among the group.

This 'discrimination' code based on purely aesthetic principles is not as prevalent as it used to be. The original synthesis of exclusive aesthetic elements has long since disappeared from the Mykonian setting, but what has survived is the rhetoric. During the eighties there was still an 'inferiority complex' vis-à-vis the space-myth of Mykonos, mostly experienced by Greek visitors. This was due to the image the cosmopolitan island obtained once it had been appropriated by the Greek media which promoted Mykonos as an easily accessible cosmopolitan-space, and eventually turned it into an 'exclusive' sign for internal consumption.[46]

Artemis' image; Artemis' self-narrative

To my mind, Artemis' image, long before I became on intimate terms with her, evoked a plethora of associations. She was the beautiful Artemis, the weird Artemis, the mysterious woman who lived in her remote cell alone with her dogs and cats, and who travelled throughout the island solely on foot.[47] She was also the daring female who overcame her well-bred fate; the naked Artemis of the Greek cult films of the early eighties; her sublime cat-like face photographed arising out of the water in the early artistic stages of Greek advertising. It was also her image dancing with unusual oriental-style movements while ecstatically performing the *tsifteteli* (belly dance) at local *paniyiria*. Then again, there was the image of the spoiled child of the bourgeoisie who refused to reproduce the *habitus* of her 'noble' origin. She would probably fit the category created as a caricature by a Greek fashion magazine of a bohemian Athenian: the pattern was an 'upper-class kid' with a glamorous family past, but quite a decadent present, selling off the family's art collection in order to survive (or buy drugs). It is not unusual for people who have experienced power and exclusivity to have a negative attitude towards material things;[48] in addition, there is a tendency among this group to address all sorts of status seekers with contempt.

Artemis follows the above pattern. She left all her family advantages behind, neglected professional and personal ambitions and lived modestly on Mykonos. Artemis belongs to a wider group of female friends of a more or less similar social background who have also 'migrated' to Mykonos. Before I even knew them personally, I had already heard about them: the group's nickname among the *Mykoniots* was *oi magisses* (the sorceresses).[49]

I remember the first time Artemis approached me. She was aggressive and cynical but yet she had her own seductive way. She took a place near me at the bar and expressed herself forthrightly. She told me that I was too beautiful to feel isolated and tense in this place and that I had to enjoy myself as well as show others that I did so. She also proposed that I should flirt a lot and enjoy my femininity: 'What is to become of you if you start your mature career as a woman by being so analytical and thoughtful? There will still be time for you to concentrate on your intellectual enquiries. It is about time to change that, otherwise, in a couple of years you will be really lonely.' Obviously she was projecting something of herself onto me, I thought then. I protected myself, I did not want to open myself up to her; she was too rough, too direct. Yet, there was something attractive in her abrupt sincerity. While I was thinking all this, Artemis started talking about her 'lifer' husband and his recent book on drugs that I happened to have read thoroughly. He had been accused of smuggling a couple of kilos of cocaine and had received a life sentence. This publication obviously made things worse: he was transferred to Corfu, the prison with the worst reputation in Greece. In his book, which is concerned with global drug politics, he mainly decries the addictive nature of Western society, blaming that rather than the substances themselves.

The second time I met Artemis, she was collecting signatures from her *Mykoniot* friends at the beach in order to protest on behalf of a local woman, named Zambelo (her name in the local dialect literally means: she who loves the animals) who had lost her supervision of the small church she had taken personal care of for many years. Zambelo was one of the picturesque characters of the island but she was considered more or less insane by the local community due to her obsession with animals. On this occasion she lost 'her' church because she let her dog give birth inside it, an act that was considered sacrilege.[50] Artemis loved Zambelo because she was like herself. She lived alone in a humble house. Outside, in her tiny courtyard, Zambelo took care of a crew of dogs and cats.

Artemis was the kind of person who could be invisible for weeks and reappear again all of a sudden with a large appetite for *kefi* (high spirits) and dope; once she achieved the 'high' that pleased her, she changed from a wildcat into an approachable creature. Every time Artemis appeared in the town's *stekia* (haunts) or at the beach where her friends used to hang about, she could not help but go beyond her limits. When the party was over, she would regret it and so disappear for some time, to lose herself in her reading and privacy.

I became on close terms with her in late autumn, nearly a year after I was initiated into the group's *habitus* and had somehow established my anthropological persona. It was only then that I managed to spend a couple of weeks socialising with her on a daily basis. Artemis was one of the rare examples among the *Mykoniots* who accepted my anthropological self. We spent most of our time indoors, talking, in her beautiful and remote miniature house, known as Artemis' *kellaki* (cell). Artemis was a different person inside her *kellaki*. She loved to read me drafts of the novel that she had been writing for the last four years or so. In her attempts to explain to me what special subject concerned her in her writing, she kept mentioning the philosophical theme of duality that arose from her two main female protagonists.

Artemis drew her novel characters mainly from mythology. The two main 'archetypal' female characters she employed were the beautiful Helen of Troy, and Mary Magdalene. The core male figure was Dionysos, the god of wine and sexual liberty, and a symbol of a male predator who seduces his victims, drawing them into an uncontrollable state of drunkenness and hedonism. The text was autobiographical and clever. The representation of the archetypal characters in modern circumstances was also realistic in terms of their experiences. In-between her readings to me, she loved to veer off into accounts of her own personal history. She spoke to me about the dynastic personality of her mother and of some of her girlfriends, their strong antagonisms and the strange men in her life. Then all of a sudden, after her confessions, Artemis liked to switch the topic and treat me to an endless flow of disjointed intellectual reflections. Artemis had read a lot. But she was especially taken with the beatnik movement, the anti-psychiatrists, the symbolic psychology of Carl Jung and the work of Eliade and Nietzsche. The archetypal characters of Jung had been of great help in her own analysis of the unconscious, and the idiosyncratic relationship she had with her past and her personal ghosts.

Artemis' *kellaki* was built without any real plan by an old Mykonian builder, *Mastro*-Michalis (i.e., master craftsman Michalis), who was also a friend of Artemis. The older Mykonians loved Artemis because she always paid a lot of attention to them. *Mastro*-Michalis built Artemis' *kellaki* in the traditional way. 'You could not find a simple right angle anywhere' as Artemis said. While stylistically this was intended to follow the local architecture, it did not seem pretentious at all. A predominant feature of the interior was a raised traditional fireplace that kept her warm, a place where she could also cook. The *kellaki* was built of thick walls and had tiny windows to keep the heat and the damp out. It was decorated with antique mirrors in elaborate wooden frames, disproportionately large for the size of her *kellaki*, old pieces that Artemis had 'stolen', as she remarked, from her grandfather's haute couture showroom (or rather from what remained of it). She had also inherited an antique desk that she made her writing table. Apart from these antiques and two art deco chairs where her dogs used to sit, the rest of the 'consumption-repertoire' of the interior consisted of some unglamorous Indian and Latin American curios and some weird pieces of handicraft that she herself had made in the past. Actually, what was left of the tiny space was occupied by Artemis' animals and books.

Artemis' daily routine was to take care of her animals, first. She then sorted out what there was left to cook for her. She lived on a minimum of food. She also lived on a minimum of money. It was not rare for Artemis to forget to feed herself. She was very peculiar in her consuming needs. She didn't ask for much. Sometimes she was happy with just some tobacco, or with just a lift to the local veterinarian. She would be always happy with a joint, though. The fact that her writing table had to have another mirror for her to look at while writing, made me curious. The reality was that Artemis did nothing to preserve her legendary beauty. She hardly looked after herself. Nevertheless, she had installed that mirror, 'the symbol of the narcissist', as she said, in front of her while writing. I asked her how she managed to write in front of a mirror since I found it impossible; she replied that mirrors had been her natural environment since she grew up in her grandfather's haute couture house. 'I had to live with all these huge mirrors and so I learned to act narcissistically, with self-awareness.' She admitted that back then she learned to be very much concerned with her beauty. While she was explaining all this to me she was facing her table mirror, instead of facing me. She leaned closer towards the mirror and brought her face very close. She detected her skin imperfections but still with self-admiration. 'I suffer from early narcissism,' she commented. 'Wilhelm Reich talked about that stage. Everything revolves so much around one's self, that the other cannot be seen. Therefore there is no communication, no relationship, only self-satisfaction.' Artemis studied dance and pantomime and that made her even more comfortable with herself and her body. Frequently, while she was talking to me, she kept staring at her image in the mirror; that made her even more confident.

What struck me about her novel, when I came to know her a little better, was that she presented her personal psychological dilemma right at the beginning. The narration starts with a strong scene of a very dangerous delivery experienced by the mother of the two 'archetypal' daughters, Helen and Mary Magdalene. Their mother fails to have an *hystero* (afterbirth). The whole story with the *hystero*, Artemis explains, is metaphorical since *hystero* linguistically shares the same roots with *hysteria*. The symbolic coming into being of the two daughters, the twins, has to be completed with the help of morphine. And this is crucial for the rest of the lives of the two daughters. Artemis explained to me that her core preoccupation with the twins, the two archetypal females, has to do with her own psychological split, between her intellectual self and her narcissist self; two aspects of her inner self in constant disagreement. She was clear that her novel was partly the story of her life. Artemis was very straightforward about her life story. Actually, she was very psychoanalytic about it. She had analyst friends and she had spent many years in self-analysis, as well as in amateur group analysis with her female friends. Nevertheless, she did not at all believe in the magical dissolving of personal problems by any means. Artemis realised and accepted what was happening to her and why. But she had no plans beyond this to improve herself.

She would speak openly to me about the persistent signs she received from her unconscious. She realised that they had their own course through the years. She told me about her dreams. There was that continuous nightmare that she had had as a child: a row of cockerels with red necks being slaughtered. The distressing feeling aroused by the cock being slaughtered returned later on in her life when she saw the cock of a flasher. She rediscovered the same feeling when she participated in a ritual she accidentally attended in Brazil with her husband.

Artemis was shockingly open about her personal libidinal details. She had no taboos. Artemis, being totally conscious of her own reality, explained all these details with reference to her personal story. She told me she had felt obliged to follow the sexual liberation movement since she had thought it important at the time to discover her orgasm. She ended up sleeping with a hundred men over a period of six months with no results. She did everything that the freedom 'movement' demanded. In New York she even attempted to get paid by a stranger. She described all this with a sense of irony. But these were the facts of her life. And she felt obliged to give to me what I was asking for: her life story. Finally, she said, she tested her orgasm with a transvestite. And later with the 'old man' (who was later her husband, subsequently sentenced to life for drug smuggling).

Artemis maintained that her mother had had an uneasy relationship with her father. The mother was the 'macho' type in the family instead of the father. In her thirties she became an alcoholic, but she kept her position as the over-dominant figure of the house. Artemis was the only child in the family. 'I can remember myself trying to cope with my constant agony. It was my mother's absence,' she explained to me. Artemis' mother left her in the care of her grandparents the moment she was born. For the first five years of Artemis' life her mother went to live with Artemis' father in Paris. Later, when Artemis was old enough, she also went to live in Paris in order to study dance. At the time, it was the late sixties, she socialised with the young members of the Greek bourgeoisie who had joined the fashionable post-Marxist intelligentsia. So Artemis had a strong intellectual influence from the 'Poulantzas group', as she called it, with reference to her then intellectual boyfriend. But she failed to succeed as a dancer; she was already too old she said. She changed her studies, she took pantomime instead. Once more, she had no real success. She returned to Athens and took over the family business since she was the only one left to do so. She blew it all. A one-way ticket to India was her next step. After taking a year off, she thought of Mykonos as the only place in Greece she could live. All these years she had been a frequent visitor to the island. She initially came as a member of the 'respected' Athenian community that used to visit the island. Later on she switched to the *hippie* group that had slowly started gathering there. At some point, her notion of a Mykonos home was realised. She sold her grandmother's house and bought a big piece of land in a remote and underdeveloped part of the island.

She told me that she used to have a car when she was younger but once she crashed it into a dry stone wall on the island. She never thought of buying another car. Artemis frequently preaches about the beneficial properties of walking: 'Well, at least, it makes me think,' she says.

I would not suggest that Artemis never complained about her loneliness. But when I asked her about it she claimed: 'As I am getting older, I need my privacy, especially after all the partying and all the communes I've been involved in.' She mentioned all the 'unsettled' friends that she used to live with. 'Now it's different,' she said, 'after a few days of the familiar intimacy, we start quarrelling.'

Every winter, Artemis has to return to her teenage room in the family house for a couple of months or so since her *kellaki* is cold and very isolated, and thus unsuitable for the heavy Mykonian winter. She talks with repulsion about those months of compromise but as she stresses: 'there is nowhere else to go really, since I've got the animals.' Artemis is already forty-three. Her best choice is to live alone in the semi-primitive conditions of her Mykonian *kellaki*. The house has no electricity supply and Artemis has done nothing more than to dig a well some years ago. Her *kellaki* may have no real facilities (she actually avoids obtaining them) but it is located safely away from her family and the conventions of the old and ruined bourgeoisie. By observing herself in the mirror, Artemis keeps stressing that she feels relieved to be getting old and ugly.

One evening, although we had arranged to repeat our reading sessions, we found ourselves attending a local ritual instead. Some of our *Mykoniot* friends, had gathered earlier in the morning in a nearby Mykonian *horio* (traditional self-sustaining household) to film the ritual of the *hoirosfayia*, the slaughtering of the pigs.[51] The courtyard of Jimmy's home whose family organised the traditional post-slaughter feast, had already been transformed from the site of an informal gathering to a spontaneous *paniyiri* (feast).[52] This was probably because Jimmy was no ordinary local. He was one of the prominent figures of the local 'mafia', one of the last remaining local legends of drunkenness and a member of the *sinafi* of the 'pirates'. Jimmy's *hoirosfayia* was by no means celebrated in any ordinary way. It follows that all the 'tough' guys and their admirers were around that evening. I tried to attend the morning ritual myself, but my male *Mykoniot* friends refused to take me with them. They said it would be 'tough'. When I entered the courtyard, I went to sit near some friends who had arrived earlier for the filming. They were extremely drunk. They had had to follow the lead of their younger Mykonian friends who had prepared by an all-night drinking session the night before the slaughter. One of them was Jimmy's son, and he was the excuse for our *Mykoniot* friends gaining access to the ritual.

By the time Artemis and I arrived, they had completed a night and a day drinking and working. The rest of their table companions were pretty much unknown to me, but were all extremely drunk. There were also many joints travelling from hand to hand. The women of the household were invisible and I soon realised I was surrounded by a lot of men. The only females around were Artemis, myself and two other foreign women, one Dutch and one German, accompanied by their boyfriends. Although the cold was really intense, nobody seemed to bother or to make a move. The participants in Jimmy's spontaneous feast had made an improvised fire inside a barrel. It was the first time and maybe the last in my fieldwork that I felt threatened (as a woman). Members of Jimmy's family, as well as friends, had prepared the seasonal *souma*, a tasty but 'dangerous' local grape-based spirit, suitable for the winter. The guests must have consumed huge quantities of Jimmy's famous drink. That night, I heard many nasty propositions directed at me. Needless to say, the situation left me no space for sober socialising. I was struck though by Artemis' attitude. She kept staring at the drunken Mykonians aggressively. She was so wild that she was provocative. She sat together with a couple of harmless alcoholic friends of hers and got involved in a peculiar kind of gossip or rather a paranoid conversation with them. Artemis felt at home. She introduced me to her friends, but she soon forgot all about me. I kept close to some other people I knew. I felt really hesitant to go near the fire where all the local males were gathered. I turned to Artemis again, she was absorbed in her loud conversation with Manolis. She was cheerfully trying to extract some memories from him concerning another local female friend of hers named Maroulina. Maroulina lived in seclusion on a hill near Artemis' land and was considered insane by the locals. She lived outdoors all year round, together with her goats. Artemis was one of Maroulina's rare human friends.

When I decided to leave, I saw Artemis had moved inside, so that she was now more comfortable to talk and drink all night long. She was among friends.

I went back to visit her the next day. The first thing she said when she saw me was: 'Wild, wasn't it?' Even the question felt satisfying to her. Then she continued: 'They all wanted to fuck every single one of us.' Artemis felt a serious bonding with any instance of subcultural behaviour. Moreover, she herself felt part of the Mykonian subculture. She liked the drinking commensality and without realising it, she shared the discourse of these local boozers. What was also striking, though, was that Artemis did not feel threatened by them. Instead she acted like a counter-patron to the 'wild' ritual.

We started that evening's session with Albert Camus. Inspired by Camus' heroes, Artemis proposed that she herself was a rebel of a 'romantic' type. 'It is a rather narcissistic type' she said, 'who admits the forbidden, while agreeing with society that not everything can be accepted.' There was also another type of rebel in Artemis' classification. It was the Nietzschian type, the 'nihilist' rebel, the one that she could not afford to be, but still the one that she most absolutely admired. 'It is the logic of a rebellion that will eventually turn against itself.' Artemis was already carried away by her tortured duality. Since rebellion was the favourite topic of her life, she continued with fervour: 'Self-destruction. Everything is allowed, everything is destroyed in order to recreate itself after death.' 'But what about our reckless anti-hero friends,' I asked, referring to the whole 'drug subculture' that dominated the *Mykoniots*' lifestyle. 'What about their self-destruction?' She replied: 'It's out of cowardliness that one begins to act in reckless terms. The junkie, for example, usually has an unresolved Oedipus complex vis-à-vis the mother. What results: a person with a weak will, someone who is subordinated and repressed by the cruel mother who subconsciously wants to take revenge. There is one good way of achieving it: simply by scaring her. Taking revenge by harming only himself, self-destruction. In a sense, that's the junkie's rebellion against the system, the society, or the family.'

Artemis was indirectly addressing the story of many of her dear friends who had ended up junkies.[53] She was actually talking about her own generation and how she experienced the 'junkie' decade of her life. She automatically switched to her own relationship with *preza* (heroin):

> Me, I got into *preza* because I wanted to lose weight! Many girls I know started like that. Food is *preza*, too. In 1976, the rebellion of the *polytechnio*[54] was over. Then *preza* comes. A new revolution arises. It was the rebellion of *preza*. *Preza* in a sense was one way to protest against the same establishment that reinvented itself via the new 'democratic' forces. In Mykonos, *preza* came quickly, since here everything was allowed; the decadent image of Morrison, the hipster movement, all of that was passing through. Mykonos was 'on the road'. In Athens, I had no idea what Rajasthan meant. But Mykonos was a progressive place; people kept coming and going from New York, from Bali, from India.

Artemis got involved in the Athenian drug scene of the late seventies and she played the 'junkie game' almost all the way. In a sense she was 'acting out' the junkie when she joined her working-class junkie friends who broke into pharmacies (*boukes*, burglaries); in reality, they were doing the job while Artemis just offered them the family car and the facility to bury the '*stuff* in her mother's garden. 'I did all that in order to gain their approval,' she concluded. Later on in her life, Artemis meets her 'old man'. He was a cocaine dealer with attitude. A 'junkie' with a strong ideology.

When she met the 'old man' her life changed. She used to read Leary, Laing and Cooper and the whole company of the 'anti-psychiatrists' but all that was just 'Harvard laboratory experiments,' as Artemis said. With the 'old man' the taste for the 'forbidden' experience begins to materialise. 'The anti-psychiatrists had reached their insights after entering the reality of Indian metaphysics by actually travelling there. But reading about them and experiencing the trip yourself were different things.' Her acquaintance with the 'old man' began a fascinating period in her life. She was absolutely charmed by him. She followed him everywhere.

They travelled a lot in Latin America. Her occasional references to snapshots of their 'dealing trips' sounded like good quality ethnographic data.

At this point I want to make something clear: although Artemis could have become a helpless junkie, she never really allowed herself to turn into one. She told me, though, about others who did. She told me the story of Elli, another daughter of the 'upper classes' who, because of her junkie habit, played the role of the prostitute for real. And the story of several other 'lost' causes: friends who either ended up insane or as organisers of groups like Narcotics Anonymous.

Artemis used to be a casual heroin user but not a junkie. She said that she avoided using a '*fix*' in order to get high, and maybe that helped. 'These days, I am not at all interested in this *stuff*'. But she admits to being 'incurably' in love with hashish: 'It helps me write. But it's a hassle to go out and find it.' In this sense, her rhetoric about heroin consumption, and in particular about *preza*'s addictive power is quite distinct from a mainstream point of view. Her opinion about *preza* might not be as radical as that which one could find among urban Greek junkies.[55] This is important, since her rhetoric about drugs is very much a shared rhetoric among the *Mykoniots* who strongly maintain that the addictive potential of a substance is something highly relative, and has nothing whatsoever to do with the pharmacology of the substance itself. *Mykoniots*' rhetoric about *preza* goes that 'for them' it was just a period of their lives that they enjoyed, maybe got a little stuck with it, but finally left it behind without much help. Their 'different' attitude towards the 'addictive' power of *preza* is an additional element in the *Mykoniots*' game of distinction.

Nevertheless, *Mykoniots* themselves, maybe without realising it, also generalise and jeopardise their own discourse of 'difference': they often refer to a '*junkie mentality*', a negative behaviour whose roots lie in the abuse of certain substances. Members of the group are usually accused of suffering from this attitude that results in indifference. The '*junkie mentality*' is characterised by an intense compulsion-cum-superstition and a highly inconsistent attitude.

The only inconsistency that I can detect on the part of the *Mykoniots* is the attitude they reserve for one another. On the one hand, they have a grandiose rhetoric of brotherhood and a boundless commensality; on the other, they may come up with an altogether opposite and very individualistic discourse. Conspiracy theories and suspicion are not rare in the interpersonal relations of the *Mykoniots*.

I think that the above mentality is exemplified in Artemis' characterisation of her *Mykoniot* group: 'Them,[56] I consider them my close relatives, I love them as such; but I have no close relations since they consider me a crazy woman. They never help me out with my work, they never ask if I want anything or read my drafts like you did. They are the kind of people who get stuck into a certain persona. They remind me of the myth of Deianeira's dress; the dress she was wearing stuck to her; when she took it off she had to peel her skin off too.' Artemis, in other words, saw her *Mykoniot* colleagues as performers who get stuck in a role play and cannot shake it off. But when they manage to free themselves, they are completely transformed.

One morning, Artemis and I were sitting in her courtyard to enjoy some of the last sunny spells of the autumn. We were chatting, or rather Artemis did the talking and I did the questioning as usual, when the so-called 'moonstruck' Maroulina appeared, walking down the nearby hill. After a while, she entered Artemis' land and followed by Artemis' dogs she approached us. When she saw me she was quite reluctant to proceed. Artemis tried to overcome her hesitation, but Maroulina insisted that she did not want to disturb us and that she only came to give her a pair of knitted socks as a present for the coming winter. Artemis happily reciprocated with all the food supplies she had in her *kellaki*. After a very speedy dialogue between them Maroulina left. Artemis loved Maroulina and must have been among the few people on the island that Maroulina communicated with at any length.

Artemis had many local friends and it was not by chance that many of the 'barmy' people loved Artemis. She took care of them but most important of all she listened to them. Artemis went on by telling me the story of this woman. In a sense when she was talking about her 'insane' local friends Artemis felt as if she was talking about her own community. Artemis' symbolic discourse of belonging went beyond the limits of locality: 'Maroulina used to be the first girl of her rank in the village of Ano Mera since she was tall and beautiful and also the best embroiderer,' she narrated. But something must have happened to Maroulina, the best embroiderer, who could have had the best man in the village but chose to renounce the world instead. She decided to live alone in the countryside. The only thing she wanted to do was to take care of her cattle. Eventually she abandoned her relationship with her family since they strongly disapproved of her disrespectful attitude. 'And mind you, Maroulina could have been a rich woman if she was a bit more sociable. She could sell her huge property and live like the rich Mykonians.'

I was puzzled by Artemis' affinity with Maroulina and Zambelo and *Mastro-Michalis*, but equally I was puzzled by her affinity with Helen of Troy, with Mary Magdalene and her girlfriends, the 'sorceresses'. Artemis could genuinely identify with people without paying any attention to their social and cultural classification. I don't think one could classify her easily according to her lifestyle.

Artemis promised Maroulina that she would find somebody to drive her yearly share of maize from the harbour to her shelter. She made that enquiry her project for the day but we both knew that she was clearly misleading Maroulina. None of her *Mykoniot* friends would ever bother to help Maroulina and certainly not as part of a project planned in advance.

That day we ended up visiting several friends' houses. Artemis' cooperation with my anthropological enquiries had increased significantly. Finally, we found ourselves in the house of a *Mykoniot* friend who was himself absent. I switched on the tape recorder for the first time and continued our discussion. In the meanwhile another friend showed up from Athens. He had just returned from India. He treated Artemis and her 'sorceress' girlfriend who appeared at the same time to some pure Indian opium. I myself only realised what had happened later on when we decided to play cards and the attempt was completely unsuccessful. Everything slowly turned into a toneless rhythm, faces went pale and contact between us was marginal: winter on Mykonos, playing cards and smoking opium.

The next day we continued on the subject of heroin and she explained to me the male eagerness to sniff *preza*: 'It's beneficial during intercourse; it helps the *kokorakia* [literally meaning the 'pricks', and metaphorically the boys who play macho but climax easily] last longer.' She then jumped to another topic and talked about the 'old man'. She mentioned something about their travelling period and then she started describing the parody of their 'engagement' ritual. She was dead stoned on heroin; the family had opened a very old barrel of strong wine for the occasion. She drank excessively. Her mother, who disapproved of the 'old man', discreetly tried to prevent Artemis' grandmother from handing her granddaughter a valuable family ring. Next morning Artemis woke up with hepatitis. A little while later she got married in a red peasant dress she had herself bought from Latin America. She married the 'old man' who was already in his sixties only in order to have the right to sell the property allocated to her as her 'dowry'. She continued to travel a lot with the 'old man', and alone.

Lately, Artemis has tired of travelling; she actually lives on very little money. She does not particularly like working and maybe she never really needed to. Back in the eighties, she earned her living for some time by making bags and selling them on Mykonos. She also dealt in old furniture. Now, she is happy reading Greek mythology and indulging herself in the divination method, using the tarot cards of the magus Aleister Crowley.[57] Artemis falls in love passionately and gets seduced by the occasional men in her life. But she always remains incompatible with other people. She has always felt obliged to follow the lifestyle of the men she was involved with. She keeps her title as a 'married' woman, but in reality she never managed to escape her mother, who is still completely identified with her daughter, as Artemis points out. She explains that her mother was from a lower-class background, but as she was ambitious she married her father. 'They have tasted some glamour together during the fifties and sixties. Now they are selling things in order to live properly. They hate working.' Her mother drinks beer and her father does the housework. The mother is currently pressing her daughter at least to divorce her dealer husband, now that he has been sentenced to life. The 'old man', on the other hand, presses his wife to complete her novel.

Artemis' theory about herself is that she is an unsuccessful rebel. She is and has always been a romantic. Once she explained to me the symbolic mapping of the town of Mykonos. 'Everything was divided by the statue of the local hero, Manto. There were those who hung about on the far side of the statue of Manto, and those who would never go beyond it.' Shields justifies the functionality of the 'differences within' his organising notion of spatialisation as follows: 'Space-myths

– aligned and opposed, reinforcing or mutually contradictory – form a mythology or formation of positions which polarises and dichotomises different places and spaces. Place- and space-myths are united into a system by their relative differences from one another even while they achieve their unique identities by being 'set-off' against one another. Even if split by inconsistencies and in continual flux, this formation works as a cosmology' (Shields 1991: 62). Artemis' polarisation of the Mykonian space is subjectively charged and reveals an alternative, 'emotionally powerful' and culturally informed counter-geography. Artemis first visited the island with the Athenian socialites who used to go beyond the statue. She then switched to the hippies who used to and still do avoid the nightspots beyond the statue. Then she switched to the mythological creatures of nearby Delos. Then she switched to the local Zambelo. And then she went further in, closer to the 'insane' Maroulina. But all the fragments of her life that torment her are here. Her rambling is there, reflected on the mapping of this tourist town. Every fragment of the mirror is there to be gazed into.

I will conclude my presentation about Artemis by quoting a piece of her inspired raving that, I think, displays all the existential angst about her fragmentary female self that she suffers so guiltily:

> The intellectuals treated me as a mere smart-setter with no further insight; the smart-setters on the other hand, treated me as a bohemian; while the bohemians treated me as an arrogant snob. But for all of them I was just a *bimbo*. I, myself, kept insisting on pointing out my intellectual abilities rather than my good looks. Today all of them say I am a loony; but at least I speak up in my own voice. Back then I was mute.

Narratives of the self: the self-image of Angelos

From Zorba to Buddha

The following autobiographical confession was made accidentally. The setting was a sixties house in the centre of Athens, a two-storey building that included an old-fashioned wine shop. I frequented this house in the intervals between my fieldwork, since Eurydice, whose parents owned it, was my close friend and another member of the *Mykoniots' sinafi* who helped me tremendously throughout the fieldwork. Eurydice frequently invited friends along when visiting her family home. The situation within Eurydice's house was 'untypical'; or at least, it was not at all consistent with 'my cultural preconception' of how a 'Greek' family home was organised. The atmosphere was easy-going, not 'conservative' at all; the mother, in her sixties, was a rather otherworldly figure who enjoyed the presence of visiting strangers.

I felt a peculiar sense of being in a commune when visiting this house, as opposed to being in a 'traditional' Greek household where the boundaries of belonging and not belonging are clear-cut, and the roles within it appear to be clearly allocated. The four offspring of the family, 'grown-ups' for some time, were still around; occasionally living there, or stopping over, or simply working in the family wine business. Eurydice herself was travelling back and forth a lot, occasionally bringing along her friends, offering them accommodation and thus extending her own communal lifestyle and transplanting it in the informal lifestyle of her own family. All this coming and going happened spontaneously, and it felt as if it caused no real disruption to the daily rhythm of the household. I can recall several occasions when Eurydice and I would happen to visit Athens and, apropos her family home.

Our arrival, although unexpected, was treated casually. In return for this casual attitude, guests, who felt immediately 'incorporated', would eventually reciprocate. Some of the friends would help by selling wine or getting involved in the family's obsessive preoccupation with planning the maintenance and renovation of the family property, while others would equally casually indulge in doing nothing. The 'idiosyncratic' accommodation offered by Eurydice's family included no further obligations, apart from a required sensitivity to their internal code of a relaxed and unconcerned sharing. There was a single bunch of keys for accessing the several entrances into the shop-cum-house. The fact that keys had to be shared had little effect on the otherwise flexible routine of its inhabitants: one would wake up early in the afternoon, while another would go for a siesta at the same time.

It was early in the evening, when my friend Eurydice arrived with Angelos; she had run into him, she said, at the flea market. She had agreed to let him stay in the house, as she explained later. Gradually, over a couple of days, Angelos moved in with all his belongings. He settled in with great care, chose the 'right' bed, cleaned the room he preferred, placed Bhagwan's picture on his bedside table together with a vase of fresh flowers, and probably burned some incense, too. Nevertheless, he looked very weak and nervous. His blurred junkie glaze kept scanning the space surrounding him impatiently. His talk was gibberish. An intense anxiety was apparent in his sad laughter. He kept changing his mind constantly, often becoming unjustifiably aggressive. He was carrying the merchandise he had acquired during his latest trip to India: a huge bag full of Indian silks, *sarongs*, cushion covers. He was trying to '*push the stuff*' as he put it directly. Once a day, usually in the afternoon, he would leave his room, come down to the wine shop where a telephone was available, and open his huge filofax that contained a long list of 'glamorous' contacts and friends, in an attempt to arrange appointments that he would then either drop or postpone. Angelos, at that point, had the symptoms of what my junkie friends called *paranoia tou asprou*. This expression literally translates as: the paranoia of the 'white stuff';[58] what this describes is a highly compulsive behaviour on behalf of the junkie who likewise disguises his fears or rather his existential anxieties. I gradually figured out that he must have been using a lot of *preza* (heroin) lately, and had now decided to begin a period of abstinence. Eurydice's family home provided a familiar, commune-like situation that allowed Angelos to be optimistic about his efforts. Entering an '*off*' (the abstinence period), during the first few nights, gave him no sleep. It also made him eat very little. Angelos would put himself through this trial quite often; it was certainly not the first time. Although he was in his early forties, Angelos had a baby face and looked very attractive. The rumour had it that he had been an extremely good-looking man.

After the fourth night of abstinence, I woke up and saw Angelos painting the walls of the empty apartment next door. He was still at the stage of trying to regain his good humour, but his *harmana* (craving due to abstinence) was no longer irresistible. He worked non-stop for a couple of hours and then paused only in order to make a funny remark: 'Together with my working-class consciousness, I might also regain the desire to fuck.'[59] The picture of Angelos, perched on the ladder, made me realise that he was back in the world 'with the rest of us'. He did not actually give up painting until he finished the whole living room. This made both Eurydice and I simultaneously think the same thing: that he was happily getting intoxicated from the paint.

The Cyclothymic Angelos

During the next few days, Angelos kept changing his mind all the time. He said he wanted to write a novel. Then he suddenly decided he wanted to go back to Ithaca, his place of origin, for some family warmth and comfort. But later on, he even considered following his occasional 'drug' mate for some new adventures: finding the money, getting stood up, getting frustrated, eventually *'getting high'*, then again frustrated, at some point deciding to abstain and so on. Ultimately, he said he wanted to return to Mykonos. But within five minutes he would be alarmed again and cancel all other alternative plans so that he could *'push'* the Indian goodies in Athens. While in this very inconsistent state, happily for its owners, he ended up painting the two-bedroomed flat next door.

At that point he had obviously shifted to a very talkative stage. He started going out with us. I wanted to know more about his relationship with Mykonos. His replies were erratic or, rather, I was still unfamiliar with the *Mykoniots'* discourse and could not interpret it. Among the many things he said about Mykonos was the following phrase: 'The charms of this place attract the appropriate people who inevitably get into its illusive *trip*.'

I first met Angelos in Mykonos about nine years ago. What struck me about him at the time was the fact that he was part of an idiosyncratic group or, rather, a romantic triangle, which included another man and a woman, called Dimitris and Eleni. Dimitris and Eleni had been married for many years and had a son. They were neither effectively nor officially divorced but they were used to 'living apart' some of the time. Now, Angelos and Eleni were a couple. Eleni herself, a strong and radiant personality was the main reason for Angelos' involvement with Bhagwan. The three of them were living and working together at that time and divided their lives between Poona (Bhagwan's ashram in India) and Mykonos.

At some point they attempted to run a winter business in Athens, but as another *Mykoniot* friend put it, its 'junkie' customers ruined its chances of success.

During his student years, Angelos was a hard-line member of the mainstream Communist Party. His years of political awareness set him apart from the rest of the *Mykoniots*, who were primarily apolitical. Angelos used to be a university student, studying physics, but he dropped out. He eventually became obsessed with the idea of not belonging anywhere. His favourite line was: 'Everybody looks for a network to get into the game, but *we* [he constantly used this mysterious plural] always try to be *xekarfotoi* [never being on the spot; for instance, by never repeatedly exercising a recognised social identity].' For Angelos, life was a chain of alternating 'highs', different experiences, further 'communes'. A shift from the 'high' of love to the 'high' of heroin and the 'high' of fresh paint, abstinence and creativity. As I saw it, his life story was all about this game of shifting his own identity; a shift from the ideological communes of the highly politicised groups of the seventies (Marxist-style) to the brotherhood of the first urban junkies. Eventually, a slick synchronistic shift from the worldly retreat of Mykonos to Bhagwan's spiritual commune and so on.

Angelos' relentless monologue

It was almost the beginning of my fieldwork and I was too shy to talk about it or ask for anything. Eurydice took the situation into her own hands and set Angelos to help. So, it all happened more or less spontaneously. During the intervals of his painting therapy, Angelos provided me with fragments of his past; the bits and pieces from his memories had no chronological order, but it is important to note that his consciously erratic but structured autobiographical narration, boiled down to easily identifiable and discrete periods of his life. This inconsistent style of narration nevertheless reflected Angelos' ideological constancy throughout his well-articulated representations of his otherwise aesthetically 'diverse' lifestyles. His account started with a description of the manifestos of his politically active student period:

> For me, university life meant only political assemblies. But none of them has ever dared to say that the key issue was the demolition of the family.[60] This is why I turned to Bhagwan. I was a survivor since I turned seventeen. I wanted to break the family ties.

During his student years in Thessaloniki, Angelos was involved in hard, manual labour; but, according to Eurydice's reconstruction of the past, he was the kind of guy who would easily spend a week's wages by offering food and drinks to a random company of 'friends' on a night out. Angelos also had another 'bad' habit; he liked to play cards with his 'other' friends, and this led to his expulsion from the Communist Party. It was not considered ideologically consistent to be simultaneously a left-winger and a gambler. At that point the 'real' lumpenproletariat in him managed to 'overshadow' his loyalty to the party line. Angelos had the following to say about this period of his life:

> Indeed *we* had our sexual revolution but *they* [the politically correct] were enormously repressed in terms of their sexual desires. When I first read *Listen, Little Man* [by W. Reich 1948], I got the message. Their dream was after all to turn us into a petit bourgeoisie. We turned our backs on the sort of hypocrisy that wanted the urban elite lecturing on the working class. We made a turn towards authenticity; we were the first to get away from class analysis and get into individuality. At that time, the first bars opened in town, and they were playing jazz ...

Angelos must have been talking about the late seventies here. By then, he was already involved in the 'subculture' of Thessaloniki which was evolving around a developing local rock scene and the emergence of a bar culture which was later related to the space-myth of the town. This bar culture eventually acquired a reputation of being 'underground' and 'progressive' according to its aesthetic prototype which was said to be the ambience of the bars in Berlin.[61] Angelos himself was involved in the consumption of illegal substances with its relevant ideologies well before heroin was mass consumed, but his serious 'drug period' must have started in the early eighties. Angelos, considering this period of his life important, continued his rambling by commenting on drugs:

> A huge trap. I had no idea what heroin could do. Heroin, as an anaesthetic, was the remedy for the *evaisthitoi* [the sensitive].[62] It turned you from 'sensitive' to senseless. The real hypocrites at that time were the so-called communists, the idealists. I am still a real communist. That's because I am forty years old and I have nothing of my own. I have no possessions. I do not have *my* child or *my* little car.

At this point he makes a vague reference to the right-wingers being more authentic in their drive to acquire wealth. Then he continues:

> The esoteric trip had begun. Moving downwards from the head to the heart. Whoever followed [this path], would eventually end up in India. I got the message from them. A different infrastructure from ours but they were still searching for the same thing. Drugs were also part of it. One was just experiencing. Taking them [the drugs] inwards. They were searching for the same thing but through a different way. Once you stick to a certain ideology, a certain background, you can never be a drug addict. This is the reason why there are nowadays 'young' and yet already 'dead' junkies. I had put myself in danger. I am the kind of person that they would like to lock up in a prison. But it is also your karma, you see. This is why I haven't been [staying] in Mykonos for the last three years.[63]

Angelos' family lives in Ithaca. His father comes from a left-wing family; a fanatic, who had been exiled in the past, he is now a tailor. His mother comes from a bourgeois background. She eloped (*kleftike*) with Angelos' father and was disinherited by her own family. Angelos describes her as a thoroughly 'lazy' woman: 'she hardly ever cooks a plate of food,' he says, and adds that she lived to regret her decision to marry his father. He remembers with nostalgia the first seven years of his life: he lived in his father's village with his four uncles, three of them left-wing, the other right-wing. He was much closer to his right-wing uncle because the latter was an open-hearted alcoholic. He continues with a narration of what he calls the 'psychiatric period' of his childhood:

> After I was seven we went to live in the town, near my mother's relatives. The house was close to a mental home. Every Saturday, I used to go to the movies with the patients. My only hobby was playing football. My charmless stage started. Up to that moment I had been living in the countryside with no fears. The period in the city is when I entered the petit bourgeois prototype. My act of resistance was to play football and my family's only problem was that my shoes used to wear out ... I then entered a new phase of my life where sexual desire awakened. I went on holidays to a small island with a female cousin. I was eleven years old. I fell in love with a young girl. By discovering love I forgot football. Falling in love was much more hedonistic. My cousin's breasts matured in my hands. This is how I first experienced lack of fulfilment. I joined the Ithaca football team but I was short and delicate. At some point, innocence was gone. My cousin had a schoolmate with whom we started kissing and not with my cousin. She was jealous. During the *preza* [heroin] period I had a lot of gaps in my memory. I lived for three months with a girlfriend, but there is no way I can recall her name ... Anyway my relation with the madmen nearby during that period [childhood] was decisive. I learned a lot.

Angelos got his certificate of exemption from the army, the *trelloharto* ('madness' certificate) as it is colloquially called, by putting on a persuasive performance. He was dressed up accordingly for the 'occasion', combed his hair like the [mad] mates of his childhood, and took some pills before going to the interview.

As far as I can tell, his relationship with Ithaca was generally traumatic and problematic, but still an open one. The fact that his father's brother was the prominent communist mayor of the island only made things worse for the uncompromising Angelos.

Angelos generally plays the role of the 'black sheep' in his family. Yet, from time to time he looks to them for shelter. His parents do not exactly welcome his presence and they refuse to give him any allowance which, in any case, they can hardly afford. Angelos recently attempted to run a bar in Ithaca, during the off-season period. He soon gave up.

From a hard-core communist to a sophisticated junkie

'Spend your whole life learning how to live' was an aphorism – Seneca cites it – which asks people to transform their existence into a kind of permanent exercise. (Foucault 1986: 48–49)

The shift in Angelos' interests from politics to the 'rock 'n' roll ideology' marks his arrival on Mykonos. Mykonos represents his quest for the 'authentic' lifestyle. The *sinafi* of the *Mykoniots* had a lesson to teach Angelos, as he himself asserts, which involved a different understanding of how people relate to money:

> *They* [implying the *Mykoniots*] were survivors, spending their money from day to day. I had never been the type that puts some money aside. Every kind of property is a burden. The lighter your luggage the better for your trip.

Once he started frequenting Mykonos, and soon after he first went out with Eleni, he was initiated by her husband Dimitris into the trade in Indian artefacts. Later on, he also started his own frequent visits to India. A new circle of adventures had begun.[64] There were times when he had to resort to really inconvenient solutions in order to realise his trip. Once he had to *loukarei* (rectally carry) good quality opium on his way back. At some point in the late eighties, the heroin fashion began to boom in Mykonos. Its use was no longer restricted to the privileged 'few' who used to come with some rare 'stuff' from the East. Opium was processed in large quantities intended for mass consumption. Mykonos slowly changed from a paradise of freedom into a trap where the most unlucky were caught. In every corner there was a cop disguised as a 'sexy chick' or a 'funky rapper'. By that time, those who were seriously involved in heroin, had disappeared, or chose to come off-season. Some made attempts to become '*clean*' (stop using heroin) while on the island. Only a few succeeded, while others left quickly to meet 'their' dealers in town. Angelos himself continued in his on/off situation, but he never really got out of it. His life circumstances resemble those of the protagonists in the novel he wants so much to write. He knows every detail about what he wants to write, he knows the story, but he never actually manages to do it. Thinking out loud:

> I get into the novel, but I can't escape. It is autobiographical. The central hero is me and my relationship with women. I call *preza* Scheherazade. In order to escape from *preza*, I have to write: [go] from an empiricist to [become] a creator … Eleni's death was the ultimate experience for me. Together we travelled for the last time to India; she was in a wheelchair. We had not been a couple for some time. The woman. The seduction. And death. Death is that thing that puts you in touch with reality. *Preza* is death. On and off. Reborn and dead again. I want to write the true story of a junkie, not Burrough's bullshit. Even if only one person reads it, I don't want more than that. I have the syndrome of the child. Maybe experiencing death has changed that in me.

> When somebody manages to pass from relationship [coupling] to friendship … for example, my relationship with Eurydice is more fulfilling. There is no sexual aspect, but what is left is real. Energy-wise, I am always going to be with her, irrespective of what she does. Total trust. No power could be founded on love. Bhagwan's ecological model succeeded in the U.S. But they finished him. The story goes on, but this time in a 'Club Méditerranée' style. For me the final straw was when they did not let Eleni have her room in the *ashram* … there was no real love then.

Angelos' sanyassi[65] name:
Deproven or Divine Love: the Bhagwan period

> 1979, India. Bombay. I was young. I had just arrived there, alone. A woman, in an orange dress approaches me; she had already obtained her *mala* [literally, a garland or necklace – and a sort of spiritual upgrading within Bhagwan's group]. She was a rather ugly German woman. She asks me: 'Where are you going? Come to Poona, you are going to have a nice time.' I chose to take the boat to Goa instead. As I smelled India, I was driven there. Don't forget it was the *drug* period, back then. People would go there for fun. Later they started *dealing* things. During that period, they would only buy their own clothing. Goa was the open secret in Mykonos. Patrick was also there. The greatest figure in the seventies. It was very cheap. You could leave the winter behind and go to the summer again. It was a way of life. A free, super free way. I discovered the freedom of wearing just a *sarong*.

In order to explain his involvement with the Bhagwan, Angelos returns to a description of his relationship with Eleni:

> My encounter with Eleni was karmic. She was the most original person of *them* all in Mykonos. I had been wandering around Mykonos and Goa but I never met her there. Once, I was preparing to work in a night bar in Thessaloniki. She appeared at the 'opening'. I never went back to work. I stayed with her for the rest of her life.

And he sets himself to describe her to me:

> Although she was not especially cultivated, being an ex-model, she was very much hooked on the Mykonian lifestyle, and she had a big heart. She would help anybody.

I could myself recall the hospitality of her house where lots of people would always visit just to relax or attain some spiritual or other 'high'. There was that big bed that Eleni put outdoors under the stars, well-protected from the Mykonian wind in the south-facing yard of her house. And the sounds of her Tibetan bells that were ringing out over the fields around all night long. Everyone would stop off at this hospitable bed. So that people would be comforted and healed. Eleni kept her hospitable disposition and high spirits until the very end of her life.

Angelos took his own *mala* after long meditation in Oregon. The acquisition of a *mala* coincided with Eleni's first treatment in the Memorial Hospital.

He became a *sanyassi*[66] on their later trip to Manali and Katmandu where he first contacted the Bhagwan. Eleni organised the Bhagwan's trip to Greece. She obtained a visa for him, at a time when the 'Americans' had denied him entry into their country. Angelos then was the most junior *sanyassi* among the Greek group. He was very close to the Bhagwan during his visit to Crete. The name he was given was Deproven, meaning '*divine love*'. He recalls this Cretan trip:

> Twenty of us were staying in this house. In fifteen days more than two thousand people came to meet him. It was a great experience. Bhagwan himself said that he was Socrates and the ones who would give him the hemlock were all around.

Even today, Angelos maintains that '*they*[67] finished Bhagwan' with a strong dose of valium.

Within the *Mykoniots*' commune, friends would refer to Angelos' and Dimitris' *sanyassi* identity in terms of some common 'behavioural' characteristics; they would refer to their 'raw directness' and 'sincerity' but also to their 'sweetness' towards other people. Angelos would describe this '*sanyassi*' quality as a special communication skill he shared with his fellow *sanyassi*. For example, he would explicitly refer to his special '*sanyassi* relationship' with Dimitris in respect of the fact that they were sharing the same woman.

According to Angelos' philosophy of life, the biggest gift offered to humanity was that of meditation as taught by the Buddha:

> Without meditation you can never call yourself an intellectual. The intelligentsia should experience meditation, in order to grasp the potential of its instrument which is the mind. What is missing in communism? Meditation. Atheism left a vacuum in intellectual discourse.

Angelos definitely believes that '*drugs*' do not suppress individuality. He referred vaguely to hereditary factors and some peculiar 'body chemistry' as a means of explaining why some people remain 'stuck' with heroin.

> If one feels that there is something one needs to go through, one has to do it. *I*, for example, could move straight to Bhagwan,[68] though I know someone who had transformed himself into a perfect *junkie*, after staying for some time with Bhagwan.

Finally, I can perhaps best sum up Angelos' lifestyle by quoting a seemingly contradictory ideal personality that was invented by Angelos' 'guru', Bhagwan; in Bhagwan's doctrine there was the ideal figure of 'Zorba the Buddha'. The whole idea of 'Zorba the Buddha' connoted to the attainment of an alternative version of *theosis* (unity with the divine) beyond the 'splitting' that the dualist Western theologies have created between the 'divine' and the 'human'. In Bhagwan's dogma, in order to reach *theosis* one had to reach one's limits. In their study of Bhagwan's movement, Thompson and Heelas attempt to 'portray' the charisma of Bhagwan's 'new man': ' He combines the qualities of Zorba the Greek and Gautama the Buddha, a life-affirming, celebratory, yet meditative person' (1986: 50). Or, otherwise, as Angelos rephrased it:

> If you have not been a Zorba, yourself, if you did not taste life with a great appetite, you can never be a Buddha.

A wardrobe of selves

> ... [S]elf-knowledge is an interpretation; self-interpretation, in its turn, finds in narrative, among other signs and symbols, a privileged mediation; this mediation draws on history as much as it does on fiction, turning the story of a life into a fictional story or a historical fiction, comparable to those biographies of great men in which history and fiction are intertwined. (Ricoeur 1991b: 188).

A very important game the *Mykoniots* play with their self-identity emerges from my reading of the above ethnographic material. It is obvious that in their self-narrations the *Mykoniots* propose for themselves multiple 'subject' positions. How is this multiplicity, a core element of their self-identity, acquired? The answer is through narrative. That means that beyond acquiring multiple subject positions they are aware of this multiplicity and furthermore they promote it. In the last self-narrative, which was actually a spontaneous narration by Angelos, the multiplicity of a concrete sign, i.e., the self-experience, is organised around the theme of multiple self/subject positions. Angelos automatically arranges his fragmented identity in chronological order; there is the politically active self; then the spiritually active; and, finally, his 'fringe' identity as a junkie. The reader must be careful not to treat these concrete categories of self-experience as different territories of Angelos' identity. What Angelos reveals to us is that he abolishes none of them. In reality, all of his past coexists in a syncretic narrative of the self. Seeds of all the above discourses can be found in Angelos' narrative. Angelos clearly doesn't suffer from any fragmentation or any real transformative revelation, but instead, transformation is for him auto-discourse.

Let us move to Hercules' discourse. Hercules is the great fragmentation theorist. He clearly has a timeless and all-inclusive discourse. Hercules is the exemplary bricoleur of the group who produces ideology out of the group's praxis. For Hercules, a fixed identity, a stable income and a single professional title attached to one's persona is synonymous with self-imprisonment. Hercules consciously plays with his own identity by making it eccentric. He accomplishes that firstly by making his professional identity indefinite in a world where specialists prevail; and secondly, by making his self-identity indefinite through constant preaching about the multiplicity of identity as the only 'ideological' source of his existential quest.

Eleonora, on the other hand, obviously cancels all the self-categories that threaten her flexible existence. She proudly recounts her sixties, seventies, eighties and nineties experiences but omits age or a fixed cultural role from her self-definition. Her class and family background remain obscure. Eleonora wants to tell us, I think, through her self-narrative that by transcending her 'fate', a lover, a style, a decade, she fully experiences herself. Everything lies a step ahead, transcending one's fate is to experience life fully without being trapped into a category.

Finally, in the case of Artemis, the experience of self-fragmentation is articulated in her self-narrative in a poetic way. Artemis is a gambler and simultaneously a victim of her own self-destruction. She gambles by provocatively playing with her identity. She enters the realms of several 'ideological' categories and admits that she is always a 'misfit'. But is she a 'misfit'? Artemis with her lifestyle and praxis abolishes every class category. In her self-narrative she embodies the grievance of all modern women, but rather than acting it out, she turns it into a self-myth.

The self in the *Mykoniots*' narrative is 'sacrificed' to a pure sign open to aesthetic manipulation. In what sense is this so? *Mykoniots* have to be creative with the self, since the self is their aesthetic capital. They are constantly working on their selves. The personal quest, or personal transformation is the heroic compulsion that governs their self-styling. They act out, they experience their eccentricity[69] by, as they stress in their narratives, employing their senses as the organising factor of their existence. They do that, moreover, by provocatively abolishing the 'sovereignty of emotions' since emotions do not fit in with their aesthetic code of ethics.

In their culture, emotions ruin the aesthetics of living. Besides, emotions, by relating them to other people in an exclusive manner, create a fixed past, a fixed identity and they thus obstruct the very fulfilling game *Mykoniots* play with the self. What is home for the *Mykoniots*? Discourse is home, since for them discourse is versatile and creates a flexible self. What else is home for the *Mykoniots*? Mykonos is home, since Mykonos can be another discourse. Mykonos is a myth, an artificial culture, a summer culture, an anarchic culture. What can the *Mykoniots* obtain through discourse? They can be creative, hence, they do not need to be fixed.

In the *Mykoniots*' discourse on the self there is an obvious repertoire, a 'wardrobe of selves'.[70] At this point I need to justify the term 'self' in the text. As is obvious by now, the self is analysed here without particular reference to an engendered self.[71] By no means do I want to imply that in the case of the *Mykoniots* there is gender equality or a gender symmetry, nor that they explicitly make such value-free statements themselves. There are obvious social asymmetries based on gender already evident in the ethnographic text. For example, the two females of the text could survive financially (and/or be [in]dependent) thanks to family or a male partner's economic resources. The two males, on the other hand, had no such facilities and/or relationships of dependency. Nevertheless, at the level of discourse, the identity game is not constructed on gender or ethnic differences but on idiosyncratic 'difference'. My ethnography tries to record one single cultural pattern, namely, how these people construct their 'difference'. Moore argues that 'deciding on differences is one way of delineating identities' (Moore 1994: 1). But there is an additional reason why I decided to concentrate on their discourse of 'difference'; simply because in my fieldwork material there was plenty of it. But how was this discourse of 'difference' constructed? In other words, what was the vehicle of the *Mykoniots*' 'difference'? I will maintain that it was not a single social class, a gender identity, or even simply a non-fixed gender identity.

In *Mykoniot* discourse, the game of 'difference' does not clearly emerge through gender or any other source of a single fragmented self, instead, I maintain that the game of 'difference' happens through bricolage. This is why the idea of a 'wardrobe of selves' is useful: it can be a wardrobe of 'engendered' selves, a wardrobe of 'social' selves, even a wardrobe of 'cultural' selves. Most importantly, fragmentation, or rather any division within, is not monolithic. Self sustains its completeness by eclectically picking up and appropriating different elements. Bearing in mind the above, the reader can probably understand by now why I have dedicated so much space to self-narrative. It is simply because my informants chose to speak about their experience strictly in personal terms. The 'I' remains the organising theme of discourse. The anthropologist is trained to 'penetrate' discourses and discover what it is that they serve. In my case, the 'self' is more than 'a representational economy' (Battaglia, 1995: 4). The category 'self' does more than actually allow one to skip any other classification. Moreover, the category 'self' in my text does more than cut across the categories of gender, culture or class. It reflects the *Mykoniots*' exploitation of the 'self' as a sign.

Unravelling my informants' discourse, I was puzzled by the deliberate absence of any collective identity category. Their interpretations struggled to overcome representations of the self as part of a family, a class, a group. I decided to give that serious consideration. Only after I had turned to Foucault's later work did I realise that, for my informants, the (discursive) object of desire was not the 'other' but the 'self': the self as a source of pleasure, as a source of transformation at any cost. The self-narratives revealed a highly elitist principle constructed as a result of their authors' endeavours to cultivate the self as an ultimate existential predicament. It seems from these narratives that the *Mykoniots* are permanent cultivators of the self. Eleonora's styling of the self could be a representative case of Marcus Aurelius' idea of 'retreat within oneself' (Foucault 1986: 51). Eleonora chooses constantly to be on 'retreat': an Indian retreat, a Californian retreat, a Mykonian retreat, a self-retreat. Artemis chooses to 'cultivate' the self by writing, a rather

Narratives of the self

autobiographical text, an *askesis* (exercise) in self-realisation (Foucault 1984b: 364). Then, there is Hercules, the bricoleur, whose *askesis* is to appropriate and create out of any resources. Finally, Angelos' transformative experience of existence is realised as Seneca's permanent exercise: 'spend your whole life learning how to live' (Foucault 1986: 49). I do not offer all these quotations from Foucault just to underline the similarity vis-à-vis the predicament of the 'self' between my informants' discourse and that of the classical philosophers. The rhetoric obviously matches, but what is more important here is that, in the *Mykoniots*' case, the 'care of the self' is transplanted into social practice and consumption.[72]

In the *Mykoniot* case, the field of action is oneself, the styling of one's self: the transformation of one's self is the object of desire. The self is the source of all knowledge. How is this styling, the change, the transformation of the self accomplished and what is the vehicle for this transformation? The main vehicle is a narrative sustained by a set of practices. The *Mykoniots* cling to a narrative understanding of themselves. They neither see themselves as a group with a marginal or distinct identity, nor as absolutely conscious agents of their deliberate extreme individuality; nor, as it might seem to us, as actors of their own life experience. On the contrary, they construct and constantly transform their identity through self-narratives and ritualised practices. It is only through self-narrative that they realise their various self-transformations and organise their personal 'drama' of an existence in a constant process of *askesis*. Ricoeur posits a narrative understanding of the self, or rather a constitutive narrative identity that can account for self-transformations through its dynamic composition. He suggests that 'our life, when then embraced in a single glance, appears to us as the field of a constructive activity, borrowed from narrative understanding, by which we attempt *to discover and not simply to impose* [my emphasis] from outside the *narrative identity which constitutes us* [original emphasis]' (Ricoeur 1991a: 32).

The *Mykoniots*' self-narratives do not only entail, but actually consciously describe the multiple nature of their subjectivity. More than actually describing, narrative in this case is conditioned by the principle of multi-subjectivity. Hercules has many alternative professional identities and various sexual preferences. Angelos has various lifestyle experiences, Eleonora exhibits a wardrobe of selves, while Artemis has different political selves which, in a psychoanalytic way, she attempts to incorporate. However, 'all locations are provisional' (Moore 1994: 2) in the *Mykoniots*' discourse. The 'I' is understood as a transitory experience. The problem remains to decide how much 'intended' agency these people have in their narrated and fragmented experience. In their self-narratives they describe, they possess, they boast about their versatility of the self.

Eleonora, for example, rejects the cultural norm of *mnimosyno*, the family gathering to commemorate her mother, but although she herself has chosen a syncretic Hindu cult, she pays tribute to her mother's memory and organises the yearly dinner in an orphanage in Athens. Why? A theory of the self needs to account not only for the fragmentation within, or the cultural differences within, but also for the contradictory discourses that coexist (Moore 1994: 56). The *Mykoniots'* self-narrative, like a bricolage, synthesises different structural elements, modern, traditional and syncretic that coexist both at the level of discourse and of practice. The project of bricolage, in turn, is always a creative process since it assumes eclectic mixing. *Mykoniots*, after all, are not devotees of anything. They are only eclectically selecting their self-fashioning.

Notes

1. I follow Giddens' definition of the term 'narrative of the self': 'the story or stories by means of which self-identity is reflexively understood both by the individual concerned and by others' (Giddens 1991: 243).
2. This cliquish narrative mechanism for re-inventing 'local' heroes ultimately promotes the space-myth of Mykonos. Waldren, in a similar fashion, narrates how her fellow Deia foreign residents perpetuate the myth of Deia, as well as reinforce their 'local' identity by retelling stories about their past (1997: 67–68).
3. For example, at first I felt patronised and distressed. Then, I started questioning myself: why do I feel that, rather than why do they do it? Much later, I realised that beyond my personal pattern of 'co-dependence' and moreover beyond my 'psychoanalytic' endeavour to analyse intimate power-relationships, lay the whole structure of the group and its only 'collective' principle. The initiation ritual commanded that once *you* successfully (i.e., alone) confronted *your* 'co-dependency', or other control-pattern, *you* will automatically be 'acknowledged' by the group.
4. More specifically, there is an alternative stream of feminist critique of the above theorists for 'reducing ethnographic encounters to texts', thus 'mystifying the power of the ethnographer', and, furthermore, for not acknowledging the long reflexive tradition of women's writings, as well as the feminist contribution to the debate on scientific objectivity (cf. Bell 1993).
5. In fact, *Mykoniots* conspicuously use the above expression in English. In order to help the reader distinguish the English expressions my informants use, I italicise them.
6. In the ethnographic context of 'traditional' Greek culture, the category of a 'Greek', 'unmarried', 'woman' is largely an unrecognised one – even in the monastic context, the unmarried nuns are symbolically portrayed to have 'betrothed [themselves to] Christ' (Iossifides 1991: 152). The power that a recognised social role assumes is acquired by 'females' mostly through marriage and is mainly re-enacted in the context of the household (cf. Loizos and Papataxiarchis 1991a). Nevertheless, Faubion's recent ethnographic account of an elite group in Athens describes a semi-fictional female, Maro; a rather bricolage character of a woman in her late forties, who happens to be an unmarried professional and a 'powerful' (social) agent (1993).
7. Gossip, in our case, is a means of building a self-myth, a process which is silently agreed upon among the *Mykoniots*. Du Boulay maintains that one of the functions of gossip in the Greek village of Ambeli is to preserve the cohesion of the community (1974: 210). Alternatively, according to the same author, gossip can become a cause of fragmentation and give way to antagonism and hostility (ibid. 212). Although *Mykoniots* rely on gossip in order to shape their self-image, its function largely remains cohesive rather than fragmentary.
8. The italics in the text within a quotation connote that Eleonora actually used the same words in English, while the rest of the quotation is a translation.
9. For Rajneeshism, the Bhagwan's religious movement, see 'the Osho movement' in Barker (1989: 201–05, appendix IV).

10. *Mnimosyna*, memorial services in contemporary Greece are ethnographically explored by Danforth (1982: 42–45, 56). Panourgia (1995) describes at some length the cultural significance of memory vis-à-vis the dead. She also interprets the ritualistic food and drink commensality after the funeral service (ibid. 115–19).
11. See, for example, Herzfeld's closely affiliated notion of performative male *eghoismos* which stands for self-regard (1985: 11), as well as du Boulay's description of the male *anexartitos* (1974: 124).
12. *Horio* is a self-sufficient household of a traditional type that autonomously covers all its needs.
13. Traditionally, the Mykonians mainly produced wine; but by that time, consuming the local produce was an exclusive pleasure, since Mykonian wine was a rare and thus fetishised item due to the development of tourism. The easy profit that came from renting out houses and providing services meant that the locals stop cultivating the land.
14. During the preparations for and the celebration of the 'Easter' rituals I felt as if I were playing the role of the 'family'. I had known Eleonora for some time but I had never got this close to her. I stayed over for the holy days, performing the role of that 'special person' with whom somebody shares the big celebrations. I was excited because I was entering Eleonora's world and she was excited because she had found a new 'disciple'.
15. As I found out later, Ganesh was Shiva's son and had the peculiarity of having a human body and an elephant head. The myth said that his father had cut off his head in anger but immediately regretted it and replaced it with the head of an elephant that happened to be passing by.
16. Meditation pillow.
17. For Eleonora, syncretism was a way of life but for me all this was something new, at least on a practical level.
18. Eleonora brings big quantities of incense for personal consumption from Vrindavan. The quality is considered exceptional and everybody is happy if Eleonora offers it as a gift.
19. During the eighties, another exclusive item was the Indian sarongs that the *Mykoniots* used to wear wherever they went. Recently, however, poor quality sarongs have been imported for tourist consumption, and the item is no longer a distinctive feature of the group.
20. Next morning, after Eleonora's purification of the house with many Vrindavan incense sticks, we proceeded with a detailed study of the annual setting of the planets on my astrological chart. Our endeavour with certain 'metaphysical' practices, could be related to a general anthropological discussion about a distinctively 'female' religious praxis on behalf of 'Greek women' that credits an (aesthetically) organising spiritual dimension to 'female identity' (Dubisch 1990; Hirschon 1983, 1989). Nevertheless, in our case, as we shall see later, similar practices are equally employed by the 'males' of the group.
21. This idea of the 'ecstatic triangle' re-emerges in chapter 4.
22. Some of Eleonora's eighties parties were reputedly glamorous. At one of them, Eleonora prepared a choreography and performed a dance with a couple of *Mykoniot* youngsters on her split-level terrace. The crowd was spread over its lower level, enjoying the full moon and Eleonora's performance.
23. For a definition of the 'girls' see n. 26.
24. *Leela* in Hindi, according to Eleonora's definition, is something like the 'game' life is playing with us. The official definition of the term, according to Carter (1990) is: the common property of all 'transient' and 'dualistic' phenomena. *Leela*, according to the same author, is classified as a term of Indian mystical ontology, the so-called *Advaita*, a non-dual, monistic mysticism. The term is designed to portray an 'external play (or dance) of cosmic consciousness' (Clarke quoted in Carter 1990: 26).
25. The term 'meeting place' was largely used in the seventies for places like Goa, Bali and Ibiza. These were the original places where the hippies met. They played the part of official stopovers on the global pilgrimage of the hippies.

26. *Koritsia*, according to Cowan, is a culturally charged term traditionally designed for all unmarried (i.e., virgin) females (cf. Cowan 1991: 180n). Interestingly, Eleonora's group of female friends called themselves the 'girls', irrespective of their marital status. Eleonora herself also employed the term extensively in order to portray her occasional female-group affiliations.
27. A favourite slang expression among the *Mykoniots* dating back to the late sixties which proposes a 'hippie' alternative to the psychoanalytic implications of the 'degenerated' relationships of modern individuals. The *Mykoniots* would normally add to the above behavioural lessons another cliché to their disciples: 'Don't let them lay a trip on you.'
28. The Mykonian basil was a highly fetishised symbolic item of consumption by my *Mykoniot* informants who were largely imitating the locals' practices in this respect. The locals cultivated basil and used it mostly for decorative reasons. The 'Mykonian' bunch of flowers would definitely include some basil, the 'Mykonian' church would be decorated with plenty of basil, and the courtyard of every Mykonian *horio* would be full of the traditional clay flowerpots, with basil in them.
29. I have invented this term to characterise a generalised '*nouveau* riche' mentality pervading Greek culture. To put it in crude terms, the 'nouveaux Greeks' compose an arbitrary aesthetic category which semantically refers to a 'cultural' longing for exclusivity and distinction (cf. Mouzelis 1978: 99).
30. My fieldwork officially started in January. I had to trace my Mykonian group in Athens via networking and via the group's various haunts. The *Mykoniots d'élection* were called the 'Mykonians' there, but they were highly marginalised in the Athenian setting. The bourgeoisie and the *Mykoniots* socialised in the same haunts, but their lifestyle parameters differed dramatically. While in Athens, I started socialising with Hercules more frequently and he suggested putting me up in his Mykonian home. By agreeing to live with Hercules I launched without realising it, my new identity as part of a 'chain of reciprocity' among the *Mykoniots d'élection*. Lodging with Hercules, who was one of the senior members of the group, gave me the official status I needed to enter the group.
31. The 'liberated' and 'beautiful' body is important aesthetic capital in the *Mykoniots*' milieu. As we see here, Hercules invests in a 'liberated' image of his body. The body, albeit 'naked', i.e., liberated, is yet another demanding task; it needs to be looked after: 'We find a new mode of investment which presents itself no longer in the form of control by repression but that of control by stimulation. Get undressed – but be slim, good looking, tanned!' (Foucault 1980: 57)
32. In Hercules' personal terminology, the English word *project* stands for any kind of job he would undertake.
33. Hercules' working pattern of intense labour, alternating with long periods of 'idleness', is culturally constituted as an alternative 'attitude' to work. Similarly, Okely's ethnography of the Gypsies (1983: 53) refers to a notion of 'shame' attached to 'canonical' wage-labour. According to Okely, for the Gypsies, self-employment is part of their distinct cultural identity. Their discourse stresses that regular jobs would 'spoil' them (Okely 1996: 48). Throughout Hercules' self-narrative, analogous discourses as well as practices towards work can be traced.
34. The word 'patronise' did not occur to me then, since I was absorbed in my role as an observer and I could not realise the dynamics of relationships which included myself.
35. Hercules was one of the 'designers' of local 'staged-authenticity'. He designed the 'staged-authenticity' of the various Mykonian haunts (cf. Boissevain 1996: 11, 12) and the 'authentic' Mykonian setting, as much as he designed his 'authentic' Mykonian self.
36. Good music at the time was hard to find, so it was something highly fetishised.
37. Hercules displays a conscious ability to play with his identity. Okely observes a similar flexibility in role playing on behalf of the Gypsies (1996: 49). One of her informants characteristically states: 'I have a thousand faces' (ibid. 51). The ethnographer explains how the Gypsies can perform to the *gorgios* (non-Gypsies) by occasionally displaying a 'degraded' ethnic image, a 'neutralised', or alternatively an 'exoticised' one. In any case, they are portrayed as

Narratives of the self

having a great ability to conceal their identity, or play with it (i.e., look poor, look non-Gypsies, look stereotype Gypsies).

38. Yet Hercules is a pseudonym.
39. According to Heelas (1996), Gurdjieff's thought heavily influenced the New Age movement.
40. One has to bear in mind that Greece has no 'welfare state' and Hercules, contrary to the norms of the Greek petit bourgeoisie, had no financial support from his family.
41. Stewart (1991) ethnographically accounts for a similar existential agony. He describes an informant commenting on the loss of his son who was 'gone' before he even joined the army, before getting married and without having left any children behind. In other words, what the Naxiot informant's rhetoric conveys is a distress over the fact that his child did not have the chance to 'complete' himself. As he characteristically stated: 'If you don't leave anything you don't count' (ibid. 58).
42. Obviously, by making a huge projection, confusing myself in the situation I was describing, I subconsciously identified with my 'informant' and created a pseudo-situation out of exaggerated fears that did not belong to the reality of Hercules.
43. Similarly, Okely's ethnography of the 'Traveller-Gypsies' suggests that: 'for the self-employed Travellers there is no concept of retirement' (1983: 55).
44. In Hercules' eclectic linguistic bricolage, English is used a lot in his abstract thinking process. In the following dialogue, I try to revive that bilingual element in Hercules' discourse by using italics for the English expressions he uses.
45. Firstly, one could obviously argue that Mykonos' increasing popularity during the first decades of the twentieth century was due to its proximity to the ancient island of Delos and its appropriation of whatever the sacred island signified. Apollo, the 'sun-god' to whom the island was dedicated, was a 'brilliant' 'love-child' of 'protean nature', a male with 'marvellous youthful' looks, considered as the god of beauty in ancient Greek mythology or, at least, this is how Durrell describes some of the properties of the 'Delian' Apollo (1978: 238). This symbolism must have played an important part in why the 'beautiful people' of the seventies picked Mykonos as one of their meeting places, as well as why Mykonos has been a renowned meeting place of male homosexuals for the last three decades. Secondly, the original evaluation of Mykonos as an exclusive cosmopolitan resort of the sixties and onwards, that initially attracted exclusive groups of people, remained another signifier open for exploitation. Moreover, for one reason or another during the seventies, Mykonos had managed to attract all sorts of examples of aesthetic vanity and mainly some of the groups that worshipped, as well as established, the narcissism of late modernity: the jet setters, the fashion people, the avant-garde artists, the emerging culture of the 'top models', the gays and the 'beautiful people' of the hippie culture.
46. The aforementioned attitude is epitomised in the headings of the special editions of the popular lifestyle magazines dedicated to Mykonos. Amongst the titles were: 'Mykonos, the island of the brave'; 'Mykonos, the new metropolis'; 'Mykonos – are you in?'; 'Mykonos Mystique', and so forth.
47. Travelling on foot is rare on the affluent tourist island, although means of transportation other than the donkey came as late as the sixties. I knew only of rare examples such as *Kyr*-Thodoris, my landlord, an elderly Mykonian, who enjoyed walking and refused any modern means of transportation. Lately, the stream of (illegal) immigrants from Albania to Mykonos changed the picture in this respect. Mykonos is full of Albanians travelling on foot in search of, or on their way to work.
48. Bourdieu argues about the ethos of the bourgeois 'elites' 'who always pride themselves on disinterestedness and define themselves by an elective distance – manifested in art and sport – from material interests' (1993: 342–43).
49. In 'traditional' ethnographic settings in Greece, it is common to associate women with 'evil' and promote a rhetoric that equates 'female' with a 'cunning' property as an illegitimate exercise of power. Papataxiarchis (1992a: 52–53) and Dubisch (1986: 17, 18) refer to ethnographers like Friedl, Handman and Herzfeld, who account for such discourses which attribute the 'latent'

negative power of women to their 'female' cunning-property. Du Boulay in her own ethnographic context of Ambeli, highlights similar discourses concerning the 'evil' potentiality of a 'woman' which can only be 'transformed' by marriage (1974: 135). In the classic ethnography of Sarakatsanoi, Campbell describes their common-sense belief that women (although they lack intelligence) are, at least, 'gifted' with cunning (1964: 277–78). Women are also reported to be affiliated with ('second-rate') spiritual practices. 'In Inner Mani', Seremetakis maintains that 'the central sites of the production of women's discourse and cultural power are the mortuary ritual and related divinatory practices' (1991: 2). This 'female' cunning property could be rephrased in Herzfeld's ethnographic account from Rhodes concerning the 'diabolic cleverness of a woman'. Herzfeld has recorded a Rhodian villager who attempted to persuade the ethnographer that he was as 'clever' as a 'woman'. He quoted an old saying about a woman who had won a wager with the Devil, since she managed to arrive home without getting wet in the rain simply by taking off her clothes. The narrator assured the ethnographer that this was the evidence of the 'diabolic cleverness of the woman' but he himself had also done something similar (Herzfeld 1987: 113–14). Herzfeld, in his attempt to approach Greek culture holistically, has been ethnographically applying the self-contradictory and all-encompassing model of *disemia*. In the case of 'female' cunning, Herzfeld brings into play a more sophisticated model in order to validate the cultural *disemic* dilemma of the Greeks vis-à-vis an established rhetoric concerning the 'inherent' 'female' quality of being both the Devil and Virgin Mary (ibid. 175). Herzfeld argues that the double image of women, if contextualised, is not necessarily contradictory. In line with the above ethnographies, there could be a 'negative' connotation associated with the nickname 'sorceresses', yet only as a 'remnant' of some (cultural) prejudice, a suspicion towards women's metaphysical practices. For example, nobody among the community of the *Mykoniots d'élection* called Hercules, a 'sorcerer'. Nevertheless, the reader should not treat the above ethnographic observation as an overall explanation, as a determinant preconception about the image of the 'gang' of Artemis' 'sorceresses'. The same 'gang' made up of female friends enjoyed a certain status among the *Mykoniots*. Their recognised power derived from alternative discourses that promoted the group's admiration for being 'independent' and 'spiritually skilled' women. In this sense, the 'female' image is neither double, i.e. good and bad, nor merely 'negative', but multiple. *Mykoniots*, especially the 'males' in the group, occasionally drawing from different discourses, i.e., traditional, feminist friendly, modernist and so forth, characterised Artemis and her group, either as 'mad' or 'progressive' or 'charismatic' or simply by employing the controversial term 'sorceresses'. According to du Boulay (1986) an autonomous or alternative female discourse is not possible in the 'traditional' Greek context, since everything is governed by an undivided (ethical) discourse concerning the 'good of the household'. In our case, the implicitly 'offensive' element in the term 'sorceresses' comes from Artemis' and her female friends' potential 'power' to create a type of female bonding whose validation could threaten a basically 'male' quality: men's privileged capacity to create and respect 'intimate' relationships outside kinship.

50. It is commonplace for a family or an individual to take personal care of one of the many local churches in the town of Mykonos. Nevertheless, the churches are considered public spaces and thus nobody's property. In recent years, the churches have become another source of income due to their popularity with tourists. This is maybe a reason for someone wanting to take over the patronage of Zambelo's church.
51. These male friends came from the younger group of exogenous locals, the 'neo-pirates' (see chapter 2 for the detailed definition of their aesthetic group). The 'neo-pirates' made a point of living and socialising with locals in winter Mykonos. When I initially expressed my desire to go with them to the pig-slaughtering, they refused by saying that it would be too hard (meaning too hard for a woman). Later on that day, Artemis passed by my place to pick me up. She was on her way to Jimmy's *paniyiri*.
52. Traditionally, Mykonian pig-slaughtering that takes place in November is reported by Stott (1982) to be a period of 'heightened sociability' for families with rural properties. Stott

Narratives of the self

mentions that in 1978, her informants observed a decline in the number of evening dinners and parties offered in association with the pig-slaughtering (Stott 1982: 263, 264). Finally, the slaughtering itself is considered a highly skilled job, which only some rare local specialists ritualistically execute (Triantafyllou 1986: 21).

53. Heroin in Greece spread during the eighties. Very early on, thanks to the Greek media, and the Greek legislation that copied an American notion of addiction (according to which, addiction was allegedly related to criminality, prostitution, sexual menace and degraded morality [cf. Tsiganou 1988]), 'drug-addiction' had been established as a 'major' social problem. As Tsili (1987: 226–27, 233) argues, this portrayal of the situation was out of proportion, and an initially 'simple' social problem was immediately fetishised. The issue of drug-addiction performed the role of the 'ideological gamble' in the Greek case. The 'tragic' and exaggerated way the newspapers represented the, only then, emerging problem of 'drug addiction' is the greatest evidence of that. Interestingly, the topic of 'drugs' was immediately categorised as belonging to the sphere of the 'dark' and the 'forbidden' (ibid. 234). As a result of this early negative fetishisation, moralising discourses developed. This was followed by a sense of counter-resistance on behalf of the various young subcultures against this moralising discourse of the 'establishment'. Tsili argues that the voice of the 'addicted' was automatically suppressed in the face of rapid developments (a series of projections and misrepresentations of a newly emerging, not yet established, social problem). The results were only intense 'discourses' about addiction, and the actual 'marginalisation' of the 'addict' himself and his discourse. Finally, the reader should know that Greek jurisprudence made no distinctions between different substances and equally applied the 'imported' views on what is 'addictive' to substances like hashish, opium, heroin, cocaine and so forth. The traditional consumption of (the nowadays illegal) substances has not been taken into account in any way whatsoever.
54. The rebellion of Greek students against the dictatorship of 1967–74.
55. For statistical data and some comments on the subject, consult the third volume of 'Drugs in Greece: the use of substances by the [Greek] population' (Madianou et al. 1992: 181).
56. It is important to underline at this point that there is no established group name among 'them' when in Mykonos. When away from the island, they tend to call each other (employing their 'derivative' identity) the *Mykoniates*, (the Mykonians).
57. According to Heelas (1996: 44), Aleister Crowley devised a 'magical' community in Sicily from which to launch the New Era (i.e., the New Age). Apart from heading an occult movement, Crowley is considered among the founders of the New Age ideology and a significant figure in the pagan and magical milieu.
58. 'White' is a code word for heroin.
59. Heroin, among other effects, depresses sexual appetite.
60. Obviously Angelos must have been well-acquainted with Engels' *The origin of family, private property and the state* (1972), which was a standard 'textbook' in the education of the Greek Communist Youth.
61. At this point, I should quote Alexis, a bar owner in both (eighties and nineties) Thessaloniki and Mykonos, who rushed to justify the reason why Thessaloniki had acquired a progressive underground and rock scene, 'ahead' of Athens and the rest of Greece. Alexis believed that this happened accidentally since, during the seventies, the so-called '*Magic Bus*' used to make its stopover in Thessaloniki on its way from Europe to the 'East'. That is how the first '*trips*' came to town, he said. This fact had aesthetic implications for the youth culture of Thessaloniki, which also happened to be a major student haunt in Greece. The audience in Thessaloniki must have been introduced into the by then fashionable 'hippie' lifestyle and the associated substances of the late seventies. The official introduction and establishment of heroin into the local market as a frequently used substance, though, happened later on during the eighties.
62. This is one of the rare occasions on which an informant offered a self-classification that also creates a generic term for a group, i.e., the group of the *evaisthitoi*, the group of the 'sensitive'.

The Nomads of Mykonos

The collective- and self-classification of 'the sensitive' kind, frequently re-emerges in the *Mykoniots*'s discourses.

63. Here, Angelos is hinting at the situation between members of the group and the Greek police, since many of the 'friends' had been busted for drug possession. Mainly during the late eighties, there had been an attempt to decimate their alternative community on Mykonos.
64. The reader should note that Angelos' self-narrative promotes an 'agonistic' identity through the self-image of the adventurer, the opportunist, the (political) fighter and the heroin survivor which, in the 'traditional' ethnographic context, is a gender-specific one (Herzfeld 1995). Papataxiarchis refers to a similar agonistic property of the Greek male. He observes the existence of *rakitzis*, the 'natural leader' of a coffee shop collectivity. *Rakitzis* is he who can 'tolerate' the competitive exchanges of *raki* offerings (1990: 339).
65. This literally means a Hindu religious mendicant. The spiritual term was later appropriated by the Bhagwan to address or somehow classify his Western 'disciples' by claiming that anyone could become a *sanyassi*.
66. This spiritual title, *sanyassi*, derives its context-specific meaning, not only from its actual use in the Bhagwan's cult, but also from the symbolic capital invested in it within the *Mykoniots*.
67. Angelos again uses the plural of conspiracy. This time 'they' are not his *own* people, but a vague group out of the 'establishment' which creates a category of 'malign' others.
68. Here Angelos means to skip the 'junkie' period.
69. This type of personal/experiential eccentricity differs significantly from Marcus' analysis of eccentricity as a class or cultural performance. *Mykoniots*' 'first-hand' eccentricity is part of a deliberate act of self-invention as personal resistance, and is not relational as in Marcus' notion of eccentricity which operates as *habitus* or awareness of one's compliance – 'awareness of how one's self is being constructed by other agencies' (1998: 166). With this in mind, Marcus' rich eccentric – who unavoidably has to reproduce his class or fame – uses eccentricity as a mechanism to exercise his power. So eccentricity is not an intrinsic property of the character of the rich and famous, but the 'distortion effect' of the awareness of this position of power. Marcus' eccentrics, although conscious players, are only actors in a performance that is being constructed by significant others; they are 'not self-aware enough to provide an interesting account of his or her own eccentricity as a personal matter' (ibid.).
70. The term is borrowed from Pico Iyer who portrays the 'privileged homeless' of the 'transcontinental tribe of wanderers' to whom he himself belongs, and highlights his eclectically multicultural self, recognising an immediately available identity-repertoire (Iyer 1997). Shields very accurately, I think, theoretically comments on the above predicament of the (post-)modern 'transient' subject who has acquired a 'subjectivity in the ironic mode': 'Rather than the individual who presents a uniform identity over time, for certain social groups this may take the form of a persona possessing multiple, mask-like identities (a dramatis persona) realised in different situations while remaining non-commital and "cool" to any one identity' (Shields 1991: 269).
71. Some ethnographies on Greek culture, influenced by the feminist critique in anthropological theory, have shifted their interests from kinship, which constructed monolithic gender identities, to various gender models outside kinship (Cowan 1990; Dubisch 1986, 1995; Herzfeld 1985; Loizos and Papataxiarchis 1991a: 25). The main reason, however, for gender becoming a fruitful theoretical issue was that researchers decided to deal reflexively with 'differences within'. Focusing on such differences, they had to deal with discourses on different gender roles, since such discourses were pre-eminent in the internal cultural game of difference. In my case, at the level of discourse, there is an alternative construction of 'difference' – simply by overriding any collective categories. Gender is definitely one of these categories.
72. We are not dealing here with some elitist discourse, at least not in terms of class. The differences in my informants' financial and cultural backgrounds are evidence of that. The *Mykoniots*' various social conditions clearly demonstrate that, in our case, the 'cultivation of the self' is not a purely elitist or phallocentric discourse, as in Foucault's classical philosophers (Foucault 1984b: 341, 344).

4
NARRATIVES OF PLACE: A SPATIAL MYTH OF OTHERNESS

The following chapters will concentrate on ethnographic manifestations of the group's idiosyncratic liminality. I describe some examples of *Mykoniot* gatherings that will help to ethnographically draw the performative boundaries around the *Mykoniots d'élection*. The material will show three aspects of the *Mykoniots'* attitude towards liminality: firstly, the *Mykoniots'* version of celebrating mainstream rituals (through a description of a wedding in chapter 5); secondly, their appropriation of and participation in local feasts; and, thirdly, the creation of a liminal 'routine' of their own, that I euphemistically call 'a ritual of our own' in imitation of the *Mykoniots'* childlike and conspicuous attitude towards their 'difference' (both described in chapter 4). During my fieldwork, I witnessed the *Mykoniots'* eagerness to invest their everyday activities with an aspect of liminality and glamour, as well as to generally abolish accepted ideas about special 'occasions' or liminal time.[1]

This was manifested in their unconventional dress and by their lack of participation in conventional Greek rituals – with the exception of the 'original' low class *paniyiria*. The *Mykoniots d'élection* had, in a sense, to invent a counter-coding of liminality, outside the established liminal context experienced by the tourist or the visitor. In other words, they had to create a counter-liminal time, their own symbolic interruption from 'work' which is essentially to be the backdrop to, and the dynamic force within, this tourist and eccentric location. The reader should bear in mind the psychological aspect of ritualising the everyday for the *Mykoniots*.

Participation mystique, scene one: 'a ritual of our own': the *Mykoniots'* version of a *paniyiri* – a trip to Delos

> Since then all the seamen of the world when passing by had to stop, as Kallimachos mentions, and join in the singing and dancing around the god's altar.'[2]

Apart from the twelve gods of the Panhellenic, they individually worshipped Dionysus, his mother Semeli, Demetra and Poseidon. For their sake, many times a year they organised *paniyiria* [feasts], sacrificing boars, lambs and rams. Maybe the tradition of the *paniyiria* and the sacrifices is relevant to the adorable Mykonian *paniyiria* that take place nowadays in the numerous chapels of the island. (Karantonis n.d.: 1)

Mykonos' spatial and historical 'otherness': an introduction or performing 'historical constructivism' for the creation of an alternative, yet exclusive, Mykonian identity

I could not hope to succeed in my attempts to recreate the local lifestyle of the *Mykoniots d'élection*, if I failed to stress the symbolic importance of the nearby island of Delos[3] in their struggle to appropriate an authentic 'local' self. Delos is synonymous with an imposing list of symbols in the *Mykoniots*' narrative. The ancient Greek and Roman shrine, and the *Mykoniots*' 'metaphysical' relationship with it, is what the local 'opinion makers' aim to promote, in order to create for themselves, an imaginary continuum with the ancient locus of Delos, as well as with the tourist locus of Mykonos. The appropriation of various localist discourses comes to the *Mykoniot* as a functional necessity, as 'entertainers' of upper-class tourists. The 'transference' of the uniqueness syndrome has a long history on the island. The reason lies in the appropriation of a glamorous historical past and a visible archaeological site to support it, a process that has played an important role in the development of tourism in the shrine's poor and unsung neighbour, Mykonos. Sutton observes that as a mechanism tourism, especially in Greece with its preponderance of 'history', has the power to transform sites semiotically, as well as to transform the local and cultural meanings of history itself (1998: 25).

Firstly, Delos constitutes one of the foremost symbols of the classical 'Greek spirit'. It represents an important 'banking centre' of the ancient world, as well as a prestigious harbour linking East and West, a central slave bazaar, but most of all (as my informants pointed out) a cosmopolitan 'core' that was one of the most hedonistic and amoral places of the known world at the time.[4] A place that notoriously enough (an informant's view), attracted that 'eccentric' personality, Jean Cocteau, to become one of the earliest visitors to modern Mykonos. By the late thirties, Cocteau, according to Antonio – a kind of cosmopolitan ambassador for contemporary Mykonos – was wandering the narrow streets of the labyrinthine Mykonian *Hora* 'with his extravagant garments and gay companions', just to get inspiration from the deserted ancient shrine on nearby Delos. 'He then produced his Delos lithographs.' At that time, Delos was the only reason why any *xenos* (foreigner) would come to the lowly harbour of Mykonos.

After the medieval period, the few historical sources that survive concerning Mykonos come from members of the English and French elite, who were curious to recreate the wonder of the 'Greek spirit' that produced their civilisation.[5] Moreover, from the travelogue of Tournefort (the most important source for eighteenth-century Mykonos), right up to the time of the modern Greek ship-owning tycoons who regularly commuted from the Côte d'Azur to Mykonos, the growing reputation for Mykonos' 'architectural miracle' seems likely to have been the means to re-appropriate a not easily accessed symbol, that of deserted ancient Delos.

All the above is, I hope, fairly clear. But what interested me more, as an inquisitive anthropologist, was the most recent rhetoric, concerning the grandiose 'power' of the ancient locus, a rhetoric that was evident in any conversation. Since we were living in the nineties, one might well expect a certain amount of 'New Age'-type rhetoric that these loci with history often attract. According to this line of thinking, Delos emits an 'energy', something that the nearby island of Mykonos inevitably shares.

At the beginning of my fieldwork, I was amazed by the consistency of the answers to my question about why Mykonos became so successful touristically. Mykonos, in my informants' view, became a legendary island in the modern Aegean, due to its proximity to Delos. This assumption, alien to purely historical and rational thinking, sometimes presupposed that Delos' myth was attracted to and emerged from the 'special qualities' of a 'unique space' that inevitably, due to the proximity, included Mykonos as well.

This section deals with ethnographic examples of my informants' statements and comments concerning Delos' myth. One must not forget that their standpoint on life is strongly influenced by a lifestyle that accommodates a visual and sensual pandemonium of pleasure. They maintain that by just physically being in this geographical area, the body and mind are constantly benefiting from the extreme sunlight and barren landscape. The *Mykoniots d'élection* are of the opinion that this very quality of everyday life gives them their *raison d'être*.

Artemis, currently attempting to complete her novel inspired by Greek myths, would state assertively: 'It is no accident that the ancients selected Delos as the centre of their known world. It was the place where all the cultures built their particular shrines. There is a certain radiation. It is a centre. A solar centre. I believe in those things. I do not believe that Delphi[6] is a random place either ... ' Artemis would go on to say how this solar energy affected visitors to Mykonos, driving them solely by their 'subconscious centres of desire', adding that: 'the Dionysiac, hedonistic type of energy and the narcissistic energy of Apollo also resides on Mykonos.' She herself came to find inspiration for her novel in this 'part of the world' having been interested in the aspect of '*dittotita*', the twofold nature of things: the bright side as well as the dark side of her personality, that emerged in her dreams. From my brief reference to Artemis' thesis on the importance of Delos, we can decipher a mixture of information about theories of myth, analytical psychology and existential philosophy, as well as a populism, that the great majority of rational academics detest. Nevertheless, Artemis is as charismatic and talented as the physical environment she occupies and no matter what her sources are, she embodies cultural 'knowledge' with passion and exclusivity.

George, a younger friend of Artemis, intensely influenced by her ideas and charisma, strongly believed that there was something 'special' about the Delos case. I remember visiting him in early spring in his 'souvenir shop', where he showed me a nationalist journal that was published at the time. National issues were hot news then, because of the resurgence of the Macedonian issue in Greece. In the 'journal' *Davlos*, a neo-nationalist conspiracy theory was being camouflaged with pagan references. George was attempting to comment on an analogous article, that also referred to Delos. In the meantime, he based his excuse for being on Mykonos not on choice, but on some mysterious attraction. He also mentioned a story of a *'simadiaki' speira* ('fateful' helix) on a stone that he had found as an *objet trouvé* a few days before on a trip to Delos. At the time, his enquiries concerned 'personal things' that were somehow considered to be linked with the symbol of the helix, and gave him a metaphysical sign that he was on the right track. George clearly believed that, by residing in this part of the world, he was accomplishing a difficult, but nevertheless inspired, ontological task.

Comments of this sort occur in a host of contexts in post- as well as pre-modern cultures, but I by no means want to imply that George was a New Age follower who spent his time thinking passionately about 'the signs'. Yet, his enquiry into the metaphysical aspect of his lifestyle choices, and his attempt to find an excuse for applying mystique to it, is indicative of the *Mykoniots*' discourse in general.

Penelope, a well-educated Mykonian woman who works for the local library, gave me the richest folkloric information while I was on the island. She also attempted to make her own analysis of the subject regarding the cultural consequences of Mykonos' proximity to Delos. The notoriety of Mykonos surfaces once again in Penelope's 'unreasonable' statements of this sort: 'Mykonian wine has a distinct taste. Everything Mykonian has a unique taste. The taste and juices are made from the light.' Penelope would also link the Delian and Mykonian cultures directly employing folkloric arguments: 'Mykonians used to worship Lineus Dionysus, the god of wine, and ancient coins have been found representing him in the excavations of Mykonos ... Our people say that Mykonos, Delos and Rhenia are skins of the same onion.' Penelope would go on to talk about the resemblance of the *apokriatika* (carnival's traditional dances and other customs) of the early decades of the twentieth century, as direct survivals from antiquity, and especially as Dionysiac *kataloipa* (remnants), from the cults that were established by the various cultures, that had occupied the area down the centuries.

It is clear that symbolic extensions from the space-myth of Delos have been used to refer to the newly formed tourist and cosmopolitan identity of Mykonos. There is a whole local rhetoric concerning the charms and 'charisma' of Mykonos that, to my mind, inter alia, exploits and imitates qualities initially attached to

Apollo's island, qualities such as Delos' mythical 'radiance'. There are extreme cases of visitors who have eventually turned themselves into local connoisseurs, who enthusiastically promote the myth's displacement. A typical example is that of Karl, a bizarre case of an alternative botanist. Karl is of German origin, but lives all over the place, and has been coming and going to and from Mykonos from the seventies onwards. During the summer of 1993, I heard Karl arguing several times that Apollo's energy had long been transferred to Mykonos, and that the sacred vibrations from Delos had transplanted themselves to the island's crowds. Karl wanted to 'purify' the Delos Bar with his incense every evening that summer, as some kind of ethical obligation to the bar's owner who gave him accommodation. In addition to all this, Karl had a manic hobby: he was forever taking pictures of the bar's customers — Delos being a bar that happened to accommodate the 'beautiful people' and their followers, a specially stylish clientele that Mykonos attracted for three decades or so (at least until recently). He would argue that in this bar one could find modern versions of Apollo and Aphrodite.[7] For Karl, Apollo was not solely a mythical persona. 'His energy still moves and inspires Mykonos. Apollo, like Shiva who had 108 different faces, lives here in different forms, inhabiting different faces.' He is vaguely planning to write a book referring to the eight sides of Apollo's persona. Finally, he used to constantly repeat his belief that 'the sacred vibrations had moved on from [ancient] Delos, to [modern] Mykonos.'

The fetishisation of the Cycladic space, especially the area surrounding Delos, may also be found in residual local notions of uniqueness. *Kyr*-Thodoris, eighty-two, a one-time farmer who had long since not needed to work to support his family, having turned to tourism, told me, in an attempt to explain why it was only Mykonos, of all the Greek islands, that managed to achieve such a notorious reputation: 'Mykonos is the centre of *Isimerinos* (the Equator). Thus, the climate of Mykonos cannot be found in any other *perifereia* (district) of the Cyclades. When a strong north wind blows and the weather is cool, if you go to the monastery up the hill you will see that only the edge of the weather gets there.'[8] *Kyr*-Thodoris would argue mysteriously, that on the one small island there are distinct climatic zones: 'When it blows up there, it will be calm here. Now, when the south wind comes, it might rain elsewhere but not here. Here we only get the edge of the rain.' For some mysterious reason, without explicitly referring to Delos, *Kyr*-Thodoris built an analogous myth of a charismatic space. By using the land of Mykonos as a charismatic space, *Kyr*-Thodoris applies metaphysics to the idiosyncrasies of nature that brought this place its success.[9] But one must not be seduced by the folkloric beauty of *Kyr*-Thodoris' theories on local weather magic or be in a hurry to judge them as the product of simple naivety. *Kyr*-Thodoris can also be rational and materialistic when discussing current Greek politics and the development projects that are going on all around him.

Artemis and the other *Mykoniots* constantly comment on how the locals effortlessly manage to put aside their own moral code in the face of the pan-hedonistic appetites of the island's visitors. She suggests that they do not actually have to make any efforts – since they themselves are predisposed to their own version of hedonism – as they are genuinely *diestramenoi* (mentally twisted). '*O Mastoras*, [the Artisan][10] fucks his wife and the sister of his wife. Old Petros does the same. Here, there traditionally exists *eklytos vios* [a liberal, amoral way of life]. The local Mykonians are heavy drinkers. They are *paradopistoi* [skinflints].'

The assumption that Mykonos is a special locus with its 'locals' possessing special qualities, with special architecture and a special 'energy' is a commonplace rhetoric of both the exogenous and the indigenous residents. It may be interesting to explore this notion of the 'charismatic space' a bit further. Antonio, a long-term and faithful aficionado of Mykonos, a cosmopolitan who lives some months of the year in Chelsea and the rest on Mykonos, occasionally flying to India in-between, believes that both Mykonos and Delos over and above 'the photogenic element', share a strong magnetic field, which derives from 'the rocky landscape and the radioactive elements it entails, and also the traces of cobalt and barite'.[11] Nevertheless, for Antonio, Mykonos remains only '*hamilis pistotitas antanaklasi*, meaning 'a poor reflection [of Delos]'.

A Greek artist friend started visiting Mykonos recently. As a left-winger and a typical product of the May '68 generation, he despised what Mykonos stood for, so avoided going there. But he was interested in the area, mostly in Delos, and mentioned to me the idea of an 'energy' triangle, situated between Delos, Mykonos and the nearby Orthodox shrine on the island of Tinos. This was the first time I had heard of the triangular theory, but soon afterwards I realised that there was a pagan trend in Greek culture which promoted theories of this sort. Paying attention to this kind of discourse made me recognise the 'triangular theory' underlying the ideas of charismatic space recorded by my own informants. Dionysis, the artist mentioned above, began to be infatuated with Mykonos' charms and repeated his visits to the 'forbidden' island of the elite, constantly seeking to establish bonds with the place (directly with Mykonos, but indirectly and more importantly with Delos). Finally, Dionysis got married one November on the island of Delos, in the presence of one witness, a priest, and the guardian of the archaeological remains. It was the first Orthodox wedding ever reported on the ancient island, I was told by his enthusiastic bride. The talented artist and thinker continued to come back and merge with the specific energising power of the triangle.

Later on, I discussed this idea with Eleonora, one of the mentors of the *Mykoniots'* milieu and a believer in religious syncretism. It was Easter Sunday but instead of celebrating the festive day, participating in the extensive all-day parties, we spent the afternoon talking about this idea. Eleonora enthusiastically volunteered to elaborate on the basic premise I offered her by attributing different qualities of ecstatic experience to the three distinct energy centres. So we took my fieldnote book and drew the 'triangle'. Thus, firstly, Tinos would be a centre for purely 'religious' ecstasy, through union with God via the mainstream Orthodox rituals.[12] The 'religious level' is synonymous for Eleonora with the 'realistic level', an ecstasis accomplished via the accepted cultural rules within the boundaries of the official *Ekklisia* (Church).[13] Secondly, Delos, according to this line of thinking, works as a centre of "pure" ecstatic experience on a 'metaphysical level'. The whole mystery that revolves round Delos' ecstatic 'energy' is protected by its unexplored past and references to vague historical sources on the annual celebrations in honour of Apollo, called the *Delia Mystiria*, once performed on the ancient island and now misused by modern Delos obsessives.[14] Finally, and more importantly for the purposes of this ethnography, there is Mykonos, the last angle of the 'energy' triangle. There the ecstatic is experienced at a 'physical level'. Pan-hedonism, maximum physical pleasure, is accomplished through swimming, drinking, eating, entertaining, intercourse, taking drugs, etc.[15]

My fieldnotes are full of metaphysical 'explanations' and quotations like the examples given above in order to explain Mykonos' *otherness*. The bottom line is that nobody comes up with a straightforward, logical explanation, such as for example that Mykonos is a normal Greek island, beautiful but spoiled. The residents of the island need the myth, justified either metaphysically, physically, or historically. Emma, an English woman who has lived permanently on the island for thirty years, maintains (as was mentioned at the opening of this book) that Mykonos functions for the nomadic and affective group of *Mykoniots* in the same way as the placenta which feeds the foetus. To her mind, Mykonos is a place where she feels secure and free: 'You feel protected and not vulnerable.' Alternatively, for Stefanos, Mykonos has *kapsouroskoni* ('infatuation dust'). 'There is a familiar element. It reminds one of being at home, an extremely comfortable feeling.' Stefanos is a hotel manager and as a professional in the tourist business he has held similar positions around the world. But once he discovered Mykonos and had lived there for a couple of years, he realised it was the first tourist place in which he had enjoyed spending more time, especially in the off season.

The common denominator to all the above theories of a spatial otherness is the fact that those who create and reproduce them adore Mykonos and spend their lives there. Some earn a lot of money, some spend their lives without or with minimal 'work', while others work hard to survive on an expensive island; but all need a theory to support the 'unorthodox' choice they have made to reside on an island which [culturally] 'produces' and reproduces nothing apart from myth and pleasure.

Why do you come to Mykonos so often? Why did you choose to live here? How you can afford to live here and still remain so passionate about this minute place? The answers to these sorts of questions were usually of a 'metaphysical' nature rather then rational explanations. Even with those who were attempting to give me a socio-economic argument, the element of fetishisation of the space was always present.[16]

September: back to the annual pilgrimage to Deles – the preparation for the most established identity ritual of the Mykoniots d'élection

Delos, the hub around which the Cyclades (Kukloi-rings) radiate, was formed by nature to be the focal point of a seaman's world. (Ernle Bradford quoted in Durrell 1978: 237)

Delos is three-quarters of an hour away from Mykonos by motorboat. Nowadays, the thousands of tourists will visit by local boats specially equipped for the cruise, a trip that starts at nine in the morning and returns at two in the afternoon. The tour includes a guide who shows you around the remains. Apart from its archaeological sites, the island of Delos consists of its 'ancient' rocks and some modern houses, no more than a dozen, I think, that belong either to the French Archaeological School or mostly to the archaeologists employed by the state to work on the excavations. What makes this archaeological site exclusive is obviously the fact that it is situated on a secluded island in the middle of the Aegean, with no current 'civilisation' or permanent inhabitants to spoil or abuse it.[17]

The island was mainly a centre for the worship of mainly Apollo and Dionysus, the god who allowed the ancients to fulfil all their profane promiscuous desires, but shrines were erected for all sorts of pagan cults and deities, of which the remains have been excavated. The nearby island of Rhenia functioned as both cemetery and birthplace for the inhabitants of Delos in antiquity since, by law, their Athenian patrons forbade birth and death on the sacred island. The current inhabitants of Mykonos refer to the complex of Delos and Rhenia with a single name, thus considering the two islands as a single unit, using the invented plural nickname 'Deles'. The Greek state rents out large infertile tracts of land to the local farmers for a peppercorn rent to rear and graze their cattle there. For that reason the Mykonian families involved with Deles have built their tiny Cycladic churches on both islands, only to add some modern shrines in the ancient sacred locus. Once a year, they hold their own *paniyiri*, to celebrate each church's name day.

For my informants, the sacredness and notoriety that the primordial myth of ancient Delos entails works as a symbolic extension of their exclusivity as a group, and more especially as 'select' and 'extreme' individuals. As I have already mentioned, the rhetoric is variable and endless, but the common denominator is that their choice to reside, or rather 'get stuck', on this Aegean island is something of a … vocation. People have attempted to express this idea of 'space seduction' in a variety of ways either as the necessity of obeying their inner voice of freedom, or as a form of welcome to the world of unlimited hedonistic choices to which they surely belong.

Led by a belief that cultural 'truth' comes from local discourses, I was constantly asking questions to try and understand the symbolic connotation

Delos had in the minds of my informants. But for the unsuspecting reader, I think it would be wiser to move from the rhetorical level to practice.

I will continue by describing how the *Mykoniots'* organise their annual feasts on Delos. We may then more readily accept the importance my informants place on Delos as a symbol and be able to interpret the idiosyncratic communal 'pilgrimages' they make each year to the complex of islands that they call Deles.

The Mykoniots' trip to Deles

When the strong local winds have calmed down, and by good fortune that usually happens when the bulk of the tourists have gone, then the ['metaphysical'] Delos 'invitation' becomes the focus of the *Mykoniots'* daily discussions. They call their ritualistic excursion 'a trip to Deles', using the indigenous' expression for the geographical area, imitating the locals' singing accent. I've been on these excursions with the same group of *Mykoniots* more than five times and the routine of the trip and its organisation was more or less identical each time.

The urge to 'worship' at the ancient and private locus will usually manifest itself during September, and an additional incentive is given by the return of old friends to the island. Alternatively, it may be an occasion to honour special guests. Both these categories of visitors usually choose the less crowded season. Trips to the sacred island are also organised in the case of some unique astronomical phenomenon, or after Orpheus' wedding (see the next chapter), or simply to celebrate the fact that the weather has calmed down. It will all start somewhat like this: on an unusually windless day at the beach, a member of the clique will remind the *sinafi*, especially the elderly patrons of the group, that it's time to visit Delos. There, on the beach, in their analogous private and symbolic space, the nudist descendants of the 'beautiful people', lying on their *pareos* (sarongs) are endlessly smoking joints while planning the night's events in Mykonos town. *Mykoniots* are usually surrounded by their 'retinue'. Those of the 'freshly arrived' or established guests who are 'accepted', or those whom the *Mykoniots* want to incorporate into their exclusive milieu, will lie down at a friendly distance but slightly farther away from the core 'patronage' group.

So when the idea for the annual excursion to Delos comes up, the *Mykoniots'* *parea* (group of friends) will react more or less as follows: Orpheus will draw heavily on the shared joint and immediately start making plans as to how to organise others to do the dirty work for all his brilliant ideas. Markos will gurgle a little with pleasure, but do nothing. George, as the youngest and least powerful among the 'patrons' will be overwhelmingly enthusiastic. Finally, after a silence, the apparently oblivious Antonis will come back to life, sit up on his *pareo* (sarong) and speak last. If he agrees with the Delos proposition, he will give information as to how he will 'instruct' his 'own' group to get organised. If the feedback on the proposition about a Deles excursion reaches that level, Hercules also gets involved. By group tradition, he is the established organiser of the ritual. He talks about the importance of inviting the 'key people', and he proceeds to make arrangements by persuading others to go to the key *Mykoniots'* homes in order to inform them. He will also announce a symbolic time of departure, and then the group of *Mykoniot* 'patrons' may proceed to their daily dips in the sea. After that the topic may be changed completely and if you happen to be sitting around them, not being familiar with the group's mentality, you may wonder if all this extensive planning is going to come to anything. But the power of the patrons' appeal to the group is that they communicate less with words and more through their own 'local' knowledge, by recognising vibrations, moods, and general trends in the weather. Somehow, the rest of the *Mykoniots* have the necessary knowledge and soberness to decipher when the above discussion and planning should be taken seriously and whether or not to appear the next day at the harbour.

If all the omens are positive, the crowd will be informed, Hercules will go to make arrangements with the boatmen, and some will decide to have an early night. The group of representative *Mykoniots d'élection* will usually be somewhere between thirty and sixty and on some rare occasions up to a hundred people. It always seemed a miracle to me how all these people were finally informed, since almost nobody really bothered to make any arrangements, except for buying lots of food and drink just minutes before departure. (But in Mykonos' small secluded world, though there was minimal telecommunication at the time, news travelled fast, and the annual ritualistic return to Deles was an attractive proposition for the *Mykoniot*.) One has to bear in mind that some members of the Mykonian *sinafia* lose daily contact during high summer, since they dislike Mykonos when it is crowded. Consequently, this is an extra reason to meet in private (they mainly lose touch since most of them are working hard for the tourists during the summer).[18]

There are some key 'recipients' of the Delos 'call', who although living in seclusion in remote houses, always appear for the group's annual symbolic gathering. Just for this occasion, Artemis will leave her dogs and cats on their own for an entire day, and Eleonora will pay some attention to the 'macho' seventies male patrons of the old-fashioned hippie group she has been meeting for the last thirty years on the island. Julie will also leave her current all-women *parea* and join the 'old' group, her original Mykonian *parea*. Antonio will suspend his public relations for the expensive and exclusive clubs, where his 'celebrity' and titled friends are hidden, and appear for once with his peers, spending the whole day with them. Antonio and Aris are both honoured guides on the sacred trip. Although Antonio *has* to visit the 'sacred' island with his celebrity friends more than thirty times a year, using private yachts, motorboats and local transportation, he will always appear on the day of his *sinafi*'s pilgrimage. Since the excursion to Delos is among the most private, and ideally collective, rituals the group performs, it sometimes gives an opportunity to solve problems in relationships within the group.

The appointment was set for ten-thirty, but the group had hardly assembled an hour later at the small harbour. Those who had been out late the night before had to run to catch the boat, while Hercules finally gave the boatmen the order to depart only to find some members of the group complaining about friends who were 'on their way'. This would always cause a little friction that evaporated as soon as the boat left the small harbour. Hercules would regain his generous smile and shine as the most primordial and experienced pagan of the annual fiesta. Hercules, who loves eating, as well as preparing food, is responsible for the shopping list, a task he voluntarily undertakes. He traditionally manages to gather aboard Thodoris' boat all the 'good quality Mykonian products' he can collect from the few 'Mykonian' gardens that exist.[19] As a chief of the Dionysiac fiesta he would give small tasks to the early comers. The 'old' would pretend to be sleepy, sipping their morning coffee in the coffee shops of the harbour. Hercules would do all his work first and then wait with a sprig of basil behind his ear, occasionally checking the hold of the boat for new supplies or bothering to give some instructions to the guests, but mainly performing his bonding with the local fisherman, and with the owner of the boat.

The most important element in this excursion that made me upgrade it to a core 'identity ritual' of the *Mykoniots d'élection* is that there is, at the moment of departure from the Mykonian harbour, a certain atmosphere of sacred commensality. The commensal element is not at all new to the group's gatherings, but what seems different here is strangely enough the level of commitment on this occasion: a commitment to a yearly self-created ritual, a bond which is conspicuously displayed by 'extreme' individuals who, otherwise, struggle by means of their idiosyncratic lifestyles to prove how commitment to any given principle is unnecessary, especially commitment to any traditional or religious ritual, and most importantly, to a group.

On our way to the source

Whoever managed to make it on-board, was already in 'Noah's Ark'. At last my *Mykoniot* group was defined. There were no *xenerotoi* (a slang expression for sober people) invited on this trip. And the first and most obvious sign of a *xenerotos* is being uncool and negative about the consumption of substances that change 'the mainstream perception of things'. The collective spirit of the group would quietly grow in the moments before reaching the sacred island. People would be silent but in good spirits, maybe still quite sleepy. Drinking would be slow before the actual 'pilgrimage' to Delos. When this 'Yioras ritual'[20] had been repeated many times in a year some members would sometimes hesitate to stop over 'one more time' at the ancient remains. Their hesitation would be overruled by the mentors of the group who would silently decide to make the stopover, maybe for the third time that year. The whole trip to Yioras 'loses its power' if a stopover at the ancient site is not included. The most experienced among them, would say to me that Delos is a place to absorb a pure 'universal energy'.

When the wind is calm, a rare pleasure for the inhabitants of Mykonos, exploration of the sacred island is quite exhausting, since there is only one tiny tree to give shade in the whole archaeological area. The outdoor remains, exposed to the sun, are surrounded by the Cycladic rocks. The whole setting is of an unprotected beauty, a piece of history that is all the more seductive to the visitor, since it is neglected by the carelessness of the Greek state. The visitor is lost in the labyrinthine experience of the open-air museum of Delos. If not in a group, one feels as if responsible for the rediscovery of the ancient temples.

The tree that Leto supposedly held onto in order to give birth to Apollo was a mythical symbol for the ancients. Today, the only tree in the ruins is an alleged replacement of this same sacred tree, a place that mentor Antonis was keen to show me as the sacred place where Apollo was born. We sat there for a while, ecstatic and speechless, and quite relieved as it was the only place offering shade to escape from the strong sun. We had an hour-and-a- half to wander around the sacred island, according to the instructions of our Delian mentor. As soon as we reached Delos, Hercules announced the departure time and moved determinedly through the gate where the archaeology students sold tickets. The *Mykoniots'* feel that this place feeds off them, I suppose, so they proudly passed the ticket office without paying for a ticket. More often than not, the supervisor would know them from Mykonos and would say nothing; if not, they would say something outrageous and again try to avoid paying. In this case, it was both a matter of 'honour' as well as a matter of acting like teenagers who manage to slip unseen through the gate. Within the group of the *Mykoniots*, there would always be an unofficial guide, who would give shocking details about the life of the ancient Delians. For the *Mykoniots*, ancient Delos is a familiar world, or even better, an aesthetic prototype that stands for a continuum through the centuries of the hedonistic lifestyle. More precisely, it is the Hellenistic period of Delos that discursively inspires the neo-pagan and cosmopolitan 'ethos' of the *Mykoniots*. Through an eclectic historical and cultural constructivism, *Mykoniots* occasionally assimilate to the cosmopolitanism of Hellenistic Delos, the marginal identity of the one-time Mykonian pirates, the 'Greek' beatnik and so on. This aesthetic principle of a cultural cosmopolitanism is reinforced by an ontologically driven one (i.e., symbolically belonging nowhere), projected onto the contemporary space-myth of Mykonos as a tourist, amoral, multicultural and thus non-threatening space.

It was not at all clear to me where all this information about Delos' extreme and Dionysiac properties came from. One thing, though, I am positive about, was the *Mykoniots'* eagerness to determine the area's history as if hedonism and amorality had been its 'metaphysical' driving force. Among the connoisseurs of the sacred Delian culture and its mysteries was Aris, a cult dandy in the streets of Mykonos during the seventies, who had expanded his knowledge on Delos enormously over the years, both intentionally and circumstantially. He came with us this particular morning and I followed his group to the ancient theatre to listen to his anti-tour narrations about the know-how of the ancient Delians. Aris currently confines himself to the twin worlds of Delos and Mykonos.

Our guide also happened to be one of the most original characters left over from the Mykonian seventies' scene and a famous DJ of that time, having completely repudiated his urban origins. He had left Athens behind for the last fifteen years and become the most conscious 'Dionysiac' resident on the island, with a fanatical devotion to Mykonos. Eventually he even lost interest in travelling. In the winter, Aris would be an English tutor. With his current girlfriend being a member of a group of architects that were, at the time, allowed to reside on the sacred island to commence some major works there, Aris spent half his time on Delos. The fact that he managed to spend time on the forbidden island gave him a certain ethnographic 'glamour'. Before retreating to the sacred island, Aris had had a long period of ten years completely assimilating the local lifestyle of the 'heroic alcoholics' of the Mykonian coffee shops at the harbour. For Aris the whole story about the idiosyncratic business of 'living in Mykonos' came down to a common denominator from ancient times right up to the present day: excessive consumption of substances, either wine or *founda* (grass), or other hallucinatory drugs that were traditionally derived from self-sown plants that were abundant in the area.

As our host on the sacred island, Aris narrated an altogether different story about the multicultural and constantly 'stoned' Delians. One might argue that it is not the substance that determines one's personality, but Aris would object: 'There is no way to enter the world of the *myimenoi* [the initiated], without this acquaintance with the substances. Locals [meaning the Mykonians] have been drinking since time immemorial. In the archaeological museum there are traces of opium consumption. There are stories of old Mykonian locals, who tried *mandraouli* [mandrake] *apo mangia* [to play it cool] or by accident.'

Aris on Delos

Aris loved to demystify the myth of continuity between ancient Delos and modern Mykonos by employing his authority as a connoisseur of Mykonian affairs: 'In ancient times, Mykonos was not even the supplier of the Delians. Tinos, instead, was the island with the closest affiliations. The only thing that Mykonos has in common with Delos is its Dionysiac personalities, these people here ... though, they do not truly understand their history and their land. They are people who are for the most part handling the situation intuitively. Substances are important, because they help them compose a Dionysiac persona (*ftiahnontai san Dionysoi*). Mykonos is not an echo of Delos, or complementary to Delos, Mykonos is only close to Delos.'

Aris, qualified with a Mykonian 'past' and a Delian 'present', was the best guide for the *Mykoniots* and their guests at the Delian remains. He used to draw an interesting parallel between Delos' name myth and the quality of people gathered on present-day tourist Mykonos: 'Delos, after a long period of being *a-delos* (invisible), a wandering island in the sea with no stable position, was turned into a stable and visible place so that Apollo, the God of light and beauty, could be born there. In mythology, Delos has its invisible side. This is exactly like the people gathered on this island nowadays. Today they live here, tomorrow they might disappear. Nothing is stable, although we try to organise things.'

Aris' tour of Delos or rather his anti-tour, saw him pick out the least mainstream remains of the archaeological sites, and concentrate mostly on details of Delians' social history. Instead of focusing on the trivial historical and archaeological information, he concentrated on the cosmopolitan and commercial aspect of the Delians' lifestyle, as well as on their hedonistic and sacred culture. He talked of their liberal sexual behaviour, their socialisation and most importantly their drug technologies. 'We', the group of select *Mykoniots*, as Aris' friends, had a distinct honour: an unofficial permit to the private part of the on-site museum. The rest of the tourists stayed on the other side of the museum, as we disappeared with an enthusiastic archaeologist, a friend of Aris who told us the stories of the new finds. It was obvious that Delos was like a home to Aris, so when it was time for us to go back to our boat, he disappeared. It was already two o'clock and the rest of the tourists were also on their way back to the boats, leaving the Delian remains to their normal peace. Our group also started assembling; some had already improved their tan, and in spite of being overtly excited and ecstatic about the silence and the 'energy' of the forgotten remains, they began to switch to the recreational part of the excursion.

The core ritual: our glendi (feasting) at Yioras beach

Hercules counted heads and the whole atmosphere magically changed to that of a normal Mykonian-style crowd, busy and loud. People started consuming beer and spirits and singing improvised songs dedicated to the secluded beach of Yioras where the group's gathering would eventually be celebrated. Indicators of a shared group identity, the first person plural 'we' and 'our' were spontaneously emerging as prefaces to the naïve lyrics that George was improvising on the spot. *Mykoniots* were acting in this instance as boy scouts who were paying honour to their own clan. It is important to note that there was no dope around so far, a highly unusual situation for these kind of 'scouts'. The absence of substances, so far, emphasised a basic element of liminality. The devout and ritualistic atmosphere connected with the *Mykoniots*' 'excursion to Delos' reached its formal climax in the walk around the ruins.

Eleonora and her group of ten other 'disciples' went all the way up to Mount Kithnos. There Eleonora, as she explained later, had witnessed a pagan baptism ritual some years earlier. She showed the group the sacred cave of Apollo. It seemed as if time was passing very slowly and I myself had the feeling that the group had been reunited after a long absence.

We still had twenty minutes to go to reach the remote beach of Yioras. Rhenia, the isle of the dead, was also uninhabited, with the exception of some locals who come and go to take care of their crops and cattle. Especially in the summer, there was a recent trend for some young Mykonians to live there in seclusion. The sea surrounding Rhenia was occupied by luxury yachts, which preferred to anchor there, keeping a low profile.

After I had participated in this trip to Yioras once or twice, I caught myself expecting to reach the remote beach that symbolises the unique experience of the 'Delian gathering' of the *Mykoniots* (a sign that, as an ethnographer, I was caught in the myth of my own informants – reproducing it and recreating it). Michalis, the owner of the boat, had recently become a specialist tour operator arranging for tourists to spend a day at the Yioras beach, probably after seeing the archaeological site. The operation is called a 'private beach party' and dates back to a tradition of the seventies. The hold of his motorboat was always full of alcohol with all the useful paraphernalia for a beach party. The beach was initially prepared to accommodate the Mykonian *parees* of the local fishermen: it had a natural barbecue space equipped with charcoal and grills protected by the rocks to nullify the wind, a small wooden dock to reach landfall which was also used to clean the fish; where Michalis and his friend, Andreas, would occasionally spend even more time fishing for a last-minute catch. Nearby shelter had been constructed to protect the fishermen from the sun. Beneath it there was a large scratched table, that could accommodate twenty or more, and several worn out plastic chairs. Next to the large table there was another lower one, probably part of an old boat found on the beach that functioned as the preparation table. There, first of all, Hercules would place the characteristically elegant bunch of 'Mykonian' wild flowers, bought earlier that day from the donkey merchants. The rest of the scenery consisted of the familiar dry landscape, with its imposing sculpted stones. Apart from a rather old, deserted *kellaki* (a miniature house, a cell) standing on the other side of the bay, nothing suggested the existence of a single living soul in the area. The sky was clear, the weather extremely hot, and the stillness was complete.

The *Mykoniots* felt immediately comfortable and the members of the group started helping one another to unload food and drinks. The preparatory table was soon crowded. A 'stereotyped' division of labour was attempted, with no great success, and initially men would prompt the women (not specifically 'their' women, since many of them 'haven't got' a woman of their own – or not on a long-term basis) to stem their hunger with snacks and salads. The greedy consumption of ouzo, wine, beer, whisky and vodka, as well as the constant rolling of joints began on the commensal table which throughout the afternoon was occupied by the mentors of the group. The 'old Indian[21] Antonis', owner of the Delos Bar, was usually accompanied by some members of 'his group' (the team of his employees for the current tourist season) and his close friend, Markos from Kansas, whose annual arrival had, until recently, provided the incentive for organising the Deles excursion.[22] Near Markos, the central focus of the Yioras ritual, I can recall seeing the two brothers, Aristos and Nikodimos, long-standing members of the *sinafi* and owners of another legendary bar on the island. They are the great exceptions to the *sinafi's* bachelor world, since they both have 'kids and a wife' who would occasionally accompany them. Aristos started playing his *toumberleki* (a traditional Turkish drum), almost as soon as the first joint had been consumed, and Markos and Apostolis joined him eventually. Other important mentors of the *sinafi*, like Hercules and Orpheus were busy making their guests feel at home. They usually played a sociable part in the group with their 'select' guests, or simply took the trouble to include some junior *Mykoniot*-to-be in the Delian excursion. Some of the women mentors of the *sinafi* were obviously attempting to avoid the focal male-dominated bonding and preferred, like Eleonora, to gather in smaller groupings and arranged their *pareos* accordingly.

The overall picture was a unified mass of naked bodies, lying across the long deserted beach. Soon after, nearly everybody would move her or his 'individuality' around and interact with the mentors' group, or join people who were swimming. A group of seventy completely naked people, some taking no trouble to 'hide' behind their *pareos*, even at the table, were moving freely, sometimes accompanied by all sorts of modern gadgets like a walkman. The focal point remained throughout the large fisherman's table where the 'mentors' kept improvising. People had to gravitate there in order to be sociable, in order to eat, and drink, in order to participate in the *kefi* (high spirits), play music and especially in order to 'get high'. The mentors just managed a brief dip, only to return to stoke the atmosphere. Aristos reached the first musical climaxes with his insistent improvisations that soon became a collective expression with instruments, voices and lyrics for the occasion, such as George's rhyme: 'Nobody enjoys it as much as we do!'

The hot sun, and the high consumption of substances intensified the improvisations and they became more primitive as time passed. Hercules took Michalis and started preparing pieces of meat and fish for the grill. Soon after, he fixed the fire and pretending he had too much to do, found volunteers to whom he handed over the difficult job of actually cooking the food. He later went back to the fisherman's table and got ready for his big moment, a solo improvisation performed on his own flute.

Hercules assumed (and moreover assumed that we assumed, too) that he got especially inspired by the 'Apollonian domain' (which also extends to the island of Rhenia). His amateur flute-playing in the sacred domain of the Deles complex took on a highly ritualistic flavour. This, at least, was the feeling he conveyed to us by the way he prepared himself. He hid for a while in the fields to pick up his precious flute-case. The way he ritualistically opened his Indian handmade case containing his flute was suggestive of his performative mood. Finally, he reappeared at the large table with a joyous expression and waited for 'his moment'. When he felt the time was right, he joined in the collective improvisation in a forceful manner, semi-naked, with the basil still tucked behind his ear. His passion brought the rest of the players to a halt and allowed him to perform solo the task of ritualistically playing to honour Apollo.

In the meanwhile hot food and *mezedes* were gradually reaching the table. Eventually Orpheus reached his own 'high' in a brilliant performance of his own improvisation. Completely naked near the fisherman's table, he invented his own percussion 'instruments' by employing practically anything he thought suitable. Eleonora also joined in, playing some other unfamiliar Oriental instruments brought along for the occasion, but mostly improvising with her fragile Indian-style singing. This was probably the only time of the year when Eleonora was ceremonially 'reconciled' with the old male mentors of the group. Since she had known them for a long time, with her being an older *Mykoniot* [as well as a female], the situation was delicate. In their eyes and discourses, although Eleonora was on the island permanently, and definitely one of them, she was occasionally 'excluded' on the pretext that she was a 'woman'. The real reason was that the (admittedly male-dominated) patronage system of initiation into the *Mykoniot* milieu was somehow disrupted by Eleonora's prestige. On her part, always reluctant to cede an inch of her 'symbolic' power in the actions of the cosmopolitan island, she was forever provoking the overwhelmingly male area of the *sinafi* just by her original moody temperament. The reader should not interpret the above as a particular gender stereotype. The 'repressed female' role is partly performative and partly cultural, as much as the 'macho female'. Among the *Mykoniots*, the rule is that the symbolic power of any category, in essence, is contested.

Towards sunset, when the situation was getting out of control, Aristos accompanied Markos' rather old and contradictory version of a traditional song, a repetitive and clearly self-deprecating verse that went like this: 'We, the old men, we, the old men are the most sensible kids ... ' I was beginning to enjoy listening to these naïve rhythms and serious improvisations, since for a participant-observer the atmosphere of the Deles 'excursion' was just what a fieldworker of such a diverse group of 'extreme' individuals longs to immortalise: a conscious, yet symbolic 'collective' act. Some signs of 'Greekness' were emerging from Aristos' initiative. He loved to 'play local', with the help of his companion, the latecomer Aris (Aris had been left behind on Delos but arrived later with another motorboat). They tried to put proper lyrics to the *glendi*, so they sang old, well-known *rembetika*, and Markos, who was born and brought up in 'Constantinople', turned out to be quite sentimental about it. During all this 'build up' time, Antonis sat quietly in the centre of the event, but nevertheless taking an active part with his sardonic smile, suggesting his own prestige as a performer by his very silent acceptance of not being the centre of attraction (an act he performs in his nightclub every night).

Artemis, with none of her dogs and cats, but nevertheless still anxious about the beloved pets she had left behind, kept collecting remnants of the food to feed them. The picture of Artemis patiently collecting food for her animals is typical of every celebration where the over-consumption of food is conspicuous, as typical as is her unwillingness to indulge herself by eating. She would always be too preoccupied with other peoples' problems and desires. During this trip she was also trying to sell her imprisoned husband's book about drugs. Artemis preferred to talk and 'get high', rather than perform solo and 'get high'. A group of women in their thirties, a male friend and his dog were gathered around Artemis, who sat in the middle lecturing. In the background were the primitive but pleasant sounds of the group. Bodies clothed in sarongs were swaying rhythmically. Occasionally, George would pronounce on their 'freedom': 'Nobody enjoys it as much as we do.' Another group were still lying on the beach. They were into a more esoteric 'trip', with a woman among them performing shiatsu on a series of devotees. In front lay the sea – the calmest I've ever seen – and behind the 'rebels', *ta remalia*, performing their favourite ritual at last: completely free with no audience, no tourists, no *xenerotoi* (sober, 'square people', an expression that covers, more or less, the rest of the world), no ethical constraints, no real culture, no real tradition. 'Eclectic memory' was the motto for the 'culture' the *Mykoniots* wanted to reproduce. Their eclectic historical and cultural constructivism centred on the idea of the pan-hedonistic liberalism of the classical period of Greek antiquity: an 'amoral' and endless existential preoccupation with 'taking care of the self'. An eclectic imaginative reproduction of the ancient 'lifestyle', that included various 'tastes', pantheism, as well as conveniently controversial multiple symbols.

The *Mykoniots'* historical constructivism can be traced to the extended phenomenon Faubion (1993) describes in his study of the Greek upper classes in the centre of Athens. Faubion treats historical constructivism as a form of cultural 'infrastructure', the collective unconscious practice of a nation. Reading back through my fieldnotes, what the *Mykoniots* were trying to imitate in this pagan ritual, reminded me of this reading of Greek modernity. Faubion characterises the Greek bourgeois discourse and practice of (aesthetically and consciously) reconstructing ethnic history and identity as a 'post-modern' version of 'Greek' cultural classicism. Yet, my informants' romantic love for antiquity apparently had a largely functional purpose: their aesthetic and strategic assimilation into the region's great 'past'. This was a conscious assimilation which served the cultural needs of the *Mykoniots'* alternative community. My *Mykoniot* informants, as both products of Greek culture and heirs to the chief representatives of the Greek 'hipster', were anchored to the least 'Greek' place in Greece.[23] Mykonos enabled them to express their 'Greekness' in a covert way in a hybridised cultural environment where a Greek could have easy access to Western aesthetic prototypes and a cosmopolitan modernity.

The *Mykoniots'* historical and cultural constructivism is eclectic in the sense that they consciously assimilate in their self-narrative the parts of history, as well as the parts of modernity, that seem to them to 'represent' their aesthetic categories. My attempt to interpret the Deles excursion as a ritual, implies that we should treat this case as another form of historical constructivism, far more aesthetic and performative than that described by Faubion, and less concerned with a teleological search for a culturally predetermined self. The *Mykoniots* live in the myths they intentionally create for themselves. They live at the edges of modern ethics, but they feed on their conspicuous explorations of being 'different' (rather then assimilating their guests' lifestyles) in order to acquire an 'unbiased' and not a 'mainstream' identity. They are not 'glamorous' proletarians for the modern intellectual observer or reader to romanticise or identify with. Instead, they are a peculiar new cosmopolitan class of eccentrics, that give an anthropologist a hard time because they do not fit any category exactly. Nevertheless, they are there and they are acting out and eclectically absorbing 'culture'. Their eclecticism, or simply their creativity, is silently spread via their mythical lifestyles. I know that the *Mykoniots* do not present a 'convenient' ethnographic case, unless you reduce them to numerous examples of bravado for tourist consumption, case studies of attractive individuals that function as local attractions, like the remains on Delos.

Afternoon on Yioras beach

During the long improvising session around the fisherman's table, some people were ignoring the *kefi* (high spirits), and engaging in small talk. One of these conversations eventually caught the collective attention of the group and so the *Mykoniot* 'patrons' began reminiscing. The topic was past experiences on the island, 'the old days', and especially the eighties on Mykonos. All of them were twenty years younger then, and literally the extremist examples of the recently 'modernised' Greek culture. The conversation was definitely male dominated, with the core topic being the period when the Greek police started having a serious presence on the island. Since the majority of the mentors had or used to have some involvement with a club or bar, as well as other businesses in the Mykonian *Hora*, explicitly bad experiences with the 'representatives of the law' were unavoidable. They talked about the old *desimata* (a slang expression referring to police 'busts' on houses, accompanied by convictions for abuse of the anti-drugs law), and the group's 'collective adventures' on the subject.[24] Comments were accompanied by sarcasms aimed at themselves and a pleasant 'recalling' of the old glory days.

I realised at that instant that the majority of women in the group, although very open-minded on the subject and completely 'independent' and present at the time of the events, stayed out of the conversation. They might be part of the memory, but they were not amongst those who had a symbolic right to openly recreate collective memories and talk about the group's 'collective' experiences.

As the sun was sinking behind the Delian hills, the primitive sounds from the large table were getting louder. Michalis, who in the meanwhile had left us with no boat for some time, reappeared. The sight of the motorboat released a second wave of 'primitive' sounds. The situation became a literally collective experience. Everybody gathered around the table being as expressive as they could within the limits of this collective improvisation. The sunset scene was breathtaking, but Michalis was excited by the beautiful girls of the company and the 'sacredness' of the exclusivity of being among the 'high-ups' of the town. He was satisfied, slowly sipping his whisky in the plastic cup he was offered. He was not at all in a hurry to take us back. The wind turned a little wilder as was always the case in this temple of light and wind. Apart from that everything in the picture was as still as the sunset, with me being the only person anxious about our return and the fact that everything was happening without any real order. Always aware of time, I kept asking Michalis how strong the local wind was, and when would be the 'right' time to go. I thought that we were ready to leave, I picked up my things and I was already uncomfortable, waiting for the 'end' of something wonderful. I was wrong though, since for the *Mykoniots* that was the best part: welcoming the dark, after an exhausting but soulful day. For them there was no end to their 'trip' to Deles. The show would go on, later in town, or later in another local *paniyiri*. In the meantime, Eleonora was drawing sounds of admiration from the group while performing her idiosyncratic *tsifteteli* (belly dance).

With the sunset on the Deles 'excursion' it was as if the heavy weight of the tourist season, that I personally experienced working in Orpheus' shop all summer, was very far away and symbolically over. The pressure of the high season was left behind, the prosperous autumn promised a series of commensal gatherings. The music and the vocal improvisations got louder, as the dark advanced across the horizon.

The fetishisation of a newly acquired 'tradition'

The Deles excursion has a long tradition in the *Mykoniots'* world. Susan, a British anthropologist who used to visit the island during the seventies remembers: 'In the old days, it was Baroutis' legendary *kaiki* (caïque), and the unforgettable beach parties of the seventies.' Baroutis was an attractive personality for the tourists because of his physical beauty and primitiveness and also due to the seductive patronage of a man that 'knew the sea'. Although the fetishisation of local heroes due to tourism was fairly new, the fetishisation of the sacred island of

Delos (and by extension Mykonos) can be traced back to Durrell's travelogues of the 1940s on the Greek islands (1978). More importantly, fetishisation can be traced to eighteenth-century travelogues where although the island of Mykonos is described as extremely boring, the traveller (Lord Charlemont) finally 'discovers' magic on Delos (Kousathanas 1989).

In turn, Durrell (ibid.) mentions something about some secret information on the healing powers of Apollo by moonlight (that he and his wife went on to enjoy), information that some generous *Mykoniot*-type friend tipped him off about. The 'ritual' of late-night provisions arriving with the motorboat that allegedly came to pick them up, and the description of a deserted beach with a magical landscape share a familiar feeling of 'sacredness', just as they share the same source of sacredness, i.e., Delos. Although staying on the island overnight was forbidden, Durrell sent back the caïque – that allegedly came to pick them up – once it had supplied him and his wife with some hot food for the night. While pretending that the motorboat had come to take them away, in reality they stayed on the (forbidden) Delian beach to spend the night and 'swam by the rising moon, the old Apollo therapy' – particularly pertinent since his wife was recovering from a grave operation (Durrell 1978: 236). Around midnight, when the moon was full, they revisited the Delian remains. Durrell describes these Delian moments with great empathy, in his literary way, offering some clues about the already established (European) fetishisation of the ancient Greek world, in which he, as a European himself was also a cultural shareholder.

Durrell talks about the exclusiveness of Mykonos's glamour, but there is nothing much about Mykonos in his explanation. Instead, it is all about Delos' attraction for unique men. The rest was the physical proximity to Delos. Why was it that Delos, and not any of the other islands among the rich Cycladic complex of the central Aegean, became so popular both ritualistically and commercially? One might wonder if this were a chicken-and-egg problem, but the important element is the fact that Mykonos in a sense 'inherited' this cultivated tradition of mystery. Why then did Delos become an important maritime centre, bearing in mind that there was a crucial absence of a good harbour on this island, Durrell kept asking. The sensation the myth of the ancient locus created, in combination with nature's aesthetics, accounts for endless misinformed or ahistorical explanations. There is an inherent challenge in solving attractive space-myths of this sort.

In nineties Mykonos, George and his *parea* also recreate their uniqueness, by rolling a joint, 'getting high' and imagining that they have reached the source of 'mystery' that inhabits the nearby ancient locus of Delos. The description of the Delos gathering reveals the persistence of pagan elements in the 'rituals of our own', an aesthetic principle that prevails as we shall see later on in the different ritual occasions of the *Mykoniots*. As I have argued already, the most important component that accounts for this semblance of paganism in these extreme individuals is their strong preference for and the endless repetition of collective experiences of transformation through substances, or via purely bodily, artistic and mental expressions. Along their haphazard and carefree lines of socialisation there is an ontological rule: a commitment to the group's *ftiaximo* (all sorts of technologies for and rhetoric about 'getting high').

Finally, the Delos gathering clearly marks the transition to a more relaxed situation, looking towards the period that comes soon after 'when the tourists are gone', and the worldwide friends of the island are welcome to rejoin the Mykonos commune which provides a grandiose alternative kinship structure, with the 'maternal' home being the symbol of '*Mykoniatiki katastasi*', or otherwise a Mykonian style of encounter.

The moral of the story

After a year or two, I attended the Delos ritual again, and given the fact that I had developed a certain amount of intimacy with the *Mykoniots d'élection*, I came to realise more about the unwritten rules of the group. For example, all the patrons of the group would be constantly sarcastic about Hercules' meticulous and impressive preparations (I did not realise until sometime later that it was well known that Hercules 'made' a certain amount of money by organising the 'shopping list' and being the 'patron' of the feast). Although he was never asked at the end of the excursion why the whole thing worked out so expensive, the patrons would laugh between themselves while paying up.[25] Nevertheless, Hercules was among the oldest members of the 'creative' milieu in tourist Mykonos and had a fantastic way of imposing his own way of doing things, which was, by the way, effective and aesthetically faultless. Hercules' bonus from the Delos excursion was something that everyone accepted as a fair reward that he decided on for himself and that varied depending on his economic circumstances. He would usually announce the amount last thing before we reached Mykonos, and collect the money upon disembarkation. Usually some would have no money or fail to pay. Hercules would then ask the old patrons to 'contribute'. Overall, economic interdependency among the *Mykoniots* exists as an unwritten rule that everyone accepts.

Participation mystique, scene two: 'a ritual of our own': Orthodoxy meets paganism – the feast of Saint Kyriaki on little Deles

In the summer of 1993, the year that the LSE gave me the approval to proceed with my fieldwork, I visited Delos with my informants four times. I suppose the group of the *Mykoniots d'élection* was reaching its second zenith (if the first one was during the late seventies); the island was full of tourists and their pockets were full of money. Moreover spirits and self-esteem were high, drug consumption was moderate, as was the threat from the 'representatives of the law'. New theoretical ideas that departed from the 'linear process of modernisation' model, moving 'backwards' to anti-modernity, were once again in tune with the hippie-oriented mentality of the *Mykoniots*. So my informants were once more 'fashionable' but less marginalised this time, in tune with the emerging new 'post-modern' ideologies and lifestyles that aimed at unifying models for *a* global culture, multiple alternative communities, alternative discourses and so on.

In this second part, I will describe what was originally a local feast, a *paniyiri*, that traditionally takes place every July in the only Orthodox church on the, once, sacred island of Delos, but now a mere remnant of a shrine. Since I want to give an account of the *Mykoniots*' appreciation and attitude towards ritual in general, I will place the notion of the local feast (*paniyiri*)[26] in the general 'ritualistic' calendar of the cosmopolitan *Mykoniots*.

The *Mykoniots d'élection* prefer the most humble *paniyiria*,[27] where one finds mainly locals, and only a few aspiring 'Mykonians' by adoption. The 'communal' space of a chapel's yard where the *paniyiri* is performed, being primarily a public space, is somehow symbolically transformed into a manifestation of a common identity that the *Mykoniots* aim to share with the local Mykonians. Their access to, knowledge and appreciation of these traditional manifestations of *endopiotita* (locality/a spatial sense of belonging) organises the *Mykoniots*' collective image by helping them to acquire an open relationship with a pseudo-traditional identity, as well as providing them with an aesthetic sense of *endopiotita*.[28] Thus the locals' 'traditional' actions in an otherwise cosmopolitan space reflect a distant continuum with a *Mykoniot*'s particular (family or community) liminal context, whilst not requiring them to be a part of this continuum, a continuum that for various reasons they do not wish to recreate. This positive attitude on the part of the *Mykoniots d'élection* towards local rituals extends to other aspects of liminality in the local community, where 'social obligations' and 'conformity' seem to be effortless. For example, by fetishishing the locals' primitivism, authenticity and amorality, they over-idealise their actual 'difference' and identify with the locals, attending their weddings, name days and other rituals with no emotional investment.

The nights before the paniyiri of Ayia Kyriaki

The *paniyiri* of Ayia Kyriaki (Saint Kyriaki) was celebrated on 6 July, just a few days after the celebration of the July full moon which lies at the heart of summer and warms the spirits for the high point of the season to come, which for the tourist area of Mykonos, and for Greeks in general, is 15 August, *tis Panayias* – the all-important 'Dormition of the Virgin' (cf. Dubisch 1995: 26).

Eleonora[29] has initiated a tradition to celebrate her dead guru's memory on that particular full moon. She would only share details about the feast with her close *Mykoniot* companions who took her seriously. Eleonora would prepare days in advance her celebration of 'Guru Purnima', by now an established tradition among the *Mykoniots*. As the reader knows already, Eleonora is not some kind of Buddhist or Hindu fanatic, creating narrow-minded celebrations for oriental 'celibacies'. On the contrary, the feast has introduced aesthetic variations over time, and each time everything is repeated from the otherworldly lifestyles of the ecstatic seventies and the self-destructive druggy eighties period on the island to the most sophisticated nights of the nineties. The whole thing is contextualised in seventies style but is also intellectualised in a nineties manner. 'The moon is in Capricorn" Eleonora said and everybody was hoping that the strong local *meltemi* would die down.[30]

The day after Eleonora's Guru Purnima, another 'successful' event is noted in my diary: the wedding of a Greek 'high society' member who had recently built an ostentatious holiday home for himself and his family. During that weekend, the *Mykoniots* would endlessly complain of how the island had lost all sense of harmony since all these 'nouveaux riches' of dubious taste had come to appropriate Mykonos, to celebrate and get married on 'their' island just for the sake of being fashionable.

In contemporary Mykonos, the once alternative culture of *koinohristoi*[31] (literally those who can be used [up] by everybody – those who orchestrated 'familiarity' with the once unfamiliar cosmopolitan space), is turned into a colony of the Athenian bourgeoisie and the rest of the global new cosmopolitans. What the island used to offer in abundance, public personas in other words, like the 'picturesque' *Mykoniots d'élection*, the decoders of the local culture who could be accessed easily through their *steki* (haunt), is disappearing. The *Mykoniots* were baptised as the *koinohristoi* because once they became the object of the tourist gaze, they turned themselves into reflexive performers. They learned quickly to reciprocate the projections and desires of their audiences. They became public personas, and slowly picturesque caricatures. The opening to mass tourism, however, marginalised their performance. From their public performances on the Mykonian streets, the *Mykoniots d'élection* ended up performing for a semi-private clique – solely for the new worldly bourgeoisie, as they were the only ones to recognise them. Their *stekia* vanished one by one; the Mykonian happenings became private, inside homes and exclusive beaches.

The biggest change in Mykonos's post-traditional culture was due to this important ideological and geographical shift from public to private space. This signified the end of an era, for 'in Mykonos, romance [was] haphazardly democratic,' as the Greek poet Seferis would put it (1974: 230). The anomalous and exaggerated expansion of Mykonos outside the confines of its two main settlements, where grossly oversized villas are being built, alienated the locals from the new settlers. The *Mykoniots d'élection* were left in the downtown *hora* with a flock of charter flight and cruise ship tourists wandering around this hippie-extravaganza mausoleum. As a result, they became invisible on their own stage; the set-up they had constructed for themselves and the new cosmopolitan space is now semiotically refashioned. In the words of Maria, another *Mykoniot*: 'it is a shame to find that everybody is buried in their elegant homes. Once upon a time we used to come here in order to meet up with strangers, bumping into one another by chance in the narrow alleys. Now you never meet friends anymore.' In Mykonos, which used to be a place of clubbing and non-discriminatory extreme socialisation, everything was happening on the streets. Now the topography of the place has been turned into isolated luxurious private homes and exclusive resorts. Today, everybody, including recent arrivals, just complains about how despoiled Mykonos is.

Why this has happened is simple: everyone eventually had the same desire to move there, to appropriate paradise, to make it their own. The indigenous novelist Melpo Axioti, bitterly exclaims: 'Did you come to build? Many come to build these days, you know. They just build' (Axioti 1986: 188, quoted in Leontis 1999: 10). Likewise, an alternative type of fetishisation emerges in the tourist space: no longer young, once nonconformist members of the cosmopolitan bourgeoisie aspire to have a house on the island, as well as to get married there. But this desire to 'perform' on location ... what does it stand for? An emotional attachment to the place that signifies the lost years of our narcissistic revolution? Everybody has turned their lifestyles into '*straight*' ones: the druggies gave up drugs, the anarchists became indifferent; I (the anthropologist) made a series of little Mykonian 'cells' for myself and my friends, got married in a privately owned chapel, near the complex of cells, and finally managed to 'colonise' my corner of the island. The *Mykoniots d'élection* came of age: they moved away from the margins, from being the nomads and they became the faceless Baumanesque vagabonds and 'hosts' by default. Is this an alternative consumption scenario orchestrated on the theme of one's lost youth? Is Mykonos our precious memory-fetish capitalising on our lost youth?

Anyway, hopefully the *Mykoniots*' attendance the next day at the Delian feast of Ayia Kyriaki reinforced their 'unique' sense of identity in the constantly changing aesthetic reality of Mykonos. For some reason that summer, this particular feast became quite fashionable among the *Mykoniots d'élection*. After Eleonora's 'rave' for Guru Purnima, the *Mykoniots* decided to 'assimilate' to local traditional culture for a change. Orpheus, commenting on Eleonora's party with his *parea* later on the next day, said that it was a *xeneroto* (square) 'nineties' party and that he should perhaps have taken the ecstasy pill offered to him, so as to feel something for the full moon and for the party. But never mind, he said, Eleonora's parties were 'tradition' and moreover there was the *paniyiri* the next day to look forward to.

The Delian paniyiri of Ayia Kyriaki

There were two religious feasts, two *Deliana* (Delian) *paniyiria*, performed on the same day. One was organised and patronised by the local Mykonians who worked on Rhenia, the second (and larger) island of the Delian cluster. According to *Kyr*-Thodoris, my landlord, this *paniyiri* should be more ostentatious, so he advised me to go. The other would be on Little Deles (as opposed to Rhenia – Great Deles), the sacred island of Apollo. The *Mykoniots* picked the second one.

Fortunately, the *meltemi* stopped and the sky was clear on the night of the *paniyiri*. At sunset, the chartered boats were hired by the modern tenant-farmers of Delos,[32] their families and friends to celebrate their yearly feast. The annual awakening on the sacred island of Apollo was patronised by those 'landless' Mykonians who traditionally worked the 'ancient' land. They celebrated their female saint, Ayia Kyriaki, in whose honour an Orthodox chapel had been built. The *Mykoniot* group obviously chose the feast on Delos and not on Rhenia, since everyone's primary aim was to enjoy the remains in the light of the great July moon, not the feast itself.

Our attendance at the feast of Ayia Kyriaki turned out to meet the expectations of Orpheus, since it was the prelude to a bout of *kraipali* (revelry). *Kyr*-Thodoris must have suggested that the Great Deles feast was the more attractive, since he himself had been renting land and had affiliations there. He emphasised that it would be 'more entertaining' since the *paniyiri* had 'more money' as well as 'electric music instruments and plenty of food and drink'. For my *Mykoniot* informants, the idea of a 'rich' *paniyiri* was simply of no interest. But the notion of a humble *paniyiri* of a more 'authentic' nature, especially if it entailed the privilege of staying all night, officially, near the forbidden remains, was a most attractive invitation. This night offered the only official possibility of staying overnight on the sacred island. In the motorboat from Mykonos the passengers were absorbed by the sunset (as was usually the case in the Cyclades), and breathless from the heatwave that had suddenly hit Mykonos after the strong *meltemi* calmed down. Leaving the busy Mykonian *Hora* behind also brought a pleasant sense of freedom. The captain of the motorboat left us on an unfamiliar part of the island. The twilight of the rising moon made it seem as empty as ever. A group of people, my fellow passengers on the motorboat, climbed the path to the chapel quietly, as if there was some silent guide ahead. I was already taken by the marvellous scene. After a silent walk along the shepherd's path, a ray of light appeared in the distance. The feeling was more mystical than I had expected. Getting closer, I saw the familiar shape of a typical Mykonian chapel. The only lighting came from the chapel's candles, a fact that communicated an extra religiosity in the early twilight of the incipient night. The people around me were quiet. Once inside the chapel each one lit a candle. On their way out, everybody took a *prosfora* (a piece of 'blessed bread', especially made for the feast) which was placed generously in a basket near the exit of the chapel. There was nothing glamorous about this house of God. None of its 'Delian' patrons were there, since the priest had performed the official liturgy for the chapel's name day earlier on, before sunset. I looked around to see my fellow travellers; the group consisted mostly of a mysterious category of locals, whose appearance and behaviour I was not familiar with. They were being as devotional as they wished and less sociable than what I used to think of the Mykonian indigenes. The icon screen inside the small chapel was extremely naïve and beautifully painted, and the saints' icon stands were dressed with flowers. Outside, the light blue on the chapel's dome was still bright in contrast to the rest of the whitewashed construction.

This encounter was what a naïve outsider would ideally expect to be confronted with: devout Greeks performing their religious rituals with piety, 'a purely fifties scene' as Orpheus, the stylist among the *Mykoniots*, would say. A class-based distinction is made obvious here: paradoxically enough, the poorest and the least 'lucky' of the Mykonians were, for this ritual occasion, the patrons of the 'sacred' island; those who did not make small fortunes out of tourism, and instead mostly stuck to agriculture and cattle rearing. These Mykonians were left with the pleasure of enjoying ancient Delos all by themselves. In their 'humble' *paniyiri*, any communication between locals and outsiders, as the reader will realise later on in this text, was almost completely absent. The excessive sociability and the obvious 'patronage', usually evident in modern Mykonian *paniyiria*, open to any guest, were absent from this one. There was something collective and really original about it. In a sense it reminded me more of the religiosity of the old traditional *paniyiria*, described to me by Penelope, the unofficial folklorist of the island, rather than the conspicuous consumption of the modern *paniyiria* of the tourist era which would feed hundreds of people. A simple factor that initially made us feel less welcome as 'outsiders' may have been that the 'patrons' of this *paniyiri* could not, on the one hand, afford the notoriety the *paniyiri* was gaining, yet on the other, they could not afford to refuse to 'treat' the guests at the *paniyiri* either, as this was the 'cultural' rule.

A Mykonian paniyiri, an ancient palaestra and an acid 'trip'

The feast's communal tables appeared after a kilometre's walk, following the path in the dark. The *paniyiri*'s setting was near the first visible ancient remains. The organisers had brought an electric generator, so there was some light at last. Multicoloured spotlights had been located for the occasion in a space that I later found used to be an ancient Greek or maybe Roman *palaestra*.[33] The ruins were composed of worn-down pieces of white marble which had once formed a long bench. Long, narrow planks of wood were set parallel to the marble bench supported on elongated pieces of rock and concrete (an improvised technique, that used an extra parallel piece of wood as a table, and which was employed for seating the guests of these Mykonian *paniyiria*). Apart from the multicoloured spotlights there was no other light. The locals were gathered around the extensive communal tables, having some soup and salads. The 'orchestra space' was set, but the musicians were absent. I looked around and thought that this *paniyiri* was definitely not a 'sociable' one. The locals remained seated around the remains of the old ring and seemed reluctant to incorporate unfamiliar people. I realised that there were more 'outsiders' than I had first thought, set apart on the far side. Others were sitting comfortably in the dark corners outside the *palaestra* on their sleeping bags.

I found my *Mykoniot* group in the far corner, some were already lying by the ancient stones. They were somehow different from the rest of the crowd, since although not quite incorporated, they were already fluently performing like an autonomous homogenised group. They seemed quite comfortable and loud. Some were already eating. A couple of friends were on an acid trip, and literally spent the whole night on top of an ancient stone wall enjoying the horizon and the *paniyiri* from a distance, with a constant smile on their faces. 'Your vision does not bound back to you, does not extract anything from [the rocks] for you. You are nothing but this ecstasy of vision' (Lingis 2002: 50). In their discourse, the *Mykoniots* very frequently make similar declarations of euphoria and contentment vis-à-vis the idiomorphic barren landscape of Mykonos with Delos as its special energy source. Beauvoir (1962: 81, quoted in Fullagar 2001: 293), who attributes to her desire to travel a visual pleasure, also refers to an 'ecstatic vision' as a visual metaphor for 'capturing' life's movement. What is exercised here, is the desire to sensually learn about the world.

I could not fail to notice the disapproving glances cast by the locals at anything exogenous. This was a rare exception to the Mykonians' usual open-minded attitude. The *Mykoniots*, on the other hand, came with great expectations and felt no threat from the locals' reluctance to incorporate them. They knew some locals, but overall it was one of the most estranged scenes I witnessed between locals and *Mykoniots*. The locals had no respect for the *Mykoniots*, but this did not seem to put off my informants, since as should be obvious by now, the *Mykoniots* had a very fixed and personal myth in their minds for that night. They were excited solely by the fact that it was being played out in the Dionysiac locus of Delos, a highly effective 'energy field' for them. The cult of Dionysus – apparently a celebrated deity in both ancient Delos and tourist Mykonos – was intangibly reincarnated at the archaeological site as an ambience promoting drunkenness, the cultivation of wine and the absence of moral boundaries; in short, a cult in favour of pan-hedonism. The *Mykoniots* reputedly considered themselves experts in the contemporary practice of their version of a Dionysian 'cult', but the local Mykonians seemed to be there for another reason altogether.

In the *Mykoniots'* opinion, the most spectacular feature of the feast's success was not the traditional commensality aspect of the *paniyiri*, nor indeed the location after all, but the band that started playing when the last sign of the day had gone and which consisted of two guitars, two *toumberlekia*, two *bouzoukia*, one *baglama* (small lute) and one accordion played by an archaeologist. When the music started and everybody had established their place at the feast, the *Mykoniots* gathered round the ancient *palaestra* and made the group's intrinsic boundaries clearer. It was obvious that the *paniyiri* had attracted more outsiders than usual, as well as people that came solely for the *paniyiri*'s special location. The core of the people who indulged in the incremental *kefi* (high spirits) gathered around the band that performed very ritualistically with an old-fashioned musical discipline that lasted till dawn. The archaeologists and their friends, as well as some local guardians of the ruins on the sacred island, acted as alternative hosts to the locals who had organised the *paniyiri* of Ayia Kyriaki. The motorboats kept coming from Mykonos (the last arrived at something like 3.30 in the morning), bringing more outsiders to the locals' feast, the 'faithful' cosmopolitan followers of any 'original' celebration. When the Dionysiac gurus and their disciples were through with partying on their sleepless island, they hired another motorboat to visit Delos at its best. And so it happened. The culminating *kefi*, or rather the unravelling of the *paniyiri*'s mystique, was extremely slow, and thus everlasting. The first elderly visitors who had come for the chapel liturgy started to depart, so there were some spaces left at the communal tables when later some fish dishes were served. Around five in the morning, a *parea* of fishermen appeared with a large barrel of local wine and a bottle of whisky now that the supply of drinks had run out. I remember I did not manage to get any, but my eyes were still open. Many of the visitors were already asleep, around the ancient *palaestra*. Orpheus and his friends preferred to roll joints continuously, enjoying the masterpiece of the large moon shining over the unexplored dark landscape. An investigation of the darkened area that surrounded the *palaestra* revealed many sleeping bodies, as well as fragments of the ancient pillars. I was as curious as the rest of the group to see what the landscape was really like on this unvisited side of the island in daylight. One could even hear the peculiar sounds of animals from afar.

Tiny spots of light were visible from the nearby islands. The band performed ritualistically with no electric amplifiers and minimal singing, from the *ballos* (a traditional dance of the region) moving gradually to the more serious *zeibekiko* (a spontaneous and dramatic male dance). The locals remaining by then were the hard-core drunkards of the Mykonian *paniyiria*. Amazingly enough, every now and then throughout the night there would be a new arrival of guests and a new supply of food or drink. Someone came with plenty of sea cockles, *kydonia*, which he had probably caught himself from the sea. Everyone was supposed to contribute, because if you run out of water in the ancient *palaestra* of Delos at four in the morning, as Aris remarked, you are pretty much stuck. Likewise, we were waiting patiently for dawn, there at the ancient Roman *palaestra*, lost in the fuzziness of the feast with no means of orientation in the dark. Whatever was on offer was welcome. In any case, the law of a *paniyiri* is that no one ever asks for food or drink but only accepts what is offered. The Mykonian *paniyiria* I attended, especially the ones outside the *Hora* of Mykonos organised by the

Mykonian farmers' *horia*, have a monastic sacredness in their unwritten commensality code. In the beginning, the sharing of food was quiet and the participants at the *paniyiri* devout. Various *parees* of the *Mykoniots* and other members of the Mykonian summer workers' group decided to explore under the moon the nearby rocks and find shelter for the night.

As the first glimpse of the sun appeared over the horizon the band started playing in a more lively fashion, and I realised that what originally had perhaps been four hundred visitors had ended up as just fifty around the *palaestra*. The memory of this dawn will be unforgettable. The multicoloured lights of the *paniyiri* were still on. Euridice was climbing up the high wall of the *palaestra* behind the communal tables to get snapshots of the musicians who played for themselves that night. The scenery started emerging in the half-light of the dawn. Bodies were all around scattered over a large part of the area in front of the *palaestra*, the size of which I could never guess in the dark, with impressive pieces of abandoned broken ancient columns reaching as far as the eye could see. Intuitively, everybody started exploring, some moving silently towards the ancient settlement. One big *parea* was just waking and appeared behind the rocks to the west of the *palaestra*. Some of the *Mykoniots* who fully participated in the Delos awakening went to find their way into the water. The ancient *palaestra* was full of leftover food and drink. In a while all this was left behind and the labyrinthine town planning of the ancient settlement was looking to seduce some new devotees. I remembered the couple who had been tripping and who had stayed staring at the *paniyiri* from afar – smiling all night. And Orpheus and his friend sleeping together on the ancient marbles of the *palaestra* on a couple of colourful Mexican blankets. Aris at this instant was the most involved of the *Mykoniots* at the Delian feast. He participated in the Delian band performing with some other musician 'freaks' from Mykonos town, probably locals. When the sun rose, it was time to go home to our beds. Boats were waiting on the 'proper' side where the harbour was waiting to welcome its tourists.

The next day was more or less lost for those not working. But for the majority who had to work, it was just another working day with not enough sleep. The endless chain of *Mykoniots*' aleatory encounters would continue on the beach at Visonas where the Mykonos freaks gathered to celebrate Aristos' birthday. As *Kyr*-Thodoris had predicted beforehand, the next morning the weather changed, as was usually the case 'after the *paniyiri* of Ayia Kyriaki'. The period of the *meltemi* had begun. Eleonora's Guru Purnima and the Delian *paniyiri* were only a brief respite from the wind. Aris, as restless as ever, was transformed into a 'rock freak' the next day, contributing to the electric sounds of the Visonas music group. '*Meltemi* helps you to sober up quickly (*na xeneroseis*),' he said, and the *Mykoniots* did not want to lose time.

The 'nomads' of Mykonos: participation mystique

> In fact, the style of daily life is criss-crossed by the aleatory that is the very property of the aesthetic, that of communal emotion, which can bring itself to bear on some object, then on some other; it can be stirred by one idea, then by another, quite opposite one ... (Maffesoli 1996b: 50)

I chose to describe the Delian *paniyiri* of Ayia Kyriaki to further explore the *Mykoniots*' liminality. There is a long tradition of local *paniyiria* on Mykonos, and they engender celebrations sponsored by private families even today. For the *Mykoniots*, participation in the local *paniyiria* justifies their 'original' self, since they accept and follow the 'local' tradition they found themselves in. Likewise, it gives them the bonding they need with the local community. To take it a step further, one could say that the frequency with which they attend local rituals – not out of religiosity but out of 'originality' – is an alternative way of acquiring the title of 'Mykonian', a definition they aspire to. Overall, what this definition does for them is to eliminate the rest of their 'Greek' or other ethnic self, which they see as a bourgeois origin they despise, or alternatively a 'repressive' petit bourgeois one. Seen from their point of view, they are 'different' and they were not there just to imitate or enjoy the way in which locals construct their rituals. At the Delian *paniyiri*, the *Mykoniots* had their own honourable role, that of contemporary patrons of a Dionysian-style worship. And for this reason solely, I believe, they put up with the locals' uneasiness, and the absence of enough food and wine, something rare in the local Mykonian *paniyiria*. A more pragmatic and alternative explanation of their tolerance would be that they were sufficiently supplied with hashish to reach their own 'high', as well as having some other hallucinatory drugs brought along especially for the occasion. *Mykoniots* belong to the category of bon viveurs and as such fail to do anything that makes them uncomfortable for whatever reason, ethical or otherwise. Inspired by their participation in the above ritual, I suspect there is a clue here to the *Mykoniots* politics of *participation mystique*. The politics and promotion of a 'Mykonian' style of commensality go beyond the quest for identity of these extreme individuals, becoming a strategic embodiment of alternative ingredients of identity, that, in turn, form a 'unique' group identity.

The sacred ritual of the aleatory encounters of the *Mykoniots d'élection* accounts for the group's 'difference' and exclusivity. This cultural strategy aims to deny the normal binary structure that separates formal ritualistic behaviour (as exceptional) from everyday activities. This reversal, aesthetically elevates the group to an apotheosis of elitist behaviour, that finds them all in a state of continually enjoyable liminality, and leaves the *Mykoniots d'élection* ecstatic about their 'difference'.

As we shall see in the following chapter where a *Mykoniot*'s wedding is described, it is clear that there is a considerable degree of ambiguity in the group's attitude towards mainstream rituals. This ideological/aesthetic position is reinforced by the pre-eminent role the members of the group play as party organisers, and mainly as conceptualisers of communal rituals of commensality (the 'haunt makers'). The *Mykoniots*' calling is mainly to organise and direct gatherings, as well as to conceptualise new reasons for creating them. Their own cultural and social liminality as a group, being fed by a cosmopolitan and strictly tourist based economy, provides examples of newly conceived, alternative, or newly created ritualistic occasions, for direct tourist consumption, as well as idiosyncratic ritual occasions solely for group consumption.

Mykoniots d'élection: consuming every culture, having virtually none

The Delos ritual immediately acquired a sacred character. Although party-wise everything was over before it started in terms of fun and intensity (and the *Mykoniots* are demanding in their party expectations), the 'nomads' displayed an outrageous perseverance and paid their respects to Apollo while waiting for it to be light again, resting their bodies on the uncomfortable stone remains. The description of an 'ecstatic' experience is exhausted already in the title: 'A Mykonian *paniyiri* awakening on the sacred island of Delos'. I am interested here in the 'symbolic capital' the *Mykoniots* acquire from this *participation mystique*, and what its narration means for the 'politics of seduction' in a tourist space.

The Delos awakening was the second awakening in a row after Eleonora's full moon party. Some of the *Mykoniots* attended both occasions, some only one of them, and some did not bother to go to either. The list of 'ritualistic' events was endless anyway, and the daily programme of 'ritualistic' meetings of a traditional or contemporary kind, whether Orthodox, Hindu, personal, pagan or simply the 'art of living ritualistically in every action', was very long. The syncretic rhetoric and the multicultural aesthetics of the *Mykoniots* as well as their exhibitionist techniques provided them with many mainstream or eccentric rituals, so as to transcend the monolithic cultures they were acquainted with, and thus recreate their unique and ever-changing 'acultural' lifestyle.

Apart from the island's myth of cosmopolitanism, which tends to be considered a common reason for the transformation of certain cultural practices in the tourist space, one has to account for the 'selling' potential of any given ritual in an economy, that survives solely on tourism.[34] But on top of everything else, 'cosmopolitanism' offers ritual an alternative and more creative option in cultural representation. In addition, it gives an emphasis to altogether alternative ritual expressions. Since my position is not positively structuralist but far more eclectic, what I would like my reader to understand from my analysis of the above mentioned rituals, is first and foremost, the essence of this aesthetic diversity as a matter of choice, and the coexistence of different stylistic elements: likewise to see the Delos *paniyiri* as a local, traditional feast, but equally as a pagan feast, or just as another tourist attraction, but above, all as a means of improvising identity.

I do not wish to suggest to the reader that I am trapped in the fallacy of assuming that one is solely dealing with a consciously innovative collective identity act here, but I think that the diversity and the embodiment of diverse stylistic and ideological choices in a single ritual in such a restricted space, shows something about 'Greek culture' as a whole. Secondly, and more importantly, it tells us something about the 'extreme' individuality displayed and experienced in the hybrid culture of Mykonos, a fact that could potentially challenge the anthropological addiction to a singular categorisation of human beings with a given collective identity and a single locality, as being either Greek, Orthodox, or otherwise simply 'deviant', and therefore, beyond the scope of anthropology. A useful theoretical framework is given by Appadurai's notion of ethnoscape, in other words, the landscape that is produced by the shifting reality of the 'moving groups' (1996: 33) created out of the dynamics of a constant deterritorialisation and global processes. Appadurai places imagination in a pre-eminent position in the social life of these new deterritorialised cultures and urges for a cosmopolitan ethnography that ultimately transforms the traditional anthropological nature of locality (ibid.: 52) – arguing, *pace* Amit and Rapport, against anthropology's 'fetish for fixity' (2002: 169).

Notes

1. By ritualising the everyday, the *Mykoniots* symbolically enter into an 'anarchic' state where time ceases to be ontologically 'threatening'. Just as 'time' is transcended, so is change, and identity categories are symbolically crossed.
2. This quote refers to the place-myth of Delos and the sacred island's 'revelation' after Apollo's birth there. Apollo was said to bring a special 'brightness' to the until then invisible island (Liavas 1992: 402).
3. Today almost uninhabited, Delos was among the most important religious and economic centres of the ancient world: the ancient Greeks considered Delos 'sacred', and, more importantly, the geometrical centre of the Cyclades complex (Roussel 1990: 10).
4. In a sense, Delos, as a shrine and a free harbour, builds its idiosyncratic history and economic development on an important infrastructural combination, being simultaneously a sacred symbol and an exclusive treasury to the ancient world (cf. Stasinopoulos n.d.: 16, 62). Bearing that in mind, it is important to see how the tourist and developed Mykonos revives Delos' cosmopolitan facet and continues to live and survive through the sacred island's space-myth. Moreover, a discursive parallel is drawn between Delos' image and the more recent history of 'sacredness' of nearby Tinos. According to Durrell, '… the Virgin of Tinos and her native land form an imaginative link with Delos, today serving as the great Lourdes of modern Greece' (1978: 243–44).
5. Among them were the English traveller and antiquarian, George Wheler, who visited Mykonos in 1676, together with the French archaeologist and doctor, J.Spon, as well as the French doctor and botanist, Joseph Pitton de Tournefort. Kousathanas (1996) also mentions James Caulfeild (*sic*), the Irish lord of Charlemont who visited the island in 1749 (cf. Stanford and

Finopoulos 1984). For a detailed bibliography on the travellers who visited Mykonos consult Kousathanas (1986, 1989).

6. In Waldren's similar ethnographic example on Deia's group of expatriots, the poet Robert Graves employed similar discourses to those of the *Mykoniots*: he attributed to Deia's surrounding mountains a 'magnetic force like that at Delphi' (1996: 179). This kind of metaphor or myth, Waldren continues: 'added an esoteric dimension to the new life some people were trying to create' (ibid.).

7. Probably it is not by chance that, beyond the homogeneously minimalist and high-tech design of the Delos bar, the only distinctly decorative element over the years was a distinguished work of art, an imitation of an ancient Greek helmet, designed and made by a New York sculptor who used to be a resident on the island.

8. *Kyr*-Thodoris expressed that as: '*erchetai mono i akri tou kairou*'.

9. It is important to note here that there is an emerging space-myth, supported by a series of sponsored editions, that promotes the uniqueness of a common Aegean civilisation, as being distinctly *anthropokentrikos*, anthropocentric and culturally pluralist. This is also reflected in several established editions (cf. Doumas 1992: 429), as well as in the attempts to plan a future space-image for the Aegean Sea. Under the aegis of the Greek Ministry of Culture, the area was designated as an ecologically conserved space and more importantly as the 'Cultural Park' of the Eastern Mediterranean, and a symbol of peace shared between Europe, Africa and Asia (Greek Ministry of Culture 1994). The aforementioned proposition was officially sponsored and was actually put forward, on behalf of the Greek government to UNESCO, by the late Melina Mercouri.

10. *Mastoras* (artisan), the generic name of a category is actually used as the established nickname of a particular person.

11. Similar discourses, concerning the 'special energy' of a retreat space, are recorded by Shields (1991) in his analysis of the liminal space-myth of the historic resort of Brighton. Brighton's growing reputation during the nineteenth century developed a myth about the 'character' of the waters that could help fecundity. Later on, a pseudoscientific theory emerged concerning the 'special' ions and ozone of the air that were said to bring 'amorous emotions and titillations' to the visitors (Manning-Sanders 1951: 47, quoted in Shields 1991: 78).

12. The miraculous icon of the Virgin Mary on Tinos is said to help when requested, to save the ill and the depressed. Dubisch analyses the miracle-working nature of the icon of the *Panayia* (Madonna) which is situated in the Annunciation Church of Tinos, the most popular pilgrimage site of Greece (1995: 69–71). She also mentions that for many Greeks, Tinos is the 'sacred centre of the Cyclades' (ibid. 122).

13. I use the term *ekklisia* (church), because some unconventional discourses in Greece might denounce the repressive establishment of official religion (i.e., the Church) but not Orthodoxy itself. Following this line of thinking, Orthodox dogma and rituals are usually referred to with the term *ekklisia*, which literally means 'the church', the building where the rituals take place, rather than the rituals themselves.

14. There are no actual descriptions of what the *Delia Mystiria* consisted of. As I was informed by the archaeologists who were working on the sites of Delos, apart from vague references, there were no written sources available on the subject. One of them was quick to stress that the reason for that was simple: the ancient Greeks were obviously being secretive about them, since they were Mysteries.

15. In line with the space-image of Delos, as a renowned pagan shrine of the ancient and Hellenistic world, as well as with that of contemporary Tinos, as an Orthodox pilgrimage site, is Markos' statement about Mykonos' space-image: 'Mykonos is … what can I say, my annual pilgrimage.' Similar discourses on the part of the *Mykoniots* reveal a sense of constantly being in a 'liminal' state, actually produced by the liminality of the space-image itself.

16. Rojek and Urry, in their edited volume (1997), argue about the 'performativity' involved in tourist-related work. According to Crang's contribution in the same volume, discourses of 'otherness' are extended to the 'nature' of tourist employment itself. Drawing on Wood's work on hotel and catering labour (1992), he maintains that: 'There is a concern then, that an unhealthy "myth of uniqueness" has grown up around much of tourist-related employment ..., a myth which obscures "the extent to which [this] work ... differs little in kind and quality from similar work in manufacturing"' (Crang 1997: 137–38).

17. The word *delos*, literally means 'visible', in ancient Greek, but the myth goes that before Delos became *delos*, 'visible', it was *a-delos*, meaning invisible (not apparent). The island had a peculiarity: it had no real basis, it was movable, with no orientation, lost in the sea, thus *adelos*. That was the reason why Leto was finally allowed by jealous Hera to give birth to the illegitimate child – that Leto had conceived with Zeus, the king of Olympus and Hera's husband – on that island, since the island was not visible, and thus non-threatening to Hera. But when Apollo, the illegitimate child, was born, since he was a child of Zeus and thus a god himself, the island was made 'visible' by Zeus and so it took its literal name and is still called Delos.

18. For the *Mykoniots*, the trip to Deles, is an intimate encounter, an authentic 'performance' for their own sakes and not a performance for an audience. Like MacCannell's (1976: 92n) back-regions, the 'authentic' trip to Delos is usually closed to outsiders and is an opportunity for the group to get 'together' and relax.

19. Nowadays, local production of food is very restricted, and local produce is sold at a high price from street donkeys under the aegis of certain local farmers. Access to the remaining agricultural households is legendary and exclusive, a privilege reserved for 'old members' of *Mykoniot* society who are well known to the Mykonian community. Hercules is among those who know the old locals, and gets their exclusive products at good prices.

20. An alternative name for the excursion, since the actual beach party will happen on a remote beach on the nearby island of Rhenia, a protected beach on the south coast called Yioras.

21. Indian was his nickname, because he had long, grey hair and strong features.

22. Markos would usually return on his yearly 'pilgrimage' to Mykonos, as he called it, during September. Things have changed since I completed my fieldwork and Markos has returned once again to his favourite retreat, sold his unisex shop in Kansas and opened a small shop on Mykonos, selling furniture that he commissions for himself, using cheap Balinese labour.

23. A fellow-Greek research student used to remind me: 'But Mykonos is not Greece!'

24. The encounters with the law were the only instances where the members of the *parea* were classified as a unified group, with their common characteristic being that of 'drug' consumers.

25. Hercules then would 'steal' with flair and personal style when he himself decided to add the extra for his labour. The mock complaints of his fellow *Mykoniots* reveal the performative character of both forms of action, both on the part of Hercules and on the part of the *Mykoniots*. The situation here is reminiscent of what Herzfeld describes for the Glendiots' animal thieves in Crete, who 'steal' for performative reasons, in order to 'make friends' (Herzfeld 1985: 47).

26. The *Mykoniots d'élection* have a feeling of disdain towards mainstream rituals. A big exception is made, however, as regards their admiration and respect for the local culture and Mykonian rituals in general, such as the island's *paniyiria*. These feasts are performed on the eve of the name day of the various saints to whom the local churches and the (approximately) 500 local chapels are dedicated. The building of the church or chapel, and hence the establishment of a *paniyiri*, is traditionally related to circumstances in which the relatives '*etaxan ston ayio*' (made a vow to the saint), to erect a chapel in her/his honour when a specific member of the family had overcome some difficulty. Mykonians also used to have these chapels in order to bury their dead, since it was customary not to be buried outside one's own household territory. Another

reason might be that they had them as the family shrine within the limits of their self-sustained households, their remote *horia*.
27. The privilege of 'appreciating' a humble *paniyiri* is distinctively *theirs*, and operates as an attribute on the basis of which they can construct their difference from the rest of the aspiring visitors or admirers of the island. The local feasts, the *paniyiria*, go on throughout the year, and together with the highly ritualistic pig-slaughtering in November, are some of the most distinctive cultural instances fetishised by the *Mykoniots d'élection*.
28. Papataxiarchis defines the term *endopiotita* (locality) as a 'notion', as well as a 'sense' of participating in a well- defined [socio/spatial] context; in other words, as a sense of 'belonging' and how this is socially and symbolically negotiated (1990: 335). Papataxiarchis attempts to explore the notion of *endopiotita* (locality) also as a symbol, beyond the social relationships it establishes. Here, we are mostly concerned with the symbolic (and aesthetic) signification of 'belonging' and how this is negotiated in the polysemic cultural space of Mykonos.
29. As already mentioned in her self-narrative in chapter 3.
30. The local seamen say that on the actual day of the full moon the weather has the potential to change, and remain the same until the moon wanes.
31. The term was coined by an eighty-year-old *Mykoniot d'élection* in a genuine attempt to give a collective label to all those people with whom he had been silently sharing an identity for thirty years or so: 'these kind of people that gather in Mykonos, I mean us, we are *koinohristoi*.' The *koinohristoi* are available local personalities for tourist consumption who operate as the secure connection with the communal space-myth of Mykonos. This imaginative expression also renders the uncommitted character of the group.
32. In other words, the Mykonians who were actually renting pieces of Delian land from the Greek state in order to cultivate it or to graze their cattle.
33. Athletics training-ground.
34. Tilley has argued about the revival and performance of cultural traditions in response to the recently fashionable 'cultural tourism' on Wala island tourist resort (1997: 73). Ritual and ceremony in tourist/cosmopolitan contexts become performative and thus there is an emerging literature on this phenomenon: (cf. Bruner 1995; Picard 1996; Crang 1997; Edensor 2000, 2001; Bruner 2001; Yamashita 2003).

5
NARRATIVES OF DIFFERENCE: AN AESTHETIC MYTH OF OTHERNESS

Participation mystique, scene three: a *Mykoniots'* version of a traditional wedding paniyiri

Mykoniots, both at the level of *praxis* and discourse tend to 'display' a creative self by virtue of creating liminality. In other words, by creating or aesthetically reinventing liminality, they establish an alternative personal myth and likewise accumulate prestige in the eccentric space-myth of Mykonos. By creating liminality and a series of communal ritual occasions, they eventually master the game of distinction in the tourist space. This chapter is focused on this kind of 'innovative liminality' through the description of a wedding ritual where the emphasis is on the aesthetic and the symbolic aspect of it operating like a Mykonian *paniyiri*, rather than on its 'transitional' character and certain established social, family or religious roles related to the wedding ritual.

The theoretical background

More afraid of oblivion than of pain or death, they always sought opportunities to become visible. (Myerhoff 1978: 33)

The opening quote of this chapter comes from an ethnography that seemingly deals with an altogether 'alien' group of informants: a number of very elderly Eastern European Jewish immigrants who formed the membership of a day centre in a Californian coastal resort. One might wonder, in the first place, what is the structural position of oblivion, or even worse, death, in an ethnographic account of a wedding ritual, a *rite de passage* for a fairly young couple? And secondly, the *Mykoniots*, so far, seem to be the reckless element of their generation, the uncompromising Greek version of the hipster. Is it then possible that they share similar existential anxieties with a group of very elderly Jews? And even if they do, how does this anxiety relate to the emotional process of a wedding ritual?

Yet Myerhoff's comment absolutely matches the existential and cultural predicament of both the *Mykoniots* as a category, as well as the *Mykoniots* as protagonists of the wedding ritual I wish to describe in this final chapter of the book.

Myerhoff describes the whole existential project of these elderly people as forming an alternative institutional order, via their creativity and syncretic skills. Instead of dwelling on her informants' Jewishness, she presents the attitude of the centre's members 'as means by which they cling on to their selfhood by demanding that others should be aware of it … selfhood is for them a tenacious reassertion of their individuality against the dreary homogeneity of their categorisation as elderly, even as elderly Jews' (Cohen 1994: 102). As Myerhoff asserts, the opposite of honour for these idiosyncratic elderly Jews was not shame but 'invisibility'. In order to fight invisibility they choose to put forward their distinct life histories as individuals rather than their common ethnic identity as *Yiddishkeit*. This antagonistic and highly individualistic attitude resulted in severe interpersonal conflicts that made the administration seek help from a behavioural therapist, though without success.

Cohen, in his analysis of Myerhoff's work, maintains that the so-called Venice Center's Jews 'provide an exemplary illustration of the skills of *bricolage* which people deploy to create and maintain their selfhood' (Cohen 1994: 103). The way they are successful in their unique case is through using their polyglot talents, their contested claims about their skills in every aspect of life and their charitable work with regard to Israel. Most importantly, I maintain that Myerhoff's creative elderly Jews are indulging in a game by now very familiar to the reader of this monograph: 'they find means of contriving plausible connections between the present and the past, *particularly by the adaptation or invention of rituals and ceremonies*' (ibid.: 103, my emphasis).

The evident age difference between the over-eighties Jews and the 'young' culture of the *Mykoniots* might be expected to produce distinct existential quests. I have devoted attention to the above ethnographic example, because I think that this 'obvious' antithesis combined with paradoxically similar practices, such as the invention of rituals and the fetishisation of the self, is provocative.

Throughout my Mykonos experience, what struck me as an observer of this community of exogenous 'locals' was the actors' preoccupation with ontological quests that were, at least at the rhetorical level, constantly magnified and thus remained 'unresolved'. Ironically, the *Mykoniots*' psychological pattern of an endless existential 'insecurity' acted as almost the only stable point of reference in my search for some 'collective consciousness'. What I mean by this is that this psychological pattern of a distinct existential predicament was the only 'structure' my anthropological enquiry could rely on due to the frequency with which I encountered it, sometimes as an explicit, but largely as an implicit state of mind or underlying motif.[1] In my eyes, my informants' mundane existential agony was usually very well hidden behind grandiose records of individual distinction, adventurous self-narratives and rhetorics in favour of solitude. What I had constantly to contend with was their passion for random spontaneous encounters that once they had 'happened' always ended up in my fieldnotes as dramatic incidents, characterised by some degree of excess. The description that follows later in the chapter will highlight the aforementioned ontological preoccupation within the framework of a controversial case, an Orthodox wedding ceremony performed by a *Mykoniot* couple. I maintain that this is the most controversial example, since it is difficult to structurally place a *rite de passage* in the case of the *Mykoniots*. If the *Mykoniots*' everyday life is an anti-structure, in the sense of an endless *communitas*, as Turner would probably argue, then clearly an Orthodox wedding is a structure, either in the form of compliance or a more sophisticated form of ideological syncretism (Turner 1974: 126). But all this holds only if we agree to place the ritualistic action of a wedding ceremony in a distinct time.

Being close to the bride as a friend and as the *koumbara* (wedding sponsor), I sensed an underlying difficulty on her part to psychologically deal with the actual wedding ceremony. A symbolic connection between marriage and death is frequently mentioned in traditional Greek ethnography[2] (Alexiou 1974: 120–21; Danforth 1982). Cowan's more recent ethnographic account of wedding celebrations in the Greek Macedonian community of Sohos presents us with a similar pattern. Reciting the sad songs performed when the groom's party comes to collect the trousseau from the kin group of the bride, shortly before the bride appears for her wedding ceremony, Cowan comments on the typical wedding songs and their images of exile and death that mark a ritual transition from the bride's old life to her new married state (Cowan 1990: 123). In the case of the *Mykoniot* bride, I witnessed a similar state of implicit grief, a fear of some transitional state that had no real implications whatsoever for the lifestyle of the bride. Save for the actual wedding ceremony, the reality before and after the ritual remained identical for the actors. Nothing really changed, including their respective economic and social positions. Although the 'modern' bride needed no justification for her actions vis-à-vis her kin and her traditional self, she had to offer some excuse to her politically aware, engendered self. After all, her discourse was opposed to traditional rituals, regarding them as being empty of existential meaning. Nevertheless, she performed the 'bride part', as we shall see, with few problems and her 'transformation' is now history. In some ways, it was myself as an anthropologist, nurtured in a Greek middle-class mentality, who was more aware of that transitional pain and symbolic 'death' of some 'modern' female identity than my avant-garde friend. As Moore has suggested: 'marriage ceremonies, for example, are sometimes situations in which sexual difference is stressed' (Moore 1994: 25). The 'lived anatomy' of Eurydice as the [female] bride-to-be, and how this is related to one of the most essential cultural performances of selfhood in the traditional Greek context, is psychoanalytically portrayed by the conscious 'female' performer through her dream. Her anxiety about her role as 'bride' produced in Eurydice's dream the image of her as a 'transvestite' in bridal clothes.

The wedding ritual, as yet another version of a Mykoniots' paniyiri

In the ethnography below, the reader will have the chance to follow a *paniyiri* organised and performed by the *Mykoniots,* inspired by the wedding ceremony of a long-established member of the *Mykoniots d'élection.* The wedding ceremony created the opportunity for another *paniyiri.* The underlying theoretical logic for this recurrent ethnographic theme should be seen in the context of the structural placement of liminality vis-à-vis the *Mykoniots'* 'sacred' and 'profane' time.

I hope I have managed so far to show the indiscriminateness in the process of selecting various cross-cultural ritual elements as well as the syncretism that builds their myth of 'originality' based on the *Mykoniots'* eclectic appropriation of these diverse elements, especially when they perform the 'rituals of our own'. The wedding of Orpheus (the groom-mentor) is the opportunity for another 'spontaneous' Mykonian encounter of the *Mykoniots' sinafi.* Most importantly, the folkloric wrapping, the form that supports the organisation of another ceremonial encounter, is the already familiar to the reader, Mykonian (i.e., traditional in its indigenous sense) *paniyiri.*

I need to stress here, that in reality what is being symbolically negotiated during this ritual occasion is the propriety of the context, rather than the actual content. The context, i.e., a local *paniyiri* fully appropriated by a *Mykoniot* (and not a Mykonian[3]) where the collective consciousness of the cosmopolitan protagonists is rehearsed and also realised to a great extent, is more important than the content, i.e., a wedding ceremony between two Greek Orthodox *Mykoniots.* Indeed, what I am reluctant to accept as the only conceptual tool for the decodification of the politics of this ceremony, is its monosemantic structural placement in a discontinuity model produced by some kind of personal liminal time. The feast celebrated on this occasion is as much a 'traditional' *paniyiri* as a folkloric reproduction of its original counterpart generated by the tourist culture of the island. The feast should also be treated as an Orthodox wedding, while retaining at the same time the ability to create another 'ritual of our own'.

I suggest that it would be misleading for the reader to focus on the wedding ritual itself, rather than on the structural placement of 'another' *paniyiri* in the sequence of the *Mykoniots'* styling of everyday life. Setting out to view this wedding with preconceived ideas about the salient structural position that a core ritual, such as a *rite de passage*, is supposed to possess, can be a great analytical fallacy.

Finally, I must take this opportunity to clarify for the reader that the descriptive collation of the *paniyiri* occasions I attended, including the wedding ritual itself, is part of the everyday activities of the *Mykoniots*, since the tourist space facilitates and calls for a constant 'liminality'. It is not so much that the *Mykoniots d'élection* inhabit a constant anti-structure – in the magical setting of 'subjectivity' and spontaneous *communitas* that Turner argues about when describing the seventies anomie of the hippies which leads to 'a feeling of endless power' (Turner 1974: 126–27) – but rather that they live in an endless 'intensive bonding' that curiously enough transcends the splitting of structure and anti-structure, the splitting of tradition from modernity. The exogenous inhabitants of Mykonos nurture a highly-fetishished 'Mykonian' way of living, which is fetishised precisely because it abolishes binary categories by incorporating the relatively appropriate and inappropriate, the spiritual and the ordinary, hence releasing their existential stress. The *Mykoniots*' stylish and sophisticated everyday living is fetishised because it denies their predicament of cultural fission, the constant oscillation from tradition to modernity. In a *Mykoniot's* lifestyle, everything is reflexive and negotiable and in this sense it is not an endless *communitas* (*à la* Turner) since there is no logic of perpetual 'liminality' on behalf of its actors.

Greek ethnographies on weddings

What has been written in Greek ethnography, as well as Greek folklore, on the wedding ritual mainly highlights its symbolic and material dimensions. This is true from the classic ethnography of Campbell (1964) to the detailed structuralist accounts of Greek folkloric literature (cf. Skouteri-Didaskalou 1984). In a later ethnographic account, Cowan (1990) focuses on the articulation of social identities and relationships mainly through bodily manifestations in the Sohoian wedding rituals. As I mentioned earlier in this chapter, Cowan's interpretation is focused strictly on the wedding ritual as a distinct structure in the Sohoian community, and being treated as such, given the 'official' status entailed in a transition ritual, its transformative power is taken for granted.

The transformative power of the wedding ritual is also exemplified at a material level, in traditional transfers of property among Greek Cypriots (Loizos 1975). Here, the role of the kinship group is divided to provide for the newlyweds: responsibility for the house falling to the groom's family, while the bride's family provide the furniture and her trousseau.

Many aspects of life seem to be transformed in the crucial moment of a wedding according to traditional and more recent ethnographies, but the domain of transformation which is of importance to us here is the self. Greek ethnographers normally focus on the 'transition' element, or rather presuppose an almost unnegotiable 'alienation' on the part of the protagonists after the ceremony vis-à-vis either a 'pre-completed' or 'uncommitted' unmarried self. Papataxiarchis maintains that 'the condition in order for one [a 'Greek'] to achieve a realistic heterodoxy, is the transcendence of the dominant appreciation of marriage' (1992a: 70). In spite of the fact that Greek ethnography has not yet shown us 'true' heterodoxy, one might wonder if a civil wedding or [a couple's] cohabitation with no official 'commitment', or even the somehow atypical wedding ceremony I am going to describe in this chapter, could be addressed as a 'true' heterodoxy. Should we base cultural concepts of 'heterodoxy' solely on the absence or existence of a ceremony? Or should we base heterodoxy on performance? In short, is the wedding, or, in our case the simulacrum of a Mykonian *paniyiri*, a 'compliance' to some tradition or to an institution? In reality, what is implied by the majority of the ethnographic accounts is an a priori loss of individuality, if there is any in the first place, or even further, the constitution of a gendered domination. This goes equally for more liberal labellings of social transformation, such as that proposed by du Boulay (1974: 133) where marriage creates a relationship of interdependence, a partnership whose harmony is, nevertheless, largely dependent on the female's efforts.

The compulsive assumption according to which the *I* is transformed into *we*, both symbolically and at the level of practice, is also adhered to by ethnographers such as Greger (1988) and Cowan (1990), though Greger describes a more complementary role between the sexes. Observing marriage practices and their ethnographic texts is an important field of enquiry for the ethnographer concerned with the concept of the self in the modern Greek context. The reason for this is that the only domain within which the notion of the self is at all defined is via its transformation. It is no accident that Cohen observes that in Greek ethnography 'consciousness of individuality' is only explicitly addressed by recent works such as Cowan's and this is still limited to the gender role of the individual and more specifically to women (Cohen 1994: 88). The central role marriage plays vis-à-vis self-identity is also evident in the broad ethnographic division that Loizos and Papataxiarchis (1991a) make: there are only two established realms of complete selfhood, engendered selves inside the household and inside marriage or otherwise the monastic life. Marriage again is implicitly a transformative structure but at least 'unmarried' selves are acknowledged beyond the context of sacred celibacy. In this sense, it is easy for the reader to conceptualise how, for the 'modern' Greek subject, the popular discourses of individuality are in conflict with the image of a 'married self', which in turn, creates counter-discourses of 'imprisonment'.[4]

I think that Greek ethnography needs to fill this gap concerning the notion of the (conscious) self coming into play. This is reflected in texts about marriage where there is a fixed presupposition that although the content of the ritual is changing – Argyrou's (1996) ethnographic study on Cypriot marriages illustrates these changes – the structural placement of the self remains more or less unnegotiated. Beyond checking the obvious – first, what ritual 'says', i.e, the content of ritual (Durkheim 1915); second, what ritual 'does', (as proposed by the British functionalist school); and third, what 'lies beyond' ritual, beyond its symbolic and egalitarian characteristics, i.e, revealing relations of power (Bloch 1974; 1986) – we need to take a step further. I think we need to abolish preconceived ideas about the individual circumstances of the actors and the change in their identity, if any, at this point in life. In other words, a wedding ritual can no longer be a homogenising mechanism of concrete cultural and personal transformations.

On the other hand, a purely performative approach to ritual (Tambiah 1979) or a purely symbolic one (Turner 1967) also ignore the actively and consciously involved actors. Giddens (1992), in his work on the 'transformation of intimacy' in modern society, puts forward an alternative definition of commitment, which actually challenges the institution of marriage as a culturally and socially predetermined act, and replaces it with a more idiosyncratic act of commitment, namely, the 'pure relationship'. This is a term broadly used by Giddens to refer to 'a relationship of sexual and emotional equality, which is explosive in its connotations for pre-existing forms of gender power' (Giddens 1992: 2). The pure relationship as a defining structure of late modernity – or in Giddens' own words 'a generic restructuring of intimacy' (ibid.: 58) – pays prime attention to the idiosyncratic past and present of the actors involved. According to Giddens, the only consistent ritualistic act allowed in the post-traditional order is a constant project of self and embodied reflexivity. Finally, in his analysis of modern 'marriages' and relationships, the life history of the actor, as it is narrated and crafted by its author, is of utmost importance. In Giddens's model, the success of the whole project of 'commitment' between individuals rests on a conscious battle on the part of the protagonists in the relationship not to accept any personal sacrifices – be they cultural, gender- related, emotional or psychological – vis-à-vis their, respective, self-reflexive life projects.

I will conclude this theoretical overview by referring to Argyrou's work (1996), which by focusing on different class strategies as regards wedding rituals, examines the subjectification of both traditional and bourgeois Cypriot culture in the constantly developing game of 'modernisation'. Argyrou maintains that wedding celebrations have been transformed from rites of passage to rites of distinction, that nevertheless still signify changes in social position and status. He draws a broad distinction between 'champagne' (i.e, the urban bourgeoisie) and 'village' weddings, emphasising their potlatch-like character as the one traditional element least affected by change, i.e., negating material inequalities at the symbolic level via the amount of money spent, the number of guests invited and entertained, and so on (ibid.: 10, 72–78). For Argyrou, contemporary Cypriot weddings 'are about cultural choices, tastes, and lifestyles' (ibid.: 111). Finally, he maintains that 'urban weddings are not fun' and they do not mean to be since 'they are involved in the serious business of reproduction and enhancing a family's name and prestige' (ibid.: 109).

Departing from the traditional notion of a wedding ritual being the most identity-wise dramatic *rite de passage* involving the 'transfer' of the actor to a different identity category, that of full adulthood, Argyrou treats contemporary weddings as social practices that 'follow the logic of "distinction" (Bourdieu 1984), a logic that raises socio-economic difference to the level of cultural significance' (Argyrou 1996: 112).

What strikes me in Argyrou's analysis is the blind conviction that similar form and style give an absolutely consistent signification vis-à-vis class and social identity. In other words, Argyrou's informants fall into different stylistic categories (champagne/village weddings) according to their already inscribed social position. The repositioning of this strictly class-based stylistic classification tends to re-establish sociological ideal types rather than emphasise conscious informants. For example, Cypriot society is described by the same author as a highly politically active and modernised one, so it is difficult for me to understand why civil weddings never appear in the text as an option. Instead of idealising tradition and accommodating the politics of an 'absolute' form of a 'traditional' wedding ritual, he idealises the stability of the actors' class position and consciousness that leaves no room for stylistic or other forms of creativity.

I initiated my research on the Mykonian cosmopolitan lifestyle by following the stylistic game of difference that Bourdieu (1984) proposes. But in the reality of Greek society which I witnessed, this game of distinction (especially vis-à-vis wedding ceremonies and its negations) went through many phases. For example, as soon as the bourgeoisie and the intellectuals adopted the civil wedding as an aesthetic and political choice, it quickly became appropriated by the petit bourgeoisie for the sake of a radical 'modernisation' process. But the former, in order to sustain their game of 'distinction' went back to practising the religious ceremony. This was not solely a stylistic, but also a philosophical turning away from Marxism and the apotheosis of modernisation and a re-affiliation to new religious and philosophical movements that looked to the Orthodox tradition and cultural consciousness as distinctive and easily affiliated with Eastern philosophies.

I could continue this game of emulation and transformation of class-based stylistic practices, as I experienced them in Greece, by extending Argyrou's modern paradigms of 'champagne' weddings to the 'chapel weddings' favoured in recent years by the Greek urban bourgeoisie. These are organised intentionally in the countryside emphasising discretion rather than conspicuousness. In the neo-urban consciousness, a 'wedding with character' is the 'ideal', according to the recent information I have collected. My own mother, in an attempt both to inform and persuade me, described to me in a long-distance phone call how a particular wedding had all this extraordinary *atmosfaira* (ambience, aura), as she characteristically put it, performed in a secret location, lit with blazing torches, giving a discreet but mystical atmosphere. What my mother was trying to communicate to me was that the more eccentric a wedding was 'nowadays', the more 'different', the more successful it was. Her comments were mostly concerned with 'style'; however, only on the surface. This detail, I think, is important beyond the connotations of 'distinction'. At a connotative level, the struggle for a highly idiosyncratic wedding style, that has recently been extended to different classes and people with very different lifestyles, shows that newlyweds have the desire, the creativity and the ultimate responsibility for keeping their individuality within the ritual. The endless list of alternative stylistic versions of 'commitment' ceremonies available actually shows the same thing. Some are still aficionados of the civil wedding, others prefer to go back to their place of origin and perform the ritual there. Others perform the wedding 'sacrament' on their own, with no guests, while others perform for friends 'only'. Others have remained faithful to the 'modern' hotel weddings. Some never marry, and some live in separate households. The great divergence in wedding practices is accompanied by strong beliefs about one's stylistic choice.

What I am trying to say is that the actual stylistic form of the commitment ritual may in the era of late modernity not be a directly revealing code. In order to clarify this point one needs, I think, to trace the personal history, the 'before' and 'after' in the lives of the actors. The style itself does not make 'traditionality' or 'modernity' or 'late modernity', at least not anymore. People can override or be indifferent to style. Nevertheless, the conscious subject can reproduce or escape his social and cultural order. I think issues of modernity are more clearly negotiated in the actual existential rhetoric of 'difference' vis-à-vis one's body or self rather than one's class, cultural ethics or customs.

One might argue that against all this is the fact that all these 'embryonic' cultural actors, my 'progressive' hippie informants included, actually indulge in a mainstream Orthodox ritual, so in a sense they reproduce 'tradition'. Where is change then? I think that this might be a trap, since it is true that aesthetics play the hidden role in a hideous moralising. But I also think that the ethnography that follows may hint at exactly the opposite. One has to bear in mind that the *Mykoniots'* existential apologia (and actually their structural reality) when 'performing' rituals offers an alternative morality code: that of pleasure. Their constant refrain is: 'for the sake of another *paniyiri*, for the sake of another party'. In this instance, the religious element (for the culture involved that is synonymous with the moral element) acts only as a backdrop, as an aesthetic detail of an altogether different orchestrated cultural representation.

Finally, to push my argument further, I need to stress the fact that my role as both an 'observer', a role that I openly discussed with my 'informants', and a wedding 'sponsor', reveals the same irony. The structure of the wedding ritual that follows and its connotations for its protagonists reads also as an inversion, whereby the *paniyiri* – the feast – is the main event and the actual wedding ceremony its by-product.

The narration of the wedding *paniyiri* or only the 'leisure class' has the right to reinvent folklore and rock 'n' roll

Orpheus and Eurydice's wedding was almost a joke; nobody could really tell when or where this ritual would take place and if indeed it would happen at all. Orpheus definitely represents the archetypal hippie for the last four Greek 'generations';[5] he and his friends personify quite a glamorous lifestyle. Orpheus is like a legend. His unique attitude is epitomised in an idiosyncratic vagueness, an unconditional relationship to time and commitment, an unpredictable temperament ranging between spontaneous high quality creativity and self-destructive or indifferent moods. An explosive creator of avant-garde scenarios, with a media profile that glorifies him as the Greek father of kitsch, Orpheus was one of the first to introduce the 'bar culture' into Greece. He was on drugs, especially heroin, for more than a decade: a habit he gradually gave up by himself. I recorded him proudly thinking back to his glorious past: 'I earned a place in *Les Beaux Arts* in Paris by sending someone else's drawings.'

Later, however, he switched to selling shish kebabs on the Parisian streets; this was the first in a series of businesses, for he had decided that no boss was good enough for him. Orpheus had continued his 'hitch-hiking' lifestyle in Europe for many years until he got engaged to an English girl and was initiated into British second-hand culture and ways of fetishising it. As a result, he has come to appreciate objects not solely in terms of their exchange and monetary value, but mostly in terms of the fanciful, odd features they possess.

It was one summer in his early twenties that Orpheus arrived unexpectedly on Mykonos. He immediately got involved in the island's social networks and set up one of the first 'groovy' shops, where second-hand, trendy seventies and extravagant clothes could be found. A couple of years later, he became the owner of a bar that established him as a member of the local 'mafia'. His highly active 'hedonistic' period has gradually slackened off over the last seven years. In this transitional stage, Orpheus transformed his Mykonian bar into an 'old' curio shop.[6] Orpheus, now in his forties, spends half the year in Mykonos and the other half in Kavala. During the winter period Orpheus lives in his hometown, organising cult events usually held in his own bar.

Orpheus considers his 'friends' solely in the context of the *Mykoniots'* milieu; this is the only group he explicitly identifies with, so much so, that lately he employed the following argument in order to convince Eurydice (his intended bride) about the nature of the wedding ritual he had in mind: 'I have to get married. I've never organised a *paniyiri* myself, I owe it to the island after all these years.'[7] Orpheus' eagerness to reproduce the *paniyiri* ritual, that acts as a chain of reciprocity in the local community, symbolises more than it actually states.

Being a *Mykoniot* for Orpheus signifies a common unconventional mentality collectively shared with other individuals; but more importantly, this *Mykoniot* 'being' is highly conceptualised in the specific locus of Mykonos. The personified Mykonos represents for the *Mykoniots* an authentic character and not some tourist folklore; the counter-petit-bourgeois 'option', and a lifestyle that goes beyond one's personal and cultural background. The *Mykoniots*, as the reader already knows, believe the locals to have inherited elements of good taste. These elements bring out a positive 'aesthetic predisposition' which is constantly recreated.

In other words, for the *Mykoniots*, whereas a wedding in one's own native village would probably be considered as kitsch, the Mykonians' 'authentic' attitude towards a ritual on Mykonos is thought to be permeated with originality. Sometimes, *Mykoniots* like to speak to one another with a particularly pretentious sing-song 'Mykonian' accent, using words from the Mykonian dialect for exhibitionist reasons. The 'Mykonian' lifestyle, is thus highly fetishised. Equally, someone's decision to get married on the island reinforces his/her relationship with the place and indirectly his/her 'originality'. Furthermore, it establishes a more official 'Mykonian' identity, since the locals and the local official community are somehow involved in the *Mykoniots*' personal lives. On the other hand, while marriage can be understood as a 'longing' for incorporation, the liberal and bachelor character of a *Mykoniot's* identity continues into the post-wedding period. For a *Mykoniot*, there are limitations to the degree of any sort of cultural embodiment. Every *Mykoniot* only feels at ease when being addressed as a 'Mykonian', but she could not equally easily agree to share a fixed identity, especially with her immediate family, such as one deriving from a village birthplace or a family name; that would detract from the *Mykoniot* actor's highly fetishised cosmopolitan identity.

The wedding ceremony that follows took place in Mykonos with the *Mykoniots* being the main protagonists and was especially performed for lost, current and old friends.

Orpheus and Eurydice: two people about to be married

The idea of a traditional Orthodox wedding ritual, if there was to be any wedding ritual at all, among the *Mykoniots* has resurfaced in recent years. The return of 'mainstream' rituals, I think, leads a general trend towards a neo-moralistic ideology in Greek society, with links to other new spiritual and crypto-nationalist ideologies, which have abandoned earlier radical reactions against Orthodoxy's conservatism. Faubion, in his ethnography on Greek practices of modernity, mentions references to theological literature proposed by a Greek bourgeois and gay activist, actually one of his core informants, in the latter's attempt to 'educate' the anthropologist on what is really 'Greek' (Faubion 1993: 237–38). Faubion particularly mentions a philosophical and theological trend under the label of 'New Orthodoxy'[8] whose philosophy underpins his notion of modern Greeks as historical constructivists. Faubion's ethnography on the modern Greeks' struggle with individuality refers to a bricolage 'project' of an historically constructivist 'making' of the self which permits equally religious and secular 'construal', a gnosticism mainly based on philosophical doctrines and the rereading of Orthodox theology, as well as other classical Greek ideas on the self (ibid.: 183).

Orpheus and his *Mykoniot* friends have recently started visiting Mount Athos, a 'men only' cluster of monasteries that symbolises the core of Orthodox tradition.[9] This act can be interpreted as Orpheus' attempt at a spiritual 'opening up' to 'traditional' religion.[10] Mount Athos nowadays acts as a winter 'retreat' for some members of the Orpheus *sinafi*, who due to personal circumstances, gave up travelling to the East. In this sense, Orpheus' 'overdue' wedding, in contrast to his 'unconventional' lifestyle of the past twenty years, might be rooted in an existential or spiritual craving which is no longer 'fed' by Eastern or rock 'n' roll ideologies, but, instead, consumes indigenous esotericism. Most of Orpheus' 'friends' are acquainted with Indian esotericism, but Orpheus, apart from a brief trip to Goa, never made it to an ashram or a guru. He was the 'stoned' boy of the *sinafi* who loved the anonymity of the big city, the excitement of the accidental and old children's toys. By the end of the eighties, he gave up *preza* (heroin), rode a bike and started wandering the city collecting cheap antiques. Basketball became his new 'addiction' to help him through the winter.

His companion, Eurydice plays a central role in his life, but they periodically spend time apart. Sometimes she can be found running his business, yet at other times she disappears. Being an open-minded feminist in her mid thirties she is politically active, but always uncommitted. Eurydice is well educated but has never used her degrees because she hates to belong anywhere. She has been 'affected' by Orpheus' addiction to collecting anything old. This habit keeps her busy during the winter months. During her Mykonian period she swims, paints, decorates the different houses she occasionally lives in, and takes care of Orpheus' social life around his 'antique' shop. Orpheus keeps his distance from the shop, especially during the height of the tourist season.

The couple have lived together on and off for more then thirteen years. The relationship developed from pure friendship to passionate love and companionship. In their view, the wedding would not change their lifestyles, everyday activities, consumption and other habits. There was no question of a dowry or any other wedding payment. After the wedding, Orpheus dared to ask her to sell a part of her parental land on another Aegean island, but Eurydice's response was negative.[11]

The Mykoniot's attitude towards a ritual: the setting

There was no such thing as a wedding list or wedding invitations. No confirmed date was given until the last moment, since the couple had postponed arranging certain official documents. After a series of postponements, one night Orpheus and Eurydice were partying at Antonis' Delos Bar – the club is famous for its lunar calendar, hung in the 'sacred' area, near the DJ. Antonis, who was going to be the other wedding 'sponsor', consulted the calendar and announced the September full moon as the auspicious date for the wedding *paniyiri*, emphasising the potential for the weather's calmness. Apart from being the leader of his Delos Bar team, Antonis also plays the part of the DJ in his club. His acting of the role of the 'harmonic navigator' who is 'in charge of the group mood/mind' is reminiscent of the 'technoshaman' of contemporary raves (Hutson 2000: 38). Antonis, with his lofty paternal figure performs here as the shaman, or even the 'god' of his flock (cf. Saldanha 2002: 51). The date was spontaneously fixed but that was about it. In the opinion of the actors, nothing more was needed; as a consequence, when the time came, the wedding preparations took place at the last moment, almost simultaneously with the guests' arrival. This wedding ritual, in terms of its cultural form can be analysed from three different perspectives: firstly, as a religious ritual; secondly, as a traditionally organised Mykonian feast, a *paniyiri* that involves the respect of the local community; and thirdly, as a big rock 'n' roll party. These levels of analysis cannot be confined to the conventional characteristics of each of them separately, since obviously they overlap. One could also argue for a parallel twofold stylistic structure: one being the simulacrum of 'traditional', 'conventional' and 'official', while the other is strongly 'unconventional', 'casual' and 'hippie-like', both being part of another simulacrum, both tending to remain anti-structural.

An overriding logic of spontaneity prevailed during the days before and after the ritual, and made the large number of guests feel as if they had been invited to an endless party.

The future bride and groom were living in a country house outside the *Hora*, on the south side of the island. Their home was located in a small residential area that consisted of an autonomous Mykonian *horio*,[12] with a private chapel, chickens, a large garden for vegetables, flowers and basil, and every July a local feast dedicated to Saint Anna. The locals who rented the house to Orpheus were very happy to let a 'foreigner's' wedding take place in their private/family chapel, and generally treated the couple as 'family'.

Eurydice told me that the couple had initially presented themselves to their local landlords as being married. One August night, when the courtyard of the Saint Anna *horio* was full of the couple's guests enjoying the generous hospitality of both households, a friend teased the couple by stating a cultural cliché: 'You should have that girl.' The phrase fitted the 'setting' of the occasion. The idea of a 'traditional' wedding setting was discussed with the couples' 'friends' at the time. But for the Mykonian landlady, who had established a close relationship with the couple, the whole thing sounded strange, and she initiated a discreet investigation to reveal the 'scandal'. This by no means meant that cases of unmarried couples were unknown to the local community. But as soon as Orpheus entered into the 'retrogressive' time of the Saint Anna *horio*, he performed a very 'traditional' role especially employed for the 'setting' that actually amused him a great deal. When the time came to decide upon the wedding ceremony, the whole thing was influenced dramatically by the picturesque situation that Orpheus and Eurydice were drawn back into in this old-fashioned Mykonian *horio*. Everything was in place to have a wedding performed 'at home': the couple, the kin group, the chapel, the provisions to feed the guests; but more importantly, Orpheus with his stage designer's mentality acquired for himself a truly 'authentic' setting. The only problem was that the landlady, even after the announcement of the wedding plans, kept asking questions in order to solve the mystery. To satisfy her, Eurydice finally came up with a vague story of a civil wedding that had taken place long ago.

The main characters of the Saint Anna *horio* were the elderly couple, Anna and Stavros; Anna was considered to be *alafroiskioti* (something like moonstruck). Aged seventy, she was the 'wealthy' member of the family. Her husband Stavros ran a vehicle all day around the town's harbour making deliveries. He was the 'beneficiary' of Anna's *proika* (dowry). Among the locals, Stavros had the reputation of being a warm-hearted person. Not yet corrupted by money and tourism, and being truly hospitable and caring, Stavros' family were considered among the last examples of the 'original' Mykonian rural lifestyle. In many respects the Saint Anna *horio* drew you back to the fifties. The uniqueness and commensality of *Kyra*-Anna, her strange physical appearance and childlike actions, made one feel that one was in another dimension of 'space and time'. Orpheus and *Kyra*-Anna had a special relationship, something like the old-fashioned image of two close female neighbours, wrapped in their own microcosm of daily cooking, gossiping and caring for the family. That relationship evolved into a gradual and mutual bond between the two *noikokyria* (conjugal households); the result was an almost communal kitchen and perpetual reciprocity. I can recall Orpheus literally spending that summer in Anna's kitchen. Usually when he woke up he would immediately go to have his coffee 'fixed' by Anna. Afterwards, he would return to the house, prepare and smoke a few joints, make plans and then suspend all his responsibilities by transferring the duties onto somebody else's shoulders, usually Eurydice's; he would then visit the vegetable garden, or his always abundantly stocked refrigerator, and come back to Anna's kitchen to discuss what should be on the menu for the day. Frequently he would cook for everybody, for his household and unexpected guests, for the old couple, their baker son and his Albanian wife – who brought all her family with her to the Saint Anna *horio* and turned the place into a 'little Albania', as Orpheus liked to put it – and for Thodoris junior, a grandchild from an earlier marriage.

The wedding-paniyiri arrangements, around the September full moon

The close proximity of the house to the church, as well as the simultaneous arrival of many visitors, and among them some members of the close kin of the couple, produced a chaotic but cheerful atmosphere. Within Saint Anna's rocky *horio* a space was arranged for the wedding according to the traditional rules of a *paniyiri*. While *Kyra*-Anna was personally preparing the church named after her patron saint, some of the girlfriends of the bride, who had arrived a week or so earlier, organised the *bonbonnieres* (the traditional wedding sugared almonds) that were placed in some '*funky*' pieces of glass, according to Orpheus' plans.

It is no longer the custom in 'modern' weddings to handcraft the wedding *bonbonnieres*, since they are usually made to order, but this was an 'antiquer's' wedding after all, so everything had to be 'traditional' and distinctive. Besides, during the winter, Orpheus had successfully bargained for a rare stock of fifties coloured glass, and they were ideal containers for the sugared almonds. The group of girlfriends literally grabbed the opportunity to come earlier, leaving their husbands and partners behind, since they had to 'play cool' and emancipated. After all, it was no common occasion: it was Orpheus and Eurydice's wedding. Orpheus took the opportunity and made them carry from his Kavala warehouse home, the stock of coloured glass, the sugared almonds and the satin ribbon, as well as many other things he considered necessary, no matter if in reality they remained useless.

The preparation of the food started two days in advance in order to feed 500 guests. The organiser of the cooking team was the sister of the bride who was also a restaurateur. She was helped by the 'girly' team that was growing ever larger, now including a wide range of guests from the numerous relationships that the sociable couple had acquired individually over the years. Cooking and house preparations occupied, among others, many volunteers but also some 'impressed apprentices' from the *Mykoniots' sinafi*, usually members of the group working in local tourism. The *Mykoniot* mentors including the groom, remained relatively uninvolved, so that they could continue rehearsing their 'Mykonian' spontaneous performance, as well as keeping fresh and immune from the chaos of the preparations. However, Antonis, the *koumbaros* (wedding sponsor) who was also a celebrated 'godfather' of the Mykonian nightlife, carefully arranged to send his 'kids' (the Delos Bar employees) to help. I think that the last-minute whitewashing of the courtyard and the church was done with their help.

For the last two days, Orpheus' elect 'apprentices' were working in Anna's or Orpheus' kitchen or in the courtyard. While all these stressful last-minute and 'spontaneous' preparations were taking place, people kept arriving. The staggered arrival of the guests produced a series of intense emotional climaxes: first was 'Uncle' Fritz, a second-hand clothes dealer from New York, an old *sinafi* member and an old-fashioned bachelor who came especially for the occasion. Second, Eurydice's girlfriend from her politically active university years, still strongly 'independent' and unmarried. Third, an old and special friend who had just discovered that he was suffering from cancer, a fact that caused great distress to the bride and made her, at the last minute, draw back from the arrangements. Then came Orpheus' cousins from the small market town outside Kavala where the groom was brought up, representing 'alien' lifestyles, expectations and a type of sentimentality that the couple was trying to avoid. Finally, the last-minute arrival of the bride's estranged elderly parents. Further, a considerable number of lifelong bachelors, that definitely outnumbered the 'committed' guests, who were either 'officially' invited or not (in fact the number of people actually invited was very small – but the news travelled fast). Some came from different parts of Greece and beyond, thus taking this opportunity to meet with their fellow 'nomads'. The guests represented a patchwork of social backgrounds. This was unavoidable due to the nature of the island's cosmopolitanism and the sociable couple's deviant but glamorous individualities. Some 'real' Mykonian locals, apart from the landlords of Saint Anna, were also invited. But an awkwardness on the locals' behalf was evident, since everything that was happening was 'familiar', yet the categories of people participating in the 'traditional' preparations of a Mykonian *paniyiri* were 'alien'. Orpheus meticulously invited only some of his favourite 'working-class' Mykonians (if such a category can be said still to exist on the rich tourist island), as well as his Albanian immigrant co-residents. But especially from the former he chose to invite those who, during his hippie and junkie years, had not blighted his existence and career on Mykonos. These were usually rural Mykonians, who had little to do with their modern 'town' counterparts who had long since shifted to tourism.

Orpheus's idealisation of the ever-changing group that alternately performs as the 'working class' or the 'outcasts' on the island – for example, his current protective attitude towards the Albanian immigrants – is contrary to the local Mykonians' perception of them, which is largely hostile. The seemingly 'classless' cosmopolitan attitude of the 'new indigenes', who idealise contemporary Mykonos as a 'single community' – *pace* Clifford (1994: 303, 308) – and attempt to redefine locality in this new transnational diasporic reality of the tourist space, is contested if one considers the fact that Albanian and other immigrant workers form an exception to the 'classless game' of this diasporic community of 'extreme individuals'. In a sense, the *Mykoniots d'élection* themselves only eventually acquired the right to 'perform' with the classless and not with the marginal. Papailias' (2003) analysis of the case of a Greek bus-hijacking by a young Albanian migrant worker, Pisli, who was eventually shot dead, together with a Greek hostage on Albanian territory – a controversial case that revealed the politics of nationalism and discussion of which eventually became anathema and to be avoided – detects an 'interesting reversal': a mirror effect vis-à-vis the rivalry between the indigenous Greeks and the Albanian newcomers who had flooded into Greece by the late nineties. The Greek media represented the Albanians as 'brutal' and 'backward'; in turn, the Albanians perceived the Greeks as savages (ibid.: 1063). Papailias argues that poor organisation and migration policies in Greece multiply the local discourses on immigrants' criminality. This is also reflected in the Mykonians' discourse on the Albanians' 'invasion', those who were, in fact, asked to come and work on their building sites and later in the villas of the arrivistes; those who were asked by the *nouveaux riches* Mykonians – who eventually abandoned manual labour to pursue touristic entrepreneurship – to take care of all the dirty work, tourist, agricultural or otherwise. The fact that Mykonos was an extremely poor island until the seventies makes for a similar ironic mirror effect between the Albanians and the Mykonians: the Mykonians see the Albanians as the 'untouchables' and make sure their own children are not in the same classrooms as the Albanians. At the same time, the Albanians feel extremely mistreated and misrepresented, especially when gangs of Mykonian youths loot the empty villas of the 'arrivistes' during their winter absence – but it is still the Albanians who get the blame.

One example of an 'outcast's' awkwardness at Orpheus' wedding, was that of the reputable *paniyiri* organiser and the island's refuse collector, the famous indigene, Spathas. Spathas was the most outrageous case of an alcohol consumer and spontaneous *paniyiri* organiser in the rural district of Mykonos. Orpheus passed through his 'Mykonian apprenticeship' while renting one of Spathas' houses a decade or so ago. I have attended several of Spathas' orgiastic spontaneous *paniyiria*, but the consumption of alcohol and dope was so heavy that the people participating in Spathas' sleepless *paniyiria* took on alienated and scary forms and behaviour, a fact that had lately made me avoid these encounters. Nevertheless, Spathas liked Orpheus and came to his wedding, as did the remaining members of the *pirates' sinafi*. Yet, I could not fail to detect an unusual behaviour, outside the normal codings of the Mykonian *paniyiria*. Spathas was dramatically modest and although he consumed enough to make him blind drunk, he did not act out his drunkenness 'freely' once drunk. Spathas was sitting at the usual sort of improvised long *paniyiri* table, listening to familiar island music, drinking wine. Yet, while the stylistic elements of the setting were so similar to the numerous Mykonian *paniyiria* he had attended, Spathas did not seem to feel a sense of belonging. Another example of an 'outcast's' awkwardness was revealed in Anna's behaviour. She disappeared at the last minute, although many of the cooking preparations were initially organised to take place in her large kitchen that was specially equipped for the occasion of a *paniyiri*, with its built-in fireplace, large enough to hold two large cauldrons that simmer simultaneously. Anna's kitchen also had the necessary equipment to serve many hundreds of guests, but when the stream of eccentric 'pilgrims' began invading the Saint Anna *horio*, she must have felt uncomfortable and thus the preparations were transferred to Orpheus' kitchen. Fortunately, she finally accepted to host the preparations on the second day.

Apart from the preparation rituals, whereby the joint venture initiated a bonding of the participants towards this 'ritual of their own', the bohemian friends who kept arriving 'uninvited' and the pre-eminent role of the *Mykoniots* were the salient characteristics of this prelude to the fiesta. There was no real coordinator and everybody had to improvise.

The 'bachelor' friends on the bachelors' night

On the eve of the wedding up to a hundred people were gathered in the *horio*; this farrago of ritual participants were milling around either to help or, mainly, to start partying. Later on in the evening, the male and female 'bachelors' attempted to celebrate initially independently in two friendly bars in the town. The exhausting drinking and dancing ended around six o'clock in the morning. On this occasion, an exception to the traditional single-sex prenuptial entertainment was permitted by the bride. After a certain point, male and female bachelors were gathered together for a joint celebration in Antonis' bar.

Every activity was very brief the following day; some attempted a quick swim. The flowers for the church did not arrive, and the wedding rings were left at the jeweller's.

The girls' 'dressing' of the bride

The girlfriends of the bride were supposed to dress her in the nearby *horio* of another *Mykoniot* friend. Hercules' bachelor home was the most favourable place for female gatherings, given his highly organised and accommodating space. The bride, continuing her unpredictable behaviour, went for a swim to relax incognito and arrived late. She came back at a point when the rest of the girls, including myself, were already arranging their attire for the ceremony. Eurydice was not particularly fond of this type of 'girlish' talk. She had bought herself a not particularly bridal outfit – but at least cream in colour – a few days earlier and avoided the chaos of the arrangements. Everybody had their opinion about her appearance, but Eurydice refused to dye her grey hair, or adopt any particular hairstyle or any typical nuptial ornaments, continuing to feel reluctant to get drawn into the 'typical' bride's anxiety. The rest of us were shaving legs and arms, exchanging clothes and massages, while at the same time organising the stylistic details of our attire, and finally deciding that white was the appropriate colour for the girls' group. In the end, I was dressed in a friend's clothes and the bride's sister was dressed in mine. At some point, the mother of the bride arrived in a garment borrowed from another friend. She played a completely secondary role throughout the whole preparation and celebration, in contradistinction to the traditionally salient and patronising position 'expected' from the 'mother of the bride'. Eurydice refused to play the game of 'fixing up' her own body, face and hair, confining herself to some limited preparation. It was not obvious at all,

Narratives of difference

from the bustle in front of Hercules' bathroom mirror, who was the protagonist in the ritual.

Hercules' bachelor but 'promiscuous' bed was spontaneously decorated with a piece of satin cloth just for the sake of a 'wedding decoration'. Neither I nor the bride had any idea who arranged this last-minute preparation. After some pleading, Hercules allowed the girls to cut some flowers from his pink climbing plant to throw on the pseudo-wedding bed, imitating a traditional ritual called the 'making of the bed'.[13] The decor of Hercules' room now looked more reminiscent of a wedding setting. Still, there was something missing. There were no hysterical kinfolk, no hairdresser, no tears, no proper 'wedding dress', but at least there was the 'bed'. The girls at some point removed themselves to the room near the 'bed' to indulge in a sobering fifteen-minute group relaxation session, with some five of them lying on their backs. That was clearly the part of the preparation the bride approved of. After the invigorating silence, the house slowly started partying with music. Hercules had already gone to meet the groom's group, and one of the girls started preparing the *yinaikeio* [literally woman's] – a code word among the female *parea,* meaning the joint that is solely consumed by the girls before putting in an 'appearance' – in order to create the essential atmosphere for performing. Both these techniques, i.e., the relaxation session and the joint helped to relieve some of the tension.

Eurydice dressed herself, since everyone else was busy preparing their own big 'Mykonian' appearance. The wedding gown consisted of a simple elegant silk skirt and a Balinese lace blouse; she also wore a classic pair of English bridal shoes brought by a friend from London. The bride followed a cross-cultural code that came to her as a piece of last-minute superstitious 'knowledge' from her cross-cultural friends. Her New Yorker-*Mykoniot* girlfriends said she should wear 'something old, something new, something borrowed, something blue'. Eurydice liked this adage; she also did not find it threatening, I think, so she followed the custom and she also wrote down the names of her girlfriends on the soles of her wedding shoes (a custom in modern Greek weddings) just before the exodus for the wedding ceremony.

Before I proceed, I wish to make some preliminary comments: in the 'making' of the wedding bed and also the 'dressing' of the bride, one can detect a tendency to parody the established cultural ritualistic elements.[14] The bride left her parents or some other relatives to sleep on her real wedding bed. During the bachelors' night, as well as the night before that, she slept over in a friend's hotel room, something that happened purely as a matter of convenience. Something analogous happened to Orpheus. On the morning of the wedding, Eurydice went to a breakfast where a *Mykoniot* photographer took pictures of the 'bride' wearing the same clothes as the night before. The important point is that some of the preparation details, that I gleaned from the bride while writing this chapter, still emphasised the familiar discourse of spontaneity.[15] This pattern, I thought, did not come solely from an insecurity about her new 'selfhood', or from some fear of being classified either as petit bourgeois, normal or traditional. It was largely a by-product of a conscious choice to follow an alternative philosophy. For example, Eurydice reminded me that the essential large-scale wedding candles had been missing, and since it was Sunday, they had to go to the grocer's house and ask him to open his shop. The grocer saved them at the last minute, offering the candles traditionally used in the Orthodox ceremony during the wedding dance of the *Isaia*, that must be accompanied by the *paranyfaki* (pageboy) who holds these candles.

Finally, the bride intentionally promoted an unpretentious style. The only jewellery she wore were the pearl earrings 'borrowed' from her sister. In general, the traditional decoration of the bride, that usually comes thanks to expensive presents given by relatives for the occasion, was absent. The bride and the groom organised, directed, paid for, and set the 'customary' rules to a large extent, though being highly eclectic for their own ceremony.

A few minutes later, the groom appeared passing by the main street with dozens of friends shouting at the house in honour of the bride.

The bride's journey to the church

The time had arrived: the father of the bride appeared at Hercules' *horio* to escort her, accompanied by a traditional (i.e., Mykonian) band, consisting of one fiddle and one *tsambouna* (a local type of bagpipe) that had already escorted the groom. We had started drinking some brandy we found in Hercules' kitchen. Soon after, the father and the daughter performed the 'first dance' together prompted by the crowd and especially by Antonis, the *koumbaros* (sponsor) who was of Mykonian descent and probably knew the local customs. The bride's retinue left Hercules' house and started climbing the hill of Saint Anna. The many guests, standing in front of the church, could see her approaching. It was an exotic scene; an Australian photographer friend was 'shooting black and white' of the bride, who continued smoking and leaning on her father's arm.

I will once more interrupt the description in order to highlight the scene: the father, a distant but proud figure, was also dressed in clothes borrowed at the last minute (i.e., not paying particular attention to his 'prestigious' position). On his left, walks the bride performing her part in the parade: she is gradually catching her audience's attention while she continues to smoke. Here, I will quote a passage from Cowan's comment on the body language of a wedding's protagonist during an equivalent moment in the Sohoian wedding ritual. Cowan points out that 'the bride assumes a pose of modest dignity in her walk to the church' (Cowan 1990: 131). For Eurydice, this underlying gender principle of 'shame' is absent; and, if Bourdieu is right, 'beyond the grasp of her consciousness', as she smokes her cigarette. In my opinion, Eurydice is totally aware of her 'traditional' performance and her atypical wedding scenario. She has already offered herself as an active performing persona.

The Orthodox ceremony

The ritual was performed at sunset. By the time the bride's retinue met the groom, the 'girls' started screaming and repeating in sisterhood fashion: 'We are not going to give her.' Eurydice, I suspect, symbolised for them a 'modern' model of female independence. At Eurydice's behest, the official wedding bouquet was also boycotted by the girls, who had arranged for another one, made from Hercules' pink flowers. By the time that the groom and bride's ceremonial meeting took place, Eurydice must have had two bouquets, since she first appeared holding the pink one, but somehow, later on, she managed to find herself holding the 'official' one while walking with the groom towards Saint Anna's chapel.

The priest performed the ceremony in the courtyard of the small church, thus enabling the colours of the Aegean sunset to overarch the 'blessed' couple. The whole event was held outdoors at Orpheus' instigation due to the hot and calm weather, a highly atypical circumstance for such a ceremony. The father of the bride sang out of tune, as he repeatedly failed to follow the second priest's chanting. At the same time, *Papa*-Yiorgis (the head-priest) was scolding Stavros junior, the *paranyfaki* (pageboy), as the latter would keep nervously waving his candle up and down. Everyone witnessing the scene was in an almost ecstatic state. Orpheus was carrying off his role with sobriety, while Eurydice smiled nervously. *Kyra*-Anna hid from the guests, as she feared the crowd. The majority of them were in a state of sentimental embarrassment. One has to bear in mind that the *Mykoniots* were unfamiliar with the *rites de passage*.

The reading of the wedding ceremony took nearly an hour since *Papa*-Yiorgis, the legendary priest of the island, wanted to keep to tradition. Orpheus fully agreed with this arrangement when it was initially proposed to him. The reading of the totality of the ritualistic passages appropriate for the wedding ceremony is something that is absent in town weddings due to 'modernist' ideas. The reason for this is mainly that the wedding ceremony is nowadays primarily confined to a social act, an enhancement of a family's prestige rather than a *mystirio*, a sacrament, as the revivalists of the Orthodox dogma and 'way of life' understand it to be.

I was standing together with the other *koumbaros* behind the couple, but for some mysterious reason my perpetual observant mode disappeared and I was drawn into the ritual. Yet, I could feel that people were still coming from afar.

The most salient feeling I had during the whole wedding *paniyiri* was that my 'informants', whom I looked up to in some respects, had symbolically accepted me. Their trust in me went beyond my anthropological identity, an identity that usually gave them the chance to reject and tease me. I felt incorporated, not only as an 'apprentice' into their cultural 'secrets' but also, in this instance, as an equal (given the bonding and traditionally patronising image of the role of the *koumbara*).[16]

At some point during the ceremony, I found myself unconsciously acting out the role of the anxious and suspicious relative, checking the church flowers since in the chaos of last-minute preparations, I heard that the flowers were missing. Some very artistic and minimal decoration using branches and Mykonian wild flowers had transformed the entrance of the chapel into its festive form. Obviously somebody must have made a last-minute arrangement to solve the problem.

When I first heard about the missing flowers, earlier on in the day, I automatically abdicated responsibility for doing anything about it, since I had to rush to Orpheus' curio shop to find an old stock of copper wedding rings, since neither the jeweller nor anybody else had brought the ordered gold ones on time. Not that the couple worried about it, but I did. I was also asked by Orpheus, the 'mentor' of the occasion, to bring an old tray and a couple of old-fashioned Greek wine glasses from his shop. This detail was a beautiful aesthetic addition, but I was furious. He didn't have the wedding rings, but he had his mind on these specific glasses. At the end of the day, wine glasses were not at all an important detail in the ceremony. Thanks to a *Mykoniot* friend, whom I found on my way to the shop and who undertook to find the jeweller, the *koumbaros* finally obtained the real rings on time.

Standing now at the side of the couple, I looked at the art nouveau bronze tray that Orpheus had envisaged especially for the setting of Saint Anna's chapel and the old, wine crystal-glass, mass produced in the fifties. He was right; it seemed as if we took it from *Kyra*-Anna's kitchen shelf. A perfect stylistic detail that matched the extremely modest decoration of the chapel.

I could see the reverence radiating from Orpheus out of the corner of my eye. Stavros junior was, as I learned later, the unofficial pageboy. The other boy, a son of a *Mykoniot* friend was wearing his best clothes and standing quietly with his candle. His eight-year-old brother Kostis was behind him, inside the church. Kostis had borrowed his photographer father's camera and had taken his role rather seriously. Stavros was feeling absolutely at home, and although he was not wearing the 'proper' clothes, he was invited by Orpheus to enter the 'sacred' circle of the ceremony at the last minute.

Eurydice did not act out the modern 'custom' of discreetly stepping on her future husband's foot when the priest said the key controversial phrase: 'and the woman should stand in fear of her man'. This practice was established some time in the late sixties in Greece, I think, and made numerous brides symbolically 'object' to their husband's future sovereignty. Arguably, this custom also implied that the bride's new powerful position as *the* wife would initiate a different dynamic into the relationship. In any case, Eurydice refused to indulge in this practice since, as she argued in her own words: 'It's too common a practice'.

After the ceremony: the organisation of the paniyiri, dressing and dancing codes

The commanding presence of the calm Mykonian landscape, the setting of the sun and the simultaneous rising of the impressive autumn full moon communicated to the guests a beautiful and authentic sensation. Furthermore, the absence of basic formalities such as the greeting ritual at the end of the ceremony, or the formal setting of a dominating wedding table, contributed to a relaxed atmosphere. This outcome resulted from a symbolic proximity of following form, such that everyone could feel close and undifferentiated. Instead, the band was situated in the centre of the feast's setting. The musicians began as soon as the priest had finished, and stopped only ten hours later. All night long they were 'fed' continuously with money by the *Mykoniots* and the kin of the couple. Later, a musical group of improvisers took over from them.

The guests were dressed with great diversity; some were dressed casually, others in their Indian semi-formal silks, some in their 501's and several in exotic garments. Two friends of the bride and the *koumbaros* were in top-of-the-line Armani suits. But this by no means set a trend for the occasion; Hercules, for example, came in his everyday clothes. As I mentioned above, the immediate kin of the bride were actually in borrowed clothes, and the groom did not bother about his appearance since he detested shopping for new clothes. He preferred to spend a 'fortune' talking about his potential outfits over the phone with his second-hand clothes dealer friend from New York, repeatedly changing his mind about the colour. Finally, his friend came empty-handed because he was 'bored' with it all, as Eurydice informed me later.

Orpheus saw himself only as another stylistic detail in his wedding setting of the Saint Anna *horio*. Readily identified with the old stuff he had been collecting for years, he treated himself as another piece of 'merchandise' that would decorate the wedding. Fortunately, he also charged the sister of the bride with finding him a fairly cheap white linen suit as a standby, which finally proved to be the solution. For Orpheus, there is no anxiety, because there is talent and last-minute inspiration that solves everything. And if this standby suit had not existed, he would have discovered an alternative rhetoric to support his appearance.

The couple ignored a nephew thought to be '*straight*'[17] (Eurydice's characterisation) when he asked them to 'pose' for the traditional photographs of the newlyweds at the end of the ceremony. Eurydice, highly suspicious of her nephew, commented on the incident when she recalled this scene: 'he dreamed of having a pretext to photograph, so that he would be able to shoot some of those dreadful media socialites'. Anyway, this ceremonial 'posing' of the couple never materialised for the nephew, or for any other photographer of the party.

The guests, soon after the end of the ceremony began to mix and started socialising; the composition of the actors in the wedding *paniyiri* was by no means typical of such occasions nor particularly homogenous. There were many types of people mixed together: I can recall middle-class relatives next to ex-coke-dealers, the New York group with rich and trendy media people, the glamorous gay group, primitive *Mykoniot* artists, honoured locals, old friends from the politically active years, many of the new Mykonos generation of ravers, some typical Mykonos socialites, Orpheus' Elvis-style younger friends who used to work in his Kavala club, some cult figures from the Greek media ... or in other words, as one informant put it, 'three generations of hippies gathered together'. The dancing, once started, was continuous. The *Mykoniots* opened the dancing as a body performing the role of the immediate kin. Eleonora captured her audience with her tightly fitted, sexy orange dress, dancing barefoot.

Soon people started dancing everywhere. The party gradually acquired the atmosphere of a 'rave', a constant flow of musical and dancing elements that were imitating 'traditional' sound patterns. The main focus from the beginning to the end of the *paniyiri* was on the area in front of the local band, an area which had been transformed into a dancing floor immediately after the wedding ceremony. Eurydice avoided dancing as much as possible, especially after obvious encouragements to do so, to play her role. The rhythm of the party was soon handed over to the connoisseurs. The wedding protagonists were dismissed.

Considering the personal backgrounds of the people gathered, the fact that a heroin 'high' was completely absent from the occasion was a crucial element. People drank homemade wine or whisky but they mostly got very high on dope. For the older members of the group there was always an alternative: the drug of celebration, namely cocaine. Joints were openly shared, sometimes creating difficulties among the odd group of kin and the uninitiated.

The sounds of the Mykonian fiddle and the magic 'strings' of Lagoudas (a famous local musician) were slowly, as the night went on, transformed into a rap beat. Some uninvited guests – 'freaks'[18] from Naxos – helped by performing at amazing tempos that kept the audience awake throughout the night. The feast's music was performed by a variety of traditional island instruments and two bouzoukis. Slowly a growing number of performers was added to the musicians who had initially started their performance with some 'traditional' music accompanying the lyrics. The *Mykoniots*' involvement in the musical performance gave the *paniyiri* an improvised flavour over its traditional equivalent, with the performers and the audience mixing their roles. The best of the Mykoniots' *touberlekia* were brought along, ready for 'performance'. The picture of the musical ensemble consisting of a 'traditional' band, the Naxian freaks and the *Mykoniots*' conspicuous percussion, symbolically represented the syncretic cultural elements which were hidden beneath the traditional structure of the wedding *paniyiri*.

One interesting moment on the dance floor was when a local woman, Aleka, who happened to have belonged for many years to the group of the *Mykoniots*, having found herself married to one of them, stood up to dance in high spirits. As soon as she started dancing, she began yelling toasts to the bride and the groom and the *koumbaroi* (plural of *koumbaros*), a form of address that has been rhetorically credited to the intimate body of the *Mykoniot* mentors and those close to them. The result was that for many days after the Saint Anna's wedding *paniyiri*, everybody in the milieu went a round calling each other *koumbare*. The communal feeling of the wedding *paniyiri* broadened the spectrum of 'the protagonists', thus symbolically transforming the ritual into a collective celebration.

Aleka at the high point of her performance attached a large amount of money onto the fiddler's shirt with a safety-pin. But this was not all. She started, as she was 'high', to persistently call on the bride for a dance. The bride tried to ignore her and finally Aleka started chasing her but with no result, since Eurydice kept finding a series of different excuses. In the end, she openly refused to 'dance' for Aleka's money.

Two additional highlights of the dance floor were, first, a brilliant saxophone performance from someone who had come with a friend, and the homemade fireworks that were probably exploded by some of Orpheus' mischievous local friends.

The hybrid element in consumption patterns: the food commensality and the wedding presents

The arrangement of the wedding-feast tables followed the typical organisation of a local *paniyiri*. As soon as the ceremony was completed the guests began occupying the long communal *paniyiri* tables. The seating was random in accordance with the practice of local *paniyiria*. Wine, bread and some 'food' was already on the tables to initiate the participants' commensality ritual.

Some of the guests remained standing near the 'performance' area. Others occupied a group of rocks near the Saint Anna courtyard where the feast's mentors welcomed them by sharing plates of food and carafes of wine. Orpheus was constantly running in and out of Anna's kitchen, organising the food supply to the tables, as well as acting as a waiter himself. The wedding *paniyiri*'s menu accommodated different culinary ideas. Different plates kept arriving at the guests' tables in no particular order. A loosely structured team of helpers was initially organised by Antonis who 'offered' his bar staff. Spontaneous helpers volunteered however, throughout the feast.

The 'main course' consisted of freshly slaughtered livestock offered by Anna's family as a wedding present. The slaughtering, which was a typical ceremonial procedure preceding every Mykonian *paniyiri*, took place in a nearby relative's *horio*, whereas, the cleaning and cutting up of the animal took place in the Saint Anna courtyard the day before the wedding. This difficult and skilled job was executed by the landlord, Stavros, a relative of his and the groom.

There were also last-minute arrangements made by Orpheus for cooking some special 'fresh' fish he had managed to obtain. This was an arrangement that made those in charge of the cooking furious since the cooking and preparation of the fish was very demanding.

The big bones of the slaughtered animal (it was probably a pig) were boiled for many hours to produce the tasty *Mykonian zomos* (a type of broth) which was traditionally offered at the Mykonian *paniyiri* tables. This broth was highly appreciated by the *Mykoniot* connoisseurs. Apart from the 'traditional' meat dishes produced from the slaughtered animal, there were also many different types of dishes based on cross-cultural recipes prepared by the restaurateur sister of the bride. Her 'progressive' recipes included baked potatoes with a special ham filling, sweetcorn and chicken salad with a mayonnaise dressing, a bean and vegetable salad, as well as a very rich salad made of ham, cheese and mayonnaise. Some modified versions of traditional 'Greek' appetisers were also served. Side-salad portions with plenty of oil and lemon were offered in large quantities, in the 'Greek' way. The different dishes were shared by the guests on each table.

The feast's menu also included some additional surprises: at dawn, the remaining 'participants' were treated to some shish kebab. The preparation of the meat was undertaken by some friends and the cooking was done outdoors on a charcoal fire. A stock of ready-made skewers of meat, another of Orpheus' initially frustrating last-minute supplies, was left out of the earlier food arrangements. The shish kebab cooked in the open air was the perfect answer to the early morning hunger pangs. Orpheus' last-minute supply turned out to be useful in the end. As well as the kebabs, there was another gastronomic surprise for the guests. A white van arrived and parked with its back facing the middle of the yard. The back was opened and buckets of *Häagen-Dazs* ice cream of different flavours were revealed; a generous wedding present from another 'participant'. The van was parked near the area where Orpheus' friends were cooking the shish kebab. As soon as the participants realised what was happening, they made a dash for the back of the van. During this amazing scene, some guests who were feeling hungry after all the dope and alcohol found themselves holding a shish kebab in one hand and an ice-cream cone in the other, sometimes eating them simultaneously. Actually, this idiosyncratic wedding present, that also came as a surprise to the newlyweds, covered the 'dessert' part of the ceremony's menu since the wedding couple were absolutely indifferent to the 'modern' idea of a wedding cake.

The groom in his white linen suit had adopted a classic Sicilian look and maintained his aesthetic perfection into the next morning; except, that is, for the black Indian eyeliner that he had painted his eyes with, which 'ran' over his face. The bride, after she had had a nap in her bridal clothes on a pile of travelling bags, changed at some point early in the morning and then reappeared at the party in her T-shirt with a sarong wrapped around her waist.

The wedding presents were almost all confined to 'funky' (i.e., positively fetishised) items. A large number of guests did not feel 'obliged' to bring a wedding present. Some used alternative methods to 'give' something to the newlyweds, such as Hercules who had recently spent some time artistically painting two rooms of their rented Mykonian home. The wedding presents of Orpheus and Eurydice mostly comprised a series of 'decorative' items that stayed untouched for many months, some on one side of the living room and others in several corners of the curio shop. I will try to describe some of these presents in order to give the reader a flavour of their style. A large part of the wedding presents looked like the kind of objects one could find in Orpheus' curio shop that have no consistent stylistic characteristics. Orpheus loved anything old and unusual. Analogous things were given to him: some flashy but inexpensive sixties 'antiques', an old Balinese clock, a pair of bronze chandeliers, an original Victorian plate made out of papier mâché, handmade embroidery, and so on. Oriental pieces of art were also popular among the wedding presents: a handmade embroidered blanket brought from India especially for the occasion; handmade gold-plated glasses; two antique gold pins, whose donors remained a mystery; a piece of antique jewellery and a large Indian silk print, most probably an antique as well.

One of the 'key' wedding presents was a pair of designer earrings given to the bride by Antonis, the *koumbaros*. This jewellery was created by an 'exclusive' Greek designer, another exogenous inhabitant of Mykonos. Eurydice thought that as a symbolic present these earrings carried something of the 'bourgeois mentality' she detested; a mentality and stylistic option she hesitated to validate, stating as an excuse that she 'hated' expensive jewellery. Her mother-in-law, who also wanted to give her something 'gold' for the occasion, was persuaded by the bride not to buy it by herself. Instead, Eurydice chose for herself a ring made by a friend who was working on the island. This ring was a simple and rather cheap reproduction of an Indian one with no obvious 'symbolic capital'. Eurydice commented that she preferred something 'inexpensive and not useless'. Her rhetoric was that sooner or later she would most probably mislay it somewhere anyway. The groom was given by his mother-in-law a pin featuring the head of Alexander the Great, a popular reproduction at the time and a symbol of re-emergent Greek nationalism.

Art objects were also frequently represented among the wedding presents. Four oil paintings were given by their creators. In one of them, the artist characteristically focused on the 'joint'-making equipment. There were the so-called 'straight' wedding gifts, such as a pressure cooker, toaster, a mixer, and a mini Hoover, sent by 'uninvited' relatives. There were also some highly atypical gifts: such as original Palestinian scarves, a couple of raincoats brought from Australia, a basket with a large string of garlic, and pieces of 'traditional' Greek needlework brought by Emma, the English *Mykoniot*, a 'funky' dressing-table mirror designed by a famous Greek painter, and an old Russian edition of a book on the Hermitage collection. The latter was Artemis' contribution to the wedding, and it was a volume stolen from the old library of her bourgeois family. Another memorable present, this time for immediate consumption, was a hand-painted box full of large joints, already rolled for the occasion.[19] A triptych of antique gravures with romantic female images was given to the bride by a university friend. A black-and-white quality print, an artistic naked pose of the bride from earlier years was especially developed and retouched for the occasion by an old male friend. Finally, a handmade mosquito net and a Tibetan metal-chime which produces a distinctive echoing sound were among the wedding presents the couple utilised immediately.

A characteristic incident with regard to the wedding presents is indicative of how the newlyweds' mentality deviates from that of their kin. The couple's home was used as an alternative seating area for the guests of the ceremony. It was kept wide open and available for different activities: at some point, one room was a hashish den but later the bride's family retreated there. The front room was mainly occupied by children but it was also used for storing some wedding presents. Most of the presents came with no special wrapping and after the ceremony one side of the room was full of them. In the middle of the party chaos, I remember entering the front room and running into an anxious relative who urged me to participate in the opening of the wrapped gifts. Without waiting for my consent she straight away launched into the pleasure of opening the presents, using my status as *koumbara* to justify her action. Her curiosity and enthusiasm were not shared by either the groom or the bride, who remained largely indifferent to their own wedding presents. They did not bother to display them or even move them from their temporary position. Another curious incident further reveals their mentality. A couple of days after the wedding, Anna was persistently asking questions about a washing machine that had been left outside her house. Eurydice replied that she had no idea about it. Anna assured her that the washing machine did not belong to her family. A little later the mystery was solved. The washing machine was another wedding present that somebody must have delivered while nobody was around. It had a postcard attached with a typical folkloric representation of Greek culture, a group of *evzones*, the 'safeguards' of the nation, marching outside the Greek parliament. The gift was sent to the couple from a group of *Mykoniot* friends. To cut a long story short, the washing machine remained out there for many weeks after it was discovered. Orpheus finally decided to carry it inside one day before departing for his winter season in Kavala, after numerous threats from Eurydice that she would 'happily' leave it to spend the winter where it was.

The wedding 'tradition' among the *Mykoniots d'élection*

The wedding 'picture'

There is no way to classify the type of practice this wedding ritual represents using its cultural (i.e., Greek) counterparts as a yardstick. This became clear to me when I recorded Eurydice commenting on another memorable wedding in the *Mykoniot* milieu – that of Antonis, her *koumbaros*. A decade earlier, Antonis got married to a top model, who was Australian in origin. Eurydice's narrative, actually a second-hand account, since she was not present at the wedding, went as follows:

> It was the early eighties, heroin was king back then and *rock 'n' roll* was the only ideology. The whole ceremony is epitomised in the classic black-and-white picture of the wedding where all the members of the gang are immortalised, while being really 'high' for the occasion [meaning stoned on heroin]. They all stand posed for the 'picture' but they keep their dark glasses on. They are all dressed in jeans. The 'picture' portrays several men and only one woman. Maria was an exception – an exceptional member of the group. It must have been at a time when she was trying to give up *preza* (heroin). That is the reason why she is the only one wearing a leather flying-jacket in the middle of August.

Eurydice, using a visual metaphor, actually portrays the 'Mykonian mentality', as she characteristically calls it. Eurydice herself was not a stable member of the group until the mid eighties. The wedding 'picture', in her rhetoric, acts as a token of this mentality. Paradoxically enough, a collection of poseurs, performing the role of the 'cool' guys of their generation symbolically make up the 'wedding picture' for Eurydice. Her borrowed memory (since she was not there in the first place) in turn recreates the *Mykoniots*' aesthetic myth. Eurydice also implied, in order to reinforce the myth, that only one woman had 'the guts' to be part of this picture.

Orpheus' wedding follows this line of mythologised ceremonial tradition. He himself attended the above wedding and is actually one of the picture's protagonists. The *Mykoniots' sinafi* performs 'rituals' only to perpetuate the myth of the group.

The wedding 'picture' lacks focus

There is a very interesting clue, I think, to this 'Mykonian mentality' that Eurydice repeatedly refers to: that is the way this mentality is implicitly reproduced through the group's manipulation of aesthetics. For example, when one observes the wedding photographs, the politics of difference become apparent. The most obvious characteristic of these pictures is the lack of focus on the wedding ceremony itself, and especially the lack of the 'expected' focus on the rituals' protagonists. Nearly twenty people were taking photographs on the night of Orpheus' wedding; all of them keen photographers, both amateur and professional. It is no accident that neither the professionals nor the amateurs produced any substantial series of pictures of the couple at the time of the ceremony (or at least there is no trace of any such series of photos). The conventional photographic approach towards a wedding ceremony, in my cultural experience, is to produce a big album with the bride and the groom in numerous close-ups and different poses. Before the ritual, after the ritual, with the father, with the mother, with the 'friends', etc. In our case, the artistic focus tends more towards an anthropological approach: the photographic evidence presents us with a continuous mixture of faces who are actively 'performing'. There is no hierarchical order in the appearance of the guests. In a sense, they are all equally important, equally glamorous. It seems that the focus is on the actors' individuality rather than on their social roles. Likewise, every conflicting element 'melts' into the special aesthetics of the group. This is the culture that glorifies any hybrid form: the kitsch 'relative', the folkloric Orthodox priest, the leftover hippie, the Armani suit, all united in order to compose our theoretical scenario of *aesthetic otherness*. This is the rhetoric, and this is how it is accomplished. The game of 'distinction' has been transformed by the *Mykoniots* into an all-inclusive game of 'difference'.

There is an additional point crucial to our understanding of the 'unconventional' element and the 'uniqueness' of the ritual that goes beyond the stylistic level: in line with the content of the photographic material of the wedding ritual, the lack of focus extends to the actual rhetoric of practice. The focus is not on the symbols of transition, but rather on the importance of merging antithetical symbols to connote a non-existent change. For example, Eurydice did not change her habits for the ritual, nor did she experience any post-ritual changes of status. She slept in several different places before the ceremony and on a pile of travelling bags after it. Her attitude was interpreted by the community as confirming her unalterable 'communal' identity.

Drugs of 'distinction'

It may be interesting to explore the drug culture of the wedding party, since, as we saw in Eurydice's narrative on the eighties wedding 'picture', the group's internal logic of memory and time is related to periods linked with different types of substance preferences.

For example, the absence of a heroin 'high' seems to signify a transitional state for the *Mykoniots*. But does this absence also signify the end of an era, leaving behind the old junkie self? Not really. The *Mykoniots*' game of distinction is constantly assuming a rejuvenated image by reshaping the self. Nevertheless, the old self is not thereby excluded from one's repertoire. As regards the group's attitude towards illegal substances, this is particularly true. The *Mykoniots'* shift to 'softer' drug habits is by no means as radical as it might seem. For example, Orpheus occasionally sniffs some 'white stuff': 'just for the sake of the flash' (a typical explanation referring to the transitory time of visualising the heroin 'rush', where for one moment the feeling of security is absolute and boundless). The ritualistic sniff takes place in order to honour the old self, in other words, as the rhetoric goes, 'to keep the memory alive'. 'To keep the memory alive' he acts like an irresponsible child at his own wedding, avoiding any 'routine' tasks. 'To keep the memory alive' he recreates a 'local' *paniyiri* where he, the 'patron', turns into a 'servant' for his own guests. But every memory he wants to 'keep alive' definitely reproduces another 'collectivity' together with his own 'personal myth'. I can recall a young town-dweller's wedding in Mykonos the year before Orpheus' took place, where heroin consumption was a pre-eminent feature due to the couple's own preferences. The old 'godfathers' of Mykonian rock 'n' roll got into this wedding's 'junkie mood' just for the occasion. They were continuously 'flirting' with the groom who was offering 'the stuff' as a wedding 'present'. Orpheus, who had given up the 'bad habit' some years ago, was one of those after him. The whole story of heroin's highly 'addictive' power is renegotiated by the *Mykoniots'* rhetoric vis-à-vis the power of self-transformation. Many members of the group indulged heavily in heroin consumption during the eighties. The beginning of the nineties found them 'health freaks'. The transformation, however, holds no rhetoric of suffering or addiction.

A cultural pattern of persistence: 'everything Mykonian is good and original' *or* the strategy of space

Let us shift our attention for a while from the specific circumstances of the ritual's protagonists to focus on the choice of the wedding space. Mykonos has become a fashionable wedding location in recent years for some elite members of the Greek bourgeoisie. Obviously, our informants do not share the same elitist background in simply following this trend. In a sense, Mykonos, in the Greek media-centred reality of the nineties and beyond, signifies an alternative elite's space of distinction. In Argyrou's analysis of modern Cypriot weddings, the stylistic game of distinction depends to a large extent upon the selection of the wedding space. The choice of wedding space is further classified in terms of Cypriot modernisation. In Argyrou's ethnography, large-scale hotels like the Hilton are chosen as wedding 'spaces' and as the characteristic locus of reproducing 'modernity' in Cyprus (Argyrou 1996: 143). Mykonos, as a cosmopolitan resort has over the last four decades acted as a bastion of modern and 'progressive' ideas in Greek culture. Mykonos is therefore signified as an elitist space, and its prestige is reflected in the bourgeois' and lately the *nouveaux riches'* urge to adopt it symbolically as a wedding space. The fact that the petit bourgeois and modern Greek intellectuals, following an anti-elitist tradition, used to be culturally 'intimidated' by the social symbol of Mykonos is no accident. Mykonos represented a case of cultural ambivalence; on the one hand, it represented the urge to indulge in modernity via tourism that brought cosmopolitanism and Western sophistication; on the other, it represented something taboo: hedonism, syncretism and the emergence of different and extreme cultures, such as the hippies and the homosexuals. A crucial additional element that supports the notion that Mykonos is an especially 'charged' space vis-à-vis internal cultural politics, is the interpretational prejudice I experienced from some members of Greek academia who were largely preoccupied with a very fixed symbolism of Mykonos. Ironically, referring to Mykonos' 'modern' setting was in itself an automatic turn-off for some intellectuals, something like a second-rate source of 'knowledge'.

Argyrou, in his ethnographic context, maintains that the process of any given group's distinction is secured by the selection of the wedding space. Referring to the modern (seventies) Hilton Hotel, a preferred locus for bourgeois Cypriot weddings, he comments: 'to many villagers and working-class people, the imagery functions as a mechanism of cultural intimidation' (Argyrou 1996: 143). It is crucial to distinguish the *Mykoniots'* pattern of distinction in this respect. The appropriation of the 'intimidating' symbol (i.e., Mykonos) by the *Mykoniots* derives from a deep-rooted 'anti-authoritarian' mentality, which stems from their 'alternative' superiority discourse rather than from a more 'modern' sense of superior class identity. In their alternative fashion, the *Mykoniots* promote their adventurous life histories, their cultivated cross-cultural aesthetics and elitist faith that leads to hedonism, liberalism, cosmopolitanism and subsequently to no identity barriers. On a different level, the *Mykoniots'* familiarity with the 'intimidating' symbol comes from their practical knowledge of the different aspects of the cosmopolitan space, a capital acquired through their 'profession'. Many members of the *Mykoniots*, started their careers as part of the newly emerged group of 'workers' engaged in local tourism. Argyrou's ethnography describes an analogous incident of an outsider's appropriation of the 'intimidating' symbol of the Hilton Hotel. A friend or relative from a 'lower'-class background, who had been invited to one of the urban 'champagne' weddings, was discovered by some members of his own class, who also happened to be invited, acting atypically. He was standing in the centre of the gathering near the large swimming pool of the hotel in a 'self-assured manner'. Argyrou quotes his informants, who claimed that the aforementioned guest literally acted 'as if he owned the place'. Upon interrogation the 'confident' actor finally confessed that he had worked there for six months on the electrical installation (ibid.).

In the *Mykoniots'* case there is a similar appropriation of the 'intimidating' symbol through their expertise. *Mykoniots* do not carry the same 'cultural capital' as the elite that created and appropriated the myth of Mykonos' exclusivity, but they do not need to possess any particular social status since they create their status by eclectically playing with all the class and cultural semantics. As their practice is one of decodifying 'distinction', they constantly leave behind previously appropriated stylistic elements by creating new ones, thus escaping the fate of an irreversible social classification and a 'fixed' identity. Orpheus' wedding thus departs from the logic of the 'cosmopolitan' Greek weddings of Mykonos, since it chooses to appropriate the local element rather than the elitist element of the bourgeois 'Mykonian' weddings. Their alternative form of symbolic capital then, is their expertise on local culture. This expertise is a long-term investment that has eventually allowed the *Mykoniots* to survive the elitist and expensive tourist space, both culturally and financially.

The wedding paniyiri: a cultural ambivalence?

A few days after the wedding ritual, I met Elsa, a long-term *Mykoniot* and a painter who spends much of her time on the island, being seen only outside the tourist season. Elsa enthusiastically commented on the wedding: 'There were three generations of hippies gathered together ... it was really unique for us. I had a wonderful time.' Comments like Elsa's concerning the aesthetic otherness of the Saint Anna wedding were a commonplace among the *Mykoniots* in the months that followed. The event rapidly took on its own mythologised structure in the consciousness of the *Mykoniots*. Accordingly, the myth went on to extend to the 'bohemian' visitors on the *Mykoniots*' scene.

The choice of a *paniyiri* wedding reflects and celebrates a specific collectivity and its ethos: that of being a *Mykoniot*. In this ethnographic study of a *Mykoniot's* wedding, although the cultural context of the protagonists is not a 'traditional' one, I do find similar elements to Cowan's Sohoian wedding where the setting, through its bodily and other symbolism, both embodies and signifies a 'specific collectivity' – that of being Sohoian (Cowan 1990: 91, 132). In our case, for Orpheus and Eurydice to become the bride and groom in the context of a Saint Anna *paniyiri*, and thus fetishise the locals' culture by employing 'folklore' elements of a traditional *paniyiri* rather than the cultural elements of a wedding 'tradition' per se, also connotes a 'specific collectivity', that of being a *Mykoniot d'élection*. In this respect, Elsa's highly sentimental comment was about this 'commensality'. Elsa, although not at all a close friend of the couple, nor one of their frequent companions, clearly related to the event. Orpheus and Eurydice's wedding meant something to her in respect of her own identity. She obviously belonged to the older hippie generation, and this wedding signified for her a symbolic continuity of her 'exclusive' category (i.e., of the 'hippies').

The wedding ritual as a celebration of the self

> The world in truth is a wedding. (Goffman 1959: 45)

Goffman (1959), in his work celebrating the performative self, turns the structural liminality of a ritual on its head. For Goffman, the world in truth is like a ritual, a constant performance. Every act for Goffman is ceremonial, is a performance, an exercise in order. Equally, in Goffman's world, every wedding represents the reality of its actors, their social and personal reality. Goffman urges us to go beyond the 'expressive bias of performance' and accept it as reality. And in so doing to eventually reposition reality as something relevant and not absolute, with aspects of performance giving some creative part to the actors who perform their social or more eccentric realities. Time in the context of 'reality', in this sense, gains a festive and liminal dimension; and he continues his argument: 'and then that which is accepted at the moment as reality will have some of the characteristics of a celebration' (ibid. 45).

For Goffman, the dramaturgical perspective of the social establishment is seen as a final way of ordering (Goffman 1959: 233). But does the case of Eurydice and Orpheus' wedding 'performance' offer another example of a self that is tyrannically overexploited in performance? Is their performance solely a paradigm of a conscious and constant social role-play? I think that the text and the transcription of the actors' narrative shows a far more conscious and creative self clearly negotiating between given structural and cultural categories. The rhetoric of spontaneity and ambivalence that runs throughout our actors' lives significantly distinguishes their notion of the self from the 'tactical moves' of Goffman's performative self (Cohen 1994: 10, 68).

The constantly performative self may be accurately programmed and socially 'wise' but offers no 'intentionality' to the actor. The *Mykoniot* wedding actors, on the contrary, are consciously involved in their own wedding parody by 'performing' roles inspired by different cultural categories.

The actor actively transforms and reshapes the norms of the ritual

> For some time now social scientists have been invited to live in a Goffmansque world where one has to recognise how much people warp their intimate interiority in order to accommodate to the expectations of others in their presentation of the self. (Fernandez 1995: 250)

> Whereas marriage was earlier first and foremost an institution *sui generis* raised above the individual, today it is becoming more and more a product and construct of the individuals forming it. (Beck and Beck-Gernsheim 1996: 33)

This wedding was mainly understood by its guests as a legitimate party. Alternatively, by maintaining an Orthodox ceremony's classical form, it can be seen as a parody of the actual rite. Ultimately, this wedding can only be appreciated as part of Orpheus' personality, that transforms the ritual into a 'handmade' piece of scenery with him as the groom, being the director of the performance, rehearsing the plot of his wedding setting, many times before the actual execution of the ritual. The groom-director distances himself from his role as the main actor, so that he can use the same setting for another type of performance. When the time for the ceremony was approaching the common joke among friends was: 'We are going to have the party anyway, even if those two do not appear!'

What makes this wedding unique as a case study is not only its hybrid form as an amalgam of different aesthetic prototypes. It is also the fact that it served as another excuse for being 'different', in that every aspect of the ritual, no matter how paradoxical or distant it may be from the 'expected', was justified by an aesthetic or idiosyncratic uniqueness based on the protagonist's 'original' character. Following this line of thinking, nobody would challenge Orpheus' own interpretation of how the idea of a wedding first occurred to him: 'I had found at the time a big stock of bonbonnieres, [20] you know, fifties stuff ... So, I thought I will have a wedding.' While planning the wedding he would use the excuse that he also owed the island a *paniyiri*. In this sense the wedding ritual was utilised in order to 'repay' his debts to the locals. But then again, in an opportunist, cosmopolitan, and tourist place like Mykonos, there is no space for 'romanticisms' of this sort. Orpheus was not a Mykonian and he would never be accepted as one by the local community. Finally, he had another idea: he found it convenient to transfer all his personal and family documents 'to a municipality with less bureaucracy', and in this respect the 'Mykonian-style' wedding might be beneficial for his newly registered 'Mykonian' profile.

It must be clear by now that the Saint Anna wedding is not a 'representative Greek wedding', modern or otherwise, or a wedding that allows us just to demystify the *Mykoniots' habitus*, but it is primarily Orpheus' wedding. And, in this respect, it is just as much a unique instance as are his Daliesque moustache, his decor and his charming stammering speech rhythm. Orpheus prefers to ride his environmentally friendly bicycle in his hometown during the winter, but sticks to his fumy trials bike when in Mykonos during the summer. He is by no means a 'responsible' person, yet can be absolutely charismatic for any given audience. Furthermore, by promoting his idiosyncratic personality, Orpheus has acquired over the years the image of a 'patron' of every cult figure around. His personal myth, likewise, finds full expression in the caricatured symbols displayed in the wedding ritual. Bearing that in mind, the creative self seems to change the image of the ritual itself. Maybe the only consistent thing about this wedding was that it actually happened.

The wedding *paniyiri* can also be seen as a characteristic example of how the *Mykoniots* perceive ritual. It does not solely reveal an emulation of either the traditional, the modern, or the petit-bourgeois cultural model. Furthermore, the case of the *Mykoniots*' wedding *paniyiri* ritual is not justified by a post-modern approach that treats it as a random patchwork of elements, i.e., a hybrid of unknown origin or composition. The wedding *paniyiri* appears to be the reflection of a new 'syncretic' culture, which happily appreciates and 'consumes' otherness while consistently promoting any eccentricity of the self. In other words, *Mykoniot* culture 'consumes' all sorts of cultural elements of 'otherness', only to create a unique 'styling' of life, that produces the species of the *Mykoniot d'élection*. Irrespective of the combination of cultural donations in the case of the *Mykoniots* (and this is individually manifested in their self-narratives), there is always a bricolage-like identity construction that morally glorifies the 'art of living' with no real social, cultural or personal constraints. In the case of this wedding, the mixture encompasses exclusive aesthetic elements, such as a seventies leftover hippie-oriented culture and a remote fifties Mykonian rural household as the 'traditional' backdrop.

Furthermore, one could argue that a counter-definition of the self is revealed through its discourse with the social realm. Self-identities are not complete in the individual's narration, or even in the individual's discourse about the self. The appropriation of diverse, even antithetical, norms or cultural practices in an idiosyncratic manner, shows an eagerness for a constant game with the self, not only in order to be reflexively 'improved' (in line with Giddens 1991), or solely to re-establish a status quo (in line with Bourdieu 1977), but also as a means of being creative beyond autistic reflexivity, through a more conscious self-realisation achieved by defying singular structures.[21] In their critique of the theorists of 'practice' (including Giddens), Cohen and Rapport stress that to limit the 'agency' of the individual to reflection and not extend it to 'motivation', is a fact that offers little realistic 'intentionality' to the individual (Cohen and Rapport 1995: 7; cf. Cohen 1994: 21).

The politics behind the series of ritual 'constructions' I have described in the last two chapters of the book, whereby the *Mykoniot* protagonists either create or appropriate several ritualistic forms, underline their angst of *belonging*. Through the *Mykoniots*' conscious intervention, their struggle for the patronage of 'locality' is justified, and a symbolic level of power is clearly achieved through their improvised feasts and spontaneous encounters.

In this sense, it is possible for them to 'consume' a ritual, and by 'consuming' it I mean that they are capable of transforming the actual context of the ritual simply because, as a sign of Mykonian tradition, it no longer bears any meaning. Rituals are, as Baudrillard argues for simulacra, 'degenerated' forms of cultural folklore (Baudrillard 1981). In our case, instead of the wedding ceremony being the focal point of reference, the central role is transferred to the 'traditional' *paniyiri*, which takes the form of the core ritual. The Orthodox ceremony is interposed in the case of the *Mykoniots d'élection* as an additional aesthetic and theatrical element of 'devoutness'. In this sense, the reader must not misinterpret the *Mykoniots*' 'returning' to the Orthodox tradition as a return to 'Greek culture' in the sense described by Faubion (1993). The newlyweds' adherence to the 'form' of the Orthodox wedding tradition does not reproduce any of the established cultural rules (the gender roles, for example, that supposedly emerge out of a common 'household'). Orpheus' and Eurydice's wedding is not a 'transition ritual'. Adhering to the form of a 'transition' ritual, the *Mykoniots* once more 'perform' their *autistic identity rituals* by selecting a series of stylistic forms: a wedding ritual, a local *paniyiri*, a trip to Delos. This type of 'identity ritual', I think, predominates in the highly reflexive age of late modernity. The element of 'sacredness' in these 'identity rituals' — in order to follow the principle of random socialising in these alternative communions — is self-consumed, as much as self-constructed. Modern individuals need to reveal and celebrate their forever negotiated 'new' self, a by-product of the self-reflexive project and these groupings' identity rituals. The self's project is to transform and verify its existence via the only possible identity source: new and alternative collectivities. Instead of having 'fixed' sources of identity like a culture, a tradition, or a nation state, alternative sources of locality and identity with hybrid forms are emerging.

In this chapter on the wedding ritual, it is clear that the 'local' as a category is a cultural construction. Furthermore, it is clear that the category of *Mykoniots d'élection* is a hybrid one. The use and abuse of the local element reveals *cultural constructivism* as the main cultural practice of the *Mykoniots*. This leads us to the 'hybrids' produced in the context of late modernity where different cultural elements merge in a 'transition ritual's' simulacrum: an 'Orthodox' wedding, a 'hippie crowd' and a 'traditional' setting. Catering and performing for 'tourists' on a Greek island is a 'self-conscious' production of culture and, in turn, 'hybrids' are, according to Harvey, 'the product of modernity that has become self-conscious' (Harvey 1996: 27). Orpheus' 'traditional' self was symbolically sacrificed on the altar of this emerging 'hybrid' culture. By celebrating his 'personal' feast, after twenty-five years of active participation on the island, he finally 'commits' to the 'other's' traditionality (not to the Mykonian tradition per se, but to its folklore) and thus he intentionally gives up his own 'traditionality'. Our 'actor', ceases to be an actor and becomes the 'director' of his conscious self-transformation, adventurously pursuing some 'other' traditionality.

The wedding was mythologised straight after and even before the ritual. The *anti-gamos* (counter-celebrations) and wedding toasts lasted more than a week. The party moved to the beach the next day, again returned later to the house, spent another day on Delos, and so on. These are things that tend to happen more or less as part of the everyday life of the *Mykoniots*.

Notes

1. This psychological pattern is often rooted in idiosyncratic upbringing, dramatic or spiritual experiences, manifested in deep metaphysical knowledge, drug-taking, an excessive lifestyle, and so on.
2. Danforth mentions that one of the most striking features of Greek funeral laments are their close resemblance to wedding (bridal) songs with regard to their musical form, narrative structure and iconography (Danforth 1982: 74). The lyrics and the basic melody of these songs remain the same. In essence, what changes is only the style of performance. According to Danforth, following Van Gennep, the key theme here is separation. In other words, it is the 'departure' of the bride from the paternal home (especially in patrilocal families) that evokes the expression of grief in the case of bridal songs (ibid.: 75).
3. The 'indigenous' local, as opposed to the *Mykoniot* who is the 'exogenous' one.
4. Nevertheless, this type of statement is absent from the relevant literature, especially as an element of female discourse (with the exception of Faubion's Maro, a female 'fictional individual' informant, described in the opening chapter of this book [Faubion 1993]).
5. According to this cultural discourse, a 'generation' is marked by a particular aesthetic disposition which changes approximately every seven years.
6. The classification of Orpheus' enterprise as a curio shop is perhaps quite close to reality. Nevertheless, the diversity of its merchandise and the frequent transformation of the style and the decoration could occasionally make it qualify as an antique shop or a junk shop, a storehouse or a souvenir shop. Accordingly, this aesthetic diversity attracted a highly heterogeneous clientele.
7. I will maintain that the principal rationale behind Orpheus' discourse is, as Harvey suggests, that: 'the realist aesthetic has become less important' (1996: 162).
8. The actual followers and theorists of this philosophical trend refuse to accept the prefix 'new'.
9. The artists' and intellectuals' recent fetishisation of Mount Athos has extended into fictional literature (Papachristos 1992; Meletopoulos 2004) and to various articles on monks, as well as repentant Marxists who adore the place, written by representatives of a 'new' journalism (cf. Tsangarousianos 1993).
10. I refer to an 'opening up', since the *Mykoniots*' relationship with the divine was until recently either non-existent or mostly syncretic.
11. Eurydice jokingly told Orpheus that there was no 'dowry' and to keep his hands off her property. According to the anthropological discussion, gender relations in the traditional Greek context concerned the hidden power of women through their dowries (cf. Dubisch 1974). In our case, Eurydice's portion of the family land is clearly her own non-negotiated power. The model here is not one of a 'hidden' power but of a substantial and acknowledged one.
12. Literally meaning a village, but in the Mykonian context metaphorically standing for separate households as self-sustaining units.
13. Argyrou, drawing on folkloric accounts and his own fieldwork in Cyprus, attempts to reconstruct the typical form of the 1930s wedding celebrations. Among them, he refers to the most established 'preparation of the bridal mattress', basically a fertility ritual that took place at the home of the bride's parents (1996: 63–64). This ritual was followed by the next rite of separation, which was called 'the changing of the bride' and was performed by the village girls, the friends of the bride.
14. For a detailed ethnographic description of Greek wedding rituals the reader should compare the account by Argyrou, who describes in detail three representative aesthetic categories of nineties weddings in Cyprus: one type is the 'village' wedding, another the 'champagne' wedding and a third the 'petit-bourgeois' wedding (1996: 114–30).
15. This text was actually edited by Eurydice, who added important aesthetic and ethnographic details.

Narratives of difference

16. The reader should appreciate the act of having two *koumbaroi* – one as the friend of the bride and the other as the friend of the groom – as an egalitarian statement between the 'male' and 'female' subcultures of the *Mykoniots*. Furthermore, my image as the female *koumbara*, with essentially no 'social' status in the *Mykoniots'* commune, and the fact that I was much younger then anybody else and only an 'apprentice' in the *Mykoniots'* microcosm – as well as literally an employee in Orpheus' curio shop – allowed Eurydice to make another statement about Orpheus' male-dominated *parea*. Actually, it was Eurydice, as she admitted later on, in the first place who 'propelled me' into the wedding setting.
17. The term 'straight', donated from the English slang expression, is widely used of any person not sharing the same 'consciousness' with that of the group of the 'like-minded'. It usually connotes a very conservative and narrow-minded, socially aware, consciousness that produces 'conventional' personalities.
18. Leftover freaks, in a hippie sense, with characteristically long hair, living on the beach under improvised constructions, carrying their property in colourful rucksacks, and so on.
19. A full account of consumption patterns at the wedding *paniyiri* should include the conspicuous consumption of '*drugs*'. According to the bride: 'The place was full of dope, people I did not know at all would come and give me *stuff* in a conspiratorial manner; one came to me and gave me a bag of grass!'
20. By *bonbonnieres*, he actually means the glass bowls in which the traditional wedding sugared-almonds are placed, rather than the sugared almonds themselves.
21. Lash and Urry have criticised Giddens' cognitive approach to the self-reflexive project of late modernity by maintaining that it crucially misses the aesthetic-expressive and bodily dimension (Lash and Urry 1994: 32, 37).

Conclusion

Mykoniots d'élection: a post-modern tribe?

The concept of neo-tribalism (Maffesoli 1996a) is highly relevant to the theoretical formation of a group like the *Mykoniots d'élection*, whose basic collective identity is synthesised through common notions of style. Maffesoli employs the concept of *tribus* in order to account for alternative group formations which are a widespread phenomenon of post-modernity. Maffesoli is the theorist who fragments mass culture. His new groups are formed from the 'remainders of a mass consumption society, groups distinguished by their members' shared lifestyles and tastes' (Shields 1996: x).

In the foreword to the English translation of *Les Temps de Tribus*, Shields warns the reader not to confuse Maffesoli's tribes with their traditional anthropological counterparts. The 'time of the tribes' is the time when the modern 'mass' is split in order to form an organised resistance through new types of communities: in short, 'the mass is tribalised' (1996: x). Maffesoli's new aesthetic group formations initially seem to leave enough space for innovation through successive and temporary identifications by the individual with a series of collectivities. Maffesoli, together with theorists like de Certeau, Benjamin and Bakhtin, explores and fetishises the quotidian, the momentary. In his work, the principles of 'being together' and of a Dionysian 'transcendent warmth' created in ordinary collectivities, establish the '*divin social*' (Shields 1996: x). Maffesoli's attachment to the notion of '*jouissance*'[1] imbues the everyday with a passionate logic, establishing the orgiastic as the principle structure 'for all sociality' (Maffesoli 1993: 1). Oddly enough, as the ethnographic body of this monograph has demonstrated, the *Mykoniots d'élection*, not only share a similar discourse on the special collective quality of warmth stemming from the group's particular type of commensality, but also maintain that they have literally 'inherited' this quality from a long 'orgiastic' tradition, mythologically established by Dionysus in the area, and aesthetically re-enacted since then in the spaces of Delos and Mykonos.

For the purposes of my analysis, it is important to look at how Maffesoli makes use of the notion of style. He employs a common-sense version of the notion of style as *aesthesis*: this aesthetic style is closer to its etymological meaning (Shields 1996: x). It is the crystallisation of an epoch. Maffesoli appropriates this notion following Shapiro's definition: 'Style is a manifestation of culture as totality; it is the visible sign of its unity. Style reflects or projects the 'interior form' of collective thinking and sentiment' (Shapiro, quoted in Maffesoli 1996b: 10). Maffesoli further proposes a definition of style not as *langue* but as *parole*, 'speech' with its 'internal order and logic, with the whole expressing itself in specific rituals and fashioning the whole of daily life' (ibid.: 15–16). Style, in Maffesoli's theoretical order, is a relational term since aesthetic judgement is always conducted in relation to something else.

Maffesoli, in a sense, disengages aesthetics from its 'romantic' tradition. Initially, he politicises the aesthetic by abolishing the dualism between the ethical and the aesthetic. This 'new' ethic of the aesthetic, although it might seem passive, is nevertheless vibrant because it creates groups with 'emotional and affective solidarities' (Maffesoli 1996b: 28). It is precisely in this new 'ethic', according to Maffesoli, that the aesthetic meets the mystical in these new forms of communion and his notion of the societal 'orgiastic' emerges. For Maffesoli, this type of 'transcendental' sociality, is not situated on the margins; it is not liminal any more. It is an ideal and anarchic state of *communitas* in Turner's sense, but finally established as the official structure. Shields argues that the slogan 'the personal is the political' is transformed in Maffesoli's work into: 'the personal is the ethical and aesthetic centre of social relations' (Shields 1996: xi).

Placing Maffesoli's work in the same tradition as Bourdieu and Baudrillard, who are the social theorists of style and consumption (Bourdieu 1984; Baudrilliard 1968, 1970, 1972), makes his work of great interest, because it directly connects style with politics, allowing the subject's serial identification with the emerging post-modern tribes to dictate identity directly, thus by-passing established structures such as social class, ethnic identity, gender and so forth.

Maffesoli's aesthetic groups are by no means subcultural, since, according to his theory, 'alternative practices' do not refer to marginal groups any more. Instead, the term 'alternative' has acquired a very broad definition which extends to a variety of interest-based collectivities (Shields 1996: xi). The important theoretical question though, is not what makes a group a Maffesolian *tribu*, but rather what is the source of the individual's identity. The answer is a wide range of sources. The individual, as a *polythetic* subject establishes a series of temporary identifications collected through her (alternative) belonging to her own idiosyncratic network of overlapping groups.

Maffesoli's notion of 'sociability' is not dictated by reason but by desire; by abandoning universal ideals, one can witness the emergence of an alternative 'collective ego' through the art of daily living (Maffesoli 1996b: 3). Maffesoli claims that we are experiencing an historical breakthrough. Departing from a modernist democratic and mass-market ideal, the emerging neo-tribal ideal should be distinguished from the stylistic recitation of post-modern nostalgia (Lash and Urry 1994: 247). Instead, Maffesoli's communitarian world of fragmented realities and 'mass subjectivity' produces a creative rather than a passive subject – as against Baudrillard's latent pessimism concerning the silence of the masses and the consumer (Baudrillard 1985: 218). The style of our 'epoch' is defined by: 'tribalisation, a culture of sentiment, the aestheticisation of life, the dominance of the mundane' (Maffesoli 1996b: 4).

Post-modern style overlaps different historical periods; styles interact in post-modernity in both a synchronic and diachronic manner. This leads to a syncretic post-modern style, 'a melange of genres' (Maffesoli 1996b: 6). According to Maffesoli, this makes post-modernity, like traditional society, a complex cultural field where (unlike the simple societal model of modernity) all domains of life interact. The boundaries between the political, the economic, the ritualistic, the everyday, the aesthetic and the moral are (con)fused (1996b: 8–9).

Maffesoli underlines, however, that in this fusion of different structural elements in a post-modern reality, the notion of style is employed only as a 'chosen methodological lever' and not as a determining factor in order to 'caricature', to 'enlarge' or to 'accentuate' what 'tends, too often, to be neglected, out of moralistic habit' (Maffesoli: 1996b: 17). In this sense, his notion of style, compared to that of Bourdieu, does not strictly speaking include a political agenda. The 'stylisation of existence' does not organise things symmetrically, as in Bourdieu's class-based principle of aesthetic 'distinctions'; style here acts rather as a conceptual tool for democratically arranging things in relation to one another. In this sense, Maffesoli's stylisation promotes a new form of creative relativism (1996b: 18).

The invented group name of the *Mykoniots d'élection* is therefore justified by a uniquely crafted stylisation on their behalf which draws on space, on local culture, on a localist historical constructivism, which in turn further promotes the group's Dionysiac elements of mystical commensality. The suffix '*d'élection*', reflects the aesthetic choice they have made to live, act in, and draw identity from this 'polymorphous' space.

Mykoniots' 'emotional ambience'

The *Mykoniots* manifest a 'communitarian ideal' mainly through aesthetics. The Maffesolian element of communitarian sensibility, although apparent, is set against an utterly individualistic discourse, according to which one belongs only to oneself. Nevertheless, as we have seen in the *Mykoniots'* trip to Delos, one of the group's private (Dionysiac) rituals, George declaims emotionally on behalf of the group: 'Nobody enjoys living as much as we do.' Equally emotionally, Hercules calls the members of his *Mykoniot* circle 'co-warriors' and 'brothers'. Artemis states that she loves them all like a family, and so, accordingly, she keeps them at a distance. Elsa, the painter, states that she has been returning to Mykonos for the last few years off-season only to be among her *sinafi*, among her 'own kind of people'. And finally, Antonis, the *koumbaros*, who has created an ecological/aesthetic manifesto to protect his idealised commune, promotes the preservation of the island's 'cleanliness': 'Whitewash, brothers; whitewash, otherwise we are lost.' This 'communitarian ideal' is more apparent in practice than in discourse, as we have seen in the last chapter's ethnographic account of the collective organisation of a *Mykoniot* couple's wedding.

The creativity of the group – less an activist theory, a discourse, a movement, a cult, a subculture and more a 'communal *passim*' – is consistent with the principle of aestheticisation of the quotidian, the art of daily living. 'The mystical is that which unites the initiated (sharing a mystery) one to another' (Maffesoli 1996b: 29).

At this point, one could reflect on the case study of the *Mykoniots* in order to decide whether to theoretically classify them as a subcultural or eccentric group, as a party of cultural survivals of a hippie prototype, or alternatively as a post-modern self-religion with New Age characteristics or, finally, treat them as a Maffesolian post-modern tribe. The line distinguishing modernist activist movements from post-modern neo-tribes seems in this case to be blurred.

Nevertheless, I will attempt for the moment to adhere to Maffesoli's aesthetic principle of group organisation in relation to the *Mykoniots'* unstructured commune. In the ethnographic case of the *Mykoniots*, I employ the neologism *tribestyle* in order to incorporate in any definition of the group's identity the concept of style as an organising and classificatory principle in the formation of a new communitarian ideal, which merges the aesthetic and the mystical with the societal. In accordance with the *Mykoniots'* praxis, in this formulation the ideological and the metaphysical acquire a performative capacity. The metaphysical escapes from its Western/modern dualism of the rational versus the irrational and becomes, in turn, aestheticised. Equally, for the *Mykoniots*, ideological signs such as the 'hippie era', a trip to India, a trip to the Dionysiac island of Delos, as well as the traditional religious and metaphysical connotations of an Orthodox wedding or a visit to an Orthodox monastery, fuse with autonomous aesthetic principles.

The emotional ambience of Maffesoli's commune bears no resemblance to the modernist notion of the ideological groups of the 'like-minded'. Rather, it is dictated by a feeling of an aleatory bonding. The avant-garde's ideal of 'acceptance' rather than the activist's seeking for 'change' re-emerges. This feeling of 'living along with others, only by accepting them' is a central principle in the

Mykoniots' socialisation in the compact space of tourist Mykonos. Vangelis describes Mykonos as an emotional ambience. He stresses that the Mykonian space works as an absolute metaphor for this communal feeling of intimacy.[2] He describes it as a boundless space, which allows 'intrusion' as well as 'autonomy': 'If you feel lonely, you just go down the main street of Matoyianni and there is everything.' For Vangelis, who was brought up in Athens, this feeling is not a given. He maintains that he has rediscovered this feeling in eighties and nineties Mykonos.

Following Maffesoli's line of thinking, what appears to be a display of individualism is 'a manifestation of tribal-hedonism' (Maffesoli 1996b: 35). The latter quotation could apply to the role aesthetic gossip plays among the *Mykoniots*. In the group's self-representations, as I have discussed earlier, the aim is to culturally place the self through the establishment of an aesthetically and experientially 'superior' identity created out of discourses, or rather mythologies, of one's mishaps and passions (chapters 2 and 3).

An additional peculiarity in Maffesoli's 'emotional ambience' is that it rests on an aesthetic ideal of communal hedonism (Maffesoli 1996b: 41). Maffesoli distinguishes this model of hedonism from its modernist counterpart where 'hedonism is an individualistic affair' (ibid.). Nevertheless, the problem with Maffesoli's theory is that everything still seems to work at the level of *habitus*. The post-modern subject turns to yet another mass cultural conversion in order to participate in the 'orgiastic'. She worships Maffesoli's aesthetic culture which rests on the principles of hedonism, the deification of the quotidian. This is the culture of the communitarian ideal which promotes the pleasure of 'togetherness', the ideal of acceptance, of communal happiness. Yet, there is no idiosyncratic level. Creativity derives from the combination of different personae attached to different performative affiliations with alternative tribestyles. Even so, different forms of identification, as well as different subject positions, could also arise from differences within categories and within subjectivities. Moreover, these differences do not necessarily depend on consciously organised decisions (without implying that the subject is losing any agency). As Lacan has shown, the inscription of social categories on the unconscious is an inter-subjective process since 'in the unconscious is the whole structure of language' (Lacan 1977: 147). Only, Lacanian subjectivity is a product of an 'unconscious' form of agency; whereas I would like to explore the possibility of an 'unconscious subject' who, for an instant, acquires agency as a consequence of an 'event' (*pace* Badiou 2005) – and thus the appending of an epilogue to this monograph.

Conclusion

The societal as bacchanalia

According to my ethnographic experience, a Dionysian type of hierarchy, similar to the organisation of the post-modern tribes that Maffesoli describes, can be discerned (Maffesoli 1993: 93). Moreover, the *Mykoniots* themselves conspicuously argue (albeit in a historically constructivist manner) that this is a predominant type of hierarchy peculiar to the Mykonian context. There is no doubt that this book has put such ideas under scrutiny and has not just taken them at face value. The *Mykoniots*' pervasive rhetoric concerning the Dionysiac, anarchic, hedonistic properties of the Mykonian space is justified in various ways, to which I have referred in detail in earlier chapters. *Mykoniots* build such discourses but, most importantly, they also feel ruled by this Dionysiac principle and experience their lives as being similarly governed. Their collective expression is permeated by the element of the 'orgiastic' as defined by Maffesoli (Linse quoted in Maffesoli 1993: xix). The *Mykoniots*, in their ritualistic daily encounters, embrace a communitarian ideal where discursively the principles of individuation and power cease to exist. Their collective life in the tourist/liminal space is dictated by a 'passionate logic' (1993: 1). *Pace* Eade and Sallnow's contestation principle of the pilgrimage site (1991), St.John (2001) attributes to the alternative Australian ConFest (Conference/Festival), a contemporary pilgrim scenario, a 'polymorphic' composition whereby participants experience and interpret the event differently. Mykonos shares with the ConFest this pilgrimage principle, as well as a Maffesolian Dionysiastic element: 'a permissive topos' where 'abandonment' and 'excess' are performed (ibid.: 56). Mykonos, as an equally polymorphic 'event-space', is the meeting place of different groups who co-inhabit without necessarily having similar ideological or aesthetic dispositions. St.John, drawing on the Dionysiastic ethics of Maffesoli's neo-tribes, portrays the ConFest event as an act of resistance against 'universal codes of morality' where its participants enter a 'sacred corporeality' (ibid.: 60). The body ceases to be itself, it becomes sensual and only an organic part of the community. 'These liminoid communities themselves become on-side "tribes", autonomous "sensual solidarities" meshed in a labyrinthine counterspace' (ibid.: 62).

As opposed to modernity where the orgiastic clearly belongs to the liminal sphere, in post-modernity it belongs to the 'whole'. It is as if the Dionysiastic principle of Nietzschean ritual as celebratory, ecstatic and transgressive (cf. Gibson 1991), is 'displaced' from the liminal to the quotidian. According to Maffesoli, although this may sound contradictory, this orgiastic element allows for the restructuring of the post-modern community (Maffesoli 1993: 2). Through Shields's (1991) analysis of the immanence of the notion of 'spatialisation' and its connection to the displacement of the notion of liminality in translocal and global consumption sites, we are already familiar with the idea that the 'liminal' is the structural. Likewise, to put it in my ethnographic terms, the tourist space of Mykonos is occupied by people who have turned liminality into structure.

Maffesoli's concept of post-modern tribalism further shares with the *Mykoniots*' discourse the deification of notions such as experience, the preoccupation with the 'here and now', the immanence of hedonism and the 'distrust of postponing enjoyment' (Maffesoli 1996b: 48). This attitude transforms the expression of the political from activism to self-satisfaction. The logic behind this shift is that when one can no longer deal with the large 'structures', the attention is diverted to the micro level, the personal, the quotidian. All 'political' action is thus transfused to controlling the 'accessible', to idiosyncratically transforming life into an artistic self-expression (ibid.: 49). The tantalising question remains: is this attitude apolitical, or, more importantly, is it catalytic? Are *Mykoniots* apolitical, or are they counter-political by experiencing the 'orgiastic'?

Maffesoli's thesis seems to bear some affiliations with the amoral aestheticisation of the Foucauldian subject, as exemplified in Foucault's principle of the aestheticisation of the everyday in the 'care of the self' (discussed in detail in chapter 3). Maffesoli historically links his theory of the stylisation of the everyday, as a dominant feature of post-modernity, with the Baroque and classical antiquity when the quotidian was equally fetishised and ritualised. The difference, I think, between his thesis and the Foucauldian subject is that Foucault stressed the principle of amoral aestheticisation of the self, by actually emphasising creative self-transformations, and in this sense he added an ideological element to the process of 'stylisation'. For Maffesoli, the 'stylisation' of the quotidian happens for the sake of the image, rather than as an inner quest (Maffesoli 1996b: 56). What is at issue here is the promotion of the 'communitarian ideal', the 'being together' rather than the autonomy of the Foucauldian subject. Thus, there is a decisive turning away from the 'modern' subject. If everything happens for the sake of the image, and the subject is capable of accumulating different 'identifications' out of successive attachments to various Maffesolian *tribus*, then the self is not a continuum; the self is only its fragments. There is no room for any syncretic project. I think that at this point the Maffesolian post-modern subject parts company with the Foucauldian notion of a self-crafted identity.

Bearing in mind the above, one can now realise why in Maffesoli's thinking the figure of the ancient god Dionysus is important: Dionysus is among the many archetypal figures in world mythology that display 'a hundred faces'. Dionysus is considered 'the god of versatility, of play, of the tragic and the loss of the self' (Maffesoli 1996b: 61). The author continues: 'with Dionysus it is the myth of ambiguity that is reborn' (1996b: 61). In other words, Maffesoli treats the post-modern subject as a serious performer of many different roles, as a neo-Goffmanesque performer who is totally aware of his performances and his continuous changes of masks.

Curiously enough, the fragmentation of the self in Maffesoli's theory re-establishes the collective. Maffesoli departs from modern individualism. In his post-modern tribalistic order the subject is saturated, she relies upon a 'mass subjectivity' which is ruled by an 'affective contagion' (Maffesoli 1996b: 134). Everything seems to operate in Maffesoli's logic at the level of *faux* dramatisation, like the effects of Brazilian *telenovelas* or the recently popular 'reality shows' (1996b: 66).

The ethnographic material has shown that my informants do undergo changes of identity, as opposed to the merely performative changes of a series of personae offered by Maffesoli. *Mykoniots*' identity changes are lived out and accumulated as a personal asset. They can always scan through their 'lived out identity repertoire', which stems from their need to politically transcend every category rather than (as the Maffesolian model dictates) to anxiously enter and idealise each and every one. The *Mykoniots*' aesthetic prototype is reflected in a life which is full of experience. Nothing is left to mere semantic associations. There is some ideological substance, some theory involved in the *Mykoniots*' self-narratives, beyond Maffesoli's affective model of orgiastic sociality.

Nomadic or *monadic* subjectivities?
Or the link between liminality and consumption cultures

Shields (1992a) adopts the Maffesolian order described above, in which a series of new types of identifications (in addition to the established categories of class, gender, regional and generational identity) emerge out of the subjects' engagement with consumption (1992a: 2). Shields shifts his focus of analysis from Maffesoli's new societal 'orgiastic' order to yet another post-modern liminal space: consumption sites and especially shopping malls. In this liminal space of post-modern consumption culture, the ritualistic consumption organised by an intense element of choice is considered by Shields as an active field for the production of selves and groups. Shields' description of the mall is of great relevance to our representational topography of Mykonos' space (which acts as a consumption site), and its capacity to include so many diverse groups, so many different tribestyles as we might say.

Mykonos is literally colonised every new (tourist) season by different tribestyles. This is reflected in the abundance of different stylistic patterns of fashionwear, for example, available in the (trans)local communal space of Mykonos 'city', which is actually transformed into a (market) consumption site. These diverse aesthetic significations which stem from different fashion styles are also part of an (architecturally) homogenous traditional setting. The ground floors of the former bourgeois houses of the Mykonian *Hora* (and more recently the houses of the many peripheral neighbourhoods), have been converted into shops where these diverse styles can be seen to operate. The diversity of style offered for consumption is amazing: from casual to punk, from fetishised leather clothing to a military look, from old-fashioned tourist folklore (a survival of the seventies) to cheap reproductions of fashionable clothes made by small Greek businesses and, finally, from imported clothing from the East (especially India and Bali) to designer boutiques. The tourist can still choose while in the picturesque resort of Mykonos which type of club, or which style of beach to consume, and what 'kind' of people to socialise with. A night out in Mykonos is like a fashion show. After midnight one can see all the different groups parading, transforming the Mykonian *Hora* into a chaotic space. Within this diversity and fusion of signs, as I mentioned earlier in the introduction to this book, the Mykonian *Hora* can be considered a busy consumption site resembling Shields' shopping malls.

Shields' notion of consumption sites is used as an all-embracing spatial notion which includes different forms of consumption spaces, public and available for the post-modern subject to 'browse through'. By appropriating the Maffesolian notion of neo-tribalism, Shields accepts that these new modes of emerging subjectivities produce a 'revalorised sense of self' (1992a: 15). Many new elements emerge out of these consumption cultures: a constantly renegotiated notion of spatialisation, new perceptions of time and space, and new perceptions of belonging to such spaces. In short, the individual, according to Shields, is 'respatialised' (ibid.: 16).

Shields' theory of spatialisation could be considered as accounting for a momentous shift: from the *monadic* subjectivity of the modern individual to a *nomadic* self, which could be explained in a Maffesolian manner as the self who appropriates a series of personae related to the available stylistic variety of neo-tribalism. The dictum is: 'from individual to persona' where this persona is like a mask which entails 'tranformative possibilities for the subject' (Shields, 1992b: 106; 107). He adopts a schema where the 'breakdown of individualism' could challenge 'if only momentarily' the analytically stable parameters of modern subjectivity, such as class, gender or ethnicity (Shields 1992a: 16).

Performativities of difference: the 'nomadic' subject in feminist theory

> Nomadism ... is not fluidity without borders but rather an acute awareness of the nonfixity of boundaries. It is the intense desire to go on trespassing, transgressing. (Braidotti 1994: 36)

The Maffesolian subject that is transmuted from an individual to a persona who, by 'wearing many hats' consciously performs on different occasions different roles, provides a link to the discussion of gender performativity, an alternative theory of difference, this time concerned with the politically performative subject of nineties' feminist and queer theory. Feminist theory is distinguished from other theories of performativity by its political aim, which is to disorganise, as Butler (1990) would have it, the well-rooted and 'naturalised' sexual and gender identities. Sex and gender are not 'given in biology or in nature'. They are social constructions, which are reproduced through the repetition and performance of socially inscribed (gender) roles (Moore 1994: 37, 39). The consciously subversive act of politically 'performing' different social roles in order to disorganise subconsciously inscribed hegemonic models of gender/sexuality is the subject of early queer theory (Butler 1993).

Butler wants to break the compulsory logic that a set of acts subconsciously 'naturalises' gender difference, and she overrides this difference performatively: by overriding the monosemantic link between a category and the 'prescribed performance' attached to it. This created 'ambivalence' is political and also entails the philosophical question that produces Butlers' theory of performativity: where does (gender) difference come from? Gender difference naturalises sexual difference, and by recreating this sexual dichotomy it reinforces relations of power. So to strategically perform ambivalently is a deeply subversive act. All the allure of Butler's theory of performativity – her notion of agency – lies in her subject's strategic 'displacement'. Performativity here is strategic rather than self-invented. But is it, ultimately, a passive performance, liberated from gender stereotypes yet deprived of any agency?

In both cases, this mode of *performativity of difference*, i.e, the performance of different roles by the subject, is seen as desirable and conscious. In the case of feminist theory, performativity takes on a political and activist twist and comes as the 'post-post-structuralist' fight back through the realisation of deeply embedded, unconscious and well-established social performances, for which a Maffesolian model of performativity could not account. In fact, activism has no place in neo-tribalism; activism is irrelevant. Moreover, the Maffesolian subject of multiple personae follows a pattern of a series of identifications which, although involving change, change only the subject's image. Hence, the model entails a passive dimension and, in essence, reproduces a pessimistic view of post-modernity where the subject, once more, is bound to be defeated by well-established hegemonic roles.

In feminist theory though, the post-modern process of different identifications is not a *faux* drama, a simulation of reality. Braidotti (1994) very clearly distinguishes between two different redefinitions of subjectivity. It is exactly where the 'dominant subjects' foresee a crisis that a feminist post-modernism can see new possibilities. There is a political (feminist) redefinition of subjectivity, on the one hand, and a more reflexive one on the other, which is yet commanding, generated out of the new consumption culture and the new era that has overcome the modern, rational *monadic* self. Feminists, in their turn, are interested in notions of performativity and difference, not solely at the level of social personae, but in the inscription of those differences on the body (i.e., the embodiment of the subject). The body is the crucial performative category where differences are re-enacted. This body is neither biological nor sociological but the 'point of overlapping between the physical, the symbolic, and the sociological' (Braidotti 1994: 4). In other words, Braidotti indicates that feminism extends the process of a series of identifications further, towards a 'radical rejection of essentialism', by involving in the *performativity of difference* the fragmented and conflicting categories manifested in the embodied feminist subject. Theorists like de Lauretis have argued against the limitations of a discourse on difference within which gender acquires the dominant role. Instead she proposes an intersubjective model where the 'I' is the site of differences, the 'field of competing subjectivities and competing identities' (De Lauretis 1986, in Moore 1994: 26).

Braidotti uses the quality of the nomad metaphorically to describe this post-post-structuralist feminist subject. She maintains that the 'nomadic subject is a myth', a 'political fiction' in order to make the subject 'think through and move across established categories and levels of experience: blurring boundaries without burning bridges' (Braidotti 1994: 4). Thus, performativity *between* categories in this case is an accepted political fiction that, according to Braidotti, might work more effectively than 'theoretical systems'. Nevertheless, even as a political fiction, her 'nomadic' subject signifies the decline of a fixed, monosemantic subjectivity. This transgressive principle vis-à-vis any given 'category' is interestingly parallel to the challenge underlying post-post-structuralist anthropological theory and is best represented by a number of writers that can be arguably called the Cliffordian 'travel-theorists': 'there' the ethnographic subject constitutes her 'transiency'; both subject and theorist become travellers, literally as well as metaphorically; 'there' fixity is challenged (*pace* Spivak 1988) and theory is no more at home in the West; there 'displacement' for both the observer and the observed becomes the regularised ethnographic topos (Clifford 1989, 1992; Said 1991; Kaur and Hutnyk 1999). This theoretical turn towards the travel-theorist has its roots in the emerging transient category of the tourist and the theorist's compatibility with such a category (cf. MacCannell 1976; Abbeele 1980): in other words a conjunctive theoretical-practical 'nomad' is realised. The literal transient category of 'the tourist' is translated into a theoretical concept: i.e., from 'a tourist' to a 'theorist' to a 'nomadic subject'. Yet, this is not in accordance with gender theories of the nomadic subject where transience is a metaphor for inner fluidity – performative fluidity within one category and amongst different categories; sabotaging dualisms such as male or female 'performance', home and away from home, stability and transience. Wolff (1993) criticises this pseudo-liberal, non-committed travelling subject as intentionally un-gendered, and thus deceptive. A generic category of the 'nomad' is rendered problematic because it masks a 'masculine' essentialising. Morris (1988) picks the motel space to metaphorically and politically 'engender' an in-between place that portrays movement, beyond the domus/mobility distinction: thus she wishes to engender this transient subject, to disturb the genderless notion of the 'nomad'.

Braidotti's Deleuzian notion of the 'nomadic' subject[3] departs from the 'transient' post-modern subject designed by theorists like Lash, Urry or Shields as the 'traveller of multisemantic spatialisations' (i.e., Urry's post-modern tourist, Lash's aesthetically reflexive subject or Shields and Maffesoli's subjectivity as multiple personae). Braidotti's 'nomadic' subjects travel, not necessarily physically, but instead *within* and *between* categories. Thus, according to her hypothesis, the change of identification is intentional. The desire is to avoid political rather than physical stagnation. Creative performance here draws from a clear-cut familiar repertoire that is strategically exploited to open up consciousness (1994: 7).

Braidotti's argument here matches the *Mykoniots*' discourses about intentional shifting between different subject positions. *Mykoniots* politically shift between categories in order not to 'get stuck'. They have developed a counter-rhetoric concerning their political performativity and self-transformation (see chapter 3). While post-modernists like Maffesoli speak of transient identifications for solely aesthetic and existential reasons, Braidotti talks about transient identifications as strategic self-transformations tailored to sustain a 'politically empowering' parody (Braidotti 1994: 7). Why do feminists play this role? Braidotti explains: 'It is not the parody that will kill the phallocratic posture, but rather the power vacuum that parodic politics may be able to engender' (ibid.).

Being political and conscious of its allegoric action, the nomadic/performative model of subjectivity, as described by Braidotti, accommodates agency. Therefore, there is an a priori potential for creativity in the subject's action. By contrast, the Maffesolian subject just moves between categories, simulating roles. Braidotti's model definitely entails a political agenda, without excluding the shifting between categories that the aesthetically reflexive post-modern subject proposes. Braidotti's 'nomad', it is argued, 'enacts transitions without a teleological purpose' (1994: 23). This is a crucial point for my own analysis, since this is an idea that predominates in the self-narratives of the *Mykoniots* and their discourses of self-transformation.

For Braidotti, post-modernism and feminism originate from the same source but follow different courses (1994: 34). I will conclude with Braidotti's view that nomadic identity manifests a politically engaged (post-modern) gaze, a premise that could equally apply to the *Mykoniots*' nomadic praxis: 'Nomadic consciousness is a form of political resistance to hegemonic and exclusionary views of subjectivity' (1994: 23).

Yet, one wonders if the prototype for Braidotti's 'nomad' descends from a Deleuzian principle of subjectivity and nomadology, is agency here axiomatic or conditional? Braidotti herself admits that a Deleuzian 'becoming' is only available to abject subjects; it is only through 'becoming minority' that one gets any chance to change and thus obtain agency (1997: 69). 'Becoming-minority' is at the heart of Deleuzean transgressive theory. But only women and other 'privileged' minorities are suitable for this conscious project of becoming (ibid.). This 'privilege' is unusually only confined to the margins. For the majority there is no 'becoming' (Braidotti 2003: 53). It is only at the margins that one can transgress and thus realise subjectivity; there is no agency available to the majority. While this is compatible with the position of the *Mykoniots d'élection* as occupiers of the margins, it makes for a controversial yet very interesting and eclectic theory vis-à-vis subjectivity and agency. Braidotti's nomadic subject is a descendant of Deleuze's anarchic principle of the multiple and the rhizomatic: this propagates a community, with neither a hierarchical order nor organising rules – its members have abandoned a tyrannical binary logic of any origin, and follow a trope of aleatory multiplicity. The Deleuzean nomad, by respecting multiplicity is politically deterritorialising space, and is subservient to no hierarchy. This nomadic model of the self is defined by a 'dislocating' subject. Gedalof (2000) criticises Braidotti for her monolithic interpretation of the Deleuzean subject as confined to a subject whose constant desire and self-definition is exhausted in movement. Deleuze and Guattari, Gedalof observes, have argued against a definition of the nomad which is solely determined by movement (ibid.: 343–44). Instead, she proposes the example of the diasporic space, which may not be a metaphor for constant movement, yet it creates ground for a constant and conscious renegotiation between a 'native' and a 'migrant' self (ibid.: 344). Emblematic of this ambivalence, is Trinh Minh-ha's definition of a 'new' subjectivity, that of the 'Inappropriate Other'. The 'Inappropriate Other', a metaphor of ambiguity vis-à-vis subjectivity, semiotically embodies the discursive hybrid space the *Mykoniots* inhabit, as well as their fluid subjectivity, a space in-between, between the 'nomads' and the 'locals' of Mykonos. Trinh Minh-ha's 'Inappropriate/d Other' is crucially defined as 'both a deceptive insider and a deceptive outsider' (1991: 74).

One is also reminded of Bhabha's notion of the 'Third Space' (1994) here. Bhabha's hybridity theorem calls for the replacement of the notion of cultural diversity with that of cultural difference: in other words, it is ambivalence that replaces relativism (ibid.: 34). The concept of culture for Bhabha, denotes not an 'object of empirical knowledge', but rather an enunciative process (ibid.). Whereas cultural diversity is 'held in a time-frame of relativism', the enunciative process of cultural difference introduces a split between a unified model of culture and the undoing of this very model; thus asserting ambivalence (ibid.: 34–35). This enunciative process challenges monolithic cultural models and familiar binary divisions: past/present, tradition/modernity, etc. The 'Third Space' is the *topos* of this 'enunciative split'. In this hybridic space an 'unconscious' personal syntax is created which perpetually paraphrases the cultural text itself by turning it into an ambivalence. In the hybrid space, rather than shame, discourses of resistance emerge: the 'half-caste' finally acquires agency (Papastergiadis, 1997: 258).

Conclusion

Mykoniots d'élection: nomads in a 'queer space'?

Concluding this monograph, I would like to comment on the initial reservations that an anthropologist might feel when engaging in an ethnographic discussion about a 'nomadic' group (with no fixed identity references). I would simply like to propose, that it is possible to ethnographically account for nomadic subjectivities as the organising principle of the collective under certain circumstances. This can be ethnographically/politically accomplished, as long as no source of identification is treated as fundamental or permanent.

I coined the term tribestyle for the *Mykoniots d'élection* in order to locate them in the post-modern spatialisation of Mykonos. *Mykoniots* construct their communal/subversive discourse and praxis through aesthetics, and a rhetoric of 'resistance' and idiosyncratic creativity. They further use their bodies to subvert; they 'exploit' desire, the unconscious and the sensual. While being critical of any organising principle of individuation, they still perform the 'orgiastic' in their long ritualistic 'trips' to Delos. They live in their heroic past and decadent present. Mykonos for them is the symbolic spatialisation of their ideological nomadic subjectivities. The first to arrive established the group by embracing the myth that Mykonos is a 'queer place'.

In order to avoid misunderstandings and hasty misjudgements, acknowledging the theoretical and political implications the term 'queer' has acquired in post-structuralist and feminist thinking, I will specify my use of the term 'queer place'. The definition of *a* space, i.e, the Mykonian space, as 'queer' works on three levels. Initially, I was inspired by something literal about this epithet that highlighted the colloquial connotations the term has long acquired, given that Mykonos is semantically associated with homosexuality. Mykonos, from the nineties, is openly advertised as a 'gay' island. Brochures available in London travel agencies dealing with holiday destinations in Greece promote this association by producing special brochures for Mykonos that are of interest to (male) homosexuals, constructing a gay world of exclusivity in Mykonos' space. The term 'queer place', in this sense, reminds us of the recently mass-developed discourse and image of Mykonos as a 'homo' pleasure dome. Yet, on another level, as one can detect in reading this book, the exploration of both 'indigenous' and 'exogenous' discourses and myths about the Mykonian space has shown that there is a salient and almost conspicuous characteristic at play: the fact that this space is prefaced with all sorts of adjectival adjuncts that connote strange, atypical, different, unconventional properties, which are in turn synonymous with the original definition of the epithet 'queer'. So far, the 'queer' semantics of the space of Mykonos as a gay place, coexist with a spatial/cultural discourse of 'abnormality' and 'craziness' allegedly 'inherent' in the quality of this space. I hope the parallels that I have drawn so far in order to connect the word 'queer' and the word 'place' in the Mykonian context are clear. But there remains a more complicated issue here, which derives from a later stream of feminist and gay thinking defined as 'queer', performative theory. The informants of this ethnography happen not to be part of a well-defined group: i.e., the much fetishised ghetto-like group of 'homosexuals' or the 'hippie' group, or the 'suffering' indigenous group. They happen also to have acquired a political discourse and a subsequent performativity very close to that which recent queer theory would reserve for its political post-post-structuralist subjects. Similarly, the subjects of this ethnography remain strategically self-unclassified. They may be eccentric modernists, or just post-modernists with diverse sexual and cultural practices that could locate them in the 'margins', or alternatively make them 'fashionable', 'queer' and glamorous. Yet their desire for an identity 'non-placeness', and, most importantly, their strategic accomplishment of this goal through organised collective practices, may possibly permit their discourse to be linked with theoretical discourses of (gender) performativity that politically or otherwise promote a blurring of boundaries, including established social and cultural categories. In this sense, feminist theories of performativity and political identity displacements, i.e., 'queer' theory (see Butler 1993: 223, for the resignification of the term 'queer', and its Brechtian 'refunction'), as a performative theory, might prove valuable for the examination of the action of groups like the *Mykoniots d'élection*. Still, the problem is that all these theoretical approaches remain extremely confined or prefer to give structural priority to gender-informed categories. Equally problematic is the question of agency vis-à-vis the subject which is highly contestable in theories of gender performativity.

Nelson (1999), for example, finds a discrepancy in Butler's notion of an 'intended' gender performativity vis-à-vis agency; if the deviation from the prescribed role is just an accidental 'slippage', how much room is left for agency on behalf of the performer (ibid.: 338–39)? Although Butler's subject resists through discourse, at the same time she paradoxically remains regulated by dominant discourses. For Butler, in the end, agency is exhausted in the intentionality of performance (Costera Meijer and Prins, 1998: 281). Power always precedes subjectivity; agency can never be consciously reproduced, even in performance. Butler is unenthusiastic apropos a Goffmanesque persona which is consciously 'putting on' a role. In other words, she is against any romantic reproductions of performance as manifestations of autonomy (ibid.: 285). McNay (1999) further scrutinises Butler's subject position vis-à-vis agency and reminds us that Butler's discursive subject is an offspring of the Foucauldian notion of subjectivation: a dialectic between autonomy and submission in identity formation (ibid.: 177). Still, Foucault is unsuccessful in integrating these two opposing tendencies. Butler is set to overcome this aporia by affirming ambivalence as 'constitutive' of subjectivity. McNay criticises Butler's conceptualisation of agency as lacking any socio-historical dimension (ibid.: 178). In addition, Butler has been extensively criticised for her treatment of sexuality/gender in the narrow prism of linguistic determinism (ibid.). There is no place for any collective or transcending resignification for Butler's 'abject body' (Butler 1993).[4]

Conclusion

Without assuming a need to undermine the structural priority of gender in feminist discourse, my research formulated the following theoretical problem: my informants would best be understood within the frame of some of these theories of performativity. Yet, the *Mykoniots'* performance involves a multidimensional blurring of boundaries that does not start with gender or place it in a supreme position. In some cases, the *Mykoniots'* discourses may even be performatively 'phallocentric' or 'subjugated'. Nevertheless, at this third level, choosing to represent the text/place as 'queer' is also a latent attempt to stretch the recent theoretical connotations of the term beyond its purely gender-related connotations. My decision to define the Mykonian space as 'queer' symbolically reflects the need for such a theoretical expansion.

Inasmuch as 'ex-centric' groups and nineties activists professed fragmented subjectivities, space acquired varying significations, and cultural discourses conveyed contradictory ideologies. Here space is employed as a more flexible organising concept upon which polyvocality and post-structuralist fragmentation are reflected. If the term 'queer' has already been successfully 'redefined' in post-structuralist theory, I hope it can tolerate yet another connotation.

Notes

1. Connoting pleasure in a broader sense than its English counterpart – see the translator's note in Maffesoli (1993: xvii).
2. The idea expressed by Emma, and quoted at the very beginning of this book, of Mykonos as a 'womb' is analogous to the 'oceanic feeling' which, according to psychiatrist Régis Airault, young Europeans are searching for in Goan raves: (with) 'the "oceanic feeling" lost in adolescence – they literally felt at home in "Mother India" (quoted in Saldanha 2002: 45).
3. Deleuze and Guattari's 'nomads' are defined by an endless displacement game vis-à-vis all taxonomies, be they ethnic, class or gender; and by sustained boundaries, be they physical, national or social (2004a, 2004b). The organising force of transformation – an end-in-itself in the Deleuzian nomadic subject – is desire. Deleuze and Guattari's 'body without organs' is a body open to possibility, and thus multiplicity; an intentionally denaturalised body – not to be inscribed. Deleuze 'uses schizophrenia as a model of *becoming other*, a fragmented multiple subjectivity, in an almost reversal of the tendency towards fixity' (Fullagar 2000: 73, my emphasis).
4. The idea of narrative identity exemplified in feminist works such as Benhabib's – following the Habermasian intersubjective model – stand opposed to Butler, who draws on the works of Derrida, Foucault and Lacan and their theories of subjectivity, where everything is constituted in language (McNay 2003). Habermas' model, on the other hand, being symmetrical and communicative, supposedly leaves space for agency. Actors themselves can generate their own interpretations. The idea of narrative identity 'emphasises the temporal and intersubjective aspects of subjectivity and agency' (ibid.: 7). Benhabib, drawing on Habermas, Ricoeur and Taylor, criticises Butler's theory for her 'abject' subject's lack of agency (ibid.: 5–9). It is not in the utterance but in the narrative that a reflexively conscious agency is realised. This alternative view, besides being criticised by McNay herself, as depoliticising and excluding the unconscious from the formation of the subject, offers a valuable critique and contra-position to Butler's 'abject body'.

Epilogue
A Beach Farewell

༄༅༅༅༅

The body without organs is not a dead body but a living body all the more alive and teeming once it had blown apart the organism and its organization'. (Deleuze and Guattari 2004b: 34)

[T]he emotion produced in performance is *real*, and dangerous. (Hughes-Freeland 1998: 14)

Throughout this book, I have avoided using anything but personal stories, representing the *Mykoniots d'élection*, as self-contained actors from diverse socio-cultural backgrounds, who rhetorically insisted that they had no real affiliation with their significant ethnographic 'others'. Those others, they argued, were just 'acquaintances', the result of aleatory encounters over the years. They were not necessarily 'friends', they were just people who happened to like and inhabit the same island: Mykonos. Thus, it was only accidentally, or as a result of spontaneous and fleeting liaisons, that they found themselves sharing the same Indian ashrams, or discrete Balinese beaches. What is hidden behind this denial of any collectivity or group identity? I would argue that it is an ontological resistance to any collective nomenclature that stabilises or stereotypes the self. A form of Nietzschean 'nomadism' *in situ* (cf. Deleuze 1985: 149).[1] But ultimately, what is hidden is a deeply involved – yet impersonal – affective community with fluid and non-committed membership. The *Mykoniots d'élection* keep returning to a series of alternative affective groups largely in order to heal a 'split': between their desire for autonomy, rebellion and aloneness and their need to affectively belong to a collectivity. The story of Patrick's return to Mykonos, after ten years, to perform his 'last goodbye' – having been diagnosed as having terminal lung cancer a few months earlier – and the ceremonial scattering of his ashes, a few months later, is emblematic of this 'split'. That's why I decided to close this book with his story.

Epilogue

When I finished writing and submitted my thesis, news came that Patrick was back in Europe. Only this time his story was not an attractive one; it was rather frightening. After he had jumped bail and escaped from Greece, he was imprisoned for a short time in Spain, from where he was later deported; again, he was deported from America – all for drug offences – ending up in Bali, trading antique furniture. Patrick was in an endless on-and-off phase with heroin. He occasionally attempted to detoxify himself. Lately, he had been to New Zealand for that reason.

But allow me to fast forward; let me recount the story starting with Patrick's 'final performance'. People who had never met him attended the ceremony Patrick had devised for the scattering of his ashes. They had, of course, heard about him. The atmosphere at the long communal table set up in Yiannis's taverna at sunset was reminiscent of an outmoded family reunion. Many of us, myself included, experienced outbursts of creativity: photographing, shooting video, improvising music. We were all in the euphoria of 'reproducing' the event. Taking pictures of each other as a form of introspection, deferring the ceremony we were there to undertake. What were we longing to capture? What was I longing to cover? Imaginative affective encounters? Emotions?

The wind was mild. It was the end of April and Patrick's birthday: with him in a jar. And the party was ready to roll. Bunches of typical seasonal flowers were brought from the 'picturesque' local growers, the parading 'donkey merchants' of the harbour. The too-many aspiring photographers, in the end, overwhelmed by the event – as Maria put it – only produced empty images. I, too, eventually abandoned shooting the event. Instead, I became totally immersed in the 'event' itself. The 'event' became me, my revelatory ethnographic moment (*à la* Badiou [2005][2]). Why all this euphoria? Maybe because I was performing for the first time beyond my sangfroid persona, something I had been constantly rehearsing during my long apprenticeship under the *Mykoniots d'élection*. I realised that – for the first time – I allowed myself to reveal signs of emotion towards them, just as they did towards one another. Paradoxically, this emotional charge was not due to the occasion, i.e., the commemoration of a lost friend, but rather due to its negation; there was no mourning vis-à-vis the deceased, no reaction vis-à-vis a finality. Yet the *Mykoniots's* 'failure' to mourn – their idiosyncratic commemoration ritual turned into a party – reveals a latent desire to maintain the continuity (of the individual and thus) of the group.[3] Patrick's persona became instantly emblematic for the self-denying group, the *Mykoniots d'élection*. Thus he could not be mourned. Yet, by denying an end for Patrick, they paradoxically accepted existence and continuation for themselves; their being part of a collectivity. They momentarily conceived of themselves as being part of something; vaguely performing their own rituals, vaguely remembering they loved, vaguely remembering they belonged.

We began to climb the hill, passing the rocks and caves which the hippies had inhabited in the seventies, on the way to the beach where we planned to perform the farewell ritual for Patrick. I noticed a used syringe discarded on the sand. I thought of the hippies and the junkies as stories belonging to the past; to the Mykonos of the seventies and eighties. But there were still some cultural remnants from that era: the caves of Paranga, a syringe, and now Patrick's ashes. The mourners lit a fire. The younger acolytes of the group, who loved music and improvising, played African rhythms. They scattered the ashes to just three elements: water – for his soul to float on the Aegean; wind – for his earthly remains to be scattered by the Mykonian *meltemi*; and fire – for his recycling, and the end of his journey. Patrick's ashes were scattered where he would have felt most at home, on a Mykonian beach.[4] For his friends, this was a day like any other day and whoever was around came along.

Flashback: Antonis, protects the ashes under his hat. As the sun sets, a large circle of about forty people hold hands around a fire. Some of them have never met Patrick. Mykonos is their common link; their annual pilgrimage to the same beach; shared sunsets and joints; shared lovers. Back in the seventies, Patrick had designed and opened what later became the group's legendary haunt, the Casablanca. But he abandoned it soon afterwards. Antonis then ran the business for a couple of seasons before handing it on to Aristos. Patrick's original Casablanca decor as well as the haunt's mythology remained intact for more than thirty years. The Casablanca, a site of emergence for the *Mykoniots*, evolved into a spatial fetish. Eventually, its – by then valuable – 'brand' ended up being bought by an aspiring Greek jeweller who euphemistically kept the name but converted the premises to a mere jewellery shop. From a communal space – a Deleuzian space of 'dynamic marginality'[5] – the Casablanca was reduced to an empty signifier of an already commercialised local 'bohemia' (cf. Wilson 1998: 124): a semiotic distortion via consumerism and unavoidably the end of an era for the *Mykoniots d'élection*. At last, everybody 'respected' the space-myth of the Casablanca.

As the Casablanca's ownership changed several times over thirty years, only a few recognised the source of its haunting charm as the essence of Patrick's mystique (with which, ultimately, this little corner of the Mykonian *hora* was endowed). In the summer of '75, having created the Casablanca, Patrick abandoned it in exchange for enough cash to travel to India. The following summer, he rented another shop – only two doors down the street – selling his handmade espadrilles. Later, he fashioned another entrepreneurial trend in the same Mykonian corner: trading in second-hand clothes and all things oriental. Patrick would soon abandon all his businesses after he created them. However, someone else would make a career out of his discarded enterprises. Over time, the neighbourhood around the Casablanca semiotically evolved into an eponymous signifier deprived of its original ambience.

Patrick was reluctant – even incapable – of sustaining any business; but he was completely capable of imagining it and skilful at setting up a shop, displaying his personal collection of beautiful second-hand artefacts together with his personal charm. While at times he would generously give away his stock as gifts to his friends and clients, he was equally capable of cheating them when in need of extra cash to buy drugs. Due to his habit, Patrick was an 'inconsistent' friend. Addiction was second nature to him; he was an emotionally seductive yet malnourished soul, a real source of affection and betrayal at the same time. At once the betrayed and the betrayer.

His personal life follows the same addictive pattern. His Greek mother had been divorced from his French father for being too amorous for a woman of her generation. She had to be 'exiled' by her family to prevent a scandal. Another version of the story was that she herself desired to escape. Could she not face her husband because she had fallen in love with another man? Or, is this recollection all just her fickleness? Anyway, both the lover and the husband eventually abandoned her. In order to forget, she left, abandoning Patrick and his sister. Patrick tried hard every night to persuade her not to leave for Germany. The moment she left, he started stuttering. He acquired a nervous tic on one side of his face which he carried with him for the rest of his life. From then onwards, his life was transformed into an endless pursuit of women who would emotionally feed the hurt child. First, his grandmother, then his sister, later his first wife – whom he then abandoned with their two children. Patrick was eighteen-years-old when he first married. From then on, he always abandoned his lovers. No woman soothed his pain. There is an obsessive revisiting to these stories of abandonment for Patrick and his family. Ironically, this autobiographical exercise is an integral part of Patrick's 'pain performance'; in a sense, by exhibiting his suffering, he is trying to exorcise his fickleness, the consequence of his pain. Women, in turn, fell for his vulnerability and seduction one after another. He loved them all, but he loved *preza* (heroin) more. He never managed to get over his mother's departure. He could not get over her betrayal and so, in turn, he betrayed them.

He also learned how to 'betray' his friends, who eventually managed not to take it personally. 'Uncle' Fritz liked to repeat this story about Patrick: in his New York years, when Patrick had to spend some time in 'Uncle' Fritz's Manhattan apartment, Patrick would occasionally – when 'Uncle' Fritz was asleep, or pretending to be – help himself to money from his pockets in order to buy drugs from the dealers in Central Park. Patrick would then disappear for a while, only to return full of his usual charm. But 'Uncle' Fritz, initially angry, would always forgive him and turn a blind eye to his bad behaviour, cheating and betrayal. Patrick's politics of seduction were performative. He entertained his friends with his talent and recklessness. It was the seventies when Patrick and his friends created their personal myths by travelling; India, beautiful women, antiques, ornamental knives – toys for boys; charmers who seduced wealthy lovers and fell for fashion models. There was an aesthetic passion – rather emotionless – for the perfect body (as if the body lacked individuality and was purely for display, victim of the gaze). The *Mykoniots* learned to exist on the gaze; their whole life is a performance. They do not survive on emotional relationships but rather on the gaze. They live in a 'liminal corporeality'.[6] The *Mykoniot,* as the object of the public gaze that keeps his performance visible in the tourist space as the cosmopolitan, the traveller, the adventurer, is turned into the performer of his own biography. As Gooldin (2003) suggests in her historical retrospective of nineteenth century performative anorexia, there is always an act of spectacle involved in the process.

Patrick's autobiographical narrative – or for that matter the group's narratives about Patrick – works along similar lines to that of the Hunger Artist's 'show': 'it was precisely about *suffering* and *ovecoming* difficulties' (ibid.: 46, original emphasis). For the Hunger Artist and for the *Mykoniot*, there is no 'front' and 'back' stage. There is no motivation behind self-performance besides the desire for visibility. The *Mykoniot* is not unlike a contemporary 'emotional anorexic'. *Pace* Gooldin's nineteenth-century Fasting Women, the *Mykoniots*' performativity is a conscious act. Yet, it is also a needy act. 'The idea of a living (social) persona in a dead (physical) body' (ibid. 42) reminds us of Patrick's orchestrated oxymoronic performance. His body is adored via its 'deadness', its 'fickleness', its 'pain'. His seductive 'junkie' body needs spectators, like the 'anorexic' body. His 'suffering' performance makes for his visibility. And visibility for the *Mykoniots d'élection* is their *raison d'être*. The performance is non-stop. Once the spectacle ceases to exist, the 'Hunger Artist' dies.

The 'boys' were passionate about harmony and immortality. Women were the prize for this existential journey. A drama of conquest that was played out in the cosmopolitan metropolises and during the long Mykonian summer nights. Patrick liked to tell me this story about a woman, Ophelia, who wanted him so badly that she had to agree to sleep with his friend Antonis first, who also desired her. In their shared Mykonian open-house, Ophelia would first sleep with Patrick and then move into Antonis's room to wait for him, in order to spend the night. In this way, Ophelia compromised her passion for Patrick; yet in return she secretly slipped into his bed. That was the only arrangement Patrick could emotionally afford, as he did not take particular pleasure in sex – and even less in commitment.

Patrick took pleasure in *preza* but not on its dependency. It made him sick. That he couldn't take, facing himself in the mirror. Maybe it wasn't him after all, it was the 'audience' who could not face his handsome face looking ghastly. Eventually he would always find someone who would be responsible for his 'salvation': 'Uncle' Fritz in New York, Juliette his sister in Texas. Sophia, his girlfriend at the time, literally saved him at the last minute from the New York heroin scene and they set off hopefully to start a new life in Bali. Every single one of this 'salvation army' of friends and lovers had (perpetually) something valuable to give: emotion. He drew it out of them because he was badly in need of it. He trusted his male friends more than any of his women. He would only betray them when in need of *preza*. As for the women, he would *always* 'betray' them. A few months before he died, he pronounced that he had always been bored with sex. Impotent now, he was finally happy, he said.

The less potent doses of the legal morphine, now supplied to him in order to kill his carcinogenic pain, liberated him in addition from his passions and addictions. Regulated morphine also liberated him from his dishonest attitude towards women; and from the perpetual, yet if meaningless, game of seduction and subsequent betrayal – and paradoxically from his heroin dependency. How peculiar for an addictive personality, on learning of the prognosis on his terminal lung cancer, to decide to 'give up' heroin and finally tolerate his pain in order to 'live' out his remaining time. The doctors were giving him little or virtually no time. Patrick thus became 'clean'. Maybe a line or two taken in Mykonos or in Portobello Road, but that became the exception: 'Just for the sake of the flash,' as Eurydice would say; or otherwise, to keep the memory of the heroin 'rush' alive. Patrick's final journey reveals an anastrophe. *Pace* Irigaray's 'sensible transcendental'[7] his existential inner movement is of a 'feminine' nature. And this is evident in how Patrick deals with his imminent death. He deals with it by multiplying 'change'. Confronted with his imminent metamorphosis, he comes up with yet another self-metamorphosis. Although Patrick's lifestyle and seduction pattern entails macho elements, the type of 'existential' freedom he pursues after hearing the news of his approaching death, reminds us of a 'feminine' teleological principle: where the 'journey' is one of becoming and self-metamorphosis and not a 'masculine' form of movement through appropriation and mastery (cf. Fullagar 2001: 290).[8] Likewise, he magically ceases to be a seducer; there is no machismo left in him anymore.

Patrick, once more, established his personal myth by 'giving up' the best painkiller when it was most needed. By discovering the certainty of death, he denied *preza*'s slow death. He moved into his sister's bedsit in Portobello, transferred from a Balinese hospital in a very bad state. Consecutive treatments followed: chemotherapies, radiotherapies … It was then that he decided to return to Mykonos for his 'last goodbye'. Patrick reappeared on the island after an absence of ten years. I had just submitted my thesis to the University of London. I had also 'passed' the apprenticeship stage of the most intimate of the *Mykoniots'* initiation rites and had successfully 'become' one of them. I had matured somewhat, and this made the 'boys' of the group accept me; they had appropriated me rather, after I appropriated their self-narratives. Through this mutual appropriation, they came to assume that we shared common memories, stories and friends. So when Patrick first arrived in London, I received several calls from the *Mykoniots* prompting me to go and visit him. But how could I visit a dying stranger? I was also extremely stressed from the completion of the thesis, as well as the changes in my personal circumstances. I was now in a stable relationship, and in a sense felt that at the same time as I was concluding my thesis, I was also making my farewell to my Mykonian world; I was departing from the ideological principles of a group who despised commitment. I became a betrayer. My potential transition to a 'professional' self also added to the stress generated by my liminal transitional state. I projected onto my self-image an aesthetically disagreeable future: a married woman, a professional with a career in anthropology. This created a conflict in me; I refused to visit Patrick.

I also felt rather exploited, at first. Nobody seemed to understand why I was not going to see him. On an earlier occasion, I had also been asked to support an elderly *Mykoniot* who was visiting London for medical tests, although his condition was not as serious as Patrick's.

It was shortly afterwards that I returned to the island. I was neurotically living on water in the final stages of writing up. As a result, I ruined my stomach. I also wanted to be slim but I ended up a wreck. Around the end of September, I heard Antonis mention that Patrick would shortly be arriving for 'the last goodbye', as he characteristically put it. The news slightly upset me. It was towards the end of the tourist season, and the *Mykoniots* were on the verge of their winter mode of withdrawal and introversion. No more lovers; no more strangers; no more wasted nights; only friends. We cultivated a habit of gathering at Antonis' home every afternoon where the *pareá*'s commensality was 'performed'. Eurydice and I would play the 'wives' and cook for the 'boys'. The nights had started drawing in. The 'boys' would roll their joints non-stop and exchange anecdotes. But the most exhaustive discussion – ritualistically repeated every night – was over what to cook the following day. The group's composition changed slightly from day to day. Yet, the rules of commensality were strict – it was only 'amongst us'. Perhaps a newcomer with no emotional baggage could be admitted to the 'charmed circle', provided they were 'cool' and 'independent' enough to participate in this communal unwinding process. The aesthetic principle was: an affective commensality with no commitment.

Then one day Patrick arrives. I first saw him on Paranga beach, sitting with the 'boys' in Yiannis' taverna where Eurydice and I joined them. Although he did not even turn his head to look at me, I was surprised by Eurydice's subsequent comment that Patrick knew exactly who I was. 'You don't know Patrick, he was checking you out,' she said. 'He even has eyes in the back of his head.' Eurydice was largely responsible for my mythologisation of Patrick. One day, amongst her many artistic black-and-white prints taken of the seventies Mykonian scene, she showed me the image of the then handsome looking Patrick. I had already often heard her recounting his adventures and how women would fall at his feet. But the fact that she – a woman I looked up to and who never played the role of prey for men – retained her admiration for Patrick, made him even more alluring in my eyes. It was not until I met Patrick again at a dinner party that I recognised the charisma Eurydice was talking about.

Dressed in his second-hand 'colonial' white linen suit, Patrick had arrived early and placed himself accordingly in an elderly, white, bamboo armchair, the only sixties remnant in this old refurbished Mykonian villa. His style was intentionally anachronistic and exotic, in order to create a fictitious idealised persona. An old Australian girlfriend had organised the party in his honour. He was radiating a definite charm to all the women in the room who eventually gravitated towards his bamboo chair; numbed still by his long absence but enchanted as always by his presence. This 'adoration scene' made me realise immediately the remarkable capacity Patrick had for performing before 'an audience'. The ghost of handsome Patrick, now a wreck, had reappeared. Enduring the pain – hidden behind his playful demeanour in his bamboo chair. Patrick's 'sartorial play' is reminiscent of the nineteenth-century traveller's romantic disguise: the traveller here plays the romantic hero whose endurance has been tested in personal trials and adventures. A self that emerges away from 'home' (cf. Adler 1989: 1385).

We slowly became friends. I eventually lost my inhibition about his illness. He even managed to make me touch his tumorous neck. Patrick was very casual about it. We were both due to come back to London on the same weekend. He had to make a stopover in Athens where he went to visit the Acropolis, probably for the last time. Soon after, I found myself in Portobello Road calling Patrick. In the few weeks we had spent together in Mykonos, he managed to draw a commitment out of me: to teach him how to use a computer. This was a way of expunging my earlier guilt about not going to see him in the first place. Patrick wanted to learn how to operate the computer in order to make digital animation stories. He was very good at drawing them by hand – even a talented artist. We first met at Juliette's bedsit. Instead of a computer lesson we cooked *fasolada* (bean soup), the Greek national dish. This was the first time I had met his sister Juliette and I immediately felt a kind of inexplicable familiarity with both of them, produced by the unusual circumstances of our recent introduction and Patrick's imminent death. It felt as if we had known each other for ever, as we shared old stories of the *Mykoniots*. We spontaneously acquired the *Mykoniots d'élection*'s aesthetic principle of uncommitted 'bonding'. The cooking continued, exactly as it would have done in Antonis's Mykonian *horio*. In between chemotherapy, our relationship evolved into confessional ethnographic sessions, computer lessons and watching old Greek comedy films. Very soon, we became oblivious to the fact that we had only just met, and Patrick was about to die. What was the point of investing in this friendship? It was no more than living for the moment, another ontological principle of the *Mykoniots*.

An impulse drives me to make an automatic – arbitrary at first – association between the metonymic Deleuzian domain of music, as a cultural form that best resembles how the world is organised, with the 'social organisation' of the *Mykoniots*. 'Music' there is defined by a self-contradictory power of deterritorialisation and belonging, a power to mobilise the body – yet change nothing in the 'systems of domination'; it is rather a 'narcissistic revolution' (Saldanha 2002: 58–59). What Deleuze and Guattari (2004b) prescribe for the instrumentality of 'music' as metaphor is a principle of a haphazardly democratic intimacy: 'music is when desire is released to change relations of power, relations enabled especially by the eye ... ' (Saldanha 2002: 59). 'Music' is when bodies – escaping from rigidity – become 'faceless' (ibid.). In this anarchic domain of 'music' there is no male-female distinction, no self-other dichotomy. Ultimately, there is no significant other; only 'alternating others'.

During Patrick's short-lived attempt to serve in the Greek army, he aesthetically immortalised himself in a stereotypical kitsch miniature self-portrait: one that all the raw recruits used to send back home – bordered by a heart-shaped floral frame and decorated with two doves. This was the kind of portrait that the conscript would normally send to his lover or mother. In Patrick's case, the reverse of this much-duplicated photographic print was signed and accompanied by the following text: 'Forever together – whoever you may be, Patrick.' The print was circulated amongst his friends. I also acquired a copy many years later. The concept of friendship here, similar to Deleuze and Guattari's reflection on the anarchic concept of 'music', is flexible vis-à-vis individuality; 'friendship' is not personified. 'Friends' are an ever-expanding group. Patrick's self-portrait is dedicated to the ones not present as well as to those who are present, or to the friends who have not yet 'become'. Occasional friends like occasional lovers, passing lovers but always beloved. This 'faceless' element of friendship is exemplified in the impersonal dedication of Patrick's miniature portrait. His text and signature on the back of the photograph also work 'metonymically' for Patrick's later aleatory commemorative gathering on a Mykonian beach. Intimacy can be 'impersonal' in this sense. The object of desire is forever interchangeable.

A Mykonian type of encounter, a '*Mykoniatiki katastasi*' as the *Mykoniots* loved to call it, was transferred to Portobello Road. As Patrick's condition worsened, two of his closest *Mykoniot* friends, Markos and Antonis came to visit. Their visit felt hurried and awkward, and they only stayed in London for a short time. As death approached, lovers and friends, the seduced, the betrayed and the beloved abandoned Patrick for the first time. His mother came to bid him farewell at Christmas, a month before he died. By the deathbed of the 'adored', stood a chorus of women: Juliette, his sister; Sophia his Spanish lover with Maria her sister, and Patricia, her mother; Cynthia, Juliette's and Patrick's English friend; and finally, Eurydice and myself. We took turns at Patrick's bedside. His mother was not there, she could not cope with it; she flew back to California before the end. His male Greek friends were absent, too – also unable to cope with it.

When Patrick passed through Athens for the last time his father refused to see him. That's why he visited the Acropolis instead. His old Athenian girlfriend was out of town as well. She preferred to be away for the weekend. Athens was hot. Patrick invented the romantic story of his visit to the Acropolis in order to endow all this neglect with mystery.

Not many of his admirers attended his cremation. One of his former lovers, whom he remembered most affectionately, sent a bunch of white flowers, with a note saying 'Farewell my love.' Everything was there from Patrick's biography: absence, love and neglect. But in reality far more people were silently mourning; the night of Patrick's death, many candles were lit around the world. Even his daughters refused to talk to him on the phone in his final days. After all, he had ignored them all his life. Patrick had a humanist funeral in London. Later, when Juliette brought his ashes to Mykonos, she performed an informal Orthodox commemoration in the main church, careful not to mention to the priest that Patrick had been cremated – as this is a forbidden practice in the Orthodox Church.

Patrick's ashes were scattered in three different places around the world. First, in Bali where his last partner performed a moving ceremony under the full moon, spreading his ashes over the ocean from a fishing boat. Second, and much later, at Laguna Beach in California. And third, in Mykonos where another 'beach farewell' took place. Neither his father or mother, nor his children ever attended any of these ceremonies.

What is 'home' for Patrick?[9] The notion of home has been symbolically turned into a versatile dispersed identity signifier; home has been transmuted into alternating homes; 'home' has been semantically and ontologically reconfigured into 'the place you get to, not the place you came from' (Monette 1991, quoted in Fortier 2001: 409). Stripped of any stability, identity has become a process of becoming. The scattering of Patrick's ashes in three different locales is a good indication of this ideological identity instability. 'Not only can one be at home in movement, but that movement can be one's very own home'[10] (Rapport and Dawson 1998: 27).

But 'how do the "homes" people move towards relate to those that are "left behind"'? Fortier asks us (2001: 408). She argues that alternative notions of home emerge in gay culture:[11] home becomes the site of emergence rather than a physical entity. Gay bars become 'sites of connection' where 'the ontological security of being "at home"' is best experienced (ibid.: 412). Outside a homophobic world, 'away from home', at home in migration, at home in movement. Like Fortier's gay bar, Mykonos metonymically stands for this type of ontological nomadism. Drawing semiotically from its ancient counterpart, Delos, whose myth of emergence entails a spatial restlessness, Mykonos also acquires an idiosyncratic fluidity. In mythology, Delos, the island of Apollo, had been condemned by the gods to be an island in constant movement. Mykonos as a signifier of a cultural nomadism, semiotically shares such assumptions. Mykonos – and, by extension, the *Mykoniots d'élection* – signifies mutability for the space/group. Mykonos acts as a 'site of emergence'. 'A "home" that is not necessarily place-based but that is grounded in the "sense of community" provided by her [in our case a group of] dispersed friends' (ibid.: 414). Likewise, Mykonos metonymically stands for a 'sense of community' of dispersed friends who only occasionally meet on the island. The sense of being 'at home', of being on Mykonos can equally be experienced outside its physical space. Mykonos is not the tourist island, nor the sunset nor the clubbing. Mykonos is the home of the 'like-minded'.

The Mykonian ceremony was initiated by his sister, Juliette, according to Patrick's meticulous instructions, and performed by his *Mykoniot* friends.

A beach farewell

Everyone who was there will always remember that day at the beach: Patrick's farewell. The scattering of the ashes took place during a spring sunset. This was a convenient time and season for the *Mykoniots*: after their daily swim, and well before the tourists' mass arrival – thus they had time to celebrate another 'ritual of our own'. Yet, nobody had bothered to attend the actual funeral. Patrick's cremation was witnessed largely by acquaintances rather than friends. 'People who had not seen each other for ten, twenty ... years met up again to bid their friend ... farewell.'[12] Curiously, this is not a quote about Patrick's 'beach farewell' ritual. Yet it refers to a farewell to another charismatic mentor, the poet Robert Graves, who since the thirties had established an artistic colony of admirers in Deia, on the Balearic island of Mallorca. Waldren (1996), the ethnographer and insider of this group, describes how Graves's death was received and appropriated by these 'bohemian eccentric ex-patriots', a group not unlike the *Mykoniots d'élection*. Waldren's 'outsiders', her '*Deianencs d'élection*', is another ethnographic version of a cosmopolitan group residing in a tourist space on the artistic/aesthetic principle of extreme individuality. The above quote was taken from Waldren's description of Graves's London wake, performed at the Royal Academy, where a certain 'Deianenc' atmosphere was palpable: 'almost everyone had been to Deia' (ibid.: 178). It is important to unravel here how the association with an idealised topos like Deia or Mykonos can create similar types of collectivities; to symbolically attribute to the tourist space a sense of affective community, a sense of otherness, built upon individuality and creativity.

In Patrick's case, a much mythologised member of the *Mykoniots*, his cremation was held at the West London Crematorium and was witnessed by very few people, virtually none of whom were *Mykoniots d'élection*. Patrick's ashes were scattered later in Mykonos, despite the fact that he had been absent from the Mykonian scene for the last ten years or so. In this sense, Patrick's farewell scenario is an inversion of that of Graves. Strangely enough, in the case of the long 'absent Patrick', membership of this 'symbolic community' – the *Mykoniots d'élection* – was being celebrated for the first time on the occasion of an 'absence'. This quality of 'absence' on the part of the group's mentor carries the intrinsic characteristic of the group itself. Graves's London wake also operated metonymically on a similar absence: what unified the mourners was simply the fact that they had at some point in their lives met in Deia. In other words, apart from Graves, what was really missing and being celebrated in the London wake was the 'Deianenc'. The Deia or Mykonos topos stands for a way of life that affectively 'collectivises'; ultimately one transgresses – beyond locality and the group itself; the 'group' is never formulated as a group; its 'members' are never consistently there.

Back in London, Eurydice and I were very angry with the 'boys'. But as Hercules would argue: death is not important, it is only a lonely passage from one situation to the next. The *Mykoniots'* corruption of the loose and ambiguous Greek term *parea* (company [of friends]), which can incorporate both acquaintance and companionship, is revealing. Whether referring to a committed or a looser association, the notion of *parea* traditionally applies to a clearly defined collectivity. The *Mykoniots d'élection* have their own idiosyncratic interpretation of the concept of *parea*: *parea* is 'whoever comes along', i.e., ontologically emphasising fluidity and randomness. *Parea* never implies for them a notion of 'closed' or nominal collectivity. Their idiosyncratic rituals have no rules of membership.

Instead, the concepts of 'liminoid communities' and 'sensual solidarities' (cf. St.John 2001) could be the starting point for the 'social organisation' of the *Mykoniots d'élection*. By turning into the hosts of the Mykonian fiesta, the 'sensual solidarities' of the *Mykoniots* and their randomness acquire a sense of permanence. Patrick's ceremony for the scattering of his ashes on a Mykonian beach was a ritual performed on behalf of an affective community of strangers; a sensual solidarity built upon principles of spontaneity and impulsive affection for a vague 'collectivity', or rather for its absence, since it has no definitive membership. Scattering the ashes of somebody who, ironically, had not been around for the last ten years reinstates the group's sensual solidarity. The absence of mourning, the existence of infinite 'aleatory encounters'- that perpetually define its new members – signify a principle of poetic impersonality in the acquisition of an 'unbodied' group membership for the sensual community. As in Derrida's aporias, where a term like 'mourning' is reconfirmed by its antithesis, i.e., not mourning, a 'liminoid community' like the *Mykoniots d'élection*, is reconfirmed in a ceremonial event for an absent member's loss performed in the presence of non-members. And the problem still remains: are the *Mykoniots d'élection* a 'community'? The *Mykoniots*' existential principle – apart from aestheticising extreme individuality – is to occasionally 'lose' their bodies and immerse themselves in haphazard 'sensual collectivities' such as *the event* of the scattering of Patrick's ashes, where a rapture between the body and the self is evident. The body, *pace* Jordan (1995: 129, quoted in St.John 2001: 62) acquires a liminoid position within this 'communal state of euphoria'. The *Mykoniots*' existential principle of being 'alone together' (Moore 1995: 207) is finally realised in a conscious performance of an 'unbodied collectivity'.

When Patrick's ashes arrived on the island, the *Mykoniots* were overwhelmed by emotion. 'Uncle' Fritz travelled from New York, Spiros from Patras, Michael from London; some old friends – who used to spend a lot of time on the island in the past – reappeared like ghosts. I was equally moved by the exceptionally collective feeling of this spontaneous event. I saw, at last, an act of belonging to this Mykonian affective community, enacted by the conscious performers of the self-image. Bonding in Patrick's 'beach farewell' was performed by the *Mykoniots d'élection* as their ideological demarcator. Soon after the ritual, the 'old friends' disappeared. Patrick's 'beach farewell' was another improvised moment of liminality for the group.

Flashback: a few weeks before Christmas in London. He was waiting impatiently for his *Mykoniot* friends. His 'great expectation'. The bedsit where they were living was cramped and the furniture threadbare. Juliette was preparing a miniature Christmas tree. Patrick could hardly get out of bed at this stage. Nevertheless, he insisted on Juliette arranging a pile of empty bags beneath the tree to look like presents; thus 'setting up' a scene of intimacy. That's what he wanted most of all. Shortly before he finally left the bedsit for the hospital, and as he lapsed in and out of a coma, I asked him what was the lesson he had learned. His answer was, bluntly, self-respect. And that he had none, he had lost it. He defined it by using the Greek word *axioprepeia* (dignity/integrity), the cultivation of self-respect through maintaining the boundaries between one and another – the only way to learn how to love and be loved. His last words, before he slipped into his final coma were: 'Nurse, please, give me something to alleviate my pain.' A life-long cry from the heart. I cannot convey Patrick's mystique and charisma in words. The withdrawal symptoms suffered by those once 'seduced' and later 'betrayed' were a demonstration of it. They would deny him the pleasure of their company in his last days, while at the same time silently suffering at the thought of his non-existence, or rather of their empty existence – without the challenge of a fickle 'other'. This was the power of his charisma; it all became apparent after his death. Everyone close to him claimed him for themselves – insisting almost to the point of violence that they were *the* intimate in his life. Patrick sensed that this was coming. To the emotional turmoil that his imminent death was causing them, he reacted with inexplicable patience. His esoteric reaction vis-à-vis pain allowed him to overcome the suspiciousness of those once more 'betrayed' with kindness; now that he was dying, finally his lifelong restlessness persevered. I felt an intense need to reveal another of Patrick's masks; this could further establish the transformative power Patrick's final trial had 'accidentally' offered him: by breaking the habit of his familiar (seductive) performance, he finally realised a conscious self-performance.

Patrick's powerful charisma was also evident in the outpouring of narratives which emerged upon his return to perform his 'last goodbye'. Collective and intimate memories resurfaced. Everyone – especially the women of the group – came up to me with a story of 'seduction', nostalgically recalling their encounters with him. They were all, without exception, overwhelmed by his reappearance. Mostly, however, they felt intimidated and kept themselves away from him and the feelings he evoked. Patrick was, after all, the manipulator of emotions for the *Mykoniots d'élection* and the hero of their best stories. What most impressed me was the reappearance of his old friends at the 'beach farewell'. After many years of absence, they only reappeared for the sake of Patrick's commemoration. Patrick's ceremony triggered a 'collective memory' of a past Mykonos and of a commensality lost; in reality, this was what was being re-enacted in Patrick's 'beach farewell' over and above his commemoration. For the *Mykoniots* this was a rare occasion where, for once, they allowed their subjective masks to slip – playing at being a 'collectivity' of a 'mourn-less' mourning. Mykonos's liminal space thus epitomises their conundrum of belonging and non-belonging.

Mourning was absent both at the time of Patrick's death and in the months that followed. Yet, now, their off-season Mykonos reunion heralded a groundswell of emotion. In fact, the only time that I was confronted with a collective sensation of emotion was then, when the most adventurous of them was lost. Everybody who happened to be present and partying that evening – even those unknown to him – were deeply moved, engaging in an unrepeatable manifestation of collective affectivity. After all, as an audience, we were only used to an ever-aloof self-performance by the *Mykoniots d'election* – displaying individuality conspicuously.

In my romantic anthropological imagination, I always thought that the *Mykoniots*' performative repertoire would invariably succeed in making them retreat from any sign of intimacy, any encounter with (the face of) death; thus forever inhabiting their emotionally sedated and constantly liminal state. The most amazing fact of all, though, was when Patrick confessed to me that he only felt alive – only regained his desire to live – after he heard the news of his imminent death. He was by then in excruciating pain; for him morphine was not strong enough, and Portobello was literally around the corner from his bedsit. He could have ended it all much sooner with an overdose.

The *Mykoniots*' performance as a Schechnerian type of embodied playing is evident here both in Patrick's return – conscious of his theatrical last appearance on Mykonos's 'stage', performing 'the last goodbye' – as well as, in the unusual emotional response of his friends' gathering a year later for the scattering of his ashes. Both acts entail the concept of a conscious performance-play. In the instance of the *Mykoniots*'s self-invented ritual and idiosyncratic *paniyiri*, the scattering of Patrick's ashes, their performance deals creatively with a crisis of loss. Patrick's loss also signifies the loss of many other things: i.e., Mykonos as they used to know and patronise it; or Mykonos – now a construction site – under the threat of an over-indulgent consumption; the conscious self-performance of the *Mykoniots* under threat from media constructed celebrities; and *their* haunts turned into impersonal spaces by the over-commercialisation of tourist services. The bohemian archetype of the wheeling and dealing adventurous bricoleur, who has been paradigmatically exemplified and 'deified' in Patrick's persona, has now been superseded by the professional trader: a caricature of an 'adventurer', a 'local' or a 'cosmopolitan'. Idiosyncrasy no longer has a place on Mykonos. You have to be mainstream in order to be tradable. The utopic Mykonos I have been describing throughout this text belongs to the past. Patrick is the embodiment of this nostalgia. The tableau of the scattering of Patrick's ashes is unlike the black-attired grieving of the Greek Orthodox commemoration. Here the ritual entails a sacrificial aura reminiscent of Girard (1977) who sees in sacrifice an act which sublimates violence; to paraphrase Girard, the *Mykoniots*' invented ritual and affective performance sublimates estrangement and further fragmentation. The scattering of Patrick ashes is yet another ritualistic neologism, akin to Schechner's hypothesis of the sacrificial property of ritual as a theatrical performative catharsis (1995: 234).

This ritual could also be seen as a communal moment of Nietzschean transgression (cf. Gibson 1991), revealing life's metaphysical and tragic face. But this is not because of its content, i.e. a death ritual, but rather due to its transformative power: a communal moment of transgression on behalf of a group whose members 'politically' deny any collective identity. Patrick's symbolic return after ten years of absence to 'leave' his ashes made his friends – and other members of the group unknown to him – realise that although they proselytise for a highly fatalistic individuality that condemns one to an isolated individual freedom, there comes a moment of respite. A tragic event makes them realise that in total loss of *self* there is the *other*, i.e., the affective community of strangers who one day in May gathered to scatter Patrick's ashes on his favourite beach. According to Gibson, Nietzsche acknowledges the element of transgression in ritual as a moment of 'philosophical revelation' where one immediately recognises and at the same time deconstructs all forms of illusion, be they 'social' or 'moral', 'cultural' or 'metaphysical' (ibid.: 1). Patrick's ritualistic tripartite exit: three distinctive ceremonies vis-à-vis his burnt body – one in Bali, one in California and one in Mykonos – incarnates his ubiquitous performance. In a sense, his body continued to travel; fragmented between different intimacies and places. There was no single self-defining collectivity for him; be it a partner, a family or a group of like-minded where Patrick 'belonged'. The Greek root of utopia stands for a fantastic space of non-topos. Since 'topos' denotes some bounded identity space, the u-topos denotes the transcendence project. But, Bauman argues, in post-modernity we already inhabit the boundless u-topos, so there is no desire for transcendence, utopia. 'The "u" of "utopia" bereaved by the "topos", is left homeless and floating, no more hoping to strike its roots, to "re-embed"' (Bauman 2003: 22).

He betrayed them, so they betrayed him, they let him die alone. Yet for me Patrick's ceremony was the first clear manifestation of commitment in the context of the *Mykoniots*' peculiar ethics-aesthetics. Patrick's paradigmatic uncommitted existence and the paradox of a 'community' of the like-minded, struck me during the beach farewell ritual as an ethographic revelatory moment. The *Mykoniots* also feel betrayed by post-modernity; they are more inclined to a utopian control of the world via their paradigmatic act of travelling and self-transformations. They ceaselessly move around the world but they hardly remain unattached; their compass being their affective communities around the globe. In their (restless sense of) movement, utopia remains as the only commitment to those left behind, as well as to a fragment of self carried within them, which is reminiscent of what they left behind.

Nietzsche's theory of performative subjectivity, according to Patton, is derived from his long preoccupation with the aestheticised subject and her 'inner craving for a role and mask, for appearance ... ' (Nietzsche 1974: 316, quoted in Patton 1991: 32). Nietzsche sees the modernist subject as a conscious actor who requires for the performances of her hybrid personality, a wardrobe of selves. Her existence is identified with her masks. Nietzsche was amongst the first to realise that the modern European self was characterised by a decentring of the subject; behind the masks 'there are only further masks' (Patton 1991: 32). The subject is multiple and is constituted in a conscious self-performance; the performer acquires agency and distance vis-à-vis her appropriated roles.[13] But in multiple performativity lies the post-modern tragedy: 'the role has actually become character', 'appearance becomes being' (ibid.: 34). In other words, the role confines the being, the performance becomes the barrier to any agency. Yet, the subject's inability to escape her role, Patton suggests, could be read as a tragedy only if we assume that she has 'a true self, an inner core of emotions and desires' that she betrays (ibid.). Since the role playing is plural, the post-modern subject does not suffer from any form of loyalty to an acquired role. Post-structural theorists in general tend to deny that there is a substantial core behind the roles. But what happens to the subject's desire if, once she is identified with her role, she becomes incapable of willpower? Patton's interpretation of Nietzsche's Zarathustra offers a way out: the 'genuine actor', who is quite separate from the unconscious and the involuntary actor (ibid.: 37). This is the actor who never takes off the mask 'even when his unhappiness or his own grief are at stake' (ibid.: 38). It seems that the genuine actor equals a conscious actor who elevates her mimetic practice into a moral exercise. There is some agency involved in this single-minded enterprise. This act of devotion is what distinguishes the great actor from lesser beings.

What happened in Patrick's case was that the role confined the being until, by a twist of fate, he experienced a reversal: his certainty of death made him realise, become conscious of his perfomance-play. Patrick's personal revelatory moment of self-transformation was later sublimated into a collective revelatory moment. Myerhoff (1990: 248), drawing on Turner's state of communitas, accepts that in performance, heightened subjective states can account for the performer's 'transformation of consciousness'. This can also acquire a 'collective dimension', i.e., also involve groups and communities. Myerhoff, *pace* Turner, also acknowledges a 'dark side' of communitas; this transformative experience may provoke intense feelings of self-loss and rapture (ibid).

Theatre, it has long been argued in anthropology, was created out of ritual. Both theatre and ritual incarnate a desire for a Turnerian 'communitas' (Schechner 1988). Hastrup – drawing on Schechner (1985) – unravels this 'liminal' property of theatrical performance, as an articulate 'double agency' on behalf of its actor (1998: 38-39). Patrick's performative 'training' entails this Schechnerian principle. He is himself and he isn't. He is always 'in-between' himself and a role. This double agency merges the 'being' and the 'becoming' of Patrick as a performer. In his performance lies the basis for agency. Patrick is calling us:

À bientôt,
Let's play!

Notes

1. Nietzsche's philosophical anti-system allows 'inventive' rebellious social actors to emerge (Deleuze 1985: 142). Nietzsche's nomad *in situ*, always acts outside institutions or any other form of imposed re-codifications, be they private or public. In Nietzsche's modernity, the process of decodification is totalising. Deleuze's interpretation of Nietzsche's aphoristic writing, which does not correspond to any textual interiority, explores – beyond the transgressive nature of Nietzschean thinking – the subject/agency that Nietzsche inspires; she who never 'barter[s] away intensity for mere representations' (ibid.:146). The reader appropriates the fragmented text, his aphorisms rather, by idiosyncratically de-fragmenting it. The reader is constantly displaced; yet, this displacement establishes her very uncompromising extreme individuality, her intensity, her 'self'. Nomadism in Nietzschean's anti-theory is a thus a constant 'splitting' act.
2. According to Hallward's reading, Baudiou's 'event' is purely haphazard; the unpredictable result of chance. An event is the opposite of structure that supplies us with repetition; it is the opposite of the expected (Hallward 2003: 114). The event makes us believe that there is the possibility of novelty in being (ibid.). What is in truth encountered through the 'event', is the 'void' of the situation; i.e., the element in this situation that has no 'interest' in preserving the *status quo*. The event sheds light on the void. Therefore every 'event', by highlighting the 'void' - be it existential, emotional or social – is always the sign of a new beginning (ibid. 114–15).
3. In his thinking on the paradoxical concept of mourning, Derrida (1989: 6) claims that 'successful mourning' is when the mourners actually fail to mourn; whereas, he who has been mourned, is essentially 'altered' by the internalisation of this mourning process. Amongst the *Mykoniots*, the dead are never acknowledged; friends are never conceived of as being dead. Thus, failure to mourn, paradoxically appears to succeed because the absent person's presence is likewise prolonged. The notion of mourning is part of Derrida's increasing preoccupation with a set of notions, called *aporias*, 'afflicted' by a contradiction: giving, hospitality, forgiving, mourning. In all these terms, a paradox lurks: the condition of their possibility is at the same time their impossibility.
4. The Mykonian beach occupies a 'liminal zone'. Similar to Shields' Brighton (1991: 82), beyond a site of 'amorality' which emerged historically, first, as a site of Cures and later as a pleasure-dome, the Mykonian beach is symbolically turned into an unoccupied, deterritorialised space. Following the Van Gennepian principle of liminality, Brighton beach was baptised as a liminal space that could accommodate life transitions: the pilgrims believed that they could cure themselves through bathing. Mykonos' cultivated quality of being a liminal space that can accommodate life transitions is, in turn, evident in the much-fetishised communal discourses on metaphysics and self change. The *Mykoniots d'élection* – who through their strong connection with the tourist space serve as 'performers' to the transient visitor – act as the role models for these life transitions. The 'beach farewell' – like a 'staged' tourist performance (*pace* Bruner 2001) – caters to the outsiders' desire to experience the 'wildness' of the *Mykoniots*' soul. At this level, the beach ritual also works as a re-enactment of their existential liminality; the beach represents the space in which liminality can be most effectively acted out.
5. Braidotti 1997: 69.
6. See Gooldin 2003: 43.
7. Irigaray 2004: 30, 109.
8. Paraphrasing Fullagar's epitome on Beauvoir's travel narratives: Patrick's 'desire to travel is also a desire to experience the movement of desire itself' (Fullagar 2001: 303). Beauvoir's experience of 'wonder' perfectly suits the *Mykoniots d'élection*'s (feminist) existential project.
9. Oddly enough, both for the 'outsider', Patrick, and for Melpo Axioti, the indigenous novelist, political and later self-imposed exile, the notion of 'home' – Mykonos in our case – operates more like an 'axiomatic' memory (see Leontis 1999).

Epilogue

10. Formerly, in anthropology, place was conceived as static. But now place – as well as the ethnographic context itself – is in a state of flux. Contemporary notions of identity parallel this fluctuating property of space (cf. Robertson et al. 1994; Trinh T. Minh-ha 1994; Jackson 1995; Ward 2003).
11. Following Turner and Turner (1978), Howe (2001) represents San Francisco 'queer land' as a contemporary example of 'communitas'. For the queer pilgrims, certain districts become a 'queer homeland'. The pilgrims find their place of origin and family home alienating; the family home is for them a place of 'spiritual exile' (ibid.: 53). They don't feel at home 'back home' so they travel to the queer homeland in search of queer authenticity. There is a similar idealised spatial discourse amongst the *Mykoniots*: Mykonos becomes 'home', more than the 'real' home, due to its amorality and tolerance.
12. Waldren 1996: 178.
13. Schieffelin warns us to dismiss an internalised (Aristotelian) logic of theatricality that determines our notion of performance as a mere illusion, a simulacra of 'real life' that dichotomises 'acting' and 'being' (1998: 200).

APPENDIX I
THE PROBLEM OF AGENCY IN THE GREEK ETHNOGRAPHIC SUBJECT

Positioning the *Mykoniots d'élection* in the context of Greek ethnography and anthropological theory

This study is not intended to offer any homogenous statements about '*a* Greek culture'. Rather, it will offer an ethnographic account which reveals cases of 'extreme' individualities within the Greek context, subjects who might deviate from gender and self-cultural stereotypes. Greek ethnography has failed so far to account for 'individual' self-identities; and by 'individual' I do not mean de-culturalised or de-traditionalised. My analytical aim is to promote contextualised synthetic subjectivities.

There are several ways to deal with the problem of 'classifying' my informants within the corpus of Greek ethnography. For instance, one could locate alternative discourses on self and gender in the 'margins' of Greek culture (Papataxiarchis 1992a: 72). Alternatively, we could incorporate the whole rhetoric of the *Mykoniots*' otherness into a broader cultural pattern based on a discourse of difference. This discourse is ethnographically represented either as masculine (gender) performativity, exemplified in the notion of *egoismos*, self-regard (see Herzfeld 1985: 11), or as a 'secretive' national pride stemming from Greek culture's 'intellectual inheritance'. The latter is a discourse of cultural 'superiority' based on a 'glorious' past (cf. Herzfeld 1986: 5).

My aim is to resist identity classifications based on cultural stereotypes of any sort. Even Herzfeld's most tempting and sophisticated models of *disemia* and cultural intimacy, a term employed in order to alleviate the concept of nationalism, are unsatisfactory (Herzfeld 1987, 1997a). Cultural explanations of this sort remain essentialist, and in any case are incompatible with the hybrid context of my ethnographic inquiry.

Instead, one could turn to theories of consumption that offer alternative systems of classification and identification, and promote an aesthetic and reflexive subjectivity. Nevertheless, these theories have not yet dealt adequately with the issue of agency.

Yet, there is another problem concerning individual agency beyond the plurality of positions that a subject can acquire. In anthropological writing, the type of agency that accounts for a conscious and creative self has been undertheorised. In Greek ethnography, issues like reflexivity, subjectivity and individual agency are rarely addressed. Where is, and furthermore, what is, the 'proper' subject in anthropology? Many scholars have attempted to challenge anthropological theory by tackling this question (Callaway 1992: 33; Cohen 1992: 225; Okely 1992: 9; Cohen 1994: 22; Moore 1994: 4; Cohen and Rapport 1995: 11; Fernandez 1995; Rapport 1997).

The problem of agency is complicated since the anthropological subject only realises herself in connection to a series of subjectivities. The point is not simply how much agency we decide to give to the subject, since the ethnographic subject is only realised through a text and its author. To contextualise the question of agency, one should also ask how much agency should be given to the actor/author and to her act of interpretation,[1] how much autonomy to the text itself,[2] as well as, how much agency the ethnographer should give to her own self as an essential tool of reflexive analysis (Okely and Callaway 1992). This chain of theoretical enquiry could extend to questioning how convincing theories of praxis (Bourdieu 1990) and structuration (Giddens 1984) are, when although initially taking into account the aesthetically reflexive subject (the former theory marginally and the latter more directly), they both allow little space for creativity and change.

However, a stream of British anthropologists maintains that ethnographers should rid themselves of Durkheimian assumptions and pay attention to and recreate discourses about conscious 'individual' informants. According to this innovative school of thought, focusing on the discourse of the consciously reflexive self rather than assuming that the ethnographic actor is a mere 'representative' of a fixed social category might bring back to the analysis the useful but overlooked concept of individual creativity (cf. Cohen 1994; Cohen and Rapport 1995; Rapport 1997). Turning back to my own ethnographic case, I strongly felt that I had to deal with the problem of self-creativity, since I was confronted with 'subjects' who were constantly transforming their discourses and selves.[3] In the early stages of writing, I experienced great difficulty in transforming my informants into anthropological subjects. For me, they were primarily Hercules, Angelos, Artemis, Eleonora. They were 'personified' subjects, and, moreover, agents of their own self-creation. Their individual identities preceded their various collective ones, and classifying them under a single label seemed an impossible task. However, this difficulty proved, I hope, to be theoretically fruitful.

Searching for the subject in Greek ethnography

> This section will inquire into an already established syncretic cultural model employed by theorists who are concerned with Greek ethnography. This type of syncretism as an absolute cultural model could be potentially criticised for leading to cultural essentialism and for treating the notion of culture in a monolithic manner. The need to question this model becomes an imperative when notions of cultural syncretism are reflected by hybrid subjects. The theoretical predicament is syncretism versus agency.

> Like the shepherds I was studying, I deformed a social and cultural convention: this was the ethnographic style of my own intellectual lineage, that of my teacher (Campbell 1964), who had in effect deformed Evans-Pritchard's (1940) model, designed for the presentation of an African society, by applying it to a European one. (Herzfeld 1997a: 23–24)

Herzfeld, a pioneer of Greek ethnography, 'excuses' his past ethnographic invention (1985) as a 'performance' that 'aestheticised' social relations. He further attempts to trace his ethnographic model back to its intellectual roots. In principle, I accept Herzfeld's assumption that all ethnography is, anyway, a performance. Nevertheless, I shall pick upon Herzfeld's self-criticism to retrace the notion of performance which is, within the framework of Greek ethnography, subjugated to cultural/ethical codes of honour and shame, gender roles and male performativity, as well as 'social poetics'. I will examine notions of self-identity in recent Greek ethnography in order to unravel the uneasy relationship between a 'Greek' subject and the overarching notion of cultural performativity.

The purpose of this line of enquiry is to contextualise my anthropological subjects who happen to be both 'Greeks' and 'different'. If I were to follow the performative tradition of authors like Campbell, Herzfeld, du Boulay and Danforth with reference to gender,[4] I would have great difficulty in incorporating my informants' 'performativity', which presents itself as an unclassified, cross-gender and aesthetic performativity, conditional on the absence of fixed gender roles. So, instead of deforming social and cultural categories, I decided to distort 'cultural selves': my anthropological subjects were left unclassified. It would have been difficult to have done otherwise. Discourses on group identity, as well as self-narratives, were constructed upon a rhetoric of inconsistency, otherness and subjective fragmentation. Initially, I saw them as a collection of forgotten 'freaks', who, nevertheless, seemed to cope very well in the post-modern tourist space. When I originally set out to study notions of style and consumption, and especially the group's relation to addictive substances, it was not only their 'marginality' or their 'avant-garde' consciousness that made them different from a conventional anthropological representation of a 'Greek' self. Rather, it was the fact that they have coexisted, and survived, not as aesthetic remnants of a subculture, but as active and adaptable agents in the ever-changing hybridic space. They were actively transforming themselves and their discourses rather than confining themselves to a 'subcultural' identity. Finally, they continued to be a 'group' consisting of 'Greeks' who were brought up and educated amongst other Greeks, but they were neither a 'uniform group' who shared a 'traditional' notion of locality, nor did they belong to a common social category.

Initially, the subject matter of my research seemed inconsistent with the larger cultural context of a 'Greek' ethnography. My informants clearly deviated from the rigid cultural representation of a 'Greek-male-shepherd-nationalist', and nor did they fit the gender prototype of a 'Greek-oppressed-shamed-female' who had hidden domestic authority or, at best, a public performative power role.

The question I asked myself was how did recent Greek ethnography account for a more syncretic identity? And the answer was, largely, by applying a homogenous and culturally specific model of syncretism, which disguised any idiosyncratic manifestations of fragmentation.

To contextualise ambivalent discourses, conflicting subject positions and inconsistent cultural practices, Herzfeld has invented the term *disemia*, a binary and often incompatible rhetoric, which according to the author defines 'Greek' identity (Herzfeld 1987). The equivocal model of *disemia* reflects the habitual way in which the Greeks have responded to their modern political predicament, namely their position on the 'margins' of Europe, both as its spiritual 'ancestor' and its political 'pariah' (Herzfeld 1997a: 18). Herzfeld finds at many levels of practice a consistent pattern of pairs of oppositions, which originate from this historical and political dilemma, and mark Greek identity. This polarity is embodied in several conflicting models of Greekness: the Classical cultural prototype (Hellenism) versus a Byzantine/Orientalist one (*Romiosini*); the official, pro-Enlightenment version of Greek history in contradistinction to rhetorics that refute a Eurocentric model of ethnic identity, and numerous, analogous pairs of opposing discourses, which Herzfeld astutely calls 'embarrassments of ambiguity'. The tension between the two sides, *Romiosini* and Hellenism, composes according to Herzfeld the dialectic of Greek identity and is 'linguistically embodied in the model of *diglossia*' (Herzfeld 1987: 114). According to the author, *disemia* as a conceptual tool is a semiotic term that accounts for multiplicity and balances the phenomenological cultural antinomy between self-knowledge and self-presentation (ibid.: 122). He maintains that in this cultural pattern there is a constant manipulation of meanings, the so-called 'political economy of the rhetoric' (1995: 130). Rather than being handicapped replicas reciting a rhetoric, subjects 'recognise a reservoir of extenuating formulae' (ibid.). In his later writings, Herzfeld replaces the concept of *disemia* with the concept of 'cultural intimacy', as an 'antidote to the formalism of cultural nationalism'

(Herzfeld 1997a: 14). Within Herzfeld's concept of cultural ambiguity, binary oppositions are not committed to their respective semantic categories, and in any case they are not manifestations of a stable set of ideologies. The model is intentionally flexible in order to accommodate the Greek self as part of a global universe. In this sense, Herzfeld treats nationalism as an effort by these cultural actors to find their 'own' space in a global and impersonal universe.[5]

Herzfeld's contribution to Greek ethnography is manifold. He abolished a great deal of cultural essentialising, i.e., the myth of the 'special' properties that the 'Mediterranean' people shared, epitomised by the analytical category of 'honour-and-shame' societies (Herzfeld 1980, 1987). Although Herzfeld stressed this problem in Mediterranean ethnography, he cannot himself escape cultural stereotyping in his own work.

The pattern of cultural stereotyping persists through the Greek specialists' refusal to deal with the problem of subjectivity. This is evident from the fact that the debate on self-identity in Greek ethnography is mainly fixed to binary gender roles (cf. Papataxiarchis 1992a; Loizos and Papataxiarchis 1991b). The post-structuralist subject has been largely overlooked. The Greek engendered being has not yet departed from gender role-playing to meet gender or subject performativity. The Greek self is portrayed as completed through marriage (Papataxiarchis 1992a: 70) and thus, kinship seems to be the organising principle of 'personhood' (Loizos and Papataxiarchis 1991b: 5–6). Additionally, by establishing an agonistic identity, the actor is placed against her/his 'eternal' rival, i.e., the opposite sex, and thus acquires a self. Here we can refer to engendered discourses of resistance manifested through transcendental male commensality (Herzfeld 1985; Papataxiarchis 1992b: 209–50), or through the female public or private expression of a 'feminine substance' that negotiates sentiments (Caraveli 1986; Seremetakis 1991).

To recapitulate, sources of Greek identity in the above-quoted ethnographies are, either 'big' structures like kinship and gender roles (with a strong emphasis on the performance of masculinity), or 'big' cultural stereotypes of an indigenous and idiosyncratic version of syncretism that 'does not fit comfortably into the duality of Europeans and Others' (Herzfeld 1987: 2).

According to Stewart, for the Greeks to recognise their 'syncretism' was ironically 'an engaged nationalist stance' (Stewart 1994: 140). In other words, accepting that Greeks have two parallel traditions, and consequently two conflicting or complementary selves or sources that influenced their ethnic identity, was their ironic resistance to an imposed marginal historical positioning in the 'developed' world and signified the emergence of a local nationalism. This historically charged semantic *diglossia* nurtured a cultural identity of two 'natures'. Herzfeld's expansionist notion of *disemia* attempts to holistically account for conflicting discourses in the Greek context, thus excluding any alternative model of exegesis. An overriding principle of cultural ambivalence, like a skeleton key, 'unlocks' gender roles, political discourses and occupational 'deviousness'.

Appendix

Faubion (1993) attempts a shift from this model: the subjects of his study are chosen not as impersonal beings, but rather as personified members of an Athenian elite. His informants have acquired individuality in depth. Faubion manages to establish anthropological subjects with a social and most importantly a personal profile (artists, gay activists and the attractive identity bricolage of Maro). Faubion's elites and gays bring different discourses to the front of the ethnographic stage. But in reality, all these distinct individuals are suffering from the same cultural disease: 'historical constructivism'. In the most serious attempt in Greek ethnography to portray a multi-subjective identity, exemplified in the portrait of the aforementioned heroine, Maro, this multiplicity is not personified (ibid.: 166–83). Faubion makes it clear that Maro is a construction, a bricolage of several personalities. But would it not be different if Maro was a real embodied character? It would certainly be an opportunity to present ethnographically an unmarried, mature professional and an occasional 'adolescent'. In other words, Faubion would have accounted for an embodied corpus of conflicting subjectivities and discourses rather than the mere quotation of a series of conflicting subject positions. Faubion builds his sophisticated argument on Maro's culturally syncretic self without realising that he is in essence stripping her of her identity (ibid.: 183). Although a very refreshing piece of ethnography, all of Maro's 'atypical' discourse is set to reveal yet another historical constructivism descended from the Cretan animal 'thieves' who steal 'to befriend', and the apprentice carpenter who 'steals skill' to become an established 'professional'.

There are many 'nationalist' discourses in modern Greece. But I seriously doubt whether all 'syncretism' is associated with a single cultural model. The multiplicity of the subject cannot be subjugated to the 'poetics' of a nation state. A model that opts to account for a hybrid identity should be highly synthetic and go beyond a one-dimensional cultural or religious based syncretism.

Stewart actually attempts to offer another dimension to the syncretic cultural model of Greek identity (cf. Stewart 1994). In their volume, Stewart and Shaw (1994) propose that the notion of syncretism should be liberated from a bias acquired by its multiple and controversial historical use. The authors attempt to reconstruct the notion of syncretism as a valuable conceptual tool for anthropological theorising. The notion is employed in order to scan through similar political uses of both syncretist and anti-syncretist cultural discourses. In their case, the model does not exclude recent cultural theories of hybridity, multiculturalism and so forth. Instead, they propose a more synthetic model that restores the notion of syncretism to cultural analysis. Stewart's personal contribution to the volume (1994) expands the notion of syncretism in the Greek context, from its rhetorical use to a pragmatic one.

Stewart, in his work on the supernatural (1989), accounts for a culturally established identity model searching through Greek selves which are acquired (more syncretically) through lifestyles and identity references related to the sphere of consumption. His model for a 'syncretic' Greek identity, following Bourdieu's

(1984) prototype of social groups strategically affiliated to reversible aesthetic preferences, appears to be more flexible. Opposed to a monolithic identity based on self-reproduced social structures like class, ethnicity or gender, a syncretic model of identity which incorporates elements of cultural consumption, appears to be closer to a polythetic subject, since consumption could be cited as a mechanism which credits choice and thus some agency to the consumer. Stewart's 'syncretic' cultural model scans through a set of reversible discourses on the supernatural in both urban and rural contexts, where the respective social actors change their taste patterns. In line with Bourdieu, he finds that in the Naxos countryside, the locals choose to employ rational and 'official' discourses, abolishing 'local' beliefs about the supernatural as a 'sign of backwardness' and turn pagan rituals into folklore (Stewart 1989: 79, 89). On the other hand, a growing number of Athenians are becoming 'irrational', so to speak, fetishising a wide range of 'imported' practices associated with the supernatural and employing 'mystical forms of explanation' like astrology, meditation, parapsychology, as well as previously obsolete discourses that re-establish traditional notions of the supernatural (Stewart 1989: 91).

I believe that Stewart's inverse model as a game of class 'distinction' is still problematic, since it does not account for more idiosyncratic modes of 'aesthetic' action and consumption choice. Nevertheless, his work signifies a departure from an all-embracing and culturally biased model of difference and offers a reading of Greek culture which could potentially look for differences within it, thus escaping a monolithic cultural 'syncretism'.

A similar approach is employed by Argyrou, who incorporates aesthetic elements in his analysis of a class-based distinction game amongst Greek Cypriots (Argyrou 1996). Argyrou portrays the different class groups through a description of their respective wedding ceremonies and spaces. Unfortunately, in this work the ethnographic subject is characterised by another identity dualism of modernisation versus traditionality. The struggle is inscribed in social actors, who at least manifest some class-based difference in their aesthetic patterns. These aesthetic patterns are, nevertheless, consistent: all middle-class people perform one kind of wedding and all 'villagers' another.

Up to now, I have intentionally taken a negative line in this literature review in order to (over)stress the ethnographic assumption that there is a consistent cultural pattern behind the plurality of discourses evident in Greek ethnography. In this book, I have to account for individuals who display extremely diverse and inconsistent patterns of social action as well as conflicting subjectivities. Yet, as 'Greek' social actors they must have their place in a 'Greek' ethnographic reality.

My research was carried out on a cosmopolitan Greek island. My nomadic informants were largely one-time or current urban inhabitants who alternatively became incorporated into an ex-rural, but currently cosmopolitan space. A persistent methodological question emerges: is my sample of people so 'different' as to be considered an exception to the cultural pattern? Did I misjudge their rhetorics of 'difference'? Or, were these rhetorics, following Herzfeld, just a cultural pattern after all? Alternatively, should the subjects of a 'Greek' ethnography be so dramatically homogenised? Why should we stick to a narrow identity definition based on a spatial distinction between urban and rural in a globalised world reality?

Gender and agency

Recent ethnographic material on gender has introduced some changes into the aforementioned theoretical setting. Theorists who concentrated on gender, frequently influenced by a politicised feminist discourse, deal with their ethnographic subjects more reflexively. Their reflexive preoccupation with the 'self' grants the anthropological subject elements of 'intersubjectivity' (cf. Dubisch 1995) and their model vis-à-vis a traditional self-identity treats the subject as capable of strategically performing alternative, although still category specific, gender roles (Cowan 1991; Papataxiarchis 1992a; Dubisch 1995). The works I refer to here, are influenced by anthropologists who have brought the 'anthropological experience' back into play. With an occasional reflexive overtone, they have attempted to question the binary opposition between the 'empirical' and the 'theoretical' as estranged realms of knowledge (Dubisch 1995). This ethnographic stream is influenced by ethnographies like Abu-Lughod's *Veiled Sentiments*, or Kondo's *Crafting Selves*, whose authors promoted an anthropology of the particular, according to which people are seen as individuals and not as mere categories (cf. Abu-Lughod 1986, 1993; Kondo 1990). Individuals' 'emotions' have become theoretical. The 'passion' in this new style of ethnography aims at alternative 'expressions' of identity within cultural contexts (cf. Behar 1996, 2003). Recent Greek 'queer' ethnography (Kantsa 2000; Kirtsoglou 2004) is illustrative of this reflexive/emotional tendency; here, alternative roles are consciously performed by Greek women and gender stereotypes thus transgressed.

More particularly, Dubisch's (1995) text involves herself and her pathos. Her ethnography is dedicated to the observation of other 'suffering' women who perform a pilgrimage to the Virgin Mary. According to Dubisch's interpretation, these Greek women, beyond their traditional gender role, perform an expressive public power role instead of a latent domestic one. Her informants acquire in the text 'personified' discourses. Dubisch concentrates on female performances in public spaces, especially in the context of pilgrimage.

The aforementioned type of anthropological discourse enables the reader to depart from a 'caricatured' cultural subject to a more syncretic one. The model is far from achieving a coherent theory of a conscious and 'syncretic' self, but, nevertheless, it incorporates an informant that has ceased to be another 'predictable' case from a homogenised category.

Cowan's ethnography is another important contribution to this line of thought, mostly because, in a more flexible model, she pays attention to and attempts to incorporate atypical gender discourses. Cowan highlights the existence of alternative female discourses in the Greek context by ethnographically processing the discourse of 'the girls' in a small Greek town (Cowan 1992). She criticises anthropological discourses that tend to 'homogenise' categories and fail to listen for what is in reality offered as an alternative discourse (ibid.: 148n).

The new style of ethnography I refer to here concentrates on gender in a different way from earlier ethnographies. On the island of Mytilini, Papataxiarchis (1992b) accounts for less 'agonistic' relations among the local males in the context of the coffee shop. His model clearly deviates from a fixed, male gender role, which portrays the subject as agonistic and flamboyant about his masculinity (cf. Herzfeld 1985). *Egoismos* (self-regard), male 'difference' and distinction is not the main issue in drinking commensality and sentiment sharing performed by males in the 'world' of the coffee house. The 'expression' of emotions (a characteristic hitherto attributed to a female gender role) is established among men (Papataxiarchis 1992b: 241).

In the second chapter of this book, the reader is introduced to a party of Greek males who share a rhetoric of 'authenticity' and 'difference'. They are portrayed as promoting a discourse of 'experience' that revolves around issues of 'recklessness' and creates an antagonistic game of distinction vis-à-vis group membership. At first glance, this performative model appears to be similar to Herzfeld's 'agonistic' masculinity. The *Mykoniots d'élection* are represented as desiring to belong to an invented 'local' category of legendary examples of 'some' male recklessness. Yet, this rhetoric, in my opinion, is a very conscious exhibition of a simulated gender 'persona'. Performative gender roles, in this case, reveal only provisional identifications. For example, a 'male' *Mykoniot* can employ a 'female' discourse and later on switch to a 'macho' one. In the *Mykoniots*' case, cross-gender rhetorics and performances of 'difference' are political. They are provisional identity choices. Difference is not exhausted in gender performativity or performance in general. In our case, difference is primarily experiential; it is a provisional performance lived through as a part of a creative and idiosyncratic self.

Trying to abolish the 'Zorba' stereotype

What made Herzfeld's work so pioneering during the late eighties was the fact that he challenged a discipline that had supposedly rejected exoticism in principle, but, nevertheless, managed to place Greek ethnography on its periphery. The 'marginal' status of Greek culture depended in essence on 'the Eurocentric ideology rather than in anything intrinsic itself' (Herzfeld 1987: 7).

Later, Herzfeld criticised his earlier work for participating in the essentialising of a Greek 'performative' and 'eccentric', but in reality 'calculative', self (Herzfeld

1997a: 22). Disclaiming the 'Zorbaesque' cultural prototype, he proceeded to a seemingly flexible post-structuralist cultural schema. But in reality, all he claims is that 'Greeks' have culturally and personally conflicting discourses because they are Greeks. The inconsistent rhetorics described in Herzfeld's ethnography are not justified theoretically, but only as a type of cultural survivalist strategy. The idea of a cultural *habitus* which justifies any inconsistent pattern only succeeds in reproducing an artificial cultural reality of lobotomised subjectivities.

The asymmetry that Herzfeld's schema attributes to Greek identity is welcomed, yet not as a culturally specific characteristic, but as a more sophisticated and all-inclusive schema that goes beyond simple notions of 'the nation'. To claim that concrete cultures produce concrete cultural identities would be an oversimplification. The project of a cultural globalisation has introduced new classificatory strategies that apply cross-culturally and most importantly translocally. I, therefore, propose that anthropological theorising should accept that global processes have affected particular localities (Fardon 1995). As Fardon rightly suggests, the terms global and local 'write off one another through mutual provocation' (ibid.: 2). In this 'new' cultural reality, the question of creativity in social theory becomes a central one.

The *Mykoniots d'élection* are constantly in transit, or rather they feel constantly in transit. The mapping of the space which they chose to occupy and use to reflect their identities is semiotically versatile. In the symbolic mapping of the transitional space there is a corner for every cross-category. Still, this is supposed to be a 'Greek' Cycladic island, inhabited by 'traditional' locals and invaded by 'modern' tourists. My ethnographic experience showed me that such a schema is monolithic. In the case of the hybrid group of the *Mykoniots d'élection*, the fact that different subjects 'occupy' the same space does not establish that they share the same (concept of) locality, or a common cultural identity.

'Greeks' in a global setting

In his more recent work, Herzfeld attempts to theoretically renegotiate 'Greek' identity as part of both local and global processes (Herzfeld 1995). For him, the very fact that several nationalisms have emerged, shows that social actors' struggle to find their own 'personal' space in a world that turns out to be a homogenised (globalised) cultural setting. He examines his concept of *disemia* in a challenging globalised context. In such a context 'Greeks', by means of the media, frequent travelling and so forth, reflect their 'Greekness' in the Others' representation of it. He re-establishes his *disemic* model on yet another discursive and political inconsistency: Greeks employ one type of discourse for themselves among themselves, and another (for themselves) when among 'others'. Likewise, he constructs the 'international' image of an ethnic self through another *disemic* model. We can trace, according to Herzfeld, a conscious self-stereotyping at an (inter)national level.

My initial objection is that, in my case, the *Mykoniots d'élection* display a translocal self. Their identity discourse has not a *di-semic* but a *poly-semic* inconsistency. In the tourist space, they are occasional identity partners with a series of multicultural 'others': the indigenous, the tourists, the permanent exogenous residents, the nomadic travellers and so forth. The 'self' of the *Mykoniots*, as well as of the diverse groups who 'survive' the polysemic Mykonian setting, converses with the 'other' in a democratic fashion. The 'self' is constantly in a state of being formed. Conversely, for Herzfeld the identity model is a unified one. There is a collective/national identity that worships the 'social poetics' of belonging. The Greeks' political economy of rhetoric is presented in the form of a collective ability to immediately recognise another Greek in an international and 'alien' context. This ability is regarded as an art, or rather, as a 'cultural' quality invested with a 'mystical' force (Herzfeld 1995: 125).

One could criticise Herzfeld for not incorporating aesthetics into his analysis of the reflexive recognition of affinity. Instead, he treats this reflexive ability as a cultural project. Herzfeld's Greeks easily switch between nationalist/communal and individualist discourses. This discursive *disemia* applies equally to divisions between notions of 'Greekness' and 'otherness', as well as divisions within the single category 'Greekness'. Herzfeld's *disemic* model appears to give flexible identities to his 'Greek' actors, but the *disemic* model can only apply to the self at the cultural level and does not account for alternative and ambivalent subjectivities within.

Herzfeld invents a cultural formula that is defined by a versatile discourse, which is, nevertheless, confined to the benefit of a political and localised self. In Herzfeld's analysis of the self, all alliances are provisional, as in feminist post-structuralist analysis of the subject 'all locations are provisional, held in abeyance' (Moore 1994: 2). The great difference between the two theoretical streams is that, in Herzfeld's model, provisionality is a culturally dictated self-strategy. The self here is a socio-cultural *actor*. In the post-structuralist model, provisionality is a constant self-reflexive process. The self in this instance is a multiple-constituted *subject*.

The *disemic* model is applied in Greek ethnography when conflicting discourses have to be theoretically accounted for. Nevertheless, what Herzfeld's theory cannot account for is the conflicting discourses of transcultural and invented identity categories, and alternative identity definitions beyond ethnic or social classifications.

I have expanded my argument on Herzfeld's *disemic* schema, in order to clarify my analytical stance with reference to my informants' performative and discursive inconsistency. Fragments of Herzfeld's representation of a 'Greek' cultural discourse (as opposed to the *disemic* model itself) can be cited in this ethnographic account. The *Mykoniots d'élection* occasionally employ a nationalist discourse, an Orientalist, a Eurocentric, or an individualist and syncretic one. Yet, the ethnographic subjects of this study equally share alternative discourses of belonging to an aesthetic group, as well as to an invented cultural space. Unlike Herzfeld's actors, the *Mykoniots* are not politically committed to a cultural project. In fact, their discourse, if culturally contextualised, is apolitical. Their model of identification is intersubjective but also an open-ended (anarchic) one, at least at the level of discourse. This can be seen most clearly with regard to their invented rituals (described in detail in chapters 4 and 5).

Syncretic and not disemic selves

The *Mykoniots d'élection* could be seen as the epitome of (religious) syncretism as described by Stewart (1989). This is exemplified in their invented rituals, metaphysical discourses and religious preferences. For instance, they might visit Mount Athos;[6] they might also practise meditation, and occasionally employ pagan neo-Orthodox and monistic religious discourses. Thus, their discursive pattern and praxis vis-à-vis the ritualistic and metaphysical is consistently inconsistent. Nevertheless, the term syncretism, as contextualised by Stewart and Shaw (1994), cannot be confined to religion, for the simple reason that the religious, the social and the political are not necessarily clearly demarcated.[7] In this sense, the authors contend, theoretical notions like cultural hybridity, or bricolage can be sufficiently represented by a wider (rather than narrowly religious) ascription of the term syncretism (ibid.: 10).

Another version of culturally eclectic syncretism, according to Stewart (1994: 141), is the way Greeks employ both an official church discourse and an antagonistic 'pagan' and popular one about the supernatural. This eclectic syncretism has been culturally 'justified' by specific historical and political circumstances. It was invented in order to strategically accommodate opposing discourses: one pagan and unofficial, and the other, sophisticated, authoritarian and official. In an earlier article, Stewart observed that within this syncretic model there is an interesting class-based inversion of aesthetic preferences in relation to the supernatural (1989). These preferences shift between symbolic territories of discourse about the supernatural, to strategically display class difference. As mentioned above, his Naxiot informants are portrayed as having largely abandoned pagan discourses on the supernatural in public and having shifted to an official and 'rational' discourse in order to avoid getting socially denounced as 'retrogressive'.

Neighbouring Mykonos is an island almost exclusively subsidised by tourism, with a considerable number of exogenous inhabitants, a large number of seasonal tourist invaders, and a different socio-economic reality to that of Naxos. For this reason, discourses on the supernatural in the polysemantic tourist space are different to those of nearby Naxos.

Appendix

Mykonos developed into a tourist attraction, from the late thirties, due to the reputation of the nearby archaeological site of Delos. Mykonians engineered a sophisticated way of representing local folklore and promoting discourses of 'indigenousness' vis-à-vis a pagan supernatural. This is also manifested in the elaborate discourse of the *Mykoniots d'élection* about spatial supernatural properties that is described at length in chapter 4.

The *Mykoniots*' (trans)local cultural pattern means they consume official Orthodox dogma, Eastern esotericism, theological monism, post-modern syncretism, paganism, traditional local discourses on the supernatural, as well as nihilistic philosophical discourses. The aforementioned discourses are not strictly territorialised and they are exchangeable between the local groups. In nineties Mykonos, there may not be a single local pagan discourse as in Stewart's ethnographic case of Naxos (1991), the place-myth, however, is charged with a complex system of metaphysical discourses. Actually, the coexistence of multiple and seemingly inconsistent metaphysical discourses is recorded, not only among the *Mykoniots*, but also amongst the many different aesthetic groups and social categories of the island. Syncretic metaphysical discourses, then, are a shared practice, rather than an element of aesthetic differentiation. This discursive and cultural 'assimilation' is not a pre-existing but an emerging one; it is an 'assimilation' in process.

Finally, the issue of monosemantically translating the syncretic profile of the tourist space into a latent 'nationalist' discourse, encouraged in a Mykonian rhetoric of spatial and aesthetic otherness is, I maintain, irrelevant, since the syncretic elements of 'local' consumption embrace a wider context of cultural semantics. Consequently, the rhetoric in question cannot fit into a strategic and narrowly 'localist' or 'nationalist' attitude. If syncretism is strategic, it is so in ontological, lifestyle and survivalist contexts alike and not as a one-dimensional cultural project.

Notes

1. Cf. with Ricoeur's notion of narrative identity (1992: 114, 152).
2. Cf. with the Derridean desire and imperative to deconstruct/reappropriate a text in order to politically downplay the authority of its producer (Spivak 1974: lxxvii).
3. I ethnographically explore this strategy in detail in chapter 3 which focuses on their self-narratives.
4. For a detailed review of the literature, see Papataxiarchis 1992a.
5. Herzfeld shares with us many instances of his urban and rural fieldwork where the *disemic* model for explaining action is rhetorically employed. For example, the Cretan animal thieves he describes, explain how they 'steal' in order to become equal (cf. Herzfeld 1985). Similarly, a carpenter's apprentice is 'stealing' the skill from his master, the craftsman (who is reluctant to teach him), in order to 'qualify' eventually for future partnership (Herzfeld 1995: 137). Needless to say, in different contexts, Greeks employ discourses based on Christian dogma

Appendix

which attribute unethical connotations to stealing. Thus, Herzfeld ascribes to the Greeks a strategically employed 'deviousness' that, I think, could lead to further essentialising.
6. Mount Athos, 'the essence of orthodox monasticism', consists of a cluster of coenobitic monasteries located on the Athos peninsula. The monastic community of Athos, today 'a state within the Greek state', was officially recognised by the Byzantines in 883 (Hellier 1996).
7. As Dubisch contends, the religious, the social and the recreational are closely bound in Greek life (Dubisch 1995: 106).

Appendix II
The emergence of the sensual post-tourist: consuming 'cultures', multisubjective selves and (trans)local spaces

The act of tourism is essentially post-modern. Urry states that 'tourism is prefiguratively post-modern, because of its particular combination of the visual, the aesthetic and the popular' (Urry 1990: 87). If one accepts Urry's contention, the project of decodifying my group's *habitus* requires admitting that the *Mykoniots d'élection* act and live in a predominantly post-modern setting.

Tourist spaces: a 'staged' performance?

The first attempts to theoretically contextualise the emerging mass of modern travellers, i.e., the tourists, placed the act of tourism in a structure similar to that of pilgrimage. Tourism was seen as the contemporary form of pilgrimage. Like the pilgrim, a subject already familiar to anthropological investigation, who pursues a normative anti-structure (similar to Turner's *communitas*) and a new form of ritual participation based more on personal choice than on organised 'tradition', the tourist, as alternative pilgrim, performs a new kind of the *rite de passage* in search of the 'sacred', the exotic, the tranformative experience, the 'authentic' (MacCannell 1976). 'A tourist is half pilgrim' (Turner and Turner 1978: 20). Urry (1990), in his review of theoretical approaches to the study of tourism, shows that soon after the invasion of this new type of pilgrim, the so-called tourists in search of authenticity, the indigenous actors of the tourist spaces organised a 'staged authenticity' (to protect the 'locals' from the outsiders' intrusion). The 'tourist

Appendix

gaze' ironically ended up corrupting the initial object of desire, namely, the 'authentic' performances of cultural 'others' (Urry 1990: 9). The notion of performativity lies at the core of an emerging literature on tourism (see Cohen 1979; Schechner 1988; Adler 1989; Crang 1997; Perkins and Thorns 2001; Graburn and Barthel-Bouchier 2001; Edensor 2001; Bruner 2001; Shepherd 2003; Cabezas 2004; Damer 2004; Hurley and Trimarco 2004). This type of theoretical dialogue though is challenged by theories which promote 'difference' rather than 'authenticity' as the organising factor of tourism, building on ideas like Turner and Turner's 'liminoid' status of the tourist (see Shields 1991). 'Difference', or so it seems, is the object of this new tourist gaze (Urry 1990: 11; Graburn 1978).[1]

In his anthropological volume on tourism, Boissevain (1996) shifts the focus of our attention to the subject position of those who actually act and 'perform' in these tourist spaces, rather than simply being the object of the 'gaze'. Embarking on the established notion of 'staged authenticity', he is interested in exploring the 'performances' and experiences of those to whom the sociology of tourism has paid little attention: the host cultures and the 'stage setters' of the tourist *attraction* (Boissevain 1996: 1). Apart from the 'mobile' body of entrepreneurs, and all those who service the tourist trade in whom the corpus of ethnography has shown little or no interest, there is the 'stable' group of 'locals', whose actions and practices Boissevain's volume attempts to address. First of all, as the author claims, locals 'use space differently'. This can be understood as a counter-strategy employed by the 'indigenous' against the invasion of tourism, and especially the 'cultural tourism' sold in recent years to a mass market (cf. Boissevain 1996: 8).

In 'cultural tourism', the object of desire is local culture, folklore, somebody else's everyday life. Boissevain offers an analysis which places the 'invaded' local subjects in a position to protect their localised life. Following MacCannell's (1976) use of the Goffmanesque terms 'front-stages' and 'backstages', he detects an indigenous organisation of resistance to the tourist penetrators in search of authenticity and to their subsequent desire to discover the locals' 'back-regions'. The tourist gaze's desire to penetrate those 'back-regions' is the characteristic of the ethnographic material in Boissevain's volume: the editor's work on Maltese communities is indicative of this tendency. The whole volume revolves around strategies of resistance. Probably the most interesting among them is the practice of a staged 'back-region', or, in other words, of a staged 'staged-authenticity', an elaborate technique directed and rehearsed by the 'indigenous' in order both to protect themselves and profit from the tourist economy.

Damer's (2004) ethnographic account of the tourist setting on the island of Symi further departs from a monolithic MacCannellesque 'staged' performativity. Instead, Damer urges us to see the performative element of tourism as a crafted dramaturgy, an improvisational performance (*pace* Edensor 2001) which entails an interactive element on behalf of both the 'faceless tourist' and her cultural decodifier, the 'local performer'. In this Schechnerian mode of interactive play, 'sincere local performances' can also take place (Damer 2004: 218). For example, Damer portrays the 'happenings' in Zorba's tourist taverna in order to illustrate a transgression from a MacCannellesque 'front-stage' and 'backstage' scenario. In Zorba's taverna a performance is orchestrated by its owner; when Zorba is in the right mood – usually after some drinking session – he alone or together with his cronies will start playing Greek music, sliding into performative personas of singing and dancing. This 'spontaneous' mode of visual entertainment – conscientiously performed for the tourist 'as an extra' to a romantic dinner after the beach – acts as a sign of a Goffmanesque 'backstage'. At last, the anonymous tourist is offered access to a more 'sincere' interaction with the local host, where he serves and performs at the same time for the tourist, while simultaneously personally unwinding. The interactional space created, in turn, becomes the site of the locals' free entertainment: they come to enjoy Zorba's dance, his interactive performance; thus turning Zorba's taverna into a local theatre (ibid.: 219). Needless to say, tourists feel excited to be invited 'backstage'.

Damer, departing from a dichotomous strategy which divides hosts and guests, introduces 'improvising' in a more idiosyncratic encounter between the tourist and the local. Thus, the boundaries between what can be defined as 'authentic' and what can be 'staged' are blurred. Within this improvised dramaturgy, that Damer calls the 'social dialectics' of tourist performance, performative roles are consciously created: 'tourist performances are constructed in a creative synthesis of human agency between locals and tourists' (ibid.: 224). Damer criticises the absence of this crucial interactive element vis-à-vis tourist performance in tourist studies in general (ibid.). Instead of using performance as a dramaturgy, i.e., defined by idiosyncratic interaction, tourist performance is reduced to a form of 'active participation' (cf. Perkins and Thorns 2001). This problem of interpretation in the reading of tourist performance stems from the lack of ethnographic focus on the interaction between different performative groups, as well as individual performances in the hybridic tourist context. Thus this improvisatory process does not become apparent. To compensate for this lacuna, I turned my ethnographic focus onto a marginal performative group in the tourist space of Mykonos.

From a romantic flaneur to a post-tourist?

The strolling *flaneur* was a forerunner of the twentieth-century tourist … ' (Urry 1990: 138)

The Romantic movement provided the tools to construct the modern tourist since its discourse was accompanied by a new ethic concerned with authenticity, recreation and the search for novelty.[2] The importance of taste, as well as the validation of the search for pleasure, emerged culturally. The new romantic ethic, moreover, as Campbell has suggested, was the basis for modern consumerism (1987).

Urry (1990) argues that the 'romantic gaze' helped tourism to spread by developing an ideology of the 'act of travelling'. Ironically, with the constitution of mass tourism the project started working against itself. Once 'discovered', places began to lose their 'authenticity'. The tourist gaze is not a consistent notion since its objects of desire have changed: from the romantic tourist and his search for authenticity, to the modern tourist to whom all the connotations of 'suffering' the inauthentic, the undifferentiated, the mass marketed have been ascribed. Ultimately, we arrive at the post-tourist who is fully aware that there are no authentic experiences. The post-tourist treats tourism as a game, as 'an endless availability of gazes' and not as an existential quest (Urry 1990: 83, 100). The post-tourist is aware of the abundance of choice. 'The world is a stage' and he is performing the part of the 'tourist' realistically, for, he will always remain an outsider.[3]

Recent theorising on tourism establishes the notion of the 'post-tourist' who is portrayed, not solely as being aware of, but, ironically, 'delighted' with the inauthenticity of the tourist space. The post-tourist is a conscious spectator who desires only to consume images of a place, in other words, to consume already prefigured space signs out of the consumption habit (Feifer 1985; Urry 1990; Lash and Urry 1994; Urry 1995; Rojek and Urry 1997; Franklin 2003). Thus, for the ethnographic deconstruction of spaces like Mykonos, the theoretical link between tourism and consumption is a very useful analytical tool.

Urry (1990) invents the notion of a post-tourist in order to explain the dramatically changing patterns of tourist practices which in effect are linked with major changes in cultural representations. The latter is evident in the dissolving of boundaries in the post-modern era when there are no distinctions between 'high' and 'low' cultures or between cultural forms such as tourism, education and shopping. Thus tourist patterns, are not organised independently but primarily through communication systems, which, nevertheless, allow the post-tourist to imagine and create her own game within the sea of signs and representations.

In the phenomenon of modern consumption as theorised by Campbell (1987), satisfaction does not solely derive from (the possession of) the actual product, but from anticipating it. Similarly, dreaming dictates the actual visiting of 'new' places; in other words, the act of travelling is demarcated by the imagined consumption of a place-image (cf. Jansson 2002; Tzanelli 2003). Even the 'green' backpacker, who has the illusion of being anti-consumerist, still consumes images of her imagined 'unspoilt' destination (see Shepherd 2003). Campbell is criticised for not accounting for the fact that these 'dreams' can indeed be constructed by certain mechanisms of emulation such as advertising and the media, which, in turn, both reproduce and generate a whole new set of signs attached to an image of a given site (Urry 1990: 13). Urry pinpoints that the shift from an organised to a disorganised capitalism (cf. Lash and Urry 1987) has created more sophisticated patterns of consumption. These patterns depart from the idea of homogenised, mass consumption practices and become more personalised as part of the project of the aestheticisation of consumption. Hence, through the act of consumption, the consumer actively forms and transforms the self (cf. Miller 1988; Carrier 1990).

The *Mykoniots d'élection:* the facilitators of the sign game

> the tourist consumes services and experiences by turning them into signs, by doing semiotic work of transformation. The tourist aestheticizes, so to speak, originally non-aesthetic objects. (Lash and Urry 1994: 15)

The recent theory on tourism has transformed the 'tourist' into a semiotician. I will use the insights of such a theoretical approach here in a rather paradoxical way. Initially, every outsider when she enters an 'alien' space, is a 'tourist' or a 'traveller'.[4]

The protagonists of this ethnographic performance are among those who decided to 'come back' perpetually or, in other words, those who incorporated the emerging sign of the ex-centric space-myth of Mykonos in the development of a new (trans)local and (trans)cultural self-identity. What these people established, partly without realising it, was a new set of cultural practices: they set the cornerstone of the discourse about an emerging place-myth that was destined to be mass consumed. Their initially improvised 'objects' of aestheticisation were slowly turned into *mythologies*. They bequeathed their skill (or they just passed it on as a hint) to their disciples, thus adding a little more, a little surplus to the myth of their ideal construction of a 'primitive', 'chaste' and 'authentic' local culture, that could convey to the newcomer their own initial feeling of anticipation. Adding a little more to the place-myth did not make it any more concrete, however. Mythologising helped eventually to turn Mykonos into a sophisticated body of signs relating to the already fetishised space, open to exploration by the prospective visitor and newcomer.

The *Mykoniots d'élection* became the founders and descendants of this emerging local body of 'exogenous' myth-progenitors. They slowly turned into experts on the 'tourist gaze' recording it from within. Ultimately, they became the facilitators of the 'semiotic work of transformation'. As Boissevain has suggested, the 'desire to penetrate' the 'back-regions' of the 'everyday' of an otherwise tourist reality is 'inherent to the structure of tourism' (Boissevain 1996: 8). Through a consistent, almost ethnographic observation of this emulative pattern, the *Mykoniots d'élection* constructed their newly acquired cultural identity in the tourist space accordingly. Originally the facilitators, the decodifiers of 'local' rules, they gradually transformed themselves into virtual 'locals' who performed their own 'backstage' (show) which remained eclectically open to some visitors. By simultaneously manipulating and fulfilling the anticipation of the tourist gaze, they turned themselves into performative 'locals'. This created a fetishised group identity which supported their personal myth of *polythetic* subjects.

Performing 'backstage' served to 'sell' precisely the image the tourist would aspire to for himself. The *Mykoniots* managed to become 'simulated' locals. In reality, it took them much longer (than they claimed) to become assimilated to the body of the new 'local' culture. As far as the 'indigenous' Mykonians are concerned, the *Mykoniots* were and are accepted as part of the scene, as long as the preparation for and the actual tourist season last. Beyond that, *Mykoniots* are temporarily stripped of their leading role on the island's scene.

The foregoing demonstrates that the processes of inclusion and exclusion are not clear-cut in the reality of a tourist space. I would, therefore, propose a schema more asymmetrical than a mere semiotic description of the tourist space. I maintain that the latter allows no room for mixing 'orthodoxy' with diverse practices, such as, for example, the combination of a romantic gaze in an otherwise semantically post-modern space. Moreover, Urry's schema does not account for subdivisions within or overlaps between the very abstract categories of the 'visitor', the 'tourist' and the 'local'. The aesthetic allocation of space has changed through time: the 'tourist' is no longer searching passionately among the narrow lanes of the *Hora* to view the wonders of the local vernacular. There is an emerging image of a less enchanted tourist who appreciates the commodification of the tourist gaze and wants to 'shop' (signs) in the main commercial arteries of the 'city'. This tourist accepts and enjoys the 'staged-authenticity' of the immediately attainable. Consequently, a new distinction game emerges: those who know the 'hidden' passages, those who still search for the 'hidden' passages or persist in decodifying them by themselves, using no 'manual'. The recent development of a sociology of tourism, strongly influenced by post-modern theorising, has created a new set of 'passive' subjectivities, like those described by Ritzer and Liska (1997), as the 'sufferers' of pre-planned tourist experiences which are 'predictable, calculable, efficient and controlled' (Rojek and Urry 1997: 3). These tourists are the victims of the so-called 'McDisneyized' tourist experience. While this might be partly true in several contexts, I feel that this theory allows little room for alternative appropriations on behalf of the individual, as well as minimum potential for creativity in a given post-modern space. It might be true that the tourist experience is a constructed one. However, I wonder if these powerful 'chefs' of the Mykonos experience (i.e., the *Mykoniots d'élection*), who (in my ethnographic case) are not 'mere' images or signs but instead exemplary individuals, could go so far as to create the accidental, reconstruct a 'one-night stand' or a drinking banquet, fake self-realisations and so forth. All these and much more can actually happen to people travelling to places with either 'authentic' or even 'staged-authentic' scenery as a backdrop.

Extending Rojek and Urry's (1997: 6) concept of tourism as the 'organised bombardment of the senses', Harrison offers an alternative view of tourism as

Appendix

mere 'sensory aesthetic' (Harrison 2001: 164).[5] Everything is reduced to its sensory surface; the simple pleasure. The notion of the aesthetic in everyday life (cf. Featherstone 1992) is reintroduced, not as a post-modern state of being, but as an inherent trait of nineteenth-century urbanism. This type of being, engaged in the 'happenings' of everyday life in the city, turns life into a work of art. The tourist's aestheticisation process, in turn, emulates this prototype: the subject's 'immersion in the experience'. This sensual/corporeal experience (cf. Veijola and Jokinen 1994; Saldanha 2002; Crouch and Desforges 2003) makes the tourist subject receptive and self-actualising; in other words – *pace* Turner's liminoid state – transcendent. This intense 'liminoid state' of the 'sensual' tourist is importantly characterised by choice.

I particularly worked with a group of informants who addressed a continuing discourse of spontaneity from 'back then', the age of the 'last romantics', the sixties. I have recorded them proselytising the same principles in the nineties. Even if we accept an extreme hybrid model of post-modernity that denies purity to any given cultural form, I maintain that tourists cannot be 'mere semioticians' (Rojek and Urry 1997: 4). 'Tourists' and 'travellers' have diverse identities, as well as diverse desires. Reviewing the sociology of tourism revealed theoretical weaknesses. I will mention here two points I consider most problematic: firstly, the establishment of a passive universal and impersonal category of the 'tourist'; and, secondly, the application of uncritical and fixed 'ideal' identity categories within a tourist space, such as the 'tourist', the 'service group', the 'local'. The ethnographic reality, under the scrutiny of anthropological 'fieldwork', revealed a greater diversity and a less consistent pattern with reference to the subjects of the tourist place. Subjects, either 'locals', 'tourists' or 'consumers' are multi-performative; they are capable of stretching their 'expansionist' self in many categories, as well as of autonomously searching for a new idiosyncratic one.

Despite the aforementioned objections, I agree that during the last decade or so, one can observe a major shift in the attitude of the 'visitors'. The nineties signified the critical 'passage' to mass tourism which brought less 'predisposed' visitors to the legendary Mykonos (experience). No matter how virtual this might sound in a so-called post-modern reality, the 'Mykonos experience' existed, either as a desire, as a construction, or as a creative state of being. Experiential or otherwise, it has been repeatedly recorded in the rhetoric of its visitors, in the beauty of its fairy tale, and remains inscribed in its spatial myth of otherness. Whether it will survive or not is another question.

Appendix

Notes

1. Franklin (2003) has criticised the long preoccupation in the tourist literature with the two key concepts: MacCannell's 'authenticity' (1976) and Urry's 'tourist gaze' (1990). These terms betray a modernist fetishisation with dualisms like local/tourist, real/fake, home/away, work/leisure. In the post-modernist distinction game rooted in the realm of consumption and the radical reorganisation of space, these dualisms are outmoded.
2. A 'disengaged freedom and rationality', the 'ethic of the ordinary life', in short the morals of the Enlightenment, together with the romantic philosophical response to the above were, according to Taylor, the two movements that have shaped modern culture (Taylor 1989: 234).
3. In all its historical stages, 'tourism', according to Urry, 'has always involved a spectacle'. That is why the act of 'gazing' is so important to his theoretical writings on the subject of touring (Urry 1990: 86).
4. In Mykonos, for example, the first 'tourist' visitors of this century (the first groups arrived in the early thirties) invaded the barren space employing the then fashionable prototype of the romantic explorer, epitomised in Urry's definition of the romantic 'tourist gaze'. These first visitors started spreading the word about the charms of the still unexplored 'white cubist (is)land'. More were to follow.
5. Jansson's (2002) counter-theorisation on the sensual tourist further departs from Urry's totalising 'end of tourism' scenario and its consequent end of (realist) hedonism; instead, an (imaginative) hedonism due to its mediatisation works as its replacement.

GLOSSARY

A-delos: invisible (ancient Greek)
agapi: love
alafroiskioti: moonstruck
andras kamaki: 'ladykiller'
andras potis: a male drinker
andrikia: 'like a man'
(to) andriliki: how to be a man
androparea: all-male society
anexartitos: independent (male)
anthropokentrikos: anthropocentric
anti-gamos: secondary wedding celebrations
apokriatika: traditional carnival dances and customs
apo mangia: 'to play cool'
askesis: (lit.) exercise
atmosfaira: ambience/aura
axioprepeia: dignity/integrity

Baglama: small lute
ballos: traditional local dance
balosia: carnival dances, an old Mykonian 'bacchanalian' custom – now defunct
bonbonieres: traditional wedding sugared-almonds
boukes: (colloq.) burglaries
briam: mixed vegetables in tomato

Café aman: traditional *kafeneio* with musicians, originally from Asia Minor
chilum: an Indian straight pipe used for cannabis (Hindi)

Daïs: powerful macho male
delos: visible (ancient Greek)
den eixe sarantisei: 'he (the deceased) hadn't completed the forty days of deep mourning'

desimata: (colloq.) police 'busts'
diestramenoi: mentally 'twisted'
dioikitis: police chief
disemia: binary – often contradictory – rhetoric
dittotita: the twofold nature of things

Eg(h)oismos: self-regard
ekklisia: church
eklytos vios: liberal amoral way of life
endopiotita: locality
erotas: falling in love
estine: setting up
estise: set up
etaxan ston ayio: 'they made a vow to the saint'
evaisthitoi: 'the sensitive'

Fasolada: bean soup
founda: (colloq.) grass/marijuana
frigana: brushwood
frikia: freaks/hippies
ftiahnontai san Dionysoi: drug-induced Dionysian 'high'
ftiaximo: means of getting high

Gamos: wedding
glendi: carousing/feasting

Harmana: (colloq.) craving due to (heroin) abstinence
hoirosfayia: pig-slaughtering
Hora: the local name for Mykonos town
horio (pl. *horia*): self-sufficient rural household
hronos: time
hystero: secundine, afterbirth

Isimerinos: the Equator
istamai: to stand

Kafeneio (pl. *kafeneia*): traditional coffee shop/café
kaiki: caïque
kapsouroskoni: 'infatuation dust'
kasina: carnival dances, an old Mykonian 'bacchanalian' custom – now defunct
kastro: fort
kataloipa: remnants
kefi: high spirits
kellaki (pl. *kellakia*): cell/small house
kleftike: eloped
koinohristoi: (lit.) 'those who can be used (up) by everybody'

kokorakia: 'pricks'
kommates: large chunks of hashish
koritsia: the 'girls'; traditionally referred to unmarried women/virgins
kosmika: gossip columns
kosmikoi Athinaioi: Athenian socialites
koumbara/os: wedding sponsor
kraipali: 'bacchanalian' crapulence/revelry
kydonia: sea cockles
kyr: an informal (rural) mode of address, lit. a contraction of Mr.
kyra: an informal (rural) mode of address, lit. a contraction of Mrs.
kyria: Mrs./madam/lady
kyrios: mister/sir

Laikes doxasies: local supernatural beliefs
leela: play – 'the play of life' (Sanskrit)
leledes: mothers' boys
liasimo: sunning
loukarei: carry rectally

Mageiritsa: Easter soup
magisses: sorceresses
mala: garland or necklace (Sanskrit)
mandraouli: mandrake
manges: (colloq.) those with 'street cred'
mangia: 'street cred'
mangika: in a 'street-cred' manner
marazi: heartache
mastoras: master artisan
maya: illusion (Sanskrit)
maya-leela: lit. illusion-play
Megali Pempti: Maundy Thursday
Megalo Sabbato: Easter Saturday
meltemi: strong local wind
meraki: artistry
merokamata: daily wage
methexi: sacred commensality
mezedes: snacks/small dishes
mia oraia lantza: a 'beautiful' motor boat
mnimosyno: commemorative ritual
myimenoi: initiated
Mykoniatiki katastasi: a Mykonian style of encounter
mystirio: sacrament
(*o*) *mythos tis palaiotititas*: the myth of 'seniority'

Na pinei: to drink
nargiledes: hookahs

na stinei: to set up
na xenerosei: 'to sober up'
noikokyria: conjugal households

Ohla: (colloq.) clamour
Ohla tou ohlou: (colloq.) 'the din of the mob'

Palaestra: athletics training-ground
palioi: 'old-timers'
pallikari/pallikaria: 'the fearless men'
Panayia: Madonna
paniyiri (pl. *paniyiria*): Orthodox rituals that coexist with traditional local 'Dionysian' feasts
paradopistoi: skinflints
paranoia tou asprou: lit. 'paranoia of the white stuff (heroin)'
paranyfaki: pageboy
parea (plural *parees*): company of friends/cliques
pareo/s: sarong/s
partouza: (colloq.) group sex
pepromeno: fate
periferia: district
pioma: (colloq.) lit. the act of drinking; the smoking of illegal substances
plani: illusion, fallacy
polytechnio: the rebellion of Greek students against the military dictatorship (1967–74)
ponos: grief
potes: consumers of illegal substances
preza: lit. snort, (colloq.) heroin
prezakia: (colloq.) heroin addicts/sniffers
proika: dowry
prosfora: 'blessed' bread
pujas: incensing and purification rituals (Hindi)

Rakitzis: natural leader of the drinking commensality/heavy raki-drinker
rakoposia: raki drinking
rembetes: members of the 'underground'/wasters
rembetika sinafia: members of the 'underground' affiliated to a group
rembetis/rembetas: a good-for-nothing person
Romiosini: a Byzantine/orientalist model of Greekness – as opposed to Hellenism
rouhla: a long bout of drunkeness; a 'bender'

Sanyassi: (lit.) a Hindu religious mendicant; a wandering ascetic (Sanskrit)
sfinakia: shots of alcohol
simadiaki speira: (a stone engraved with a) 'fateful' helix
sinafi (pl. *sinafia*): group of 'like-minded'; 'gang'- clique
souma: traditional grape-based spirit
steki (pl. *stekia*): haunt

steko: to stand
stinei: set up/design
stisimata ton magazion: setting up businesses
stisimo: set up
strosimo: setting up, preparing the house for the new season
sympotiasmos: (drinking) commensality

Ta remalia: rebels
(i) tehni tou stisimatos: the art of 'setting up'
theosis: unity with the divine
theriaklides: substance abusers
toumberleki: small Turkish drum
trelloharto: 'madness' certificate
tsambouna: indigenous bagpipes
tsifteteli: belly dancing
tyhi: luck

Varagan fixakia: (colloq.) 'they would get a fix'
vasikous: founder members
vasilikous: basil
vipasanas: breathing techniques (Sanskrit)

Xekarfotoi: (colloq.) those whose identity cannot be pinned down
Xeneroto/s (pl. *xenerotoi*): sober/square
xenos (pl. *xenoi*): foreigner

Yia na tin vgazoune: in order to 'get by'
yinaikeio: lit. women's; code word for a women-only 'joint' (marijuana cigarette)

Zafou: meditation pillow
zeibekiko: a spontaneous and dramatic male dance
zomos: broth

BIBLIOGRAPHY

Abbeele, Georges van den. 1980. Sightseers: the tourist as theorist. *Diacritics* 10 (4), 2–14.
Abu-Lughod, Lila. 1986. *Veiled sentiments: honor and poetry in a Bedouin society.* Berkeley: University of California Press.
―――― 1990. Can there be a feminist ethnography? *Women and Performance* 5 (1), 7–27.
―――― 1993. *Writing women's worlds: Bedouin stories.* Berkeley: University of California Press.
Adler, Judith. 1989. Travel as performed art. *American Journal of Sociology* 94, 1366–91.
Alexiou, Margaret. 1974. *The ritual lament in Greek tradition.* Cambridge: Cambridge University Press.
Amit, Vered and Nigel Rapport. 2002. Nigel Rapport responds to Vered Amit. In *The trouble with community: anthropological reflections on movement, identity and collectivity.* London: Pluto Press.
Appadurai, Arjun. 1996. *Modernity at large: cultural dimensions of globalization.* London: University of Minnesota Press.
Argyrou, Vassos. 1996. *Tradition and modernity in the Mediterranean: the wedding as symbolic struggle.* Cambridge: Cambridge University Press.
Augé, Marc. 1995. *Non-places: introduction to an anthropology of supermodernity.* London: Verso
Axioti, Melpo. 1986. *Το σπίτι μου.* Athens: Κέδρος.
Backos, A. 1992. *Local endogenous development through tourism in Southern Europe: case study of Mykonos.* Unpublished Ph.D. thesis, University of London.
Badiou, Alain. 2005. *Being and event.* London: Continuum.
Bakalaki, Alexandra. 1997. Students, natives, colleagues: encounters in academia and in the field. *Cultural Anthropology* 12 (4), 502–26.
Bakhtin, Mikhail. 1984. *Rabelais and his World.* Bloomington: Indiana University Press.
Barker, Eileen. (ed.) 1982. *New religious movements: a perspective for understanding society.* New York: Edwin Mellen Press.

Barker, Eileen. (ed.) 1983. *Of gods and men: new religious movements in the West*. Macon GA: Mercer University Press.

Barker, Eileen. 1984. *The making of a Moonie: choice or brainwashing?* Oxford: Basil Blackwell.

———— 1989. *New religious movements: a practical introduction*. London: HMSO.

Battaglia, Debbora. 1995. Problematizing the self: a thematic introduction. In *Rhetorics of self-making* (ed.) Debbora Battaglia. Berkeley: University of California Press.

Baudrillard, Jean. 1968. The system of objects. Reprinted and translated in Mark Poster (ed.) (1988) *Jean Baudrillard: selected writings*. Cambridge: Polity Press.

———— 1970. Consumer society. Reprinted and translated in Mark Poster (ed.) (1988) *Jean Baudrillard: selected writings*. Cambridge: Polity Press.

———— 1972. For a critique of the political economy of the sign. Reprinted and translated in Mark Poster (ed.) (1988) *Jean Baudrillard: selected writings*. Cambridge: Polity Press.

———— 1981. Simulacra and simulations. Reprinted and translated in Mark Poster (ed.) (1988) *Jean Baudrillard: selected writings*. Cambridge: Polity Press.

———— 1985. The masses: the implosion of the social in the media. Reprinted and translated in Mark Poster (ed.) (1988) *Jean Baudrillard: selected writings*. Cambridge: Polity Press.

Bauman, Zygmunt. 1998. Postmodern religion? In *Religion, modernity and postmodernity* (ed.) Paul Heelas. Oxford: Blackwell.

———— 2003. Utopias with no topos. *History of the Human Sciences* 16 (1), 11–25.

Beauvoir, Simone de. 1975 [1962]. *The prime of life*. Harmondsworth: Penguin.

Beck, Ulrich and Elisabeth Beck-Gernsheim. 1996. Individualization and 'precarious freedoms': perspectives and controversies of a subject-oriented sociology. In *Detraditionalization: critical reflections on authority and identity* (eds.) Paul Heelas, Scott Lash and Paul Morris. Oxford: Blackwell.

Behar, Ruth. 1996. *The vulnerable observer: anthropology that breaks your heart*. Boston: Beacon.

———— 2003. Ethnography and the book that was lost. *Ethnography* 4 (1), 15–39.

Bell, D. 1993. Introduction: the context. In *Gendered fields: women, men and ethnography* (eds.) D. Bell, Pat Caplan and W.J. Karim. London: Routledge.

Bendix, Regina. 2002. Capitalising on memories past, present and future. *Anthropological Theory* 2 (4), 469–87.

Benjamin, Walter. 1986. On the mimetic faculty. In *Reflections* (ed.) P. Demetz. New York: Schocken Books.

Bhabha, Homi. 1994. *The location of culture*. London: Routledge.

Bloch, Maurice. 1974. Symbols, song, dance and features of articulation: is religion an extreme form of traditional authority? *European Journal of Sociology* 15, 55–81.

———— 1986. *From blessing to violence: history and ideology in the circumcision ritual of the Merina of Madagascar*. Cambridge: Cambridge University Press.

Boissevain, Jeremy. (ed.) 1996. *Coping with tourists: European reactions to mass tourism*. Oxford: Berghahn Books.

Bourdieu, Pierre. 1977. *Outline of a theory of practice*. Cambridge: Cambridge University Press.

———— 1978. Sport and social class. *Social Science Information* 17, 819–40.

———— 1984. *Distinction: a social critique of the judgement of taste*. London: Routledge.

Bourdieu, Pierre. 1986. The forms of capital. In *Handbook of theory and research for the sociology of education* (ed.) J. Richardson. New York: Greenwood Press.
_____ 1990. *The logic of practice.* Cambridge: Polity Press.
_____ 1993. How can one be a sports fan? In *The cultural studies reader* (ed.) S. During. London: Routledge.
Braidotti, Rosi. 1994. *Nomadic subjects: embodiment and sexual difference in contemporary feminist theory.* New York: Columbia University Press.
_____ 1997. Meta(l)morphoses. *Theory, Culture and Society* 14 (2), 67–80.
_____ 2003. Becoming women: or sexual difference revisited. *Theory, Culture and Society* 20 (3), 43–64.
Brettell, Caroline B. 1997. Blurred genres and blended voices: life history, biography, autobiography, and the auto/ethnography of women's lives. In *Auto/Ethnography: rewriting the self and the social* (ed.) Deborah E. Reed-Danahay. Oxford: Berg.
Bruner, Edward M. 1995. The ethnographer/tourist in Indonesia. In *International tourism identity and change* (eds.) Marie-Françoise Lanfant, John B. Allcock and Edward M. Bruner. London: Sage.
_____ 1996. My life in an ashram. *Qualitative Inquiry* 2 (3), 300–19.
_____ 2001. The Masai and the Lion King: authenticity, nationalism and globalisation in African tourism. *American Ethnologist* 28 (4), 881–908.
Butler, Judith. 1990. *Gender trouble: feminism and the subversion of identity.* London: Routledge.
_____ 1993. *Bodies that matter: on the discursive limits of sex.* London: Routledge.
Cabezas, Amalia L. 2004. Between love and money: sex, tourism and citizenship in Cuba and the Dominican Republic. *Signs: Journal of Women in Culture and Society* 29 (4), 987–1015.
Callaway, Helen. 1992. Ethnography and experience: gender implications in fieldwork and texts. In *Anthropology and autobiography* (eds.) Judith Okely and Helen Callaway. London: Routledge.
Campbell, Colin. 1987. *The romantic ethic and the spirit of modern consumerism.* Oxford: Basil Blackwell.
Campbell, J.K. 1964. *Honour, family and patronage: a study of institutions and moral values in a Greek mountain community.* Oxford: Oxford University Press.
Caplan, Pat. 1988. Engendering knowledge: the politics of ethnography. *Anthropology Today* 4 (5), 8–12; 4 (6), 14–17.
Caraveli, Anna. 1986. The bitter wounding: the lament as social protest in rural Greece. In *Gender and power in rural Greece* (ed.) Jill Dubisch. Princeton: Princeton University Press.
Carrier, James G. 1990. The symbolism of possession in commodity advertising. *Man* (N.S.) 25, 190–207.
Carter, L. 1990. *Charisma and control in Rajneeshpuram.* Cambridge: Cambridge University Press.
Certeau, Michel de. 1984. *The practice of everyday life.* London: University of California Press.
Chadjifotiou, Zachos. 1992. *Clouds over Mykonos.* Athens: Efstathiadis Group.
Clifford, James. 1986. Introduction: Partial truths. In *Writing culture: the poetics and politics of ethnography* (eds.) James Clifford and George E. Marcus. Berkeley: University of California Press.

―――― 1988. On ethnographic surrealism. In *The predicament of culture: twentieth-century ethnography, literature, and art*. London: Harvard University Press.
―――― 1989. Notes on travel and theory. *Inscriptions* 5, 177–88.
―――― 1992. Traveling cultures. In *Cultural Studies* (eds.) Lawrence Grossberg, Cary Nelson and Paula A. Treichler. London: Routledge.
―――― 1994. Diasporas. *Cultural Anthropology* 9 (3), 302–338.
―――― 1997. *Routes: travel and translation in the late twentieth century*. Cambridge MA: Harvard University Press.
Cohen, Anthony P. 1992. Self-conscious anthropology. In *Anthropology and autobiography* (eds.) Judith Okely and Helen Callaway. London: Routledge.
―――― 1994. *Self consciousness: an alternative anthropology of identity*. London: Routledge.
Cohen, Anthony P. and Nigel Rapport (eds.) 1995. *Questions of consciousness*. London: Routledge.
Cohen, Erik. 1979. A phenomenology of tourist experience. *Sociology* 13 (2), 179–201.
Costera Meijer, Irene and Baukje Prins. 1998. How bodies come to matter: an interview with Judith Butler. *Signs: Journal of Women in Culture and Society* 23 (1), 275–86.
Cowan, Jane K. 1990. *Dance and the body politic in northern Greece*. Princeton: Princeton University Press.
―――― 1991. Going out for coffee? Contesting the grounds of gendered pleasures in everyday sociability. In *Contested identities: gender and kinship in modern Greece* (eds.) Peter Loizos and Evthymios Papataxiarchis. Princeton: Princeton University Press.
―――― 1992. Η κατασκευή της γυναικείας εμπειρίας σε μια μακεδονική κωμόπολη. In *Ταυτότητες και φύλο στη σύγχρονη Ελλάδα: ανθρωπολογικές προσεγγίσεις* (eds.) Ε. Παπαταξιάρχης and Θ. Παραδέλλης. Athens: University of the Aegean. Καστανιώτης.
Crang, Philip. 1997. Performing the tourist product. In *Touring cultures: transformations of travel and theory* (eds.) Chris Rojek and John Urry. London: Routledge.
Crapanzano, Vincent. 1980. *Tuhami: portrait of a Moroccan*. Chicago: University of Chicago Press.
Crouch, David and Luke Desforges. 2003. The sensuous in the tourist encounter. Introduction: the power of the body in tourist studies. *Tourist Studies* 3 (1), 5–22.
Dahles, Heidi. 1996. The social construction of Mokum: tourism and the quest for local identity in Amsterdam. In *Coping with tourists: European reactions to mass tourism* (ed.) Jeremy Boissevain. Oxford: Berghahn Books.
Damer, Seán. 2004. Signifying Symi: setting and performance on a Greek island. *Ethnography* 5 (2), 203–28.
Damianakos, Stathis. 1976. *Κοινωνιολογία του ρεμπέτικου*. Athens: Ερμείας.
Danforth, Loring M. 1982. *The death rituals of rural Greece*. Princeton: Princeton University Press.
De Lauretis, Teresa. 1986. *Feminist studies/critical studies*. London: Macmillan.
Deleuze, Gilles. 1985. Nomad thought. In *The new Nietzsche* (ed.) David B. Allison. Cambridge MA: The MIT Press.
Deleuze, Gilles and Félix Guattari. 2004a. *Anti-Oedipus: capitalism and schizophrenia*. London: Continuum.
―――― 2004b. *A thousand plateaus: capitalism and schizophrenia*. London: Continuum.

Derrida, Jacques. 1974. *Of grammatology*. London: Johns Hopkins University Press.
_____ 1989. *Memoires: For Paul de Man*. New York: Columbia University Press.
Dick, Anthony and Thomas Robbins. 1982. Contemporary religious ferments and moral ambiquity. In *New religious movements: a perspective for understanding society* (ed.) Eileen Barker. New York: Edwin Mellen Press.
Doumas, C. 1992. Το πρώιμο Αιγαίο και η συμβολή του στην ανάπτυξη της δυτικής σκέψης. In *Το Αιγαίο επίκεντρο ελληνικού πολιτισμού*. Athens: Μέλισσα.
Du Boulay, Juliet. 1974. *Portrait of a Greek mountain village*. Oxford: Clarendon Press.
_____ 1986. Women-images of their nature and destiny in rural Greece. In *Gender and power in rural Greece* (ed.) Jill Dubisch. Princeton: Princeton University Press.
Dubisch, Jill. 1974. The domestic power of women in a Greek island village. *Studies in European Society* 1, 23–33.
_____ 1983. Greek women: scared and profane. *Journal of Modern Greek Studies* 1, 185–202.
_____ 1986. Introduction and preface. In *Gender and power in rural Greece* (ed.) Jill Dubisch. Princeton: Princeton University Press.
_____ 1990. Pilgrimage and popular religion at a Greek holy shrine. In *Religious Orthodoxy and popular faith in European society* (ed.) Ellen Badone. Princeton: Princeton University Press.
_____ 1995. *In a different place: pilgrimage, gender, and politics at a Greek island shrine*. Princeton: Princeton University Press.
Dumont, Jean-Paul. 1978. *The headman and I: ambiguity and ambivalence in the fieldworking experience*. Austin: University of Texas Press.
Durkheim, Émile. 1915. *The elementary forms of the religious life*. London: Allen and Unwin.
Durrell, Lawrence. 1978. *The Greek islands*. London: Faber and Faber.
Eade, John and Michael J. Sallnow. 1991. Introduction. In *Contesting the sacred: the anthropology of Christian pilgrimage* (eds.) John Eade and Michael J. Sallnow. London: Routledge.
Edensor, Tim. 2000. Staging tourism: tourists as performers. *Annals of Tourism Research* 27, 322–44.
_____ 2001. Performing tourism, staging tourism: (re)producing tourist space and practice. *Tourist Studies* 1 (1), 59–81.
Engels, Freidrich. 1972. *The origin of family, private property, and the state*. New York: Pathfinder Press.
Evangelidis, T.E. 1912. *Η Μύκονος: ιστορία της νήσου από των αρχαιοτάτων χρόνων μέχρι των καθ' ημάς*. Athens: Βιβλιοφιλία.
Fardon, Richard. 1995. Introduction: counterworks. In *Counterworks: managing the diversity of knowledge* (ed.) Richard Fardon. London: Routledge.
Faubion, James D. 1993. *Modern Greek lessons: a primer in historical constructivism*. Princeton: Princeton University Press.
Featherstone, Mike. 1991. *Consumer culture and postmodernism*. London: Sage.
_____ 1992. Postmodernity and the aestheticisation of everyday life. In *Modernity and identity* (eds.) Scott Lash and Jonathan Friedman. Oxford: Blackwell.
Feifer, M. 1985. *Going places*. London: Macmillan.

Fernandez, James W. 1995. Amazing grace: meaning deficit, displacement and new consciousness in expressive interaction. In *Questions of consciousness* (eds.) Anthony P. Cohen and Nigel Rapport. London: Routledge.

Fortier, Anne-Marie. 2001. Coming home: queer migration and multiple evocations of home. *European Journal of Cultural Studies* 4 (4), 405–24.

Foucault, Michel. 1978. *The history of sexuality vol. 1: an introduction*. Harmondsworth: Penguin.

―――― 1980. Body/power. In *Micheal Foucault: power/knowledge. Selected interviews and other writings, 1972–1977* (ed.) Colin Gordon. Brighton: Harvester.

―――― 1984a. What is Enlightenment? In *The Foucault reader* (ed.) Paul Rabinow. Harmondsworth: Penguin.

―――― 1984b. On the genealogy of ethics: an overview of work in progress. In *The Foucault reader* (ed.) Paul Rabinow. Harmondsworth: Penguin.

―――― 1985. *The use of pleasure: the history of sexuality vol. 2*. Harmondsworth: Penguin.

―――― 1986. *The care of the self: the history of sexuality vol. 3*. Harmondsworth: Penguin.

Frank, Katherine. 2000. 'The management of hunger': using fiction in writing anthropology. *Qualitative Inquiry* 6 (4), 474–88.

Franklin, Adrian. 2003. The tourist syndrome: an interview with Zygmunt Bauman. *Tourist Studies* 3 (2), 205–17.

Fullagar, Simone. 2000. Desiring nature: identities and becoming in narratives of travel. *Cultural Values* 4 (1), 58–76.

―――― 2001. Desire, death and wonder: reading Simone de Beauvoir's narratives of travel. *Cultural Values* 5 (3), 289–305.

Gedalof, Irene. 2000. Identity in transit: nomads, cyborgs and women. *European Journal of Women's Studies* 7, 337–54.

Geertz, Clifford. 1973. *The interpretation of cultures*. New York: Basic Books.

―――― 1988. *Works and lives: the anthropologist as author*. Cambridge: Polity Press.

Gefou-Madianou, Dimitra 1992. Exclusion and unity, retsina and sweet wine: commensality and gender in a Greek agrotown. In *Alcohol, gender and culture* (ed.) Dimitra Gefou-Madianou. London: Routledge.

Gibson, James E. 1991. Celebration and transgression: Nietzsche on ritual. *Journal of Ritual Studies* 5 (2), 1–13.

Giddens, Anthony. 1984. *The constitution of society: outline of the theory of structuration*. Cambridge: Polity Press.

―――― 1991. *Modernity and self-identity: self and society in the late modern age*. Cambridge: Polity Press.

―――― 1992. *The transformation of intimacy: sexuality, love and eroticism in modern societies*. Cambridge: Polity Press.

Girard, René. 1977. *Violence and the sacred*. Baltimore: Johns Hopkins University Press.

Goffman, Erving. 1959. *The presentation of self in everyday life*. Harmondsworth: Penguin.

Gooldin, Sigal. 2003. Fasting women, living skeletons and hunger artists: spectacles of body and miracles at the turn of a century. *Body and Society* 9 (2), 27–53.

Graburn, Nelson H.H. 1978. Tourism: the sacred journey. In *Hosts and guests: the anthropology of tourism* (ed.) Valene L. Smith. Oxford: Basil Blackwell.

Graburn, Nelson H.H. and Diane Barthel-Bouchier 2001. Relocating the tourist. *International Sociology* 16 (2), 147–58.
Greek Ministry of Culture, 1994. *Aegean archipelago: international programme for cultural development*: Κοινό πρόγραμμα των Υπουργείων Πολιτισμού, Αιγαίου και Περιβάλλοντος (επιστημονικός σύμβουλος: University of the Aegean). Athens.
Greger, S. 1988. *Village on the plateau: Magoulas, a mountain village in Crete*. Studley: K.A.F. Brewin Books.
Hallward, Peter. 2003. *Badiou: a subject to truth*. Minneapolis: University of Minnesota Press.
Harrison, Julia. 2001. Thinking about tourists. *International Sociology* 16 (2), 159–72.
Harvey, David. 1989. *The condition of postmodernity: an enquiry into the origins of cultural change*. Oxford: Basil Blackwell.
Harvey, Penelope. 1996. *Hybrids of modernity: anthropology, the nation state and the universal exhibition*. London: Routledge.
Hastrup, Kirsten. 1987. Fieldwork among friends: ethnographic exchange within the Northern civilization. In *Anthropology at home* (ed.) Anthony Jackson. London: Tavistock.
―――― 1998. Theatre as a site of passage: some reflections on the magic of acting. In *Ritual, performance, media* (ed.) Felicia Hughes-Freeland. London: Routledge.
Hebdidge, Dick. 1979. *Subculture: the meaning of style*. London: Routledge.
Heelas, Paul. 1982. Californian self-religions and socialising the subjective. In *New religious movements: a perspective for understanding society* (ed.) Eileen Barker. New York: Edwin Mellen Press.
―――― 1993. The New Age in cultural context: the premodern, the modern and the postmodern. *Religion* 23 (2), 103–16.
―――― 1996. *The New Age movement: the celebration of the self and the sacralisation of modernity*. Oxford: Basil Blackwell.
Hellier, Chris. 1996. *Monasteries of Greece*. London: Tauris Parke Books.
Herzfeld, Michael. 1980. Honour and shame: problems in the comparative analysis of moral systems. *Man* (N.S.) 15, 339–51.
―――― 1985. *The poetics of manhood: contest and identity in a Cretan mountain village*. Princeton: Princeton University Press.
Herzfeld, Michael. 1986. *Ours once more: folklore, ideology, and the making of modern Greece*. New York: Pella.
―――― 1987. *Anthropology through the looking-glass: critical ethnography in the margins of Europe*. Cambridge: Cambridge University Press.
―――― 1995. It takes one to know one. Collective resentment and mutual recognition among Greeks in local and global contexts. In *Counterworks: managing the diversity of knowledge* (ed.) Richard Fardon. London: Routledge.
―――― 1997a. *Cultural intimacy: social poetics in the nation state*. London: Routledge.
―――― 1997b. *Portrait of a Greek imagination: an ethnographic biography of Andreas Nenedakis*. Chicago: University of Chicago Press.
―――― 1997c. The taming of revolution: intense paradoxes of the self. In *Auto/Ethnography: rewriting the self and the social* (ed.) Deborah E. Reed-Danahay. Oxford: Berg.

Hirschon, Renée. 1982. Territoriality and the home environment in a Greek urban community. *Anthropological Quarterly* 55 (2), 63–73.

―――― 1983. Women, the aged and religious activity: oppositions and complementarity in an urban locality. *Journal of Modern Greek Studies* 1, 113–30.

―――― 1985. The women-environment relationship: Greek cultural values in an urban community. *Ekistics* 52, 15–21.

―――― 1989. *Heirs of the Greek catastrophe: the social life of Asia Minor refugees in Piraeus*. Oxford: Clarendon Press.

Hobsbawn, Eric. 1992. Introduction: inventing traditions. In *The invention of tradition* (eds.) Eric Hobsbawn and Terence Ranger. Cambridge: Cambridge University Press.

Holst, Gail. 1975. *Road to rembetika*. Athens: Denise Harvey and Company.

Howe, Alyssa C. 2001. Queer pilgrimage: the San Francisco homeland and identity tourism. *Cultural Anthropology* 16 (1), 35–61.

Hughes-Freeland, Felicia. 1998. Introduction. In *Ritual, performance, media* (ed.) F. Hughes-Freeland. London: Routledge.

Hurley, Molly and James Trimarco. 2004. Morality and merchandise: vendors, visitors and police at New York City's Ground Zero. *Critique of Anthropology* 24 (1), 51–78.

Hutnyk, John. 1996. *The rumour of Calcutta: tourism, charity and the poverty of representation*. London: Zed Books.

Hutson, Scott R. 2000. The rave: spiritual healing in modern western subcultures. *Anthropological Quarterly* 73 (1), 35–49.

Iossifides, A. Marina. 1991. Sisters in Christ: metaphors of kinship among Greek nuns. In *Contested identities: gender and kinship in modern Greece* (eds.) Peter Loizos and Evthymios Papataxiarchis. Princeton: Princeton University Press.

Irigaray, Luce. 2004. *An ethics of sexual difference*. London: Continuum.

Iyer, Pico. 1997. The nowhere man. *Prospect* 5 10, 6–8.

Jackson, Anthony. (ed.) 1987. *Anthropology at home*. London: Tavistock.

Jackson, M. 1995. *At home in the world*. Durham NC: Duke University Press.

James, Allison, Jenny Hockey and Andrew Dawson. 1997. Introduction: the road from Santa Fe. In *After writing culture: epistemology and praxis in contemporary anthropology* (eds.) Allison James, Jenny Hockey and Andrew Dawson. London: Routledge.

Jansson, André. 2002. Spatial phantasmagoria: the mediatization of tourism experience. *European Journal of Communication* 17 (4), 429–43.

Jordan, T. 1995. Collective bodies: raving and the politics of Gilles Deleuze and Felix Guattari. *Body and Society* 1 (1), 125–44.

Kantsa, Venetia. 2000. *Daughters who do not speak, mothers who do not listen: erotic relationships among women in contemporary Greece*. Unpublished Ph.D thesis, University of London.

Karantonis, A. (n.d.) *Μύκονος-Δήλος*. Athens: Πεχλιβανίδης.

Katsoudas, K.D. 1998. Η αβάσταχτη ελαφρότητα του κομφορμισμού: μιρουπάφσιμ ... θα πει καλή αντάμωση. *Μυκονιάτης*, 245, 1–14.

Kaur, Raminder and John Hutnyk. (eds.) 1999. *Travel worlds: journeys in contemporary cultural politics*. London: Zed Books.

Keffaliniadis, N. 1984. *Πειρατεία: Κουρσάροι στο Αιγαίο*. Athens: Φιλιππότη.

Kenna, Margaret E. 1992. Changing places and altered perspectives: research on a Greek island in the 1960s and in the 1980s. In *Anthropology and autobiography* (eds.) Judith Okely and Helen Callaway. London: Routledge.
Kirtsoglou, Elizabeth. 2004. *For the love of women: gender, identity and same-sex relations in a Greek provincial town.* London: Routledge.
Kondo, Dorinne K. 1990. *Crafting selves: power, gender and discourses of identity in a Japanese workplace.* Chicago: University of Chicago Press.
Koppassi-Ikonomea, Elsa. 1995. *Work among urban gypsies of Greece.* Unpublished Ph.D. thesis, University of Wales.
Kousathanas, P. (ed.) 1986. *Ορτσ' αλα μπάντα: αναδρομικός διάπλους στην παλιά Μύκονο.* Mykonos: Δήμος Μυκονίων.
―――― 1989. *Ενας λόρδος στη Μύκονο και τις Δήλες το 1749.* Mykonos.
―――― 1996. Με το μάτι των περιηγητών. In Η άλλη Μύκονος. *Επτά Ημέρες/Καθημερινή* 25 8, 14–15.
Kyriazopoulos, V. 1972. Ιστορική εξέλιξις της νήσου Μυκόνου. In *Δήλος, Ρήνεια: χωροταξική και ρυθμιστική μελέτη* (eds.) Α. Καλλιγάς, Α. Παπαγεωργίου, Ι. Πολίτης και Α. Ρωμανός. Athens: Υπουργείο Κυβερνητικής Πολιτικής.
Lacan, Jacques. 1977. *Écrits: a selection.* London: Tavistock.
Lasch, Christopher. 1991. *The culture of narcissism: American life in an age of diminishing expectations.* London: Norton.
Lash, Scott and John Urry. 1987. *The end of organized capitalism.* Cambridge: Polity Press.
Lash, Scott and John Urry. 1994. *Economies of signs and space.* London: Sage.
Leontis, Artemis. 1999. Primordial home, elusive home. *Thesis Eleven* 59, 1–16.
Lévi-Strauss, Claude. 1978. Race and history. In *Structural Anthropology 2.* Harmondsworth: Penguin.
Liavas, Lampros. 1992. Η μουσική του Αιγαίου. In *Το Αιγαίο επίκεντρο ελληνικού πολιτισμού.* Athens: Μέλισσα.
Lingis, Alphonso. 2002. Petra. *Journal of Visual Culture* 1 (1), 47–55.
Loizos, Peter. 1975. Changes in property transfer among Greek Cypriot villages. *Man* (N.S.) 10, 503–23.
―――― 1981. *The heart grown bitter.* Cambridge: Cambridge University Press.
―――― 1994. Confessions of a vampire anthropologist. *Anthropological Journal of European Cultures* 3 (2), 39–53.
Loizos, Peter and Evthymios Papataxiarchis. (eds.) 1991a. *Contested identities: gender and kinship in modern Greece.* Princeton: Princeton University Press.
Loizos, Peter and Evthymios Papataxiarchis. 1991b. Introduction: Gender and kinship in marriage and alternative contexts. In *Contested identities: gender and kinship in modern Greece* (eds.) Peter Loizos and Evthymios Papataxiarchis. Princeton: Princeton University Press.
Loukissas, Philppos. 1977. *The impact of tourism on regional development: a comparative analysis of the Greek islands.* Unpublished Ph.D. thesis, Cornell University.
Lutz, C. 1988. *Unnatural emotions: everyday sentiments on a Micronesian atoll and their challenge to western theory.* Chicago: Chicago University Press.
Lynch, K. 1973. *What time is this place?* Cambridge MA: The MIT Press.
MacCannell, Dean. 1976. *The tourist: a new theory of the leisure class.* New York: Schocken Books.

Madianou, D. et al. 1992. Τα ναρκωτικά στην Ελλάδα: η χρήση ουσιών στο γενικό πληθυσμό, τόμος γ΄. Athens: Ψυχιατρική Βιβλιοθήκη.

Maffesoli, Michel. 1993. *The shadow of Dionysus: a contribution to the sociology of the orgy.* New York: State University of New York.

―――― 1996a. *The time of the tribes: the decline of individualism in mass society.* London: Sage.

―――― 1996b. *The contemplation of the world: figures of community style.* Minneapolis: University of Minnesota Press.

Manning-Sanders, R. 1951. *Seaside England.* London: Batsford.

Marcus, George E. and Michael J. Fischer 1986. *Anthropology as cultural critique: an experimental moment in the human sciences.* Chicago: University of Chicago Press.

Marcus, George E. 1998. On eccentricity. In *Ethnogaphy through thick and thin.* Princeton: Princeton University Press.

McDonald, M. 1988. Reply to S.P. Sangren (1988) Rhetoric and the authority ethnography: 'postmodernism' and the social reproduction of texts. *Current Anthropology* 29 (3), 429.

McNay, Lois. 1992. *Foucault and feminism: power, gender and the self.* Cambridge: Polity Press.

―――― 1999. Subject, psyche and agency: the work of Judith Butler. *Theory, Culture and Society* 16 (2), 175–93.

―――― 2003. Having it both ways: the incompatibility of narrative identity and communicative ethics in feminist thought. *Theory, Culture and Society* 20 (6), 1–20.

Meletopoulos, Tasos. 2004. *Ήρθε η σειρά σου.* Athens: Φερενίκη.

Miller, Daniel. 1988. Appropriating the state on the council estate. *Man* (N.S.) 23, 353–72.

Monette, Paul. 1991. *Half-way home.* New York: Avon Books.

Moore, D. 1995. Raves and the Bohemian search for self and community. A contribution to the anthropology of public events. *Anthropological Forum* 7 (2), 193–214.

Moore, Henrietta L. 1994. *A passion for difference.* Cambridge: Polity Press.

Morris, Meaghan. 1988. At Henry Parkes Motel. *Cultural Studies* 2 (1), 1–47.

Mouzelis, Nicos P. 1978. *Modern Greece: facets of underdevelopment.* London: Macmillan.

Myerhoff, Barbara G. 1978. *Number our days.* New York: Simon and Schuster.

―――― 1990. The transformation of consciousness in ritual performances: some thoughts and questions. In *By means of performance: intercultural studies of theatre and ritual* (eds.) Richard Schechner and Willa Appel. Cambridge: Cambridge University Press.

Nazou, Despina. 1996. Η ταυτότητα του νησιού. In Η άλλη Μύκονος. *Επτά Ημέρες/Καθημερινή* 25 8, 16–18.

Nelson, Lise. 1999. Bodies (and spaces) do matter: the limits of performativity. *Gender, Place and Culture* 6 (4), 331–53.

Nietzsche, Friedrich. 1974. *The gay science.* New York: Vintage.

Okely, Judith. 1975. The self and scientism. *Journal of the Social Anthropology Society of Oxford* 6 (3), 171–88.

Okely, Judith. 1983. *The traveller-Gypsies.* Cambridge: Cambridge University Press.

_____ 1992. Anthropology and autobiography: participatory experience and embodied knowledge. In *Anthropology and autobiography* (eds.) Judith Okely and Helen Callaway. London: Routledge.

_____ 1996. *Own or other culture*. London: Routledge.

Okely, Judith and Helen Callaway. (eds.) 1992. *Anthropology and autobiography*. London: Routledge.

Panourgia, Neni. 1995. *Fragments of death, fables of identity: an Athenian anthropography*. Madison: University of Wisconsin Press.

Papachristos, Dimitris. 1992. *Το άγριον όρος της ψυχής*. Athens: Νέα Σύνορα-Λιβάνη.

Papailias, Penelope. 2003. 'Money of *kurbet* is money of blood': the making of a 'hero' of migration at the Greek-Albanian border. *Journal of Ethnic and Migration Studies* 29 (6), 1059–78.

Papastergiadis, Nikos. 1997. Tracing hybridity in theory. In *Debating cultural hybridity: multi-cultural identities and the politics of anti-racism* (eds.) Pnina Werbner and Tariq Modood. London: Zed Books.

Papataxiarchis, Evthymios. 1988. *Kinship, friendship and gender relations in two Aegean Greek communities*. Unpublished Ph.D. thesis, University of London.

_____ 1990. 'Διά την σύστασιν και ωφέλειαν της κοινότητος του χωρίου': σχέσεις και σύμβολα της εντοπιότητας σε μια αιγαιακή κοινωνία. In *Κοινότητα, κοινωνία και ιδεολογία: Ο Κωνσταντίνος Καραβίδας και η προβληματική των κοινωνικών επιστημών* (eds.) Μ. Komninou and Ε. Papataxiarchis. Athens: Παπαζήσης.

Papataxiarchis, Evthymios. 1991. Friends of the heart: male commensal solidarity, gender, and kinship in Aegean Greece. In *Contested identities: gender and kinship in modern Greece* (eds.) Peter Loizos and Evthymios Papataxiarchis. Princeton: Princeton University Press.

_____ 1992a. Από τη σκοπιά του φύλου: ανθρωπολογικές θεωρήσεις της σύγχρονης Ελλάδας. In *Ταυτότητες και φύλο στη σύγχρονη Ελλάδα: ανθρωπολογικές προσεγγίσεις* (eds.) Ε. Παπαταξιάρχης and Θ. Παραδέλλης. Athens: University of the Aegean. Καστανιώτης.

_____ 1992b. Ο κόσμος του καφενείου: ταυτότητα και ανταλλαγή στον ανδρικό συμποσιασμό. In *Ταυτότητες και φύλο στη σύγχρονη Ελλάδα: ανθρωπολογικές προσεγγίσεις* (eds.) Ε. Παπαταξιάρχης and Θ. Παραδέλλης. Athens: University of the Aegean. Καστανιώτης.

Parkin, David, Lionel Caplan and Humphrey Fisher. (eds.) 1996. *The politics of cultural performance*. Oxford: Berghahn Books.

Patton, Paul. 1991. Postmodern subjectivity: the problem of the actor (Zarathustra and the Butler). *Postmodern Critical Theorising* 30, 32–41.

Perkins, Harvey C. and David C. Thorns. 2001. Gazing or performing: reflections on Urry's tourist gaze in the context of contemporary experience in the Antipodes. *International Sociology* 16 (2), 185–204.

Petropoulos, Elias 1972. *Ρεμπέτικα τραγούδια*. Athens: Κέδρος.

_____ 1987. *Το Άγιο χασισάκι*. Athens: Νεφέλη.

Pettifer, James. 1993. *The Greeks: the land and people since the war*. Harmondsworth: Penguin.

Picard, Michel. 1996. *Bali: cultural tourism and tourist culture*. Singapore: Archipelago Press.
Possamaï, Adam. 2002. Cultural consumption of history and popular culture in alternative spiritualities. *Journal of Consumer Culture* 2 (2), 197–218.
Pratt, Mary Louise. 1992. *Imperial eyes: travel writing and transculturation*. London: Routledge.
Rabinow, Paul. 1977. *Reflections on fieldwork in Morocco*. Berkeley: University of California Press.
Rapport, Nigel. 1992. From affect to analysis: the biography of an interaction in an English village. In *Anthropology and autobiography* (eds.) Judith Okely and Helen Callaway. London: Routledge.
_____ 1997. *Transcendent individual: towards a literary and liberal anthropology*. London: Routledge.
_____ 2003. *I am dynamite: an alternative anthropology of power*. London: Routledge.
Rapport, Nigel and Andrew Dawson. 1998. Home and movement: a polemic. In *Migrants of identity: perceptions of home in a world of movement* (eds.) Nigel Rapport and Andrew Dawson. Oxford: Berg.
Reed-Danahay, Deborah E. (ed.) 1997. *Auto/Ethnography: rewriting the self and the social*. Oxford: Berg.
Reich, Wilhelm. 1948. *Listen, little man!* New York: Farrar, Strauss and Giroux.
Ricoeur, Paul. 1991a. Life in quest of narrative. In *On Paul Ricoeur: narrative and interpretation* (ed.) David Wood. London: Routledge.
_____ 1991b. Narrative identity. In *On Paul Ricoeur: narrative and interpretation* (ed.) David Wood. London: Routledge.
Ricoeur, Paul. 1992. *Oneself as another*. Chicago: University of Chicago Press.
Ritzer, George and Allan Liska. 1997. McDisneyization and post-tourism: complementary perspectives on contemporary tourism. In *Touring cultures: transformations of travel and theory* (eds.) Chris Rojek and John Urry. London: Routledge.
Robertson, George, Melinda Mash, Lisa Tickner, Jon Bird, Barry Curtis and Tim Putnam. (eds.) 1994. *Travellers' tales: narratives of home and displacement*. London: Routledge.
Rojek, Chris and John Urry. (eds.) 1997. *Touring cultures: transformations of travel and theory*. London: Routledge.
Romanos, A. 1983. *Ελληνική παραδοσιακή αρχιτεκτονική: Μύκονος*. Athens: Μέλισσα.
Roussel, P. 1990. *Δήλος: η πανίερη νήσος*. Athens: Δημιουργία.
Said, Edward. 1991. Traveling theory. In *The world, the text and the critic*. London: Vintage.
Saldanha, Arun. 2002. Music tourism and factions of bodies in Goa. *Tourist Studies* 2 (1), 43–62.
Sangren, S.P. 1988. Rhetoric and the authority of ethnography: 'postmodernism' and the social reproduction of texts. *Current Anthropology* 29 (3), 405–24.
Schechner, Richard. 1985. *Between theater and anthropology*. Philadelphia: University of Pennsylvania Press.
_____ 1988. *Performance theory*. London: Routledge.

―――― 1990. Magnitudes of performance. In *By means of performance: intercultural studies of theatre and ritual* (eds.) Richard Schechner and Willa Appel. Cambridge: Cambridge University Press.

―――― 1995. *The future of ritual: writings on culture and performance*. London: Routledge.

Schechner, Richard and Willa Appel. 1990. Introduction. In *By means of performance: intercultural studies of theatre and ritual* (eds.) Richard Schechner and Willa Appel. Cambridge: Cambridge University Press.

Schieffelin, Edward L. 1998. Problematizing performance. In *Ritual, performance, media* (ed.) Felicia Hughes-Freeland. London: Routledge.

Seferis, George. 1974. *Δοκιμές*, τόμος β΄. Athens: Ικαρος.

Seremetakis, C. Nadia. 1987. Women and death: cultural power and ritual process in Inner Mani. *Canadian Women Studies* 8, 108–10.

Seremetakis, C. Nadia. 1991. *The last word: women, death, and divination in Inner Mani*. Chicago: University of Chicago Press.

Shepherd, Robert. 2003. Fieldwork without remorse: travel desires in a tourist world. *Consumption, Markets and Culture* 6 (2), 133–44.

Shields, Rob. 1991. *Places on the margin: alternative geographies of modernity*. London: Routledge.

―――― 1992a. Spaces for the subject of consumption. In *Lifestyle shopping: the subject of consumption* (ed.) Rob Shields. London: Routledge.

―――― 1992b. The individual, consumption cultures and the fate of community. In *Lifestyle shopping: the subject of consumption* (ed.) Rob Shields. London: Routledge.

―――― 1996. Masses or tribes? Foreword in *The time of the tribes: the decline of individualism in mass society* Michel Maffesoli. London: Sage.

Shilling, Chris. 1993. *The body and social theory*. London: Sage.

Skouteri-Didaskalou, N. 1984. *Ανθρωπολογικά για το γυναικείο ζήτημα*. Athens: Πολίτης.

Spivak, Gayatri Chakravorty. 1974. Translators preface. In *Of grammatology* (1974) J. Derrida. London: The Johns Hopkins University Press.

―――― 1988. Can the subaltern speak? In *Marxism and the interpretation of culture* (eds.) Cary Nelson and Lawrence Grossberg. Urbana: University of Illinois Press.

Spyer, Patricia. 1998. Introduction. In *Border fetishisms: material objects in unstable spaces* (ed.) Patricia Spyer. London: Routledge.

Stanford, W.B. and E.J. Finopoulos. (eds.) 1984. *Lord Charlemont in Greece and Turkey 1749*. London: A.G. Leventis Foundation.

Stasinopoulos, E. (n.d.) *Η Δήλος: ιστορία, εικόνες και χάρτες του αρχαίου ιερού*. Athens.

Stewart, Charles. 1989. Hegemony or rationality? The position of the supernatural in modern Greece. *Journal of Modern Greek Studies* 7, 77–104.

―――― 1991. *Demons and the Devil: moral imagination in modern Greek culture*. Princeton: Princeton University Press.

―――― 1994. Syncretism as a dimension of nationalist discourse in modern Greece. In *Syncretism/Anti-syncretism: the politics of religious synthesis* (eds.) Charles Stewart and Rosalind Shaw. London: Routledge.

Stewart, Charles and Rosalind Shaw. 1994. Introduction: problematizing syncretism. In *Syncretism/Anti-syncretism: the politics of religious synthesis* (eds.) Charles Stewart and Rosalind Shaw. London: Routledge.

St.John, Graham. 2001. Alternative cultural heterotopia and the liminoid body: beyond Turner at ConFest. *Australian Journal of Anthropology* 12 (1), 47–66.

Stott, Margaret. 1982. *The social and economic structure of the Greek island of Mykonos. 1860–1978: an anthropological perspective.* Unpublished Ph.D. thesis, University of London.

Strathern, Marilyn. 1987. The limits of auto-anthropology. In *Anthropology at home* (ed.) A. Jackson. London: Tavistock.

Sutton, David E. 1998. *Memories cast in stone: the relevance of the past in everyday life.* Oxford: Berg.

Svensson, Birgitta. 1997. The power of biography: criminal policy, prison life, and the formation of criminal identities in the Swedish welfare state. In *Auto/Ethnography: rewriting the self and the social* (ed.) Deborah E. Reed-Danahay. Oxford: Berg.

Tambiah, Stanley. 1979. A performative approach to ritual. *Proceedings of the British Academy* 65, 113–66.

Taussig, Michael. 1993. *Mimesis and alterity: a particular history of the senses.* London: Routledge.

―――― 1998. Crossing the face. In *Border fetishes: material objects in unstable spaces* (ed.) Patricia Spyer. London: Routledge.

Taylor, Charles. 1989. *Sources of the self: the making of the modern identity.* Cambridge: Cambridge University Press.

―――― 1991. *The ethics of authenticity.* London: Harvard University Press.

Tedlock, B. 1991. From participant observation to the observation of participation: the emergence of narrative ethnography. *Journal of Anthropological Research* 47 (1), 69–94.

Thompson, Judith and Paul Heelas. 1986. *The way of the heart: the Rajneesh movement.* Wellingborough: Aquarian Press.

Tilley, Christopher. 1997. Performing culture in the global village. *Critique of Anthropology* 17 (1), 67–89.

Triantafyllou, K. 1986. Μυκονιάτικα ήθη και έθιμα. In *Μύκονος, Δήλος: χθές και σήμερα.* Athens: Toumbis.

Trinh T. Minh-ha. 1991. *When the moon waxes red: representation, gender and cultural politics.* New York: Routledge.

―――― 1994. Other than myself/my other self. In *Travellers' tales: narratives of home and displacement* (eds.) G. Robertson et al. London: Routledge.

Tsakos, K. 1996. Η ιστορία του νησιού. In Η άλλη Μύκονος. Επτά Ημέρες/Καθημερινή 25 (8), 3–5.

Tsangarousianos, Stathis. 1993. Ιερομόναχος Συμεών Γρηγοριάτης: ο θεός είναι σαν το καλό χαβιάρι. *Τέταρτο* 6, 63–68.

Tsiganou, J. 1988. *The development of politics regulating drug use in Greece.* Unpublished Ph.D. thesis, University of London.

Tsiki, D. 1981. Ιδεολογία και ψυχολογία του ρεμπέτη. *Επιθεώρηση Κοινωνικών Επιστημών* 4–5, 131–36.

Tsili, S. 1987. Τοξικομανία μια άλλη προσέγγιση. *Επιθεώρηση Κοινωνικών Ερευνών* 66, 226–39.

Turner, Victor. 1967. *The forest of symbols: aspects of Ndembu ritual.* Ithaca: Cornell University Press.
_____ 1974. *The ritual process: structure and anti-structure.* Harmondsworth: Penguin.
Turner, Victor and Edith Turner. 1978. *Image and pilgrimage in Christian culture: anthropological perspectives.* New York: Columbia University Press.
Tzanelli, Rodanthi. 2003. 'Casting' the Neohellenic 'other': tourism, the culture industry, and contemporary Orientalism in 'Captain Corelli's Mandolin' (2001). *Journal of Consumer Culture* 3 (2), 217–44.
Urry, John. 1990. *The tourist gaze: leisure and travel in contemporary societies.* London: Sage.
_____ 1995. *Consuming places.* London: Routledge.
Veijola, Soile and Eeva Jokinen. 1994. The body in tourism. *Theory, Culture and Society* 11 (3), 125–51.
Vlachos, E. 1987. *Στιγμιότυπα ... φωτογραφικές αναμνήσεις της Ελένης Βλάχου.* Athens: Καθημερινή.
Wagner, Roy. 1981. *The invention of culture.* Chicago: University of Chicago Press.
Waldren, Jacqueline. 1996. *Insiders and outsiders: paradise and reality in Mallorca.* Oxford: Berghahn Books.
_____ 1997. We are not tourists – we live here. In *Tourists and tourism: identifying with people and places* (eds.) Simone Abram, Jacqueline Waldren and Donald V.L. Macleod. Oxford: Berg.
Ward, Sally. 2003. On shifting ground: changing formulations of place in anthropology. *Australian Journal of Anthropology* 14 (1), 80–96.
Wilson, Elizabeth. 1998. Bohemian love. *Theory, Culture and Society* 15 (3–4) 111–27.
Wolff, Janet. 1993. On the road again: metaphors of travel in cultural criticism. *Cultural Studies* 7 (2), 224–39.
Wood, R.C. 1992. *Working in hotels and catering.* London: Routledge.
Yamashita, Shinji. 2003. *Bali and beyond: explorations in the anthropology of tourism.* Oxford: Berghahn Books.
Yangakis, G. 1985. *Η αντίρροπη πληθυσμιακή και οικονομική εξέλιξη της Μυκόνου και της Τήνου.* Athens: Σπανός.
Yangakis, G. et al. 1986. *Μύκονος, Δήλος: χθές και σήμερα.* Athens: Toumbis.
Zarkia, Cornelia. 1996. Philoxenia receiving tourists – but not guests – on a Greek island. In *Coping with tourists: European reactions to mass tourism* (ed.) Jeremy Boissevain. Oxford: Berghahn Books.
Zinovieff, Sofka 1991. Hunters and hunted: *kamaki* and the ambiguities of sexual predation in a Greek town. In *Contested identities: gender and kinship in modern Greece* (eds.) Peter Loizos and Evthymios Papataxiarchis. Princeton: Princeton University Press.

INDEX

A
Abbeele, George van den, 225
Abu-Lughod, Lila, 62n35, 71, 256
Adler, Judith, 238, 264
aesthetics
    aestheticisation of the quotidian, 218
    and autonomy, 26
    metaphysics and, 218
    Mykoniots and, 28, 217, 219, 231
    reflexivity, 21, 22–23, 27
affective communities
    Mafessoli, 76, 216, 222
    Mykonian haunts as, 61n21
    Mykonos as, xii, 18, 47, 48, 145, 231, 237, 241–42, 245
agency
    Foucault on self and, 75–76
    in Greek ethnography, 250
    individuality and, 21, 260
    performance and, 229, 246
    ritual construction and, 210
    and subjectivity in anthropological theory, 250
    unconscious, 219
Airault, Régis, 230n2
Albanians
    in the Greek media, 188, 190–91
    in Mykonos, 4, 135n47
aleatory, the
    encounters in Mykonos, 57, 168, 169, 231, 239, 242
    Mafessoli on, 169, 218
    multiplicity and, 227
Alexiou, Margaret
    on death and marriage, 177
ambiguity
    Dionysus, 221
    Greek identity and, 252–53
    Mykoniots and, 169
    space and, 16
    subjectivity and, 227
Amit, Vered and Nigel Rapport, 32n10, 171
amorality
    aestheticisation of, 221
    Brighton as site of, 172n11, 247
    the Mykonian beach as site of, 247n4
    and the Mykonian space, 13
    of the Mykonians, 40, 161
    of the *Mykoniots*, 26, 90, 96, 144, 156
Ano Mera, 31n2, 83, 116
anthropology
    of emotions, 62n34, 62n35, 69, 256–57
    and fluidity, 248n10
    of friends, 68

Apollo
  Delian Mysteries, 145
  Delos/radiance, 14, 143, 171n2
  hippies and, 37, 41
  and the *Mykoniots'* narcissism, 134–35n45, 141–42, 143, 154–55
  therapy, 159
aporias, 247n3
Appadurai, Arjun
  on cosmopolitan ethnography, 171
Appel, Willa, 2
'apprenticeship'
  ephemeral patronage, 96, 154
  in the Mykonian networks, 37, 67–68, 160, 213n16
Argyrou, Vassos, 181–82, 205–06, 212n13, 212n14, 255
  on Cypriot weddings, 182, 205
Athenian bourgeoisie
  invasion of Mykonos, xii, 9, 36–37, 38, 40–41, 46, 60n10, 83, 91, 99, 162, 191, 206
Athens
  connection to Mykonos, xii, 6, 40, 46, 55, 88, 103, 112, 115, 121, 133n30, 151, 219, 238
Augé, Marc, 32n9, 57
  on non-places, 57
authenticity
  beauty and, 106
  criticism of MacCannell's notion of, 270n1
  ethnography and, 72
  narration and, 51, 62n28
  queer 'home', 248n11
  and the Romantic movement, 265
  staged, 7, 14, 134n35, 263–64, 268
  stylistic, 38
  Taylor on, 76
  tourism and, 266
auto-anthropology/ethnography, 65–66, 68–69
  auto-ethnographic writing, viii
  Greece and, 1
  performative, 1–2
autobiography, 68–69, 109, 125, 130, 234–35

and ethnography, 7, 65–66, 71, 119, 122
Axioti, Melpo, 163, 247n9

B
Backos, A.., 4
Badiou, Alain, 219, 232
  on the 'event', 219, 232, 247n2
Bakalaki, Alexandra, 68, 69
Bakhtin, Mikhail, 6, 215
Bali, 6, 30, 33n13, 61n25
Barker, Eileen, 33n16, 132n9
Barthel-Bouchier, Diane, 264
Battaglia, Debbora, 130
Baudrillard, Jean, 10, 21, 22, 210, 216, 217
Bauman, Zygmunt, 30, 56–57, 163, 245
  and the 'tourist syndrome', 56
  on the transient subject, 56
Beauvoir, Simone de, 166, 247n8
Beck, Ulrich, and Beck-Gernsheim, Elisabeth, 208
Behar, Ruth, 66, 256
Bell, D., 72, 132n4
Bendix, Regina, 51
Benhabib, Seyla, 230n4
Benjamin, Walter, 13, 215
Bhabha, Homi, 227
  on hybridity, 227
Bloch, Maurice, 181
Boas, Franz, 101
body, the
  abject body (Butler), 229, 230n4
  (*Mykoniots'* s) aestheticisation of, xiii, 12, 78, 79, 88, 95, 99, 100, 101, 105–8, 110, 111, 134–35n45, 141, 143, 147, 154, 155, 158, 192, 194, 202, 234, 235, 245
  anorexic, 235
  body without organs (Deleuze and Guattari), 230n3, 231
  burnt body/split body, 245
  music and (Deleuze), 238
  naked, 12, 94, 101, 108, 134n31, 154, 155, 202
  and performativity, 224

Index

as physical capital (Bourdieu), 106, 107
in post-structuralist theory, 22–23, 75
and self (rapture), 242
sensual, 220
Bohemia, 9, 118, 233, 241, 244
Boissevain, Jeremy, 134n35, 264, 267
on 'host community' and performance, 7
Bourdieu, Pierre, 32n10, 33n14, 135n48, 210, 216, 250
on distinction, 11, 24, 63n40, 70, 182, 217, 255,
habitus, 16, 22, 107, 194
physical capital, 107
Braidotti, Rosi, 223–27, 247n5
on agency, 226
on nomadism, 225, 226
on subjectivity, 224
on the transient subject, 226
Brettell, Caroline B., 71
Bruner, Edward M., 7, 174n34, 247n4, 264
Buddhism, 23, 82, 89, 119, 127, 162
Butler, Judith
'abject body', 229, 230n4
and agency, 229
and gender performativity, 24
political performativity, 224, 229

C
Cabezas, Amalia, 264
Callaway, Helen, 69, 250
Campbell, Colin, 266
Campbell, J.K., 96, 101, 135n49, 179, 251
Campbell, Joseph, 101
Camus, Albert, 114
Caplan, Lionel, 12
Caplan, Pat, 69
Caraveli, Anna, 82–83, 253
Carrier, James, 267
Carter, L., 133n24
Caulfeild, James, 171n5
Certeau, Michel de, 57, 215
Chadjifotiou, Zachos, 45, 62n38, 63n39

Charlemont, Lord, 171n5
Clifford, James, 71, 72, 190, 225
Cocteau, Jean, 140
Cohen, Anthony, P., 68, 70, 176, 180, 208, 210, 250
Cohen, Erik, 264
commemoration, xiv, 51, 81, 132n10, 232, 239, 243, 244
commensality
ceremonial, 38, 166, 170, 188, 216, 243
drinking, 37, 46–47, 114, 199
in Greek ethnography, 59n7, 62n34
in Greek memorial services, 132n10
male, 253, 257
random, 28, 90, 95, 96, 103, 116, 169, 207, 237
sacred, 36, 97, 149, 217
in the traditional Mykonian *paniyiris*, 168
ConFest (Australia), 30, 32n6, 220
constructivism
cultural, 150, 156–57, 211
historical, 140, 156–57, 217, 254
consumption, xii, viii, 23
imagination and, 266
Mafessoli on mass consumption, 215
movements, 31
Mykoniots' consumption practices, 18, 26, 31, 35, 82
Mykonos as consumption site, 8, 10, 24, 61n15, 108, 222–23, 244
post-tourist and, 266
self and, 24, 73, 107, 130
self-religions and, 30, 33n17
Shields on consumption sites, 16, 17, 220, 222, 223
Cooper, David, 115
Costera Meijer, Irene and Baukje Prins, 229
Cowan, Jane, 133n26, 138n71, 177, 179, 180, 194, 207, 256, 257
Crang, Philip, 173n16, 174n34, 264
Crapanzano, Vincent, 68, 71
Crouch, David and Luke Desforges, 269

D

Damer, Seán, 7, 9, 32n3, 264–65
Damianakos, Stathis, 37, 47
Danforth, Loring, 62n29, 132n10, 177, 212n2, 251
De Lauretis, Teresa, 69, 72, 225
death, xiv, 69, 81, 82, 125, 175
   on Delos, 146
   and marriage, 176, 177, 212n2
   Mykoniots and, xiv, 50–51, 53–55, 62n29, 62n35, 236, 238, 239, 243, 244, 246
   Robert Graves, 241
Deleuze, Gilles, 226–27, 231, 247n1
   on desire, 217
   on dynamic marginality, 233
   on subjectivity and agency, 226–27
Deleuze, Gilles and Félix Guattari, 7, 226–27, 230n3, 231, 238, 239
   on facelessness, 238
   on nomadism and desire, 230n3
Delos
   as amoral space, 80, 140, 150
   and beauty, 134–35n45
   and death, 146
   as fetish space, 143, 158–59
   as invisible, 152, 173n17
   and movement, 240
   and the *Mykoniots*, 173n18
   and Mykonos' space-myth, 142–43, 171n4
   as sacred island, 40, 134n45, 146, 147, 149, 151, 158–59, 164, 171n2
   space-myth of, 140–41
   tourism, 146
Delphi
   as a 'solar centre', 141, 172
Derrida, Jacques, 22, 73, 230n4, 242, 247n3
   aporias, 242, 247n3
   deconstructionism, 21, 73, 261n2
desire
   for community, 57
   for exclusion, 3
   for fluidity, xiii, 26, 67, 223, 224, 225
   Mafessoli on, 217

and marginality, xii
and the Mykonian image, 15, 141, 269
Mykoniots discourse of, 20, 24, 75, 107, 122–23, 130, 228, 231
self and, 30
tourist and, 7, 247, 264, 266, 267
and travel, 247
for visibility, 235
difference
   as fetish, 161
Dionysianism
   contemporary collectivities (Maffesoli), 215, 220–21
   Delos, 80, 146, 150, 216
   and the *Mykoniots*, 37, 39, 100, 141, 151, 166, 217, 218
   on Mykonos, 41, 80, 87, 142, 220
   Rajneesh and, 79
   remnant celebrations, 25, 139–177, 142, 166, 169
displacement, viii
distinction, xiii
   and beauty, 105, 107
   and class, 133n29, 165, 181–83, 206, 255
   and drugs, 115, 204
   masculinity and, 25, 257
   music as, 8
   and 'Mykonian' identity, 3, 24, 28, 70, 204, 207
   in Mykonos space, 15, 25, 63n40, 99, 175, 205, 268
Doumas, C., 172n9
dramaturgy
   tourism and, 264–65
drugs
   and ancient Delos, 145, 151
   ConFest, 30
   and Greek legislation, 136–37n53, 137n55
   Mykonian 'gangs', 26, 36, 37, 45, 49, 50, 52–55, 58–59, 59n3, 79, 158–59, 184
   the *Mykoniots*'s discourse on, 80, 86, 87, 104, 108, 109, 115–16, 122,

296

123, 127, 149, 152, 154, 156, 157, 163, 169, 204–5, 213n19, 223, 234
and Mykonos, 42–43
as protest, 53
in seventies Greece, 137n61
women and discourses on, 158
Dubisch, Jill, 3, 62n35, 69, 93, 133n20, 135n49, 138n71, 161, 172n12, 212n11, 256, 262n7
on female performance, 256
Du Boulay, Juliet, 132n7, 132n11, 135–36n49, 180, 251
Dumont, Jean-Paul, 19, 71
Durkheim, Émile, 181, 250
Durrell, Lawrence, 14, 31n1, 40–41, 60n14, 135n45, 146, 159, 171n4
definition of the *Mykoniots d'élection*, 31n1, 40–41
on Delos excursions, 159
on Greek islands, 159
and the myth of modern Mykonos, 14, 40–41, 134–35n45
on Tinos, 171n4

E
Eade, John and Michael J. Sallnow, 220
eccentricity
and fetish, 2, 12
and habitus, 138
Mykoniots' self-myth of, 65, 56, 129, 210
and performance, 13, 137–38n69
Edensor, Tim, 174n34, 264
Eliade, Mircea, 11
'energy'/'magnetic force'
Brighton, 172n11
Delos, 141–43
Mykonos, 144
triangle (Mykonos-Delos-Tinos), 144–45
Engels, Freidrich, 137n60
ethnography
experimental, 69, 70–71, 72
and fiction, viii, 7, 19, 66, 72, 132n6, 212n4
as invention, 19, 71, 251
and surrealism, 19

Evans-Pritchard, E.E., 251
ex-centricity
ex-centric group, 18
and performativity, 20

F
family
extended, 96
Mykoniots avoidance of, 29, 42, 43, 46, 67, 100, 101, 108, 112, 122
Fardon, Richard, 258
Faubion, James D., 185, 186, 211, 212n4, 254
on modern Greek's historical constructivism, 156, 254
Featherstone, Mike, 21, 269
Feifer, M., 266
feminism
and ethnography, 69
Fernandez, James W., 208, 250
fetish, vii, 6, 26
eccentricity and, 13
marginality as, 18, 60n13
masculinity and, 45, 48
and self, viii, xii, 11, 12, 13, 20, 28, 65, 176, 268
self-transformation as, 12
(Mykonian) space as, xi, xii, 3, 4, 8, 9, 11, 15, 16, 20, 40, 57, 60n11, 145, 163, 267
time as, 20, 184
Finopoulos, E.J., 172n5
Fisher, Humphrey, 12
fluidity, xiii
in ethnography, 69
and *Mykoniots*' rules of socialisation, 241
Mykonos space and, 96, 240
as performative self-identity, 61n21, 67, 100, 225
and post-modern nomadism, 223
and subjectivity/collectivity, 12, 19, 227, 231
Fortier, Anne-Marie, 240
Foucault, Michel, 31, 74–75, 124, 130, 134n31, 138n72, 221, 229, 230n4

Index

on the 'aesthetics of existence', 74, 75
on autonomy, 221
on self and pleasure, 130
Frank, Katherine, 7–8
Franklin, Adrian, 56, 266
front and backstage performance, 7, 173n18, 263
Mykoniots as decodifiers of Mykonos', 267
Fullager, Simone, 166, 230n3, 236, 247n8

G

Gedalof, Irene, 227
critic of Braidotti's nomad, 22
diasporic space, 227
Geertz, Clifford, 72
Gefou-Madianou, Dimitra, 59n7
gender
anthropology, 1, 138n71
in Greek ethnography, 180, 212n11, 249–57
Greek stereotypes of, 81, 211
Mykoniots' aesthetics of, 29, 35, 44, 81, 82, 90, 97, 101, 129, 137n64, 155, 177, 194
performance of pain, 82, 83, 85–86, 177, 234–35
and performativity, viii, 24, 25, 63n42, 223, 224, 225, 229, 249, 257
reflexive ethnography, 68, 69
structural significance of (vis-à-vis the *Mykoniots*), 10, 18, 25, 50
Gibson, James E., 220, 244, 245
Giddens, Antony, 21, 22, 27, 71, 131n1, 181, 210, 213n21, 250
on commitment, 181
on gender, 181
Girard, René, 244
'girls', the/the 'sorceresses', 38, 87, 89–90, 108, 117, 133n26, 135–36n49, 192–95
Goffman, Erving, 7, 229, 264, 265
on performance, 208, 221
Gooldin, Sigal, 234–35, 247n6

gossip, 9, 55
Mykoniots and, 27, 67, 78, 98, 113, 132n7, 188, 219
Graburn, Nelson, H.H., 51, 264
Graves, Robert, 62n33, 172n6, 241
Greek ethnography
ideals of masculine 'independence', 77, 81
Greek islands
the tourist image of, 32n8
tourists' semiotics of, 32n8
Greek Ministry of Culture, 172n9
Greger, S., 180
group
invented (i.e., the *Mykoniots*), viii, xi, xiv, 3, 18, 19, 23, 217
transient, 18
Guattari, Félix, 7, 227, 230n3, 231, 238, 239
Gurdjieff, G.I., 30, 101, 134n39

H

Habermas, Jürgen, 230n4
habitus
Bourdieu on, 16, 22, 107
eccentricity, 138
Herzfeld, 258
Maffesoli on, 219
Mykoniots', 12, 13, 14, 19, 107, 108, 109, 209, 263
Hallward, Peter, 247n2
Harrison, Julia, 268–69
Harvey, David, 73
Harvey, Penelope, 9–10, 17, 211, 212n7
hashish
as female bonding, 193
as group bonding, 233
local Mykonians and, 53, 56
and male-bonding, 37, 159, 167, 237
Mykoniots' fetishisation of, 59n3, 85, 93, 102, 110, 113, 115, 147, 154, 169, 188, 198, 201, 202
rembetes and, 47
Hastrup, Kirsten, 68, 246
Hebdidge, Dick, 26

298

hedonism
    of Delos and, 141, 150, 166
    excessive drinking, xii, 53, 63, 109
    Maffesoli on tribal, 219, 221
    and marginality, xiii
    Mykoniots and, 26, 75, 109, 206
    Mykonos and, xiii, 6, 16, 37–38, 42, 47, 63n43, 141, 144, 145, 166, 206
    and the sensual tourist, 270n5
Heelas, Paul, 27, 28–29, 30, 33n17, 33n19, 127, 134n39, 137n57
Hellier, Chris, 262n6
Hera, 173n17
heroin
    addiction as negative fetishisation, 136n53
    in Greece, 136–7n53, 137n61
    and masculinity, 117
    on Mykonos/amongst the *Mykoniots*, 48, 54, 86, 114–15, 120–21, 123–25, 127, 137n64, 184, 186, 198, 203–5, 232–36, 254
Herzfeld, Michael, 11, 25, 44, 61n17, 68, 71, 96, 132n11, 135n49, 137n64, 138n71, 173n25, 249–50, 251, 252–53, 256, 257–60, 261–62n5
    disemia, 249, 252, 258
    masculine performativity, 249
    on 'performative' Greek ethnography, 251–53
    on performative 'stealing', 173n25, 261n5
heterogeneity
    Lévi-Strauss's cultural, 31
    textual, 73
heterotopia, 17
    cultural, 7, 30–31, 32n6
Hinduism, 23
hippies, 133n25
    Mykonos and, 20, 21, 23, 30, 37, 42, 46, 60n11, 67, 79, 98, 118, 179, 198, 206, 207, 232
    and performance, 78
Hirschon, Renée, 9, 133n20
Hobsbawn, Eric, 33n13
Hockey, Jenny, 72

Holst, Gail, 47
'home', 5
    anthropology at, 68
    and movement viii, 138, 225, 240, 245, 270n1
    Mykonos as, 3, 26, 36, 41, 45, 46, 129, 145, 160, 230n2, 233, 240, 247n9, 248n11
    and queer identity, 9, 248n11
    and travel theory, 225
homosexuality
    Mykonos and, xiii, 41, 45, 135n45, 206, 228–29
host community, 7
Howe, Alyssa C., 9, 248n11
Hughes-Freeland, Felicia, 231
Hurley, Molly and James Trimarco, 264
Hutnyk, John, 9, 225
Hutson, Scott R., 78, 187
Huxley, Aldous, 30

I
identity
    as bricolage, 20, 23, 96, 103, 129, 131, 132n6, 176, 186, 210, 254
immigrants
    cosmopolitan, 44
    in Mykonos, 4, 39, 42, 135n47, 190
India, 20
    ashram in, 50, 79, 121, 125, 186
    as fetish, 13, 88
    and Mykonos, 78, 79
individuality
    extreme individuality, viii, 13, 65, 241
    fetishised, 11
Iossifides, A. Marina, 132n6
Irigaray, Luce, 236, 247n7
Iyer, Pico
    on the 'privileged homeless', 138n70

J
Jackson, Anthony
    anthropology at home, 68
Jackson, M., 248n10
James, Allison, 12
Jansson, André, 266, 270n5

299

Index

Jordan, T., 242
Jung, Carl G., 30, 110

K
Kantsa, Venetia, 256
Karantonis, A., 60n12, 140
Katsoudas, K.D., 4
Kaur, Raminder, 225
Keffaliniadis, N., 60n13
Kenna, Margaret, 68
Kirtsoglou, Elizabeth, 256
koinohristoi, 162, 174n31
Kondo, Dorinne K., 256
Kousathanas, P., 159, 171–72n5
Kyriazopoulos, V., 32n2, 32–33n11

L
Lacan, Jacques, 219, 230n4
  inter-subjectivity, 219
Laing, R.D., 115
Lasch, Christopher, 27, 107
Lash, Scott, 17–18, 21–23, 27, 32n8, 33n14, 213n21, 217, 226, 266–67
Leary, Timothy, 115
leela, 89, 133n24
  and *maya*, 12
Leontis, Artemis, 163, 247n9
Leto, 150, 173n17
Lévi-Strauss, Claude, 31
Liavas, Lampros, 171n2
liberality
  as *Mykoniots*' fetish, 2, 206
  Mykoniots' liberation of libido, 28, 111, 156
  Mykonos as sign of, 4, 40, 60, 144, 152
  from the social constrains, 29
liminality
  and consumption sites, 222
  and corporeality, 234
  and drugs, 152
  as fetish, 16
  Maffesoli on, 216
  Mykonian beach and, 247n4
  and *Mykoniots*, 86, 139, 161, 169–70, 175, 178–79, 220, 234, 242, 244

Mykonos' space, xi, xii–xiv, 13, 16, 63n43
  and the orgiastic, 220
  and performance, 18, 246
  and productivity, 6
  and reflexivity, vii, ix, xiv, 236
  and ritual, 208
  and space, 30
  as structure, 220–21
  and time, 139, 178, 208
  and the tourist space, xiv, 6–7, 43, 51, 96, 172n11, 172n15, 179, 243
Lingis, Alphonso, 16
Linse, Cindy, 220
locality
  as belonging, 174
  in cosmopolitan ethnography, 171, 190, 211, 252
  Mykonian locals' idea of, 37
  Mykoniots discourse of, xiv, 20, 116, 161, 210, 258
  Mykonos and, xii, 5, 8, 10, 25, 171
  Mykonos as transgressive locality, 241
Loizos, Peter, 68, 71, 132n6, 138n71, 179, 180, 253
Loukissas, Philppos, 60n10
Lutz, C., 62n35

M
MacCannell, Dean, 173n18, 225, 263, 264, 265, 270n1
macho, 25, 112
  anti-, 97
  female, 155
  in Greek culture, 29, 97
  and heroin, 117
  amongst the *Mykoniots*, 148, 236, 257
Madianou, D., 137n55
Maffesoli, Michel, 21, 22, 76, 169, 215–24, 226, 230n1
  on 'aesthetic style', 76
  and the 'communitarian ideal', 217
  on desire, 217, 230n1
  on the Dionysian orgiastic, 215–16
  emotional ambience, 219

300

on marginal groups, 216
neo-tribalism, 215–16, 223, 224
and performance, 221
and the quotidian as fetish, 215, 221
and the transient subject, 226
mandragora
    Mykonian myth of, 37, 54, 59n5, 151
Manning-Sanders, R., 172n11
Marcus, George E., 12–13, 71, 130, 137–38n69
marginality
    aesthetic, 23
    and the Albanian migrants on Mykonos, 190
    and Greek identity, 68, 252, 253, 257
    and masculinity, 56
    and the *Mykoniots*, 1, 17–18, 19, 42, 56, 57, 99, 130, 133n30, 150, 161, 162, 265
masculinity
    aestheticised, 44–45, 63n43
    agonistic, 25, 137n64, 257
    and drugs, 37
    mythical, 37
    performance of, 35, 253
masks and performativity, 245
    as fetish, 12
    Goffman, 221
    Mafessoli on Dionysus and, 221, 223
    of the *Mykoniots*, 222, 239
    and subjectivity, 12
McDonald, M., 72
McNay, Lois, 74, 75–76, 229, 230n4
Meletopoulos, Tasos, 212n9
meltemi, 91, 93, 162, 164, 168, 233
Mercouri, Merlina, 41, 172n9
Miller, Daniel, 267
Monette, Paul, 240
Moore, D., 242
Moore, Henrietta L., 21, 69, 71, 72–73, 129, 131, 178, 224, 225, 250, 259
Morris, Meaghan, 225
Mount Athos, 104, 186, 212n9, 260, 262n6

mourning, 49–50, 54, 62n29
    absence of, 62n35, 232, 239, 242–43
    Derrida on, 247n3
Mouzelis, Nicos P., 96, 133n29
movement, viii
    and desire, 166, 247n8
    and the feminine, 236, 247n8
    identity and, 227
    Mykoniots and, 20, 240
Myerhoff, Barbara G., 2, 175–76, 246
Mykonian apprenticeship, 38, 191
    and self-transformation, viii
Mykonian basil
    as fetish, 133n28
Mykonian beaches
    as fetish, 247n4
Mykonian haunts, 4, 8–9, 10, 15–16, 42, 47, 48, 49, 52, 55, 61n21, 98, 99, 143, 162, 172n7, 187, 244
    as Deleuzian spaces of 'dynamic marginality', 233
    as fetish, 233
Mykonian houses
    and communal life, 163
    legendary aesthetics of, 78, 93, 102, 110, 237
Mykonian landscape
    as fetish, 14, 39, 85, 91, 106, 153, 166
Mykonian lifestyle
    as fetish, 179, 185
Mykonian locals
    as heroes, xi, 36, 37, 39, 44, 45, 46, 50, 54, 56, 57, 58, 62n38, 113, 151, 158
    as 'queer'/eccentrics, 143–44
Mykonian *paniyiri*
    as expression of syncretism, 25
    as fetish, 207
    and the girls, 87, 108
    and the *Mykoniots*, 45–46, 113, 136n51, see chapter 4, 244
    wedding as, see chapter 5
Mykonian pig-slaughtering feast
    as fetish 174n27
Mykonian police

as fetish, 42, 49, 53, 123, 137n63, 157, 141, 144, 166
Mykonian space
  as intimate and protected, 3, 32n2, 145
Mykonian time, 13
  as fetish, 13, 15–16, 20, 82, 91, 102, 128, 171n1, 178
Mykonian wine
  as fetish, 83–84, 132n13, 142
Mykoniots d'élection, see also 'invented group'
  and the 'art of living', 37, 75, 101, 170, 210
  as genderless, 81, 97, 129, 155
  as solitaires, 41, 78, 80, 82, 88, 98, 101–103, 108, 112, 125, 231, 242, 245
  as 'unbodied collectivity', 242
Mykonos
  as amoral space, xii, 13, 26, 60n12, 80, 144, 150
  as anarchic space, xii, 19, 23, 129, 220
  as Apollonian domain, 154
  [vernacular] architecture of, 8, 13, 14, 32n2, 33n12, 39, 91, 110, 144
  as construction site, 244
  (Mykonos town) as a democratic public space, 9, 162–63, 136n50
  dressing code of, 9, 61n25, 78, 80, 84, 99, 139, 193, 197, 198, 203, 237–38
  as feminine, 88
  history of, 32n11, 60n14, 61n15
  as homosexual pleasure-dome, xiii, 41, 45, 135n45, 206, 228–29
  as liminal space, 172n11, 220, 222, 243, 247n4
  as marginal space, xii–xiii, 17–18, 19, 24, 63n43, 80
  as 'meeting place', 41, 89, 100, 135n45, 220
  as [axiomatic] memory/memory-fetish, 163, 243, 247n9
  mythology, 9, 59, 140, 145, 152, 185
  as a non-place, xiv, 57
  as pleasure zone, 6–7, 16
  as a polythetic sign, 15, 24
  present day reality, xiv, 5, 9, 13n60, 14, 40, 45, 78, 99, 162, 163, 190–91, 233, 244
  primitivism of, 13, 38–39, 158, 161
  as 'queer' space, xiii, 228, 230
  as rurban space, xi, 5, 14
  as sign of cosmopolitanism, xiv, 10, 17, 170
  [the]town of (Hora), 4, 8–10, 31–32n2, 32n7, 222–23, 268
  as transient space, xi, 3, 4
  as the womb (engendered female), 3, 88, 145, 230n2

N

narcissism
  Mykoniots', 107, 110–11
  Mykonos as a symbol of, 135n45, 141, 163
  and revolution, 238
  and the romantic rebel, 114
narrativity
  and appropriation of Mykonos' mythical past, 43, 47, 55, 58, 62n33, 235, 243
  identity and, 230n4, 261n1
  loss, xiv
  self, 2, 12, 65–67, 70, 71–73, 127–31, 131n1, 222
  and travel, 51–52, 57–58
Nazou, Despina, 4
Nelson, Lise, 229
New Age, 25, 26–31, 33n16, 33n19, 80, 134n39, 137n57, 141, 142, 218
  new religious movements, 20, 26–31, 33n16
New Orthodox movement, 182, 186, 195, 260, 261
Nietzsche, Friedrich, 20, 110, 220, 231, 244, 245–46, 247n1
  and 'nomadism', 247
  on performative subjectivity, 245–46
nihilist rebel, 114
nomadism

Index

and agency, 247n1
and the *Mykoniots*, xi, xiii, 3, 6, 26, 45, 70, 228, 240, 259
and performativity, 223
as resistance, 231
nostalgia
   Mykonos and, 54, 61n15, 244
   post-modern, 217
   in the tourist space, 20

O

Okely, Judith, 33n15, 68–69, 71, 73, 134n33, 134n37, 134n43, 250
orgiastic
   on Delos and Mykonos, 216
   drug-taking, 37
   Maffesoli on societal, 215–16, 219, 220–22
   Nietzsche on, 220
   paniyiri, 191, 228
   pig-slaughtering *paniyiri*, 36
Orthodox church (Greek), 8, 84, 161
   Orthodox chapel, 164
Orthodox monastery, 218, 262n6
Orthodox ritual (Greek), 25, 83, 84–85, 144–45, 170, 183, 239
   wedding as, 144, 177–78, 185, 194–95, 209–11, 218
Orthodox tradition (Greek), 54, 182
Orthodoxy (Greek), 25, 160, 172n13
   shrine of, 144, 172n15
otherness
   ethnography and, 68, 251, 259
   Mykoniots as representative of an aesthetic, 4, 28, 57, 204, 207, 241, 249, 251
   Mykonos' myth of spatial , xi–xiii, 13, 31, 39, 58, 59, 145, 241, 261, 269
   as self-myth of the *Mykoniots*, 65, 210
   and the tourist, 57
   in tourist employment, 39, 173
'outsider'/ 'insider', viii
   and ethnographic reflexivity, viii, 5, 8, 68, 227

   in the Mykonian context, 41, 42, 56, 59, 62n27, 98, 99, 165–67, 173n18, 247n4, 247n9
   in the tourist context, 7, 32n3, 263, 266, 267
   Trinh Minh-ha's 'Inappropriate/d Other', 227
   Waldren's, 5, 62n33, 241

P

paganism
   Aleister Crowley, 137
   ancient Delos and, 146, 150, 172n15
   modern Greece and, 142, 144, 156, 255
   Mykoniots as neo-pagans, 25, 74, 149, 153, 159, 260–61
Panourgia, Neni, 62n29, 69, 132n10
   on death rituals, 69
Papachristos, Dimitris, 212n9
Papailias, Penelope, 190–91
Papastergiardis, Nikos, 227
Papataxiarchis, Evthymios, 44, 47, 59n7, 61n21, 62n34, 82–83, 93, 132n6, 135n49, 137n64, 138n71, 174n28, 180, 249, 253, 256, 257, 261n4
parea (group of friends), 6, 47, 52, 173n24, 237, 241–42
   and death, 247n3
   female, 38, 108, 133n26, 135–36n49, 193
   Mykonian *androparea*, 37, 45, 46, 53–55, 58
   Mykoniots, 86, 88, 91, 92, 101, 102, 109, 117, 125, 233, 234, 237, 239, 240, 243–45
Parkin, David, 12
partying on Mykonos, xii, 109, 112, 170
   bachelor, 192
   beach, 153, 173n20
   breakfast, 99, 105
   and clubbing, 187
   commemorative party/beach farewell, 232, 244
   Delos, 167
   dinner party, 237

disco, 78
Easter, 85
full moon, 81, 84, 85, 86–87, 163
 as *paniyiri*, 183
 preparing the bride as, 193
 rave, 198
 wedding, 201–11
Patton, Paul, 245–46
performance
 anorexia and, 235
 conscious, viii, 221, 226, 242–43, 244–46
 as embodied playing, 2, 89, 244
 emotion and, 231
 ethnographic, ix, 1, 251
 front and backstage, 7, 235, 247n4, 263–65, 268
 and gender, viii, 63n42, 178, 195
 liminality and, xi–xiv
 of loss, 244
 Mykoniots', 12, 162, 173n18, 189, 198–99, 209, 230, 232, 234–35, 244, 245
 in Mykonos, 9, 78
 ritual and theatre, 2, 246
 self-performance, viii, xiv, 2, 12, 13, 244
 tourist, 7, 263–65, 247n4
 and (cultural) tradition, 33n13, 174n34, 211
 as transformation, 2, 246
performativity
 and gender, viii, 24, 25, 223, 224, 229, 249
 and pain, 82, 83, 234–35
 political, 1, 224, 226, 229
 spatial, 33n13
Perkins, Harvey C. and David C. Thorns, 264, 265
Petropoulos, Elias, 47
Pettifer, James, 60n14
philhellenism, 60n14
Picard, Michel, 174n34
pilgrimage
 and female performance, 256
 and tourism, 263
pirates/piracy, 60n13

Pitton de Tournefort, Joseph, 171n4
polysemia
 Mykonos as a polysemic sign, 8, 9, 15, 16, 24, 32n7, 174n28, 259
 Mykoniots' polysemic inconsistency, 259
 Shields on space polysemy, 16
Possamaï, Adam, 29
post-modernity
 and the subject, 138n70, 226
 and tourism, 263
Pratt, Mary Louise, 69
purification
 incense burning, 51, 84, 85, 93, 120, 132n18
 Mykoniots' purifying confrontations, 80
 Mykoniots' rituals of, 50, 87, 92, 101, 133n20, 143

Q

queer
 in Greek ethnography, 256
 and 'home', 9, 248n11
 performativity, 229
 space, 9, 228, 230, 248n11
 theory, 9, 223–24, 228, 229, 230

R

Rabinow, Paul, 72
Rajneesh, Bhagwan Shree/Osho, 50, 79, 120, 121, 122, 125–27, 132n9, 137n65, 137n66
Rapport, Nigel, 18, 20, 21, 32n9, 69, 71, 171, 210, 250
Rapport, Nigel and Dawson Andrew, 240
rapture
 between body and self, 242
 in *communitas*, 2, 246
raves
 Goan, 230n2
 Mykonos, 78, 87, 163, 187, 198
Reed-Danahay, Deborah E., 68
Reich, Wilhelm, 30, 111, 122
rembetika, 36, 37, 47, 55, 61n20, 155

restlessness
  and extreme individuals, 57
  Mykoniots' psychological/ideological, 168, 243, 245
  Mykoniots's spiritual, 45
  as personal and political performativity, 1
  spatial (Delos), 240
  and tourists, 56
Rhenia, 142
  the isle of the dead, 146, 153, 154
  paniyiri, 146, 164
Ricoeur, Paul, 72, 127, 130–31, 230n4, 261n1
ritual
  commemorative, 81
  death, 69, 132n10, 135n49
  and the everyday, 170
  invented, xii, 18, 19, 28, 260, chapters 4,5 and epilogue
  local rituals and the *Mykoniots*, 161, 169
  pagan, 153, 156
  and performance, 12, 212
  Mykonian pig-slaughtering, 113–4, 136n52
  Mykoniots' breakfast, 98
  Mykoniots' celebration of mainstream, 139
  Mykoniots' identity, 149
  Mykoniots' initiation, 131n3
  Mykoniots' personal, 28, 70, 92, 97, 101, 102, 130
  syncretism and, 25
  transgressive (Nietzschean), 220, 244–45
Ritzer, George and Allan Liska, 268
Robertson, George et al., 248n10
Rojek, Chris, 173n16, 266, 268, 269
Romanos, A., 32n2, 60n13
Romantic movement, 23, 265
  and tourism, 265–66
romantic/tourist gaze
  Mykoniots and, 267–68
  Mykonos, 14, 15, 162, 268, 270n4
  tourism, 10, 13, 266
  Urry on, 264, 266, 270n1, 270n4

Romantic traveller, 18, 60, 238
Roussel, P., 171n3
rurban
  Mykonos as, 5, 14

S
Said, Edward, 225
Saldanha, Arun, 187, 230n2, 238, 269
Sallnow, Michael J., 220
Sangren S.P., 72
sanyassi/sannyasin, 79, 125–26, 137n65, 137n66
sarong (*pareo*)
  as fetish, 12, 13, 49, 61n25, 92, 95, 99, 120, 125, 133n19, 147, 154, 156, 201
Schechner, Richard, viii, 2, 7, 12, 89, 244, 246, 264
  and Girard, Renè, 244
  on performance, 2, 244
  on ritual, (Turner), 2
  self-play, viii
Schechner, Richard and Willa Appel, 2
  on performance, 2
Schieffelin, Edward, 248n13
  on performance, 248n13
second-hand (Mykoniots' culture of)
  clothes, 36, 52, 189, 197, 233, 237
  shops, 38, 184, 233
seduction
  Delos, 146
  Mykoniots', 70, 78, 89, 90, 91, 99, 108, 118, 125, 233, 234, 235, 236, 239, 243
  Mykonos and, xiii, 40, 67, 85–86, 88, 89, 146
Seferis, George, 162
self-fragmentation
  discursive, 73
  in Greek ethnography, 251
  and Mafessoli, 222
  Mykoniots', 128–29, 131
  performative, 73
self-image
  consumption of, 2, 24, 38, 100, 106, 107, 108, 111, 132n7, 134n31

self-narrative
　of the *Mykoniots*, 12
self-play, viii
self-reflexive, vii, viii, xiv, 21, 66, 181,
　211, 213n21, 259
　ethnography, 70–71
self-religions, 26–27, 28
　consumption and, 30
self-transformations, 12
　and agency, 131
　Braidotti on strategic, 226
　and the Foucauldian subject, 76,
　　221
　Mykoniots' xiii, 12, 26, 130, 245
seniority
　myth of, 38, 42, 48, 58
sensuality
　Beauvoir on, 166
　and the body in contemporary
　　ethnographic space, 220
　and collectivity, 220, 242
　Mykonos' aesthetics/politics of, xii,
　　6, 26, 31, 141, 228, 242
　and non-places, 57
　and performance, 7
　and the post-tourist, 7, 269, 270n5
Seremetakis, C.Nadia, 62n29, 82,
　135n39, 253
sexuality
　and Delos, 109
　liberality of the *Mykoniots*, xii, 36,
　　79, 90, 96, 97, 152
　and revolution, 109, 111, 122
Shapiro, M., 216
Shaw, Rosalind, 254, 260
Shepherd, Robert, 264, 266
Shields, Rob, xii, 6, 16–17, 118,
　138n70, 172n11, 215, 216, 220,
　222, 223, 226, 247n4, 264
　on post-modern consumption and
　　agency, 222
　on tourist places, 16
　on the transient subject, 138n70
Shilling, Chris, 107
sinafi, 6, 32n4, 36, 37, 39–41, 43–55,
　58, 59, 59n1, 62n28
　rembetika, 61n20, 61n21

Skouteri-Didaskalou, N., 179
space
　transient, 20
　transient tourist, vii, viii, 6, 32n8
space-myth
　of the Aegean, 172n9
　amoral Delos, 80, 140, 150
　amoral Mykonos, xii, 13, 60n12,
　　150, 248n11
　of Delos, 142, 159, 171n4
　of Mykonian haunts, 233
　of Mykonos, xii, 19, 59, 60n11,
　　61n15, 63n43, 108, 131n2, 142,
　　150, 174n31, 267
　and mythology, 17, 118
spatialisation, xii, 16–17, 118, 220, 223
　compared to the nomadic, 226
　post-modern, Mykonian, 228
　Shields on, 16–17, 118, 220, 223
Spivak, Gayatri Chakravorty, 225,
　261n2
Spon, J. 171n5
Spyer, Patricia, 11
Stanford, W.B., 171n5
Stasinopoulos, E., 171n4
Stewart, Charles, 134n41, 253, 254–55,
　260, 261
　Greeks and syncretism, 253,
　　254–55, 260
St. John, Graham, 30–31, 32n6, 220,
　242
　on cultural heterotopia, 30–31,
　　32n6, 220
Stott, Margaret, 5, 32n2, 136n52
Strathern, Marilyn, 68
style, viii
　Baudrilliard on style and
　　consumption, 10, 210, 216, 217
　Bourdieu on, 11, 24, 32n10, 33n14,
　　63n40, 216, 217, 254–55
　and consumption in post-modernity,
　　30
　Maffesoli on, 216–17, 218, 221
　Mykoniots' stylisation, 217
　Shapiro on, 216
　subculture and, 26

subject
  polythetic, 20, 21, 23, 24, 216, 255, 268
  transient, 7, 56, 138n70, 225–26, 247
subjectivity
  reflexive, 21, 22, 29
Sutton, David, E., 140
Svensson, Birgitta, 71
syncretism
  Greek ethnography, 251–56, 260–61
  Hindu, 79, 131
  ideological, 177
  Mykoniots and, 25, 74–75, 79, 131, 144, 170, 178, 198
  Mykonos and, 206, 210
  New Age, 28
  self and, 83, 128

T
Tambiah, Stanley, 181
Taussig, Michael, 11–12, 13
  on fetish, 11–12
Taylor, Charles, 21, 22, 23, 27, 28, 76, 106, 230n4, 270n2
Tedlock, B., 71
Thompson, Judith, 127
Tilley, Christopher, 174n34
time, 13–14
  in consumption spaces, 223
  cyclic notion of, 82
  drugs and, 80
  Hronos [Time], 86
  as timelessness, 14, 56, 88, 90
  in the tourist space, 14, 77
  and transgression, 171n1
Tinos, 3, 87, 144, 151, 171n4, 172n12, 172n15, 256
tourism, 9
  and employment, 173n16, 145
  history and development of (Mykonos), 40–43, 60n14, 61n15, 100, 171n4, 244, 260, 270n4
  and history in Greece, 140
  Mykonos and, 4–5, 8–10, 13–16, 37–45, 60n10
  and performativity in tourist related work, 173n16
  tourist employment as 'emotional work', 6
tourist, the
  performative fluidity and, 225
  places, 16
  post-modern, 226
  'post'-tourist, 17, 265–66
  as semiotician, 267–69
  sensual, 268–69, 270n5
  space, vii, viii, xi
  as a transient category, viii, 32, 225, 247
  as voyeur, 7
travelling
  on foot, 108, 135n47
  modern, 51, 259, 263, 266, 267, 269
  Mykoniots and, 3, 18, 36, 42, 43, 51–52, 57, 61n25, 81, 88, 92, 94, 115, 117, 125, 151, 186, 233, 234, 238, 245, 247n8, 259
  Mykonos and, 41, 42, 59, 60n14, 171–72n5
travel-theory, 225
Triantafyllou, K., 136n52
'tribestyle', xii, 13, 15, 31, 219, 222
Trinh T. Minh-ha, 227, 248n10
Tsakos, K., 60n13
Tsangarousianos, Stathis, 212n9
Tsiganou, J., 136n53
Tsiki, D., 47
Tsili, S., 136n53
Turner, Edith, 248n11, 263, 264
Turner, Victor, 2, 30, 177, 179, 181, 216, 246, 248n11, 263, 264, 269
  on ritual performance, 2, 246
Tzanelli, Rodanthi, 9, 14, 266

U
Urry, John, 5, 6, 9, 13, 14, 16, 17–18, 21–23, 27, 32n8, 33n14, 173n16, 213n21, 217, 226, 263–64, 265,

266–67, 268, 269, 270n1, 270n3, 270n4, 270n5
utopia
   as homelessness, 245
   and marginality, 17
   Mykonos as, 244

V
vagabond, the
   Bauman on, 56–57, 163
Van Gennep, Arnold, 212n2, 247n4
Veijola, Soile and Eeva Jokinen, 269
visual pleasure
   Beauvoir and, 166
   Mykonos landscape and, 166
Vlachos, Helen, 40, 41

W
Wagner, Roy, 19
Waldren, Jackie, vii, 5, 58, 62n33, 99, 131n2, 172n6, 241, 248n12
Ward, Sally, 248n10
'wardrobe of selves', 12, 138n70
   multi-faciality, 143
   the *Mykoniots* identity repertoire, 1, 12, 82, 121, 129, 134n37
   and narrativity, 127–28
   and Nietzsche, 245
wedding, the
   Greek bridal songs and funeral laments, 212n2
   in Greek ethnography, 179–80
   as identity ritual, 211
   as *Mykoniots*' emblematic collectivity, 207
   as performance, 204
   as self-performance, 209
Wheler, George, 171n5
Wilson, Elizabeth, 9, 233
Wolff, Janet
   critic of travel-theorists, 225
Wood, R. C., 173n16

Y
Yamashita, Shinji, 33n13, 174n34
Yangakis, G., 32n2, 61n15
yoga
   Mykonos and, 38, 80, 82, 87, 90

Z
Zarkia, Cornelia, 14–15
Zeus, 173n17
Zinovieff, Sofka, 59n2
Zorbaesque (the) and performativity
   Bhagwan on, 119, 127
   Damer on, 265
   Herzfeld on, 257–58
   on Mykonos, 38